DICTIONARY
Of Essential English

DICTIONARY
Of Essential English

Compiled by
Marion L. McGuire

COMPILER

Marion L. McGuire earned her Ph.D. at the University of Connecticut in reading education. She has an extensive background in the study of English, Latin, and French. Dr. McGuire served as a classroom teacher, a district reading consultant, and then as a state reading consultant. She spent many years as a professor of education and director of the Graduate Reading Program at the University of Rhode Island. Her publications include the Croft Word Attack Skills Program and the Croft Comprehension Program. Her work on this dictonary stemmed from her long association with the language arts; her interest in words, their structure, and meaning; and her experience in teaching dictionary skills.

CONSULTANTS

Carolyn W. Knox, M.Ed.
English Specialist
Baltimore City Public Schools
Baltimore, Maryland

John L. Flynn, M.A.
English Instructor
Anne Arundel Community College
Arnold, Maryland

Benjamin G. Davis, D.Min.
Institute for Human Studies
Columbia, Maryland

Editors: Barbara Pokrinchak, Ed.D.
Beryl D. Little, B.A.
Lynna Bright, B.F.A.

Art: Gregory Broadnax
Rimma Reyder
Mark-Jay Brown

ISBN: 0-86601-624-4 Printed in the United States of America.

12 89 VG/ATB 5.0

About This Dictionary

This dictionary will help anyone to become familiar with the 5,000 most frequently used and most essential words in the English language. It will be especially helpful to students who are learning English because of its short, clearly written definitions; its clean entries, uncluttered by word histories and cross references; and its wealth of examples showing how words are used in phrases and sentences.

The words in this dictionary are words that are encountered over and over again in many kinds of reading matter. They are found in school textbooks, library reference material, literature, newspapers, and popular magazines. In selecting the entries for this dictionary, over 10,000 frequently-used words were screened to find those that are most useful to readers who are gaining proficiency in English.

How to Locate an Entry Word

The words in a dictionary are arranged according to the order of the letters of the alphabet. The twenty-six letters of the alphabet are:

a b c d e f g h i j k l m

n o p q r s t u v w x y z

It may be necessary to alphabetize to the second, third, or fourth letters of a word to locate it exactly. To aid in the location of a word, guide words are given on each page of the dictionary. The first word appearing on every left-hand page is given in bold print at the top of that page. The last word appearing on the right-hand page is given in bold print at the top of that page. The task of locating a word is more efficient if the reader can quickly determine whether or not the word sought falls alphabetically between the guide words. If so, the reader scans down the page until the entry word is found.

Understanding the Entry

In general, each of the selected words is listed only once as an entry word, even though it may be used as different parts of speech, for instance, as a verb and a noun.

Example:

a·ban·don (ə ban′ dən) *vb.* to give up; to leave forever (*abandon* the ship) —*n.* free expression of feelings (He laughed with *abandon.*)

However, when a word stands for two different sets of meanings, they are presented separately.

Examples:

sow (saů) *n.* an adult female swine

sow (sō) *vb.* **sowed**; **sown** or **sowed**; **sow·ing** to scatter or spread widely (*sow* seeds)

Spelling and Syllabication

Each entry word, given in boldface type, is spelled correctly and divided into syllables by raised dots. This syllable division is the way words should be divided and hyphenated at the end of a line of writing when part of the word must run over to the next line.

Pronunciation

After the entry word, a phonetic spelling is given to aid pronunciation. The Guide to Pronunciation on page xii indicates the sound given to each letter and symbol through the use of key words.

In the English language, some syllables are given more stress than others when they are pronounced. Every word of two syllables or more has at least one accented syllable. Accent marks are placed after the syllables that are to be stressed in the phonetic spelling.

In words that have just one accented syllable, an accent mark is placed after that syllable. The one or more remaining syllables are said without stress.

Example: **hab·it** (hab′ ət) The accent is on the first syllable.

However, in some words, two or more syllables are accented. In this case, a heavy accent mark shows which syllable receives the heavier stress.

Example: **no·ti·fy** (nōt′ ə fī′) Give a heavy accent to the first syllable and a light accent to the last syllable.

In cases where two syllables in a word receive equal stress, two light accent marks are used.

Example: **soy·bean** (sȯi′ bēn′) The two syllables receive equal stress.

Word Meanings

Short definitions are given for all the common uses of the entry word. These are supplemented by examples to show how words are used in phrases and sentences. When words represent more than one part of speech, definitions are given for each of the parts of speech.

Example:

grasp (grasp) *vb.* **1.** to grab and hold with the hand **2.** to grab onto with the mind (*grasp* an understanding) —*n.* **1.** the act of grasping **2.** possession (The diploma is within his *grasp.*) **3.** understanding (Her *grasp* of the subject is excellent.)

In finding the meaning of a word taken from a text, choose one that makes sense in the sentence in which the word was found. Notice whether the word was used as a noun, a verb, or one of the other parts of speech. The meaning selected has to be for the same part of speech as the word you are looking up.

The parts of speech are identified immediately before the meanings in the entry. Following is a list of the eight parts of speech:

Noun (*n.*) Names a person, place, or thing.

Verb (*vb.*) Shows action or state of being.

Pronoun (*pron.*) Takes the place of a noun.

Adjective (*adj.*) Describes a noun or pronoun. The special adjectives, *a*, *an*, and *the* are called *articles*.

Adverb (*adv.*) Describes a verb, adjective, or other adverb.

Preposition (*prep.*) Shows the relationship between the noun or pronoun that follows it and some other word in the sentence.

Conjunction (*conj.*) Joins words, phrases, or clauses

Interjection (*interj.*) An exclamation showing an emotion such as surprise or happiness.

How Certain Entry Words Were Selected

Proper Names

In order to present the most useful words, proper names of people, places, and things were not included.

Words with Endings

The words that appear as entry words are in their base form. They do not have endings. Most words with endings follow rules for their formation. If a word is irregular in its endings, the irregular forms are shown in the dictionary entry. The rules for adding endings are given here.

Nouns. Endings on nouns show their number and possession. Nouns regularly form the plural by adding "s" or "es." The possessive is usually formed by adding "'s" in the singular and "s'" in the plural.

Example:	*Singular*	*Singular Possessive*
	boy	boy's
	Plural	*Plural Possessive*
	boys	boys'

Irregular plural forms are given in the dictionary entry.

Pronouns. The plural and possessive forms of pronouns are given in a table in Appendix B on page 447.

Adjectives and Adverbs. Endings on adjectives and adverbs show comparison. The comparative and superlative forms of adjectives and adverbs are usually constructed by adding "er" and "est," respectively, to the positive forms.

Example:	*Positive*	*Comparative*	*Superlative*
	fast	faster	fastest
	soon	sooner	soonest

Exceptions to this rule are given after the entry word.

Example:	*Positive*	*Comparative*	*Superlative*
	big	bigger	biggest
	noble	nobler	noblest
	tasty	tastier	tastiest

The exceptions to the rule listed above follow certain spelling rules that also affect nouns and verbs. In the first example (big), the single final consonant (g) follows a single short vowel (i) and is therefore doubled before adding the ending. In the second example, the final silent "e" is dropped before adding the endings "er" and "est." In the third example, the final "y" is changed to "i" before adding the endings "er" and "est." While these words do follow rules in their formation, the rules differ from the one simple rule of adding "er" or "est." They are therefore listed after the entry word in the dictionary.

Sometimes, however, the words *more* and *most* are used in front of the adjective or adverb instead of the inflectional ending.

Example:

Positive	*Comparative*	*Superlative*
beautiful	more beautiful	most beautiful
fortunate	more fortunate	most fortunate

Verbs. Endings on verbs show person and tense. Verbs regularly add "ed" to the present tense to form the past tense and the past participle, and "ing" to form the present participle.

Present Tense	*Past Tense*	*Past Participle*	*Present Participle*
work	worked	worked	working

Readers will notice, however, that many verbs are irregular in the way their principal parts are formed. These irregular formations are given after the entry word. Also, the principal parts of many irregular verbs are given in a table in Appendix C on page 451.

Another form of a verb involves the third person, singular number, present tense. An "s" is regularly added to make this form.

Example: I walk

you walk

he (she, it) walks

Number Words

Another class of words excluded as entry words are the number words. For the person who has to look up *fifteen*, for instance, it is not usually helpful to find that it means one more than fourteen or five more than ten. It is much more helpful to see the numeral as it occurs in numerical order. Thus, the cardinal (1, 2, 3) and the ordinal (1st, 2nd, 3rd) numbers are given in Appendix A on page 443 with their names and pronunciations.

Guide to Pronunciation

a	**a**nt, b**a**t
ā	**a**id, g**a**me
ä	**a**rm, f**a**ther, p**o**nd
au̇	**ou**t, c**ow**
b	**b**at, ca**bb**age, jo**b**
ch	**ch**ild, ca**tch**, pic**tu**re
d	**d**og, pa**d**
e	**e**nd, l**e**t
ē	**e**ven, funn**y**, cur**i**ous
f	**f**it, lau**gh**, **ph**oto, pu**ff**
g	**g**irl, ta**g**, ti**g**er
h	**h**and, be**h**ave
hw	**wh**ip, a**wh**ile
i	**i**t, l**i**p
ī	**i**ce, l**igh**t, tr**y**
j	**j**elly, **g**ym, ri**dge**
k	**k**i**ck**, **ch**emi**c**al
l	**l**itt**l**e, **l**ive**l**y
m	**m**other, ho**m**e
n	**n**ose, li**n**e**n**
ng	ri**ng**, ri**n**k, si**ng**i**ng**
ō	**o**ld, cr**ow**, c**o**mb
ȯ	cl**o**th, p**aw**
ȯi	b**oy**, f**oi**l
p	**p**a**p**er, shi**p**
r	**r**un, fu**r**
s	**s**au**c**er, fa**c**e, le**ss**on
sh	**sh**e, ca**sh**, na**ti**on
t	**t**icke**t**, ba**tt**er
th	**th**ing, ba**th**
t͟h	**th**at, ra**th**er
ü	sch**oo**l, t**u**ne
u̇	b**oo**k, p**u**ll, j**u**ry
v	**v**al**v**e, co**v**er
w	**w**in, be**w**are
y	**y**ear, **y**es
yü	f**ew**, v**iew**, m**u**sic
yu̇	**u**nite, p**ure**
z	**z**oo, prai**s**e
zh	trea**s**ure, deci**s**ion
ə	**a**bout, g**er**m, circ**u**s, m**o**ther, pupp**e**t

Note:
The symbol "ə" is called a *schwa.*

Abbreviations Used in This Dictionary

adj. = adjective

adv. = adverb

conj. = conjunction

interj. = interjection

n. = noun

pl. = plural

prep. = preposition

pres. = present

pron. = pronoun

sing. = singular

vb. = verb

A

a (ə, ā) *indefinite article* **1.** one (*a* child) **2.** any (too hard for *a* nine-year-old) **3.** in each (twice *a* day)

ab·a·cus (ab′ ə kəs) *n., pl.* **ab·a·cus·es** a frame with beads on wires used for counting

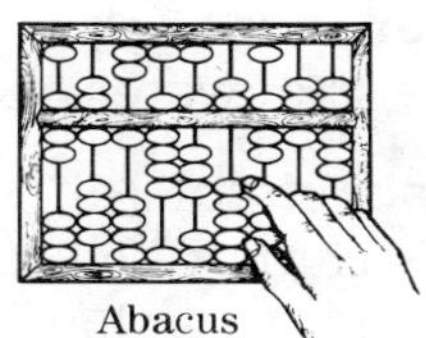
Abacus

a·ban·don (ə ban′ dən) *vb.* to give up; to leave forever (*abandon* the ship) —*n.* free expression of feelings (He laughed with *abandon.*)

ab·bre·vi·a·tion (ə brē′ vē ā′ shən) *n.* a short form of a word or phrase

ab·do·men (ab′ də mən) *n.* the mid part of the body that holds the stomach and other digestive organs

a·bil·i·ty (ə bil′ ə tē) *n., pl.* **a·bil·i·ties** the skill, talent, or power to do something

a·ble (ā′ bəl) *adj.* **a·bler**; **a·blest** having enough skill, talent, or power to do something

a·board (ə bōrd′) *adv.* on or in a ship, train, or other vehicle (welcome *aboard*) —*prep.* on or in (*aboard* the van)

a·bout (ə bau̇t′) *adv.* **1.** around **2.** nearly **3.** in the opposite direction (*about* face) —*prep.* **1.** around **2.** near to **3.** concerning

a·bove (ə bəv′) *adv.* in or to a higher place —*prep.* higher than

a·broad (ə brȯd′) *adv.* or *adj.* **1.** out in the open **2.** to a foreign country

a·brupt (ə brəpt′) *adj.* **1.** hasty **2.** rude **3.** steep

ab·sence (ab′ səns) *n.* **1.** being away (checked on his *absence*) **2.** lack (*absence* of reading books)

ab·sent (ab′ sənt) *adj.* not present or not paying attention (*absent*-minded)

ab·so·lute (ab′ sə lüt′) *adj.* **1.** complete (*absolute* power) **2.** pure (*absolute* joy) **3.** without exception (*absolute* requirement)

ab·sorb (əb sȯrb′) *vb.* **1.** to take in or soak up (*absorb* the water) **2.** to take over (*absorb* her interest)

ab·stract (ab strakt′) *adj.* **1.** describing a quality that cannot be seen or touched (Loyalty is an *abstract* quality.) **2.** hard to understand —*n.* (ab′ strakt) a brief summary of a written work

ab·surd (əb sərd′) *adj.* silly; not reasonable

a·bun·dance (ə bən′ dəns) *n.* a lot of something; plenty

a·bun·dant (ə bən′ dənt) *adj.* more than enough

ac·cel·er·a·tion (ak sel′ ə rā′ shən) *n.* increase in speed

ac·cent (ak′ sent) *n.* **1.** the way a person speaks (a New England *accent*) **2.** the stress given to a syllable (the *accent* on the first syllable) **3.** the mark that shows where to place the stress —*vb.* **1.** to stress **2.** to mark with an accent

ac·cept (ak sept′) *vb.* to take willingly

ac·cept·a·ble (ak sep′ tə bəl) *adj.* good enough

ac·cept·ance (ak sep′ təns) *n.* the act of accepting

ac·cess (ak′ ses) *n.* a way to enter or get to (*access* to the building)

ac·ci·dent (ak′ sə dənt) *n.* **1.** a happening by chance **2.** a mishap (a bus *accident*)

ac·com·pa·ny (ə kəm′ pə nē) *vb.* **ac·com·pa·nied**; **ac·com·pa·ny·ing** **1.** to go or travel with **2.** to play background music for (*accompanied* on the piano)

ac·com·plish (ə kam′ plish) *vb.* to finish with success

ac·com·plish·ment (ə käm′ plish mənt) *n.* **1.** something that is well done **2.** a skill that has grown to be excellent with practice

ac·cord (ə kord′) *n.* **1.** agreement **2.** willingness

ac·count (ə kaủnt′) *n.* **1.** a record of money received and paid out **2.** an explanation or report of work done —*vb.* to give an explanation

ac·cu·mu·la·tion (ə kyü′ myə lā′ shən) *n.* a collection or pile

ac·cu·rate (ak′ yə rət) *adj.* correct; free from error

ac·cuse (ə kyüz′) *vb.* **ac·cused**; **ac·cus·ing** to say a person has done something bad, such as stealing

ache (āk) *vb.* **ached**; **ach·ing** **1.** to have a pain **2.** to long for —*n.* a pain that lasts

a·chieve (ə chēv′) *vb.* **a·chieved**; **a·chiev·ing** **1.** to do something well **2.** to win

a·chieve·ment (ə chēv′ mənt) *n.* **1.** the act of doing something well **2.** something that is won by hard work

ac·id (as′ əd) *adj.* **1.** sour or sharp tasting **2.** sharp in temper (*acid* nature) —*n.* a sour-tasting substance

ac·knowl·edge (ak näl′ ij) *vb.* **ac·knowl·edged**; **ac·knowl·edg·ing** **1.** to admit to the truth **2.** to respond to the sender of a gift or invitation

a·corn (ā′ kȯrn) *n.* the nut of the oak tree

ac·quaint·ance (ə kwānt′ ns) *n.* **1.** personal knowledge **2.** a person one has met a few times but doesn't know well

ac·quire (ə kwīr′) *vb.* **ac·quired**; **ac·quir·ing** to gain or get hold of with effort

a·cre (ā′ kər) *n.* a land area equal to 160 square rods or 4,840 square yards

a·cross (ə krȯs′) *adv.* from one side to the other —*prep.* on or to the opposite side

act (akt) *n.* something one does —*vb.* to perform (*act* in a play); to behave (*acts* tired today)

ac·tion (ak′ shən) *n.* the doing of something (taking legal *action*; causing chemical *action*)

ac·tive (ak′ tiv) *adj.* quick or lively

ac·tiv·i·ty (ak tiv′ ət ē) *n., pl.* **ac·tiv·i·ties** actions that one carries on or participates in

ac·tor (ak′ tər) *n.* a person who plays a role on the stage, in a motion picture, or in a television show

ac·tress (ak′ trəs) *n.* a female actor

ac·tual (ak′ chə wəl) *adj.* truly happening

a·cute (ə kyüt′) *adj.* sharp or severe

a·dapt (ə dapt′) *vb.* to change or modify something to make it more useful

ad·ap·ta·tion (ad′ ap ta′ shən) *n.* something adjusted to present needs

add (ad) *vb.* **1.** to join things together **2.** to combine numbers to get a sum or total

ad·dend (ad′ end) *n.* a number that is added to another number

ad·di·tion (ə dish′ ən) *n.* **1.** the act of adding **2.** something added

ad·dress (ə dres′) *vb.* to speak or write to —*n.* **1.** a speech or lecture **2.** the place where mail can be delivered

ad·e·quate (ad′ i kwət) *adj.* enough

ad·he·sive (ad hē′ siv) *adj.* sticky —*n.* paste or glue

ad·ja·cent (ə jās′ nt) *adj.* near or next to

ad·jec·tive (aj′ ik tiv) *n.* a word used to describe a noun or pronoun

ad·join (ə join′) *vb.* **1.** to attach **2.** to be next to

ad·just (ə jəst′) *vb.* **1.** to help to settle a disagreement **2.** to make parts of a machine work better

ad·min·is·tra·tion (əd min′ əs trā′ shən) *n.* **1.** management of the affairs of a system (as of a town or school) **2.** the persons who manage the affairs

ad·mi·ral (ad′ mə rəl) *n.* an officer in the navy who commands a fleet

ad·mi·ra·tion (ad′ mə rā′ shən) *n.* excitement about the beauty or excellence of something

ad·mire (əd mīr′) *vb.* **ad·mired; ad·mir·ing** to respect something because of its beauty or excellence

ad·mis·sion (əd mish′ ən) *n.* **1.** the right to enter (*admission* to the club) **2.** the price of entrance **3.** agreeing to something not proven (*admission* of guilt)

ad·mit (əd mit′) *vb.* **ad·mit·ted; ad·mit·ting** **1.** to let in **2.** to confess

a·do·be (ə dō′ bē) *n.* a mud brick dried in the sun

ad·o·les·cence (ad′ əl es′ əns) *n.* the years between childhood and adulthood

a·dopt (ə däpt′) *vb.* to take over as one's own (to *adopt* a child or a plan of action)

a·dult (ə dəlt′, ad′ əlt) *adj.* fully grown —*n.* a fully grown person or animal

ad·vance (əd vans′) *vb.* **ad·vanced; ad·vanc·ing** to move forward —*n.* **1.** a forward movement **2.** an improvement

ad·van·tage (əd vant′ ij) *n.* a favorable position for gain or profit

ad·ven·ture (əd ven′ chər) *n.* an activity that involves risk or excitement —*vb.* **ad·ven·tured; ad·ven·tur·ing** **1.** to take a risk **2.** to look for excitement

ad·ven·tur·ous (əd ven′ chə rəs) *adj.* daring or risky

ad·verb (ad′ vərb) *n.* a word used to modify a verb, adjective, or other adverb

ad·ver·tise (ad′ vər tīz′) *vb.* **ad·ver·tised**; **ad·ver·tis·ing** to announce to the public by printed notice or broadcast

ad·ver·tise·ment (ad′ vər tīz′ mənt, ad vərt′ əz mənt) *n.* an announcement to draw public interest or sway public opinion

ad·vice (əd vīs′) *n.* an opinion given to influence another person's plan of action

ad·vise (əd vīz′) *vb.* **1.** to give an opinion **2.** to notify

af·fair (ə faər′) *n.* personal, social, or business activity

af·fect (ə fekt′) *vb.* to change or alter something or someone

af·fec·tion (ə fec′ shən) *n.* a feeling of fondness or love

af·ford (ə ford′) *vb.* able to bear the cost or effort

a·float (ə flōt′) *adv.* or *adj.* **1.** on board ship **2.** adrift

a·fraid (ə frād′) *adj.* full of fear

af·ter (af′ tər) *adv.* behind in time or place —*prep.* **1.** later in time, place, or rank (*after* the holiday) **2.** in pursuit of (chase *after* the dog) —*conj.* later than (*after* the egg hatched) —*adj.* **1.** coming later **2.** toward the back

af·ter·noon (af′ tər nün′) *n.* the hours between lunch and the evening meal

af·ter·ward (af′ tər wərd) or **af·ter·wards** (-wərdz) *adv.* later

a·gain (ə gen′) *adv.* **1.** once more (tried *again*) **2.** on the other hand (then *again*)

age (āj) *n.* **1.** the number of years a person has lived **2.** a particular time in history (the Stone *Age*) —*vb.* **aged** (ājd); **ag·ing** to grow old

a·gen·cy (ā′ jən sē) *n., pl.* **a·gen·cies** **1.** action taken to help someone else **2.** a person or organization doing business for someone else

a·gent (ā′ jənt) *n.* **1.** a person who is given the power to do business for another **2.** a thing that has an effect on something else (a chemical *agent*)

a·go (ə gō′) *adj.* or *adv.* before the present time

ag·o·ny (ag′ ə nē) *n., pl.* **ag·o·nies** severe pain in mind or body

a·gree (ə grē′) *vb.* **a·greed**; **a·gree·ing** **1.** to have the same opinion or belief **2.** to approve what someone else has done **3.** to harmonize

a·gree·ment (ə grē′ mənt) *n.* **1.** having the same opinion **2.** a legal contract

ag·ri·cul·ture (ag′ ri kəl′ chər) *n.* **1.** growing crops **2.** raising farm animals

ah (ä) *interj.* a cry of joy, relief, fear, or other strong feeling

a·head (ə hed′) *adv.* or *adj.* **1.** toward the front (to run *ahead*) **2.** for the future (to plan *ahead*)

aid (ād) *vb.* to help —*n.* assistance

aide (ād) *n.* a person who acts as a helper

ail (āl) *vb.* **1.** to have trouble **2.** to be ill

aim (ām) *vb.* **1.** to point a weapon at a target **2.** to intend to reach a goal —*n.* **1.** goal or purpose **2.** the pointing of a weapon

air (aər) *n.* the mixture of colorless, odorless, tasteless gases that surround the earth —*vb.* **1.** to hang out in the air (*air* the draperies) **2.** to bring to public attention (*air* her views)

air·craft (aər′ kraft′) *n., pl.* **aircraft** a flying machine (as a balloon, airplane, or helicopter)

air·line (aər′ līn′) *n.* **1.** a system for carrying people and goods by aircraft **2.** a company that runs an airline

air·plane (aər′ plān′) *n.* a propeller- or jet-driven heavier-than-air craft that is held up by the action of the air against its wings

Airplane

air·port (aər′ pōrt′) *n.* a place with runways and terminal buildings used for the operation of airlines

aisle (īl) *n.* a space for walking between rows of seats (as in a theater) or displays (as in a store)

a·larm (ə lärm′) *n.* **1.** a sudden fear of danger **2.** a warning signal, such as a siren, horn, or bell —*vb.* frighten

a·las (ə las′) *interj.* a word showing sadness or concern

al·bum (al′ bəm) *n.* **1.** a book with blank pages used for arranging and storing a collection of things such as stamps or photographs **2.** a folder storing one or more phonograph records

al·co·hol (al′ kə hȯl′) *n.* **1.** the intoxicating liquid found in fermented and distilled drinks **2.** a liquid sometimes used as a solvent or cleaning agent

al·co·hol·ic (al′ kə hȯl′ ik) *adj.* related to alcohol (*alcoholic* mixture) —*n.* a person affected with alcoholism

a·lert (ə lərt′) *adj.* wide awake and paying attention —*n.* a signal to warn of possible danger

al·ga (al′ gə) *n., pl.* **al·gae** (al′ jē′) simple plants including seaweed and pond scum

al·ge·bra (al′ jə brə) *n.* a branch of mathematics in which letters are used in place of certain numbers

a·lien (ā′ lē ən) *adj.* foreign or strange —*n.* a person who is not a citizen of the country in which he or she lives

a·like (ə līk′) *adj.* the same in many ways (father and son were *alike*) —*adv.* in the same way (they worked *alike*)

a·live (ə līv′) *adj.* **1.** having life **2.** full of activity

all (ȯl) *adj.* **1.** the whole of **2.** as much as possible —*adv.* completely (*all*-important) —*pron.* the whole quantity or number (*all* of us)

al·le·giance (ə lē′ jəns) *n.* **1.** loyalty to one's country **2.** faithfulness to a person

al·ley (al′ ē) *n., pl.* **al·leys** **1.** a narrow space between buildings **2.** the narrow lane on which a ball is rolled in bowling

al·li·ance (ə lī′ əns) *n.* an agreement between people or nations to unite for their common good

al·li·ga·tor (al′ ə gāt′ ər) *n.* a reptile in the crocodile family; its snout is shorter and blunter than a crocodile's

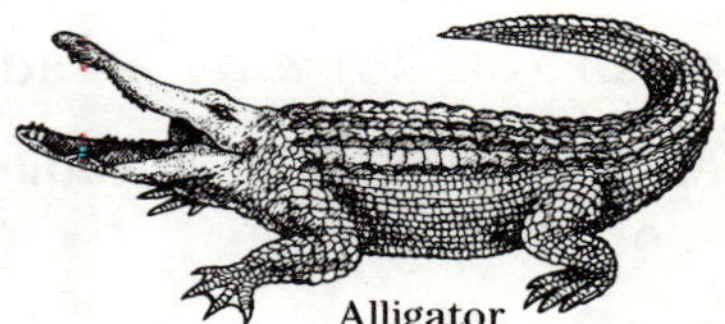
Alligator

al·low (ə lau̇′) *vb.* **1.** to permit (to *allow* the visitors to go swimming) **2.** to accept as reasonable (to *allow* ten dollars for repairs) **3.** to take into account (They *allow*ed for his weakness.)

al·low·ance (ə lau̇′ əns) *n.* **1.** the amount agreed upon **2.** money given for expenses (a weekly *allowance*) **3.** considering things that may change something (made an *allowance* in the price for the amount of fat on the meat)

al·loy (al′ ȯi′) *n.* a mixture of two or more metals melted together (Bronze is an *alloy* of copper and tin.)

al·ly (ə lī′, al′ ī′) *vb.* **al·lied**; **al·ly·ing** to join or unite —*n.* (al′ lī, ə lī′) *pl.* **al·lies** one person or nation united with another in a common purpose, especially in time of war

al·most (ȯl′ mōst′) *adv.* nearly, but not quite

a·loft (ə lȯft′) *adv.* or *adj.* high in the air, as in flight (The glider stayed *aloft* on the air currents.)

a·lone (ə lōn′) *adj.* by oneself (Ted is *alone* tonight.) —*adv.* without help (She works *alone.*)

a·long (ə lȯng′) *prep.* on the length of (*along* the river bank) —*adv.* **1.** forward (run *along* now) **2.** on the same course (brought friends *along*) **3.** throughout the time (knew all *along*)

a·long·side (ə long′ sīd′) *adv.* by the side

a·loud (ə lau̇d′) *adv.* so as to be heard (read aloud)

al·pha·bet (al′ fə bet′) *n.* the letters used in writing a language, especially when arranged in their special order

al·read·y (ȯl red′ ē) *adv.* before the expected time

al·so (ȯl′ sō) *adv.* in addition; too (He came *also.*)

al·tar (ȯl′ tər) *n.* a table used as a center of worship or ritual

al·ter (ȯl′ tər) *vb.* to change something in some way (*alter* the sleeves on a shirt)

al·ter·nate (ȯl′ tər nət) *adj.* every other time or place (*alternate* rows of red and blue) —*vb.* (ȯl′ tər nāt′) **al·ter·na·ted**; **al·ter·nat·ing** to take turns (They *alternate* working on Saturday night.) —*n.* (ȯl′ tər nət) a person named to take the place of another whenever necessary (*alternate* to a convention)

al·ter·na·tive (ȯl tər nə tiv) *adj.* another choice which may be taken (*alternative* schedule) —*n.* one of the things which may be chosen

al·though (ȯl thō′) *conj.* **1.** even if **2.** regardless of the fact that

al·ti·tude (al′ tə tüd) *n.* height above sea level or ground level

al·to (al′ tō) *n.*, *pl.* **al·tos** **1.** a low female singing voice **2.** an instrument having the range of an alto voice

al·to·geth·er (ȯl′ tə geth′ ər) *adv.* **1.** entirely **2.** on the whole

a·lu·mi·num (ə lü′ mə nəm) *n.* a silvery metal that is light-weight, easy to shape, and does not rust

al·ways (ȯl′ wāz, -wəz) *adv.* **1.** at all times **2.** forever

am (am) *v.* present, first person singular of BE

am·a·teur (am′ ə tər′) *n.* **1.** one who works or plays a sport for pleasure, but not for money **2.** a person who lacks experience or skill in something

a·maze (ə māz′) *vb.* **a·mazed**; **a·maz·ing** to surprise or puzzle

a·maze·ment (ə māz′ mənt) *n.* surprise or wonder

am·bi·tion (am bish′ ən) *n.* **1.** strong desire to do well (the *ambition* to work for good grades) **2.** the thing a person wants (My *ambition* is to be a photographer.)

am·bi·tious (am bish′ əs) *adj.* having a strong desire to reach a goal

am·bu·lance (am′ byə ləns) *n.* a vehicle for carrying sick or injured persons

a·mend·ment (ə mend′ mənt) *n.* **1.** a change made to correct or improve something **2.** a formal change of a law or bill **3.** a change in the constitution of a country

am·e·thyst (am′ ə thəst) *n.* a purple quartz stone used in jewelry

a·mid (ə mid′) *prep.* in or into the middle of

am·mo·nia (ə mō′ nyə) *n.* a sharp-smelling, colorless gas that is used in making ice, household cleaners, and explosives

am·mu·ni·tion (am′ yə nish′ ən) *n.* explosive things such as bullets and shells

a·mong (ə məng′) *prep.* **1.** in the midst of (*among* friends) **2.** through all of (*among* the townspeople)

a·mount (ə maủnt′) *vb.* **1.** to add up (The repairs *amount* to six dollars.) **2.** to be equal to (That *amounts* to half a truckload.) —*n.* the total of things added together

am·phib·i·an (am fib′ ē ən) *n.* **1.** an animal that lives in the water and on land (Frogs are *amphibians.*) **2.** an airplane that can take off and land either on water or land

Amphibian

am·ple (am′ pəl) *adj.* more than enough

a·muse (ə myüz′) *vb.* **a·mused**; **a·mus·ing** to entertain

a·muse·ment (ə myüz′ mənt) *n.* something that entertains or provides a pleasant pastime

an (ən, an) *indefinite article* one—used before words beginning with a vowel or silent *h* (*an* apple, *an* honest person)

a·nal·y·sis (ə nal′ ə səs) *n., pl.* **a·nal·y·ses** (-ə sēz′) a close study of the parts of something

an·a·lyze (an′ l īz) *vb.* **an·a·lyzed**; **an·a·lyz·ing** to study the parts of something to see how they are related

a·nat·o·my (ə nat′ ə mē) *n.* a study of the bodies of people and animals

an·ces·tor (an′ ses′ tər) *n.* one from whom a person is descended, such as a grandfather or great-grandmother

an·ces·try (an′ ses′ trē) *n., pl.* **an·ces·tries** ancestors

an·chor (ang′ kər) *n.* **1.** a heavy object attached to a ship by a chain or cable and used to dig into the sea floor to keep a ship in place **2.** a person or object that holds things steady (the *anchor* on a television news show) —*vb.* **1.** to hold in place **2.** to fix securely

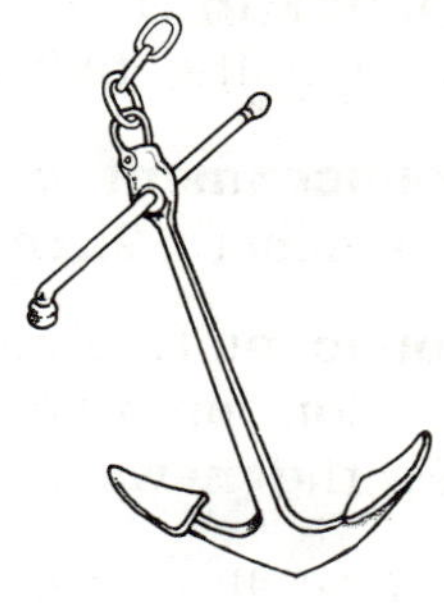

Anchor

an·cient (an′ shənt) *adj.* about a time long ago —*n.* a very old person

and (ənd, and) *conj.* **1.** added to **2.** as well as

an·ger (ang′ gər) *n.* **1.** a very unfriendly feeling **2.** rage —*vb.* to make someone angry

an·gle (ang′ gəl) *n.* **1.** two lines that come together at a point (a right *angle*) **2.** viewpoint (look at it from a new *angle*) —*vb.* **1.** to move something at an angle **2.** to fish with hook and line **3.** to use tricks to get what one wants

an·gry (ang′ grē) *adj.* **an·gri·er**; **an·gri·est** feeling resentment, rage, or wrath

an·gu·lar (ang′ gyə lər) *adj.* **1.** having sharp corners **2.** thin and bony

an·i·mal (an′ ə məl) *n.* **1.** all living things except plants **2.** a living thing that moves about to get its food **3.** a brutish person who behaves like a lower form of life

an·kle (ang′ kəl) *n.* the joint between the foot and the leg

an·nex (ə neks′) *vb.* to attach —*n.* (an′ eks) something added, as a wing on a building

an·ni·ver·sa·ry (an′ ə vər′ sə rē) *n., pl.* **an·ni·ver·sa·ries** the return each year of the date of a special event (wedding *anniversary*)

an·nounce (ə naůns′) *vb.* **an·nounced**; **an·nounc·ing** **1.** to tell the public **2.** to serve as an announcer

an·nounce·ment (ə naůns′ mənt) *n.* **1.** the act of announcing **2.** the message that is announced

an·nounc·er (ə naůn′ sər) *n.* the person on a radio, television, or other program who introduces people or gives the news

an·noy (ə nȯi′) *vb.* to disturb or bother

an·nu·al (an′ yə wəl) *adj.* once a year —*n.* **1.** a book or magazine produced once a year **2.** a plant that lives for just one growing season

an·oth·er (ə nəth′ ər) *adj.* **1.** some other **2.** one more (*another* book) —*pron.* one more (one on Monday and *another* on Tuesday)

an·swer (an′ sər) *n.* a reply or response —*vb.* **1.** to speak or write a reply **2.** to act in a responsible way (*answer*ed for their safety)

ant (ant) *n.* a small insect that lives in a colony and works hard

ant·arc·tic (ant ärk′ tik) *adj.* relating to the South Pole (A penguin is an *antarctic* bird.)

an·te·lope (ant′ l ōp′) *n.* an animal, such as a gazelle or gnu, with horns that sweep upward and backward

Antelope

an·ten·na (an ten′ ə) *n., pl.* **an·ten·nae** (-ten′ ē) **1.** a feeler on the head of an insect **2.** a rod or wire for sending or receiving radio waves

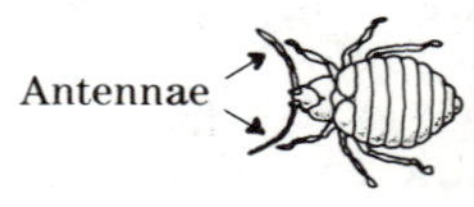

an·them (an′ thəm) *n.* a sacred or patriotic song of praise

an·ti·bi·ot·ic (ant′ i bī ät′ ik) *n.* a germ-killing substance such as penicillin

an·tique (an tēk′) *adj.* belonging to an olden time —*n.* an object made a long time ago

ant·ler (ant′ lər) *n.* the horn of an animal in the deer family

anx·i·e·ty (ang zī′ ət ē) *n.*, *pl.* **anx·i·e·ties** fear of what may happen in the future

anx·ious (angk′ shəs) *adj.* worried or fearful

an·y (en′ ē) *adj.* taken without a definite aim (*any* person) or without a definite quantity (*any* clothing) —*pron.* unselected people (*any* of us) —*adv.* at all (feel *any* happier)

an·y·body (en′ ē bäd′ē) *pron.* anyone

an·y·how (en′ ē haů′) *adv.* in any case

an·y·more (en′ ē mōr′) *adv.* at the present time

an·y·one (en′ ē wən′) *pron.* any person or thing

an·y·thing (en′ ē thing′) *pron.* any kind of thing or happening

an·y·way (en′ ē wā′) *adv.* in any manner

an·y·where (en′ ē hweər′) *adv.* in any place whatever

a·part (ə pärt′) *adv.* separate from each other in time or place

a·part·ment (ə pärt′ mənt) *n.* a separate part of a building used as a place to live

a·phid (ā′ fəd) *n.* a plant louse

a·piece (ə pēs′) *adv.* for each one

a·pol·o·gy (ə päl′ ə jē) *n.*, *pl.* **a·pol·o·gies** an expression of sorrow for making a mistake or being rude

a·pos·tro·phe (ə päs′ trə fē) *n.* a mark (’) used to show ownership (Leo’s coat) or that one or more letters or numbers have been left out (I’m going in ’92.)

ap·pa·rat·us (ap′ ə rat′ əs, -rā′ təs) *n., pl.* **apparatus** or **ap·pa·rat·us·es** the equipment for doing a special kind of work (exercise *apparatus*)

ap·par·ent (ə par′ ent) *adj.* **1.** easy to see (Her joy is *apparent.*) **2.** seeming to be real (Their *apparent* interest soon faded.)

ap·peal (ə pēl′) *n.* **1.** a call for aid or sympathy **2.** attraction (the *appeal* of a good story) —*vb.* **1.** to ask to have a legal case reviewed by a higher court **2.** to ask for aid **3.** to be pleasing (The color *appeal*ed to them.)

ap·pear (ə piər′) *vb.* **1.** to come into sight **2.** to come before the public (*appear*ed on the stage) **3.** seem (*appear*ed well-rested)

ap·pear·ance (ə pir′ əns) *n.* **1.** the act of becoming visible **2.** outward look (a ragged *appearance*)

ap·pe·tite (ap′ ə tīt) *n.* **1.** a desire for food or drink **2.** a desire to satisfy a longing (an *appetite* for flying)

ap·plause (ə plȯz′) *n.* hand clapping to show approval

ap·ple (ap′ əl) *n.* a fruit with red, yellow, or green skin that grows on a tree

ap·pli·ca·tion (ap′ lə kā′ shən) *n.* **1.** the act of putting or spreading something on a surface **2.** a request for something (a job *application*, a college *application*)

ap·ply (ə plī′) *vb.* **ap·plied**; **ap·ply·ing** **1.** to put to use **2.** to put on the surface **3.** to give full attention (*apply* myself to my studies) **4.** to request

ap·point (ə pȯint′) *vb.* to name someone for a job or office

ap·point·ment (ə pȯint′ mənt) *n.* **1.** the act of naming someone to a job or office **2.** agreement to meet (doctor’s *appointment*)

ap·pre·ci·ate (ə prē′ shē āt′) *vb.* **1.** to notice the worth or quality of **2.** to be grateful for (*appreciate* their kindness) **3.** to grow in value (The bank account *appreciat*ed in value.)

ap·pre·ci·a·tion (ə prē′ shē ā′ shən) *n.* the act of appreciating

ap·pren·tice (ə prent′ əs) *n.* a person learning a trade by working under a skilled worker

ap·proach (ə prōch′) *vb.* to come closer —*n.* the act of coming closer

ap·pro·pri·ate (ə prō′ prē āt) *vb.* **ap·pro·pri·at·ed**; **ap·pro·pri·at·ing** to take control of something —*adj.* (ə prō′ prē ət) suitable or proper

ap·prov·al (ə prüv′ l) *n.* an act of agreement

ap·prove (ə prüv′) *vb.* **ap·proved**; **ap·prov·ing** to be in favor of something

ap·prox·i·mate (ə präk′ sə mət) *adj.* nearly correct or quite accurate

a·pron (ā′ prən) *n.* **1.** a garment worn to protect the front of clothing from soil **2.** a paved area for parking airplanes

apt (apt) *adj.* **1.** suitable (an *apt* remark) **2.** likely (*apt* to cry) **3.** quick to learn (an *apt* student)

a·quar·i·um (ə kwer′ ē əm) *n., pl.* **a·quar·i·ums** or **a·quar·i·a** a tank or bowl in which fish are kept

aq·ue·duct (ak′ wə dəkt′) *n.* a structure that carries water from place to place

arc (ärk) *n.* **1.** something that is curved **2.** a glowing light across a gap in an electric circuit

arch (ärch) *n.* the curved top of an opening in a building or other structure

Arch

ar·chae·ol·o·gy or **ar·che·ol·o·gy** (är′ kē äl′ ə jē) *n.* the study of ancient people as shown by the monuments and remains that are dug from the earth

ar·chi·tect (är′ kə tekt′) *n.* a person who designs buildings and gives advice to builders

arc·tic (ärk′ tik) *adj.* relating to the region around the North Pole

are (ər, är) second person singular form of the verb BE

ar·e·a (ar′ ē a) *n.* **1.** a flat surface or piece of ground **2.** the number of square units on the surface **3.** region (grazing *area*)

a·re·na (ə rē′ nə) *n.* a large enclosed area used for sports or entertainment

ar·gue (är′ gyü) *vb.* **ar·gued**; **ar·gu·ing** **1.** to give reasons for or against **2.** to have a heated disagreement

ar·gu·ment (är′ gyə mənt) *n.* **1.** a reason for or against something **2.** a quarrel

ar·id (ar′ əd) *adj.* dry or barren with little or no rainfall

a·rise (ə rīz′) *vb.* **a·rose** (ə rōz′); **a·ris·en** (ə riz′ n); **a·ris·ing** (ə rī′ zing) **1.** to go up **2.** to get up **3.** to come up

a·ris·to·crat (ə ris′ tə krat′) *n.* a member of the ruling class

a·rith·me·tic (ə rith′ mə tik′) *n.* **1.** the science of numbers **2.** computing by adding, subtracting, multiplying, or dividing

ark (ärk) *n.* a safe place, such as a place of refuge (Noah's *ark*), or a strong box (*ark* of the Covenant)

arm (ärm) *n.* **1.** an upper limb from shoulder to wrist **2.** a part of something that juts out like an arm (*arm* of the chair; *arm* of the machine) **3.** area of influence that extends outward (*arm* of the law) —*vb.* to provide with weapons

ar·mor (är′ mər) *n.* a strong covering as of metal to protect the person within (suit of *armor*, *armor*ed truck)

Armor

ar·my (är′ mē) *n.*, *pl.* **ar·mies** a large body of men and women trained for land warfare

a·round (ə raủnd′) *adv.* **1.** in a circle (ten feet *around*) **2.** in or to many places (travel *around*) **3.** nearby (stay *around*) **4.** in the opposite direction (turn *around*) —*prep.* **1.** along the outer boundary of an area (*around* the block) **2.** near

a·rouse (ə raủz′) *vb.* **a·roused**; **a·rous·ing** **1.** to waken from sleep **2.** to excite

ar·range (ə rānj′) *vb.* **ar·ranged**; **ar·rang·ing** **1.** to put in order **2.** to plan for **3.** to modify a musical score (*arrange* the music)

ar·range·ment (ə rānj′ mənt) *n.* **1.** the order in which things are put **2.** a plan **3.** an adapted musical score

ar·ray (ə rā′) *vb.* **1.** to set out in an impressive order **2.** to dress in beautiful clothing —*n.* **1.** regular display **2.** beautiful clothing

ar·rest (ə rest′) *vb.* **1.** to stop the progress (*arrest* the disease) **2.** to take away freedom (*arrest* the robber) —*n.* the act of taking into custody by the police

ar·riv·al (ə rī′ vəl) *n.* **1.** the act of reaching a place **2.** a person or thing that has arrived

ar·rive (ə rīv′) *vb.* **ar·rived**; **ar·riv·ing** **1.** to reach a place **2.** to reach a goal (*arrive* as a stage star)

ar·row (ar′ ō) *n.* **1.** a thin rod with a pointed head made to be shot from a bow **2.** a mark used to show direction

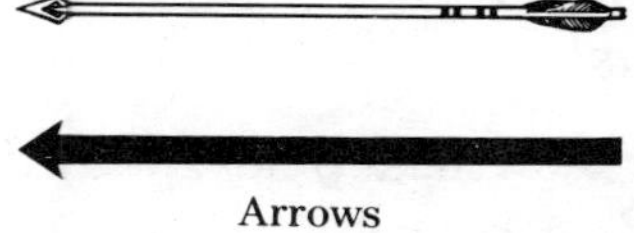
Arrows

art (ärt) *n.* **1.** talent, ability, or skill **2.** the use of these in making beautiful things

ar·ter·y (ärt′ ə rē) *n., pl.* **ar·ter·ies** **1.** a tube that carries blood from the heart to other parts of the body **2.** any great channel or passageway (That highway is the main *artery.*)

ar·ti·cle (ärt′ i kəl) *n.* **1.** a separate part of something **2.** a selection published in a magazine (*article* about health foods) **3.** one item of a class (*article* of clothing) **4.** a word used before a noun such as *a*, *an*, or *the*

ar·ti·fi·cial (ärt ə fish′ əl) *adj.* **1.** made to look like something in nature (*artificial* flowers) **2.** not what it seems to be

art·ist (ärt′ əst) *n.* **1.** a person with special talent, skill, or ability in one of the arts such as music, dance, painting, writing, or sculpture **2.** one who shows great ability in doing something difficult

ar·tis·tic (är tis′ tic) *adj.* relating to art or artists

as (əz, az) *conj.* **1.** equal to **2.** in the same way that **3.** while **4.** because or since —*adv.* **1.** to the same degree **2.** for example —*pron.* that —*prep.* like

as·cent (ə sent′) *n.* **1.** the act of going up **2.** an upward slope

ash (ash) *n.* **1.** a type of tree that has seeds with wings **2.** what is left when something is burned

a·shore (ə shōr′) *adv.* or *adj.* on or to the shore

a·side (ə sīd′) *adv.* **1.** to or toward the side **2.** out of the way

ask (ask) *vb.* **1.** to request something **2.** to invite (*ask*ed to dinner) **3.** to look (*ask*ing for attention)

a·sleep (ə slēp′) *adj.* **1.** sleeping **2.** numb (My foot is *asleep.*) —*adv.* into a state of sleep (fall *asleep*)

as·pect (as′ pekt′) *n.* **1.** view (look at it from this *aspect*) **2.** appearance

as·sault (ə sȯlt′) *n.* a violent attack

as·sem·ble (ə sem′ bəl) *vb.* **as·sem·bled**; **as·sem·bling** **1.** to gather together **2.** to fit together (*assemble* the parts)

as·sem·bly (ə sem′ blē) *n., pl.* **as·sem·blies** **1.** a gathering of people **2.** a law-making body

as·sign (ə sīn′) *vb.* **1.** to appoint **2.** to state in detail (*assign* homework) **3.** to transfer in legal terms, as property

as·sign·ment (ə sīn′ mənt) *n.* **1.** the act of assigning **2.** the thing assigned

as·sist (ə sist′) *vb.* to give help —*n.* the act of helping

as·sist·ance (ə sis′ təns) *n.* help

as·sist·ant (ə sis′ tənt) *adj.* serving as a helper to someone else —*n.* a person who helps

as·so·ci·ate (ə sō′ shē ət) *n.* a person connected with another through sharing the same work or belonging to the same organization

as·sume (ə süm′) *vb.* **as·sumed**; **as·sum·ing** **1.** to take over **2.** to suppose **3.** to pretend

as·sure (ə shůr′) *vb.* **as·sured**; **as·sur·ing** **1.** to make sure **2.** to give one's word **3.** to insure

as·ton·ish·ment (ə stän′ ish mənt) *n.* great surprise

as·tro·naut (as′ trə nȯt′) *n.* space traveler

as·tron·o·my (ə strän′ ə mē) *n.* the study of the stars, moons, planets, and other objects in space

at (ət, at) *prep.* used to indicate a point in time (*at* 2:00 P.M.) or space (*at* the top), a condition (*at* work), or a reason (laughed *at* the joke)

ath·lete (ath′ lēt′) *n.* a person who is skilled at games and exercises requiring strength and ability

at·las (at′ ləs) *n.* a book of maps or charts

at·mo·sphere (at′ məs fiər′) *n.* **1.** the surrounding air (Earth's *atmosphere*) **2.** the surrounding influence (*atmosphere* of the school)

at·om (at′ əm) *n.* **1.** the smallest particle into which an element can be divided **2.** a tiny bit

a·tom·ic (ə täm′ ik) *adj.* relating to atoms (*atomic* energy)

at·tach (ə tach′) *vb.* **1.** to connect one thing to another (*attach* a picture to the wall) **2.** to take with legal authority (*attach* her salary)

at·tack (ə tak′) *vb.* **1.** to begin a fight or struggle **2.** to say or write unfriendly words **3.** to begin to work vigorously (*attack*ed the pile of work)

at·tain (ə tān′) *vb.* to reach a goal or an important point in development (*attain* manhood)

at·tempt (ə tempt′) *vb.* to try —*n.* a trial or an effort

at·tend (ə tend′) *vb.* **1.** to go to (*attend* an air show) **2.** to pay attention (*attend* to your work) **3.** to wait on (volunteers *attend* the elderly)

at·ten·tion (ə ten′ chen) *n.* careful thought

at·tic (at′ ik) *n.* a space under the roof of a building

at·ti·tude (at′ ə tüd′) *n.* a disposition or feeling toward a person or thing

at·tract (ə trakt′) *vb.* to pull something toward oneself or itself (a magnet *attract*s iron; bright colors *attract* attention)

at·trac·tion (ə trak′ shən) *n.* the act or power of drawing toward

at·trac·tive (ə trak′ tiv) *adj.* pleasing

au·di·ence (ȯd′ ē əns) *n.* the group that watches or listens

au·di·to·ri·um (ȯd′ ə tōr′ ē əm) *n.* a large room where an audience sits

aunt (ant′) *n.* a sister of one's father or mother

au·thor (ȯ′ thər) *n.* one who writes books, stories, or articles

au·thor·i·ty (ə thȯr′ ət ē) *n., pl.* **au·thor·i·ties** **1.** the power to give orders **2.** a person who is an expert

au·to (ȯt′ ō) *n., pl.* **au·tos** automobile

au·to·mat·ic (ȯt′ ə mat′ ik) *adj.* **1.** done without an operator (*Automatic* lights go on at sunset.) **2.** done without thought (breathed an *automatic* sigh)

au·to·mo·bile (ȯt′ ə mō bēl′) *n.* a four-wheeled car for carrying passengers along a road

au·tumn (ȯt′ əm) *n.* the season between summer and winter

a·vail·a·ble (ə vā′ lə bəl) *adj.* **1.** usable **2.** at hand

av·e·nue (av′ ə nü′) *n.* **1.** a road **2.** a way to an end

av·er·age (av′ ər ij) *n.* **1.** something common or ordinary **2.** a score showing typical performance (batting *average*; spelling *average*) —*adj.* usual (*average* person) —*vb.* **av·er·aged**; **av·er·ag·ing** to find the average of

a·vi·a·tion (ā′ vē ā′ shən) *n.* the science of flying airplanes

a·void (ə vȯid′) *vb.* to stay away from

a·wait (ə wāt′) *vb.* to wait or watch for

a·wake (ə wāk′) *vb.* **a·woke** (-wōk) or **a·waked; a·wak·ing** to stop sleeping —*adj.* alert

a·ward (ə wȯrd′) *vb.* to give to —*n.* a grant or prize

a·ware (ə waər′) *adj.* watchful

a·way (ə wā′) *adv.* **1.** on the way (get *away* fast) **2.** in another direction (drive *away*) **3.** absent (stay *away*) —*adj.* gone (be *away*)

awe (ȯ) *n.* a solemn feeling of respect —*vb.* **awed**; **aw·ing** to fill with respect or fear

aw·ful (ȯ′ fəl) *adj.* causing great respect or fear

a·while (ə hwīl′) *adv.* for a short time

awk·ward (ȯk′ wərd) *adj.* **1.** lacking skill or balance **2.** lacking tact

ax or **axe** (aks) *n.* a tool for chopping and splitting wood

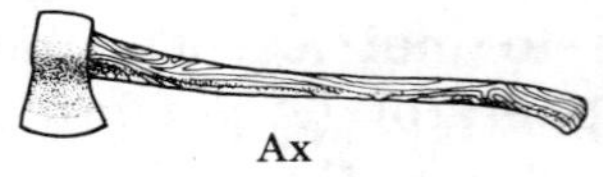
Ax

ax·is (ak′ səs) *n.*, *pl.* **ax·es** (ak′ sēz′) a line around which a figure rotates or spins (the Earth's *axis*)

ax·le (ak′ səl) *n.* a rod on which a wheel spins

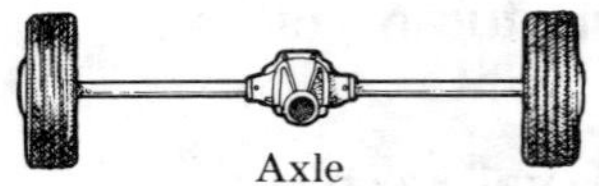
Axle

B

ba·by (bā′ bē) *n., pl.* **ba·bies** **1.** an infant **2.** a childish person —*adj.* young (*baby* bear) —*vb.* **ba·bied**; **ba·by·ing** to treat as a baby

back (bak) *n.* rear part of body from neck to end of backbone —*adv.* toward the rear, or to a time or place gone by —*adj.* **1.** at the back **2.** overdue —*vb.* **1.** to give help **2.** to move in reverse

back·bone (bak′ bōn′) *n.* spine

back·ground (bak′ graůnd) *n.* **1.** the distant part of a scene or picture **2.** a person's education and experience

back·ward (bak′ wərd) or **back·wards** (-wərdz) *adv.* **1.** toward the back **2.** in a way opposite to normal (slide *backward*) —*adj.* slow in development

ba·con (bā′ kən) *n.* salted and smoked meat from a pig

bac·te·ri·um (bak tir′ ē əm) *n., pl.* **bac·te·ri·a** (-ē ə) very tiny living things, some of which are harmful (Some *bacteria* cause disease.)

bad (bad) *adj.* **worse** (wərs); **worst** (wərst) **1.** severe (*bad* storm) **2.** spoiled (*bad* meat) **3.** evil (*bad* person) **4.** incorrect (*bad* manners) **5.** without legal effect (*bad* check)

bag (bag) *n.* **1.** a paper, cloth, or plastic sack for carrying something **2.** handbag **3.** suitcase **4.** a square white canvas sack to mark a base in baseball —*vb.* **bagged**; **bag·ging** **1.** to put into a bag **2.** to capture

bag·gage (bag′ ij) *n.* suitcases; luggage

bait (bāt) *vb.* to nag or tease (to *bait* the speaker) —*n.* something used to lure an animal to a hook or trap (the *bait* on the fishhook)

bake (bāk) *vb.* to cook in an oven —*n.* **1.** the act of baking **2.** gathering where baked food is served (the clam*bake*)

bak·er·y (bā′ kə rē) *n., pl.* **bak·er·ies** a place where breads, cakes, and pastries are baked or sold

bal·ance (bal′ əns) *n.* **1.** a machine for weighing; a scale **2.** equal totals or weight on each side **3.** the amount by which one total is greater than another

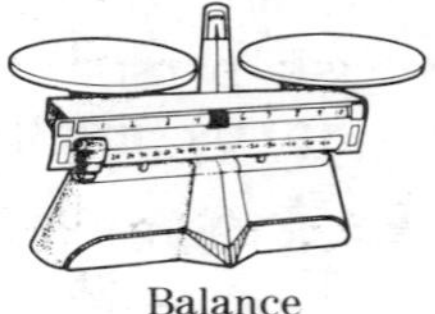
Balance

bal·co·ny (bal′ kə nē) *n., pl.* **bal·co·nies** **1.** a platform with railing built out from the side of a building **2.** a gallery in a building

bald (bȯld) *adj.* **1.** having no hair on the head **2.** without natural cover; bare (Gypsy moths left the tree *bald.*)

ball (bȯl) *n.* **1.** a round object (*ball* of string, soccer *ball*) **2.** a game played with a ball (play *ball*) **3.** a baseball pitch outside the strike zone that the batter lets go by **4.** the wide part on the bottom of the foot (*ball* of the foot) —*vb.* to form into a ball

bal·lad (bal′ əd) *n.* a poem that tells a story, often set to music

bal·let (bal′ ā′) *n.* a graceful dance, done with costumes and music, that tells a story

bal·loon (bə lün′) *n.* **1.** a large bag that rises and floats when filled with hot air or gas **2.** a soft case that can be blown up to use as a toy or decoration —*vb.* to puff up

bal·lot (bal′ ət) *n.* a paper or mechanical system used in voting —*vb.* to vote by ballot

bam·boo (bam bü′) *n.* a woody grass with jointed stems used for making furniture and other objects

ban (ban) *vb.* **banned**; **ban·ning** to forbid by official order —*n.* an official order to stop something (a *ban* on the sale of certain products)

ba·nan·a (bə nan′ ə) *n.* the long yellow or red fruit of the banana plant

band (band) *n.* **1.** something that goes around (hat*band*) **2.** something that holds things together (rubber *band*) **3.** a group of performers (a dance *band*) **4.** a group that works together (a *band* of patriots) —*vb.* **1.** to put a band on **2.** to gather into a group

ban·dage (ban′ dij) *n.* a strip of cloth used to wrap a cut or sore —*vb.* **ban·daged**; **ban·dag·ing** to cover with a bandage

bang (bang) *vb.* **1.** to hit or slam something (*bang* the door) **2.** to cut hair short across the forehead —*n.* **1.** a loud noise **2.** hair cut short across the forehead

ban·jo (ban′ jō) *n., pl.* **ban·jos** a musical instrument with a round body and strings

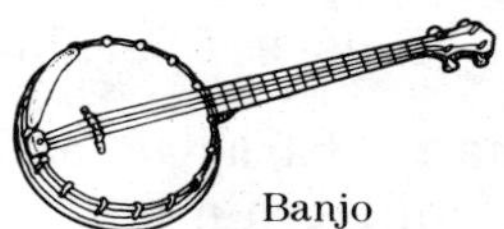
Banjo

bank (bangk) *n.* **1.** a heap of something (snow*bank*) **2.** the land along a river (*bank*s of the river) **3.** a shallow part of the sea (fishing *bank*s) **4.** a place where you can save or borrow money **5.** a place to save or store things (dime *bank*; blood *bank*) —*vb.* **1.** to put money into a bank **2.** to heap things up **3.** to store something

ban·ner (ban′ ər) *n.* a flag or a sign painted on cloth (carry a *banner* in a parade) —*adj.* excellent (a *banner* crop)

ban·quet (bang′ kwət) *n.* a special meal to celebrate a happy occasion (a *banquet* for the queen)

bar (bär) *n.* **1.** a thin rod **2.** a block (a *bar* of soap) **3.** court of law **4.** a counter where drinks are sold —*vb.* **barred**; **bar·ring** **1.** to fasten with a bar (*bar* the gate) **2.** to put up a barrier (*bar* the road)

bar·bar·i·an (bär ber′ ē ən) *n.* an uncivilized person

bar·ber (bär′ bər) *n.* a person who cuts hair

bare (baər) *adj.* **bar·er**; **bar·est** naked, empty or plain

bare·foot (baər′ füt′) *adv.* or *adj.* with nothing on the feet

bare·ly (baər′ lē) *adv.* just enough to satisfy

bar·gain (bär′ gən) *n.* **1.** an agreement (make a *bargain*) **2.** a thing bought at a good price (to find a *bargain*)

barge (bärj) *n.* a flat boat used to carry goods (a *barge* loaded with iron ore)

bark (bärk) *vb.* to make a loud, sharp noise —*n.* **1.** the sound made by a dog **2.** the covering of a tree **3.** a small sailboat

bar·ley (bär′ lē) *n.* a cereal grain used to feed animals or as a filler in soup

barn (bärn) *n.* a place to keep animals and to store hay and grain

ba·rom·e·ter (bə räm′ ə tər) *n.* a device for measuring air pressure

bar·rel (bar′ əl) *n.* **1.** a round container with flat ends used to store things **2.** the long, round part of a gun

Barrel

bar·ren (bar′ ən) *adj.* not able to bear offspring —*n.* an area of land where nothing will grow

bar·ri·er (bar′ ē ər) *n.* something that blocks the way

base (bās) *n.* **1.** the bottom **2.** the main ingredient **3.** a place where the navy keeps people and supplies —*vb.* **based**; **bas·ing** to put on a base or foundation —*adj.* **bas·er**; **bas·est** low or inferior

base·ball (bās′ bȯl′) *n.* **1.** a popular game played with a bat and ball **2.** the ball used in baseball

base·ment (bās′ mənt) *n.* the part below the main floor of a building, usually below ground level; cellar

bas·ic (bā′ sik) *adj.* relating to the foundation or base of something —*adv.* **ba·si·cal·ly**

ba·sin (bās′ n) *n.* **1.** a shallow round dish for holding water **2.** the land drained by a river

ba·sis (bā′ səs) *n.*, *pl.* **ba·ses** (-sēz) base

bas·ket (bas′ kət) *n.* **1.** a container made by weaving straw or strips of wood together **2.** an open net used as a goal in basketball

bas·ket·ball (bas′ kət bȯl′) *n.* **1.** an indoor game played by two teams **2.** the ball used in basketball

bass (bas) *n.*, *pl.* **bass** a type of fish used for food —*adj.* (bās) deep and low-toned

bat (bat) *n.* **1.** a solid club (baseball *bat*) **2.** a mouse-like animal with wings —*vb.* **bat·ted**; **bat·ting** to hit with a bat (*bat* the ball)

bath (bath) *n.*, *pl.* **baths** (bat͟hz) **1.** the act of washing the body **2.** a container for water for bathing **3.** a liquid in which objects are to be soaked (a cleansing *bath* for the jewelry)

bathe (bāt͟h) *vb.* **bathed**; **bath·ing** **1.** to take a bath **2.** to give a bath (*bathe* the baby) **3.** to go swimming **4.** to cover, as if with water (*bath*ed with light)

bath·room (bath′ rüm′) *n.* the washroom or lavatory

bat·ter (bat′ ər) *vb.* to beat again and again (*batter*ed by wind and rain) —*n.* a mixture of flour and other ingredients used to make such things as cakes and waffles

bat·ter·y (bat′ ə rē) *n.*, *pl.* **bat·ter·ies** **1.** one or more cells used to furnish electric current (*batteries* for the radio) **2.** a group of machines or devices (a *battery* of cameras clicked) **3.** pitcher and catcher of a baseball team

bat·ting (bat′ ing) *n.* **1.** the act of one who bats **2.** the ability to use a bat **3.** filling for a quilt

bat·tle (bat′ l) *n.* **1.** a fight between people or armies **2.** a contest —*vb.* **bat·tled**; **bat·tling** to fight

bay (bā) *n.* **1.** part of a large body of water forming an inlet in the land **2.** a shrub such as the laurel **3.** a reddish-brown horse **4.** the howl of a dog

be (bē); **is** (iz); **are** (är) *vb.* **1.** to equal (Ann *is* my friend.) **2.** to exist (There *are* deer here.)

beach (bēch) *n.* the land around the edge of a body of water —*vb.* to push ashore (The strong tide *beach*ed the boat.)

bea·con (bē′ kən) *n.* **1.** a signal light that can be seen at a distance **2.** radio signals to guide airplanes

bead (bēd) *n.* a small lump of material strung on a thread (a string of *beads*)

beak (bēk) *n.* the bill of a bird

beam (bēm) *n.* a long metal or wooden crossbar used to support a building or ship

bean (bēn) *n.* the seed or pod of a plant

bear (baər) *n.* **1.** a large mammal with shaggy fur **2.** a rude, surly person —*vb.* **bore** (bōr); **borne** (bōrn); **bear·ing** **1.** carry (*bear* a burden) **2.** produce (*bear* fruit) **3.** endure (*bear* the pain) **4.** press (*bear* down on your pencil)

beard (biərd) *n.* hair on the face

bear·ing (baər′ ing) *n.* the way a person carries himself (He has the *bearing* of a general.)

beast (bēst) *n.* a four-footed wild or farm animal (a *beast* of burden)

beat (bēt) *vb.* **beat**; **beat·en** (bēt′ n) or **beat**; **beat·ing** **1.** to strike again and again **2.** throb (the heart *beats*) **3.** stir (*beat* the eggs) **4.** to overcome (*beat* the enemy) —*n.* **1.** a blow **2.** a pulse —*adj.* exhausted

beau·ti·ful (byüt′ i fəl) *adj.* lovely

beau·ty (byüt′ ē) *n.*, *pl.* **beau·ties** qualities that give pleasure to the senses

bea·ver (bē′ vər) *n.* a rodent living in water and on land having sharp teeth, webbed feet, and a broad, flat tail

be·cause (bi kȯz′) *conj.* for the reason that

be·come (bi kəm′) *vb.* **be·came** (-kām′) **be·come**; or **be·com·ing** **1.** to grow to be **2.** to suit

bed (bed) *n.* **1.** a place to sleep **2.** a place to grow flowers **3.** the bottom or base of something (*bed*rock)

bed·ding (bed′ ing) *n.* bedclothes such as sheets and blankets

bed·time (bed′ tīm′) *n.* the time one should go to bed

bee (bē) *n.* an insect related to the wasp that lives in colonies, gathers pollen, and makes honey and wax

beech (bēch) *n.* a large shade tree with smooth gray bark and edible nuts

beef (bēf) *n., pl.* **beeves** (-bēvs); or **beefs** the meat of a steer or cow

bee·hive (bē′ hīv′) *n.* a hive for honeybees

beet (bēt) *n.* a plant with a sweet root used as a vegetable or as a source of sugar

bee·tle (bēt′ l) *n.* an insect with two stiff outer wings that cover the soft wings when folded

be·fore (bi fōr′) *adv.* **1.** in front **2.** in the past **3.** sooner —*prep.* **1.** in front of **2.** in advance —*conj.* ahead of the time when

beg (beg) *vb.* **begged**; **beg·ging** to ask earnestly as a favor or as a kindness to the poor

beg·gar (beg′ ər) *n.* a poor person who lives by begging

be·gin (bi gin′) *vb.* **be·gan** (-gan′); **be·gun** (-gən′); **be·gin·ning** **1.** to start **2.** to get the first part done

be·have (bi hāv′) *vb.* **be·haved**; **be·hav·ing** **1.** to act **2.** to manage oneself in a correct way

be·hav·ior (bi hāv′ yər) *n.* the way a person manages himself

be·hind (bi hīnd′) *adv.* **1.** in a place someone has left (left my billfold *behind*) **2.** toward the back **3.** not up to the standard (*behind* in my work) —*prep.* at, to, or toward the back

be·ing (bē′ ing) *n.* **1.** a living person or thing **2.** life

be·lief (bē lēf′) *n.* **1.** faith **2.** trust **3.** opinion

be·lieve (bə lēv′) *vb.* **be·lieved**; **be·liev·ing** **1.** to have faith **2.** to trust **3.** to think

bell (bel) *n.* **1.** a hollow metal cup-shaped object that makes a ringing sound when struck **2.** the sound of a bell

bel·ly (bel′ ē) *n., pl.* **bel·lies** stomach or abdomen

be·long (bə lȯng′) *vb.* **1.** to be in the right place (you *belong* here) **2.** to be owned by someone (that *belong*s to Tom) **3.** to go with (*belong*s with this set)

be·lov·ed (bə ləv′ əd, -ləvd′) *adj.* dearly loved

be·low (bə lō′) *adv.* in or to a lower place —*prep.* beneath

belt (belt) *n.* **1.** a band worn around the waist, sometimes through belt loops on pants **2.** something formed in a circle (a green *belt* around the city) **3.** an endless band for machinery (a fan *belt*)

bench (bench) *n.* **1.** a long seat (park *bench*) **2.** a strong table (work*bench*) **3.** a judge or the seat for a judge in court

bend (bend) *vb.* **bent**; **bend·ing** to curve —*n.* something that is curved

be·neath (bi nēth′) *adv.* in a lower place —*prep.* under

ben·e·fit (ben′ ə fit′) *n.* a profit or advantage (*benefit*s of healthy living) —*vb.* **ben·e·fit·ed**; **ben·e·fit·ing** **1.** to be useful **2.** to receive an advantage

bent (bent) *adj.* **1.** curved **2.** determined —*n.* a mental leaning (She has an artistic *bent.*)

ber·ry (ber′ ē) *n., pl.* **ber·ries** a small fruit —*vb.* **ber·ried; ber·ry·ing** to pick berries

berth (bərth) *n.* **1.** a bed on a ship or railroad car **2.** a place where a ship lies at anchor

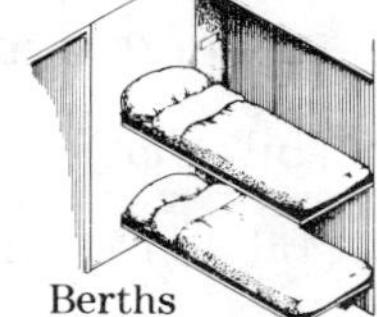
Berths

be·side (bi sīd′) *prep.* **1.** near by **2.** in comparison with **3.** in addition to **4.** away from (*beside* the point)

best (best) *n.* the person or thing that is most excellent

be·stow (bi stō′) *vb.* to present as a gift

bet (bet) *vb.* **bet; bet·ting** to take a chance by risking something if one is wrong

be·tween (bi twēn′) *prep.* **1.** in the space or time which separates **2.** from one to another **3.** by the shared action of

bev·er·age (bev′ ər ij) *n.* a drink

be·ware (bi waər′) *vb.* to be careful

be·wil·der (bi wil′ dər) *vb.* to puzzle or confuse

be·yond (bē änd′) *adv.* at or on the farther side —*prep.* **1.** on the other side **2.** out of the reach of (*beyond* hope)

bi·as (bī′ as) *n.* **1.** a line on a slant across the threads of cloth **2.** a definite opinion —*vb.* **bi·ased; bi·as·ing** to favor one opinion over another

bib·li·og·ra·phy (bib′ lē äg′ rə fē) *n., pl.* **bib·li·og·ra·phies** a list of books or resources about a subject

bi·cy·cle (bī′ sik′ əl) *n.* a two-wheeled vehicle propelled by pedaling

bid (bid) *vb.* **bade** (bad); **bid·den** to order or command —*vb.* **bid; bid** to offer to buy —*n.* an offer to pay a sum for something or to do certain work for a stated fee

big (big) *adj.* **big·ger; big·gest** large or important

bill (bil) *n.* **1.** the beak of a bird **2.** an early version of a law presented to lawmakers for their consideration —*vb.* to send a notice of money owed

bil·lion (bil′ yən) *n.* a thousand millions

bil·low (bil′ ō) *n.* a great wave —*vb.* to swell out

bin (bin) *n.* a box or boxed-off area used for storage

bind (bīnd) *vb.* **bound** (baůnd); **bind·ing** **1.** to hold together by tying or putting into a cover **2.** to bandage

bind·ing (bīn′ ding) *n.* **1.** the cover of a book **2.** a strip of cloth stitched to the cut edges of a garment to prevent fraying

bi·og·ra·phy (bī äg′ rə fē) *n., pl.* **bi·og·ra·phies** a story written about a person's life

bi·ol·o·gy (bī äl′ ə jē) *n.* the study of living things

birch (bərch) *n.* a tree with smooth bark that may be removed in large sheets

bird (bərd) *n.* an egg-laying animal with wings and feathers

birth (bərth) *n.* **1.** the act of being born **2.** an origin

birth·day (bərth′ dā′) *n.* the day of the year on which a person was born or something began

bis·cuit (bis′ kət) *n.* a cracker or a small disk of bread baked in the oven

bit (bit) *n.* **1.** a tool for boring holes **2.** the part of a bridle that goes in a horse's mouth **3.** a small piece of anything

bite (bīt) *vb.* **bit** (bit); **bit·ten**; **bit·ing** to cut into with the teeth —*n.* a wound or sting made by biting

bit·ter (bit′ ər) *adj.* **1.** harsh to the taste, puckering the mouth **2.** hard to accept (a *bitter* experience) **3.** hard to bear (a *bitter* failure) **4.** causing pain (*bitter* cold)

black (blak) *adj.* **1.** entirely without light and of the darkest shade **2.** dark-skinned **3.** dirty (*black* with dirt) **4.** gloomy or hostile —*n.* **1.** the color of soot or coal **2.** a member of a dark-skinned race

black·board (blak′ bōrd′) *n.* a smooth, dark surface for writing with chalk

blad·der (blad′ ər) *n.* a sac into which urine passes from the kidneys

blade (blād) *n.* **1.** a leaf of grass **2.** the cutting part of a knife **3.** the wide part of a paddle

blame (blām) *vb.* **blamed**; **blam·ing** to place responsibility for a fault

blank (blangk) *adj.* **1.** having no marks or printing on it **2.** having empty spaces to be filled in **3.** having no expression on one's face —*n.* an empty space in a line of writing

blan·ket (blang′ kət) *n.* **1.** a heavy covering for a bed **2.** a covering layer (a *blanket* of snow) —*vb.* to cover

blast (blast) *n.* **1.** a strong gust of wind **2.** an explosion

blaze (blāz) *n.* **1.** a hot flame **2.** an outburst **3.** a display

bleak (blēk) *adj.* cold and cheerless

bleed (blēd) *vb.* **bled**; **bleed·ing** **1.** to lose blood **2.** to feel sympathy (my heart *bleeds* for you)

blend (blend) *vb.* to put things together so that they are evenly mixed —*n.* a product that is well mixed

blind (blīnd) *adj.* **1.** unable to see **2.** unable to understand **3.** unable to get through (*blind* alley) —*vb.* to make blind (*blind*ed by headlights) —*n.* something that stops vision (window *blind*s) —*adv.* blindly (fly *blind* in the fog)

blink (blingk) *vb.* **1.** to close and open the eye quickly **2.** to put a light on and off (*blink* the light)

bliz·zard (bliz′ ərd) *n.* a severe storm of high wind and heavy snow

block (bläk) *n.* **1.** a solid piece of material with one or more flat sides **2.** something that stops progress (traffic *block*) **3.** something large that is made up of separate units (city *block*, apartment *block*, business *block*, railroad *block* — a length of track with its own signals) —*vb.* **1.** to stop progress (*block* the driveway, *block* a play in football, *block* a bill in the Senate) **2.** to set out in units (*block* out a plan)

blond (bländ) *adj.* having light hair and skin —*n.* **blond** or **blonde** a blond person

blood (bləd) *n.* **1.** the red liquid that travels through the body **2.** relatives from a common ancestor (of the same *blood*)

bloom (blüm) *n.* **1.** a flower **2.** a state of freshness and energy (the *bloom* of health) —*vb.* **1.** to produce flowers **2.** to develop to the state of high quality (to *bloom* as an athlete, a beautiful person, an excellent student, or other high goal)

blos·som (bläs′ əm) *n.* flower or bloom —*vb.* **1.** to bloom **2.** to develop well in any field

blouse (blaủs) *n.* a garment worn from the neck to the waist, similar to a shirt

blow (blō) *vb.* **blew** (blü); **blown** (blōn); **blow·ing** to send a strong current of air (the wind *blew*, *blow* your nose, *blow* glass) —*n.* **1.** a hard hit with the hand **2.** a sad event that causes misfortune

blue (blü) *n.* the color of a clear, sunny sky

bluff (bləf) *adj.* rising steeply with a flat front —*n.* a cliff —*vb.* to mislead

blunt (blənt) *adj.* **1.** dull (a *blunt* knife) **2.** outspoken (*blunt* remark)

board (bōrd) *n.* **1.** a long, thin piece of wood **2.** a group of people who manage something (the school *board)* **3.** a flat object used for a special purpose (chess *board*) —*vb.* to get on a plane or ship (to *board*)

boast (bōst) *vb.* **1.** to praise one's own deeds **2.** to brag

boat (bōt) *n.* **1.** a small vessel pushed forward by oars or paddles **2.** a ship —*vb.* to use a boat

bod·y (bäd′ ē) *n., pl.* **bod·ies** **1.** the whole of a person or animal, living or dead **2.** people working together as a group (student *body*) **3.** the main part of something (*body* of a letter, *body* of the ship)

boil (bȯil) *n.* a lump in the skin that contains pus and germs —*vb.* **1.** to heat something until it bubbles **2.** to cook in boiling water (*boil* potatoes)

boil·er (bȯi′ lər) *n.* **1.** a tank where steam is produced for driving engines **2.** a tank holding hot water

bold (bōld) *adj.* **1.** daring **2.** saucy

bolt (bōlt) *n.* **1.** a flash of lightning **2.** a pin that is fastened with a nut to hold together machinery (nut and *bolt*) **3.** a roll of cloth (about 40 yds. on a *bolt*) —*vb.* **1.** to move suddenly (*bolt*ed into the hall) **2.** to fasten with a pin (*bolt* the door)

bomb (bäm) *n.* **1.** a case containing explosives **2.** a container of bug killer under pressure

bond (bänd) *n.* **1.** something that holds things together **2.** something that holds a person responsible to pay at a certain time (He bought a government *bond.*) or if an agreement is not kept (People in security jobs work under *bond.*) —*vb.* to hold things together (to *bond* the bricks with mortar)

bone (bōn) *n.* **1.** the hard material that forms the skeleton of most animals, including people **2.** one of the parts of the skeleton (thigh *bone*)

bon·y (bō′ nē) *adj.* **bon·i·er**; **bon·i·est** **1.** having visible bones (a thin, *bony* person) **2.** looking like bones (*bony* material) **3.** having many bones (*bony* fish)

book (bu̇k) *n.* sheets of paper bound together in a volume containing a written work (our *book, English to Use*), or blank paper (scrap *book*), or lined paper (record*book*, note*book*)

boom (büm) *n.* **1.** a long pole used to support or guide something (the *boom* on the sailboat) **2.** a deep, hollow noise —*vb.* to increase rapidly (The economy is *boom*ing.)

Boom

boost (büst) *vb.* **1.** to raise or push up (*boost* him over the wall) **2.** to increase (*boost* home sales) —*n.* the act of boosting (give them a *boost*)

boot (büt) *n.* footwear that covers the foot and part of the leg —*vb.* kick (*boot* the ball)

booth (büth) *n., pl.* **booths** (büthz) **1.** a small shelter or private stall, such as a place for displaying goods at a fair **2.** a stall with a public telephone **3.** a private enclosure for voting **4.** a section of a restaurant with a table and two benches **5.** a movie projection room

bor·der (bȯrd′ ər) *n.* the edge of anything (the Mexican *border*; the *border* of flowers along the walk; the red *border* on the scarf)

bore (bōr) *vb.* **bored**; **bor·ing** **1.** to make a hole in something (*bore* a hole in the wood) **2.** to tire others by being dull —*n.* **1.** the inside of a tube (the *bore* of a gun) **2.** a tiresome person

born (bȯrn) *adj.* **1.** brought into life by birth **2.** since birth (*born* rich)

bor·row (bär′ ō) *vb.* to take something with the promise of returning it (*borrow* a book)

boss (bȯs) *n.* a person in charge of workers —*vb.* to give directions or orders

both (bōth) *adj.* **1.** the two together (*both* teachers) **2.** the two (*both* of them)

both·er (bäth′ ər) *vb.* to annoy or cause trouble (That barking *bothers* me.) —*n.* annoyance

bot·tle (bät′ l) *n.* a narrow-necked container without handles usually made of glass —*vb.* to put into bottles

bot·tom (bät′ əm) *n.* the lowest part, the base

bough (baù) *n.* a large branch of a tree

boul·der (bōl′ dər) *n.* a large stone, rounded with wear

bou·le·vard (bül′ ə värd′) *n.* a wide avenue, often divided by a strip of grass with trees

bounce (baùns) *vb.* **bounced**; **bounc·ing** to cause something to spring back

bound (baùnd) *adj.* **1.** covered with binding (a *bound* book) **2.** certain (*bound* to improve) —*vb.* to mark the boundary —*n.* a boundary line (ball went out of *bounds*)

bound·a·ry (baùn′ də rē) *n.*, *pl.* **bound·a·ries** a line that marks the limit

bou·quet (bō kā′, bü kā′) *n.* a bunch of flowers

Bouquet

bow (baù) *vb.* to bend in greeting or respect —*n.* the front part of a ship

bow (bō) *n.* **1.** a curved rod bent by a cord, for shooting arrows **2.** a ribbon tied in loops —*vb.* **1.** to curve like a bow **2.** to play a musical instrument with a bow

bowl (bōl) *n.* **1.** a hollow dish without handles **2.** the contents of a bowl (a *bowl* of fruit) —*vb.* to play a game of bowling

box (bäks) *n.* **1.** a container with a lid **2.** an enclosed place (the *box* office; the guard's *box*) **3.** an evergreen shrub used for hedges —*vb.* **1.** to enclose in a box **2.** to strike with the hand or fist

boy (bȯi) *n.* a male child

boy·hood (bȯi′ hu̇d′) *n.* the time of being a boy

brace (brās) *n.* a support that holds something firm *brace*s on her teeth, a *brace* for the screen door) —*vb.* to support or strengthen

brace·let (brās′ lət) *n.* a band of jewelry for the arm

brack·et (brak′ ət) *n.* **1.** a shelf support **2.** marks to enclose one or more words, i.e., square brackets [ ] or angle brackets < >

brain (brān) *n.* **1.** the mass of nervous tissue in the skull that controls mental and physical actions **2.** *(pl.)* intelligence

brake (brāk) *n.* a device for slowing or stopping a wheel —*vb.* **braked**; **brak·ing** to slow down or stop by using a brake

branch (branch) *n.* a subdivision or part of something larger (*branch* of a tree, *branch* of the library) —*vb.* to divide into separate parts (*branch* out)

brand (brand) *n.* a mark to show ownership (*brand* on the cattle, *brand* of canned goods) —*vb.* to mark with a brand or trademark

brass (bras) *n.* a metal alloy made by melting copper and zinc together (*brass* doorknob)

brave (brāv) *adj.* **brav·er**; **brav·est** bold and courageous —*n.* a North American Indian warrior —*vb.* to act with courage (to *brave* it out)

bread (bred) *n.* a baked loaf of raised dough made mostly of flour

break (brāk) *vb.* **broke** (brōk); **bro·ken** (brō′ kən); or **break·ing** **1.** to separate into pieces **2.** to force a way into or through (*break* through the ice) **3.** to fail to obey (*break* the rule) **4.** to interrupt (*break* the silence) **5.** go beyond (*break* a record) —*n.* an act of breaking

break·fast (brek′ fəst) *n.* the morning meal

breast (brest) *n.* a gland that produces milk

breath (breth) *n.* air taken in and let out of the lungs

breathe (brēth) *vb.* **breathed**; **breath·ing** to use the action of the lungs to take in and send out air

breed (brēd) *vb.* **bred** (bred); **breed·ing** **1.** to increase the number of plants or animals by reproduction **2.** to bring up —*n.* a kind or class of plant or animal (*breed* of dogs)

breeze (brēz) *n.* a moderate wind

brick (brik) *n.* a molded block of baked clay used as a building material

bride (brīd) *n.* a newly married woman or one about to be married

bridge (brij) *n.* **1.** a structure built to carry a road or railroad across a river or bay **2.** the high bone on the nose **3.** the arch that holds the strings on a violin

brief (brēf) *adj.* short

bright (brīt) *adj.* **1.** shining with light **2.** a strong, sharp color **3.** a clever, witty person **4.** sunny and cheerful

bril·liant (bril′ yənt) *adj.* sparkling or talented

brim (brim) *n.* the edge (*brim* of the cup, wide *brim* on the hat) —*vb.* **brimmed**; **brim·ming** to fill to the upper or outer edge

bring (bring) *vb.* **brought** (brȯt); **bring·ing** **1.** to carry (*bring* a book) **2.** to get someone to come along (*bring* a friend) **3.** to cause something to happen (The wind *brought* power lines down.)

brisk (brisk) *adj.* **1.** lively or quick (a *brisk* walk) **2.** burning quickly (a *brisk* fire) **3.** clear and stimulating (a *brisk* morning)

brit·tle (brit′ l) *adj.* **brit·tler**; **brit·tlest** firm but fragile or crisp (thin, *brittle* glass)

broad (brȯd) *adj.* **1.** wide (*broad* avenue) **2.** open or clear (*broad* fields) **3.** open to suggestions (*broad-minded*) **4.** touching only main points (*broad* outline)

broad·cast (brȯd′ kast′) *vb.* **broad·cast**; **broad·cast·ing** to spread far and wide

broom (brüm, brům) *n.* a long-handled, stiff brush for sweeping

broth·er (brə<u>th</u>′ ər) *n., pl.* **broth·ers** or **breth·ren** (bre<u>th</u>′ rən) **1.** a male related to someone by having the same parents **2.** a fellow member of an organization

brow (braů) *n.* **1.** the arch of the face above the eye **2.** the top of a hill

brown (braůn) *adj.* of the color brown (*brown* jacket) —*n.* a color between orange and black —*vb.* to brown (*brown* the meat in a frypan)

bruise (brüz) *vb.* **bruised**; **bruis·ing** to crush without cutting —*n.* a black and blue mark on the skin

brush (brəsh) *vb.* to scrub or stroke with a brush (*brush* your shoes, *brush* your hair) —*n.* a heavy growth of wild bushes

bub·ble (bəb′ əl) *vb.* **bub·bled**; **bub·bling** to make bubbles —*n.* a round film of liquid filled with air or gas (soap *bubbles*)

buck (bək) *n.* the male of some animals such as the deer or goat —*vb.* **1.** to charge ahead (*buck* traffic) **2.** to resist (*buck* the new rules)

buck·et (bək′ ət) *n.* **1.** a pail **2.** a deep, round container (*bucket* of feed for the horse)

buck·le (bək′ əl) *n.* a fastener for a belt

bud·get (bəj′ ət) *n.* a plan for spending money that is received

buf·fa·lo (bəf′ ə lō′) *n.*, *pl.* **buf·fa·lo** or **buf·fa·loes** a wild ox, especially the American bison

Buffalo

bug (bəg) *n.* **1.** insect **2.** defect (get the *bug* out of the computer)

bug·gy (bəg′ ē) *n.*, *pl.* **bug·gies** a small carriage pulled by one horse

bu·gle (byü′ gəl) *n.* an instrument like a trumpt but without valves, used for military signals like "taps" at bedtime

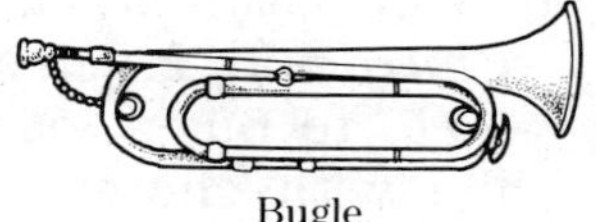
Bugle

build (bild) *vb.* **built** (bilt); **build·ing** to construct or put together (to *build* a bridge, to *build* a business)

build·ing (bil′ ding) *n.* a structure for living, working, storage, or protection

bulb (bəlb) *n.* the underground part of certain plants that is shaped like an onion (a lily *bulb*)

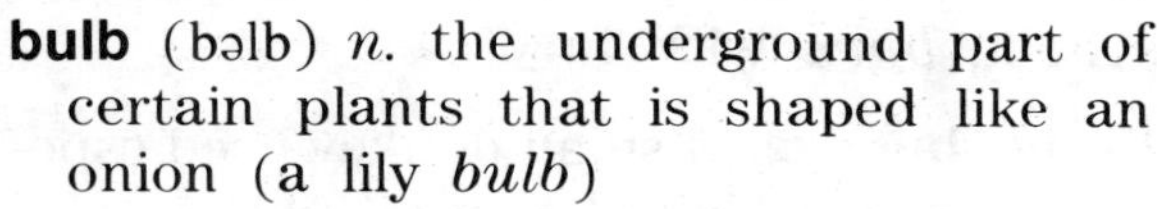

Bulb

bulge (bəlj) *n.* a rounded part that sticks out (*bulge* of his muscle) —*vb.* **bulged**; **bulg·ing** to swell or curve outward

bulk (bəlk) *n.* **1.** the size of an object **2.** the main mass of the object

bull (bu̇l) *n.* the male of certain animals such as the ox, cow, elephant, and whale

bul·let (bu̇l′ ət) *n.* a piece of metal made to be fired from a gun

bul·le·tin (bu̇l′ ət n) *n.* a short notice about a matter of public interest

bump (bəmp) *vb.* to strike, or clash, with something —*n.* **1.** a heavy blow **2.** a swelling

bunch (bənch) *n.* **1.** things growing in a cluster (a *bunch* of grapes) **2.** a group (a *bunch* of carrots) —*vb.* to bring together in a group

bun·dle (bən′ dl) *n.* **1.** a package **2.** things that are tied together or in a package (a *bundle* of clothes)

buoy (bü′ ē, bȯi′) *n.* a floating object used to mark a channel for ships

Buoy

bur·den (bərd′ n) *n.* **1.** a heavy load (the suitcases were a *burden*) **2.** the weight of grief (a *burden* of sorrow) —*vb.* to put a load on someone or something (*burden* him with chores)

bu·reau (byu̇r′ ō) *n.* **1.** a chest with a mirror for storing clothes in the bedroom (A *bureau* is not as high as a chest of drawers.) **2.** a specialized department

burn (bərn) *vb.* **burned** (bərnd) or **burnt** (bərnt); **burn·ing** **1.** to destroy by fire **2.** to feel as if on fire (*burning* up in this heat; *burn* with fury)

bur·ro (bər′ ō) *n., pl.* **bur·ros** a small donkey used especially in the southwestern United States

bur·row (bər′ ō) *n.* a hole in the ground dug by an animal such as a rabbit for a home —*vb.* **1.** to make a burrow **2.** to hide or enclose oneself as if in a burrow (*burrowed* down into his work)

burst (bərst) *vb.* **burst**; **burst·ing** to break suddenly or to explode —*n.* a sudden outbreak (a *burst* of clapping)

bur·y (ber′ ē) *vb.* **bur·ied**; **bur·y·ing** **1.** to put in the ground and cover over (*bury* the dead; *bury* the time capsule; *bury* the asparagus roots) **2.** to hide (*bury* her face in her hands)

bus (bəs) *n., pl.* **bus·es** or **bus·ses** a vehicle which will hold many passengers

bush (bu̇sh) *n.* **1.** a shrub or woody plant with branches **2.** a large, uncleared area where very few people live (Australian *bush*)

bush·el (bu̇sh′ əl) *n.* a measure of dry goods equal to four pecks or thirty-two quarts (a *bushel* of apples)

busi·ness (biz′ nəs) *n.* **1.** a company that works to make a profit (a cleaning *business*) **2.** personal activities (tend to some *business* at the bank) **3.** what one does to make a living or be successful (I have to get down to *business* now.)

bus·y (biz′ ē) *adj.* **bus·i·er**; **bus·i·est** actively working (Ellen is *busy.* The telephone line is *busy.*) —*vb.* **bus·ied**; **bus·y·ing** to keep busy

but (bət) *adv.* only (He is *but* a beginner at this job.) —*prep.* except or besides (no one *but* Ava Brown) —*conj.* however (fished *but* didn't catch anything)

butch·er (bu̇ch′ ər) *n.* one who cuts and sells meats

but·ter (bət′ ər) *n.* the fatty food made from cream by churning —*vb.* to spread with butter (*butter* the toast)

but·ter·fly (bət′ ər flī′) *n.* a daytime flying insect with colorful wings

but·ton (bət′ n) *n.* a small round object used for holding clothes together by passing it through a buttonhole —*vb.* to close with buttons

buy (bī) *vb.* **bought** (bȯt); **buy·ing** to receive something in exchange for money —*n.* something bought at a good price (a good *buy*)

buzz (bəz) *n.* a humming noise like that of bees —*vb.* to make a humming sound (The hall *buzz*ed with the news.)

by (bī) *prep.* **1.** near (stood *by* the desk) **2.** past (drove *by* an exit) **3.** at (cross the desert *by* night) **4.** according to (his *by* law) —*adv.* **1.** near at hand **2.** past

C

cab (kab) *n.* **1.** taxi (call a *cab*) **2.** the driver's compartment of a locomotive or truck

Cab

cab·bage (kab′ ij) *n.* a plant with a thick head of leaves, used as a vegetable

cab·in (kab′ ən) *n.* **1.** a small cottage (our *cabin* in the mountains) **2.** a private room on a cruise ship (slept in our *cabin*) **3.** a large area in an airplane where passengers ride

cab·i·net (kab′ ə nət) *n.* **1.** a piece of furniture for storing records or supplies (file *cabinet*) **2.** a group of persons who serve as advisers to the President or other heads of countries

ca·ble (kā′ bəl) *n.* **1.** a large, strong rope or chain **2.** a cablegram **3.** an insulated bundle of wires for carrying electricity —*vb.* **ca·bled**; **ca·bling** to send a telegram by underwater cable

cac·tus (kak′ təs) *n., pl.* **cac·tus·es** or **cac·ti** (-tī′) one of many kinds of fleshy, flowering plants, usually with sharp spines, that grow in dry regions

ca·det (kə det′) *n.* a student in training for the military or Civil Air Patrol

caf·e·te·ri·a (kaf′ ə tir′ ē ə) *n.* a lunchroom or restaurant where people serve themselves

cage (kāj) *n.* **1.** a box with bars for keeping an animal **2.** an enclosure like a cage —*vb.* **caged**; **cag·ing** to confine

cake (kāk) *n.* **1.** a baked food made from a sweet batter **2.** a flat, solid mass (a fish *cake*)

cal·ci·um (kal′ sē əm) *n.* a metallic element found in lime, marble, and chalk that is important to plants and animals

cal·cu·late (kal′ kyə lāt′) *vb.* **cal·cu·lat·ed; cal·cu·lat·ing** to get an answer by adding, subtracting, multiplying, or dividing

cal·en·dar (kal′ ən dər) *n.* a method of keeping track of the days of the month and months of the year

calf (kaf) *n., pl.* **calves** (kavz) **1.** the young of the cow and certain other large animals **2.** the skin of the calf

cal·i·co (kal′ i kō′) *n., pl.* **cal·i·coes** or **cal·i·cos** a cotton cloth, usually with a colorful pattern printed on one side

call (kȯl) *vb.* **1.** to speak in a loud voice (to *call* for help) **2.** to name someone (to *call* her Nancy) **3.** to telephone (*call* her aunt) **4.** to announce (*call* a meeting)

calm (käm) *n.* a quiet, peaceful period —*adj.* still (a *calm* day) —*vb.* to become calm

cal·o·rie (kal′ ə rē) *n., pl.* **cal·o·ries** **1.** the amount of heat required to raise one gram of water one degree centigrade **2.** a unit used to measure the energy content of food

cam·el (kam′ əl) *n.* a large hoofed animal with one or two humps on its back, used in the desert to ride or for carrying loads

Camel

cam·er·a (kam′ ə rə) *n.* a device for taking pictures

camp (kamp) *n.* **1.** a large area with tents or huts for shelter where people can spend a vacation **2.** a place where military personnel stay temporarily

cam·paign (kam pān′) *n.* a series of activities done for a special purpose (a political *campaign*)

cam·pus (kam′ pəs) *n.* the grounds of a school, college, or university

can (kən, kan) *helping verb, past* **could** (kəd, kůd); *pres. sing. & pl.* **can** **1.** know how to (She *can* speak French.) **2.** be able to (He *can* dive.) **3.** be permitted to (They *can* go to the concert.) —*n.* a metal container

ca·nal (kə nal′) *n.* a waterway built to connect two bodies of water (the Panama *Canal*)

ca·nar·y (kə ner′ ē) *n., pl.* **ca·nar·ies** a small songbird usually kept in a cage

can·cer (kan′ sər) *n.* a deadly growth in the body

can·di·date (kan′ də dāt′) *n.* **1.** a person who runs for office **2.** a student who is studying for a college or graduate school degree

can·dle (kan′ dl) *n.* a wick surrounded by wax that is burned to give light

can·dy (kan′ dē) *n., pl.* **can·dies** a sweet treat made by boiling sugar and flavorings —*vb.* **can·died**; **can·dy·ing** to coat with sugar (*candied* carrots)

cane (kān) *n.* **1.** a walking stick **2.** a tall, woody plant (sugar *cane*) —*vb.* **caned**; **can·ing** to make with cane

can·non (kan′ ən) *n., pl.* **can·nons** or **can·non** a large gun

can·not (kan′ ät′, kə nät′) is not able to

ca·noe (kə nü′) *n.* a long, light boat with a pointed prow at each end, that is moved by paddles

can·vas (kan′ vəs) *n.* a coarse, strong cloth used for sails, tents, and as the base for oil paintings

can·yon (kan′ yən) *n.* a deep, narrow passage with steep sides

cap (kap) *n.* **1.** a hat with a visor **2.** a cover (bottle *cap*) —*vb.* **capped**; **cap·ping** to cover or put on a cap

ca·pa·ble (kā′ pə bəl) *adj.* being able to do something

ca·pac·i·ty (kə pas′ ət ē) *n.*, *pl.* **ca·pac·i·ties** power to hold (The gym has a seating *capacity* of 600.)

cape (kāp) *n.* **1.** a short or long garment without sleeves that is worn over the shoulders **2.** a piece of land that juts out into the water (visit *Cape* May)

cap·il·lar·y (kap′ ə ler′ ē) *n.*, *pl.* **cap·il·lar·ies** the smallest of blood vessels —*adj.* relating to capillaries

cap·i·tal (kap′ ət l) *n.* **1.** seat of government (*capital* city) **2.** an upper-case letter (*capital* letter—A, B, etc.) —*adj.* punishable by death (*capital* crime)

cap·i·tol (kap′ ət l) *n.* **1.** the building in which a state legislature meets **2.** when capitalized, the building in Washington, D.C. in which the United States Congress meets

cap·sule (kap′ səl) *n.* **1.** a case or pod holding plant seeds or spores **2.** a case of soft material, such as gelatin, holding medicine to be swallowed **3.** a closed compartment for travel in space

cap·tain (kap′ tən) *n.* **1.** the head person on a team **2.** a commissioned officer in the army **3.** the commanding officer of a ship —*vb.* to command or lead

cap·tive (kap′ tiv) *n.* **1.** a prisoner, especially in war **2.** one tied to another by affection or admiration

cap·ture (kap′ chər) *n.* the act of taking as a prisoner —*vb.* **cap·tured**; **cap·tur·ing** to take by force or by surprise

car (kär) *n.* **1.** a vehicle that runs on wheels **2.** the basket under a balloon in which people ride

car·bo·hy·drate (kär′ bō hī′ drāt′) *n.* the energy-producing nutrients in sugar and starch

car·bon (kär′ bən) *n.* a chemical element

card (kärd) *n.* **1.** a playing card **2.** a stiff piece of pasteboard (a 3×5 *card*)

card·board (kärd′ bōrd) *n.* a material thicker than paper, used for cards

car·di·nal (kärd′ n əl) *adj.* very important (*cardinal* rules) —*n.* **1.** a bright red American finch with a crest **2.** an official in the Roman Catholic Church

care (keər) *n.* **1.** a cause for concern **2.** supervision (under the *care* of a therapist) —*vb.* **cared**; **car·ing** **1.** to feel concern **2.** to give attention and service (*care* for her sick mother) **3.** to be fond of (to *care* deeply about her friend)

ca·reer (kə riər′) *n.* an occupation a person follows to make a living

care·ful (keər′ fəl) *adj.* watchful to avoid trouble

care·less (keər′ ləs) *adj.* without taking proper care

car·go (kär′ gō) *n.*, *pl.* **car·goes** or **car·gos** goods carried by ship, airplane, or vehicle

car·i·bou (kar′ ə bü′) *n.* a large reindeer native to northern North America

car·ni·val (kär′ nə vəl) *n.* a festival with amusements

car·pen·ter (kär pən tər) *n.* a worker who builds things of wood

car·pet (kär′ pət) *n.* a thick fabric floor covering

car·riage (kar′ ij) *n.* **1.** posture (he has good *carriage*) **2.** a wheeled vehicle for carrying people or things (horse and *carriage*, baby *carriage*, gun *carriage*)

car·rot (kar′ ət) *n.* **1.** an orange root used as a vegetable **2.** a weed that grows wild in fields

car·ry (kar′ ē) *vb.* **car·ried**; **car·ry·ing** **1.** to take from one place to another **2.** to transfer a number from one column to another (write the units and *carry* the tens) **3.** to have on one's person (to *carry* a passport) **4.** to sing in tune (*carry* a melody)

cart (kärt) *n.* a two or four-wheeled vehicle for carrying loads (grocery *cart*)

car·ton (kärt′ n) *n.* **1.** a cardboard container **2.** a sturdy box

car·toon (kär tün′) *n.* a drawing representing a well-known person or event that is marked by comedy or satire

carve (kärv) *vb.* **carved**; **carv·ing** **1.** to cut meat into slices **2.** to cut a design into material such as wood or ivory

case (kās) *n.* **1.** an event under investigation (a legal *case*) **2.** a place to store something (book*case,* a *case* for your glasses, a trophy *case*)

cash (kash) *n.* money —*vb.* to get money for a check (*cash* a check)

cast (kast) *vb.* **cast**; **cast·ing** **1.** to throw **2.** to mold (*cast* in steel) —*n.* **1.** the act of throwing **2.** the actors and actresses in a play (she was in the *cast*) **3.** a protective form for a broken bone (arm in a *cast*) **4.** a form for molding metal (poured molten metal in the *cast*)

cas·tle (kas′ əl) *n.* a place where a royal family lives, often large and grand, and sometimes protected by high walls and a moat

ca·su·al (kazh′ ə wəl) *adj.* **1.** happening by chance **2.** showing little concern (a *casual* attitude)

cat (kat) *n.* a small feline, kept as a pet, that is good at catching mice and rats

catch (kach) *vb.* **caught** (kȯt); **catch·ing** **1.** to get hold of (*catch* the ball) **2.** to come in time for (*catch* the bus) **3.** to overtake (*catch* up) **4.** draw attention (*catch* someone's eye) **5.** snag (get *caught* on a nail) —*n.* **1.** a game (playing *catch*) **2.** quantity (the *catch* of fish) **3.** a fastener

cat·e·gory (kat′ ə gōr′ ē) *n., pl.* **cat·e·go·ries** class or variety

cat·er·pil·lar (kat′ ər pil′ ər) *n.* a worm-like larva of a butterfly or moth

cat·fish (kat′ fish′) *n.* a large-headed fish with long whisker-like feelers near the mouth

cat·tle (kat′ l) *n.*, *pl.* **cat·tle** cows, bulls, and calves that are tame farm animals

cause (ko̊z) *n.* **1.** a reason for something **2.** an activity that deserves support (a worthy *cause*) —*vb.* to make happen

cau·tion (ko̊′ shən) *n.* carefulness to avoid trouble —*vb.* to warn

cau·tious (ko̊′ shəs) *adj.* careful

cave (kāv) *n.* a hollow place in the side of a hill —*vb.* **caved**; **cav·ing** to fall in or collapse

cav·ern (kav′ ərn) *n.* a cave

cav·i·ty (kav′ ət ē) *n.*, *pl.* **cav·i·ties** a hole (*cavity* in a tooth)

cease (sēs) *vb.* **ceased**; **ceas·ing** **1.** to bring to an end **2.** to stop

ce·dar (sēd′ ər) *n.* an evergreen tree in the pine family with reddish wood that is fragrant and that lasts a long time

ceil·ing (sē′ ling) *n.* **1.** the inner part of the top of a room **2.** the height from the ground to the lowest layer of clouds (the cloud *ceiling*)

cel·e·brate (sel′ ə brāt′) *vb.* **cel·e·brated**; **cel·e·brat·ing** to mark the memory of an event with carefully planned activities

cel·e·bra·tion (sel′ ə brā′ shən) *n.* the act of carrying out the events planned in memory of some event

cel·er·y (sel′ ə rē) *n.* a garden plant used as a vegetable

cell (sel) *n.* **1.** a small room or compartment **2.** a very small mass of living matter **3.** one component of a battery

cel·lar (sel′ ər) *n.* the bottom floor of a house or building which is at or below ground level

ce·ment (si ment′) *n.* a compound that, when water is added, hardens into a firm mass

cem·e·ter·y (sem′ ə ter′ ē) *n., pl.* **cem·e·ter·ies** a place to bury the dead

cen·sus (sen′ səs) *n.* an official count of the people who live in a certain area, with information about each person's level of education and other conditions

cent (sent) *n.* one penny

cen·ter (sent′ ər) *n.* the middle —*vb.* to place at or near the middle

cen·tral (sen′ trəl) *adj.* **1.** placed at the middle **2.** important or high-ranking

cen·tu·ry (sen′ chə rē) *n., pl.* **cen·tu·ries** a hundred years

ce·re·al (sir′ ē əl) *adj.* relating to grain —*n.* **1.** a plant that yields grain **2.** food prepared from grain, especially breakfast food

cer·e·mo·ny (ser′ ə mō′ nē) *n., pl.* **cer·e·mo·nies** formal activities to observe a religious or public occasion

cer·tain (sərt′ n) *adj.* fixed, settled, specific, or stated

chain (chān) *n.* **1.** a series of links joined together **2.** anything strung out like a chain (a *chain* of mountains)

chair (cheər) *n.* **1.** a movable seat with a back and four legs **2.** an official seat for a person in charge

chair·per·son (cheər′ pərs n) *n.* **1.** a man or woman who is in charge of a meeting **2.** a person who is in charge of a department or committee

chalk (chȯk) *n.* a soft marker of limestone or similar material for writing on a chalkboard or other surfaces

chalk·board (chȯk′ bōrd′) *n.* a blackboard

chal·lenge (chal′ ənj) *vb.* **chal·lenged**; **chal·leng·ing** to question a record —*n.* an offer to compete in a contest

cham·ber (chām′ bər) *n.* a room, often referring to a private area, such as a bedroom, an office, or a small meeting room for a government body

cham·pi·on (cham′ pē ən) *n.* **1.** a person or team that wins the highest award in sports **2.** a person who defends another person

chance (chans) *n.* **1.** an unplanned event **2.** a ticket for something that will be raffled off —*vb.* **chanced**; **chanc·ing** to take a risk —*adj.* to happen by chance (a *chance* meeting with an old friend)

change (chānj) *vb.* **changed**; **chang·ing** **1.** to make something different in some way **2.** to put on different clothes —*n.* **1.** the act of changing **2.** a fresh set (a *change* of clothes) **3.** coins (*change* in my pocket)

chan·nel (chan′ l) *n.* **1.** the deep part of a river or harbor **2.** the route by which something moves (send the message through *channels*) **3.** a radio or television frequency for a station —*vb.* **chan·neled** or **chan·nel·ing** **1.** to form a channel **2.** to send through a channel

chant (chant) *vb.* to recite a hymn of praise in a sing-song voice with a modified melody using one tone for several words —*n.* a hymn of praise, usually sung without an instrument for accompaniment

chap·el (chap′ əl) *n.* a place of worship

chap·ter (chap′ tər) *n.* **1.** a part of a book **2.** a branch of a society

char·ac·ter (kar′ ək tər) *n.* **1.** a person's mental and moral qualities **2.** *pl.* marks, signs, and symbols (such as letters) that are used in writing or printing

char·ac·ter·is·tic (kar′ ək tə ris′ tik) *n.* a special quality of a person —*adj.* marking the person as different from others (his *characteristic* pleasant manner)

char·coal (chär′ kōl′) *n.* a carbon made by charring wood for use as fuel

charge (chärj) *vb.* **charged**; **charg·ing** **1.** to give or restore the electric charge in a battery by passing an electric current through it **2.** to accuse (*charge* him with driving without a license) **3.** to attack **4.** to buy with a credit card —*n.* **1.** a task or duty **2.** a cost (a service *charge*) **3.** an attack (the *charge* against the fort)

char·i·ot (char′ ē ət) *n.* a two-wheeled, horse-drawn vehicle used by soldiers in ancient times

Chariot

char·i·ty (char′ ət ē) *n., pl.* **char·i·ties** **1.** giving to the needy **2.** kindness toward others **3.** a fund to help the needy

charm (chärm) *n.* **1.** attractiveness **2.** a small metal object worn on a bracelet **3.** something thought to bring good luck —*vb.* **1.** to fascinate **2.** to influence as if by magic

chart (chärt) *n.* **1.** a map **2.** a table giving information such as tides or weather —*vb.* **1.** to make a map or table **2.** to plan an activity

char·ter (chärt′ ər) *n.* an official paper granting certain rights and privileges

chase (chās) *vb.* **chased**; **chas·ing** **1.** to try to overtake **2.** to drive away (the dog *chase*d the woman) —*n.* pursuit

chat·ter (chat′ ər) *vb.* **1.** to talk a lot about little things **2.** to make quick sounds like talking (monkeys are *chatter*ing) **3.** to make quick clicking sounds (teeth *chatter*) —*n.* the act of chattering

cheap (chēp) *adj.* **1.** low in cost (*cheap* shoes) **2.** at a sale price (*cheap*er than usual) **3.** embarrassed (felt *cheap*) **4.** without much effort (learned a *cheap* lesson) —*adv.* at low cost

cheat (chēt) *n.* **1.** an act of cheating **2.** a fraud —*vb.* to deceive or trick someone

check (chek) *n.* **1.** a written order to a bank to pay out money (pay by *check*) **2.** a claim ticket (a baggage *check*) **3.** a bill (a restaurant *check*) —*vb.* **1.** to slow down (*check* your speed) **2.** to see if something is correct (*check* your addition) **3.** to mark an answer (*check* the right answer)

check·ers (chek′ ərz) *n.* a game played on a board with small squares

cheek (chēk) *n.* the side of the face between nose and ear

cheer (chiər) *n.* state of mind (be of good *cheer*) —*vb.* to shout words of encouragement (to *cheer* the team)

cheese (chēz) *n.* the pressed curds of milk, a high-protein food

chem·i·cal (kem′ i kəl) *n.* a substance produced by or used in a chemical process

chem·is·try (kem′ əs trē) *n.* a science that deals with the nature and composition of different kinds of matter

cher·ish (cher′ ish) *vb.* to protect and treat tenderly

cher·ry (cher′ ē) *n., pl.* **cher·ries** a small red fruit related to the plum

Cherries

chess (ches) *n.* a board game played by two players

chest (chest) *n.* **1.** the upper part of the body containing the lungs **2.** a storage box for safekeeping

chest·nut (ches′ nət) *n.* a nut that grows in a prickly bur on a tree related to the beech

chew (chü) *vb.* to bite and crush with the teeth

chick·en (chik′ ən) *n.* a young hen or rooster

chief (chēf) *n.* leader (fire *chief*, *chief* of police) —*adj.* highest in rank (*chief* justice)

child (chīld) *n., pl.* **chil·dren** (chil′ drən) a young person

child·hood (chīld′ hůd′) *n.* the period of a person's life between birth and youth

chill (chil) *vb.* to cause something to become cold (to *chill* the lemonade) —*adj.* cold (a *chill*ing wind) —*n.* a feeling of coldness (felt a *chill*)

chim·ney (chim′ nē) *n., pl.* **chim·neys** the flue of a furnace or fireplace, usually made of brick or stone, which carries the smoke away

chin (chin) *n.* the center of the jaw below the mouth —*vb.* **chinned**; **chin·ning** to hang by the hands and pull oneself up until the chin is as high as the hands

chi·na (chī′ nə) *n.* in general, any kind of dishes, but sometimes referring to those made of porcelain

chip (chip) *n.* **1.** a small piece of wood, stone, or glass that has broken off **2.** a disk used as a counter in a game **3.** a thin, crisp piece of fried food (potato *chip*) —*vb.* **chipped**; **chip·ping** **1.** to cut with an edged tool **2.** to break off in small pieces

chirp (chərp) *n.* the short, shrill sound of a cricket or small bird —*vb.* to make a chirping sound

chlo·rine (klōr′ ēn′, -ən) *n.* a strong-smelling gas used in bleach and in purifying water

chlor·o·phyll (klōr′ ə fil′) *n.* the green material in plants by which they change light into chemical energy

choc·o·late (chäk′ ə lət, chȯk′-) *n.* a food made by roasting and grinding cacao seeds, and used in a beverage (hot *chocolate*), candy (*chocolates*), and many other sweets

choice (chȯis) *n.* **1.** the act of selecting **2.** the person or thing chosen —*adj.* better than most

choir (kwīr) *n.* **1.** a group of singers, especially in a church **2.** the part of the church where the group sings

choke (chōk) *vb.* **choked**; **chok·ing** **1.** to cut off air by blocking the windpipe **2.** to clog (The drain was *choke*d with leaves.)

choose (chüz) *vb.* **chose** (chōz); **cho·sen** (chōz n); **choos ing** to pick or select

chop (chäp) *vb.* **chopped**; **chop·ping** **1.** to cut with sharp blows (to *chop* off a limb) **2.** to cut into small pieces (*chop* nuts) —*n.* **1.** a cut of rib meat (pork *chop*) **2.** a downward stroke of an ax (one more *chop*)

chord (kȯrd) *n.* **1.** a set of tones that sound in harmony **2.** a straight line joining two points on a curve

chorus (kōr əs) *n.* **1.** a group of singers and dancers who perform special numbers in stage shows **2.** a part of a song that is repeated after each verse —*vb.* to speak or sing together as a group

chro·mo·some (krō′ mə sōm′) *n.* one of the rod-like bodies in the nucleus of a cell that contain genes that determine a person's characteristics

chuck·le (chək′ əl) *vb.* **chuck·led**; **chuck·ling** to laugh quietly to oneself —*n.* a quiet laugh

chunk (chəngk) *n.* a short, thick piece of something (a *chunk* of cheese)

church (chərch) *n.* **1.** a building for public worship **2.** the entire body of Christian believers

ci·der (sīd′ ər) *n.* the juice pressed from apples

cin·na·mon (sin′ ə mən) *n.* a spice made from the inner bark of certain East Indian trees

cir·cle (sər′ kəl) *n.* **1.** a round shape **2.** a ring (chairs were set up in a *circle*) —*vb.* **cir·cled**; **cir·cling** **1.** to draw a circle around (*circle* the vowel) **2.** to revolve (The moon *circle*s the earth.)

cir·cuit (sər′ kət) *n.* **1.** the path of an electric current (The fuse blew on that *circuit.*) **2.** the route a person follows in doing his or her work (The salesman finished his *circuit* this week.)

cir·cu·lar (sər′ kyə lər) *adj.* **1.** shaped like a circle (a *circular* flower bed) **2.** going around in a circle (take a *circular* route) —*n.* a notice for general distribution (the ad in the *circular*)

cir·cu·la·tion (sər′ kyə lā′ shən) *n.* **1.** moving around (blood *circulation*) **2.** movement from person to person (library books in *circulation*) **3.** average number of copies sold for each issue (magazine *circulation*)

cir·cum·fer·ence (sər kum′ fər əns) *n.* the outside boundary of a circle

cir·cum·stance (sər′ kəm stans′) *n.* other activities or conditions that have bearing on an incident

cir·cus (sər′ kəs) *n.* a traveling show with acrobats, animal acts, clowns, and other feats

cit·i·zen (sit′ ə zən) *n.* a native or naturalized member of a country

cit·i·zen·ship (sit′ ə zən ship′) *n.* the status of being a citizen

cit·y (sit′ ē) *n., pl.* **cit·ies** a large, important town with local self-government

civ·il (siv′ əl) *adj.* **1.** relating to the affairs of citizens (*civil* war, *civil* liberties) **2.** polite (speak in a *civil* way)

civ·i·li·za·tion (siv′ ə lə zā′ shən) *n.* **1.** a state of refinement in arts and culture **2.** the manners and customs of a people (Chinese *civilization*)

claim (klām) *vb.* **1.** to demand something that is due (*claim* one's belongings) **2.** to say that something is true (She *claims* she paid the bill.) —*n.* **1.** the demand for a right **2.** something claimed

clam (klam) *n.* a shellfish with a soft body in a hinged shell —*vb.* **clammed**; **clam·ming** to dig for clams

clap (klap) *vb.* **clapped**; **clap·ping** **1.** to applaud **2.** to move suddenly (to *clap* his hands over his ears) —*n.* **1.** a loud noise (a *clap* of thunder) **2.** applause

class (klas) *n.* **1.** a group at the same level of society (the working *class*) **2.** a group of students who receive instruction together (my woodworking *class*) **3.** a course of study (Sign up for dancing *class*es.) **4.** a classification or category (Fruits and grains belong to different *class*es of food.)

clas·sic (klas′ ik) *adj.* **1.** of the highest rank in literature or art (a *classic* example) **2.** related to the fine books, statues, buildings, and ideals of ancient Rome and Greece **3.** about the traditional study of the humanities (a *classic* program)

clas·si·fi·ca·tion (klas′ ə fə kā′ shən) *n.* the process of putting things into classes (the *classification* of animal life)

class·mate (klas′ māt′) *n.* another student in the same class

clat·ter (klat′ ər) *vb.* to make quick clicking sounds (The cups and saucers *clatter*ed.) —*n.* a clicking or rattling sound (the *clatter* of chains)

clause (klȯz) *n.* **1.** a part of a sentence having its own subject and predicate (*while I waited*) **2.** a separate part of a will or other document

claw (klȯ) *n.* **1.** a hooked nail on the toe of an animal (the cat's *claw*) **2.** something that looks like a claw —*vb.* to dig with claws (The animal *claw*ed its way under the wall.)

clay (klā) *n.* a type of earth used in making pottery and bricks

clean (klēn) *adj.* **1.** not dirty (a *clean* towel) **2.** smooth and neat (a *clean* cut in the wood) **3.** well-shaped (having *clean* lines) —*adv.* in a clean manner (Keep your teeth *clean*.) —*vb.* to make something clean (*Clean* your room.)

clear (kliər) *adj.* **1.** bright and uncloudy (*clear* day) **2.** without blemishes (*clear* skin) **3.** without confusion (*clear* mind) —*n.* an open space (parked in the *clear*) —*vb.* to clean something away (*clear* the dishes) —*adv.* in a clear manner (make that *clear* to me)

clerk (klərk) *n.* **1.** a salesperson in a store (pay the *clerk*) **2.** someone who keeps records (an office *clerk*)

clev·er (klev′ ər) *adj.* **1.** skillful (a *clever* computer operator) **2.** quick to learn (a *clever* student) **3.** witty (*clever* with words)

click (klik) *n.* a quick sound (the *click* of the camera) —*vb.* **1.** to make something click (*click*ed his heels) **2.** to work well (things really *click*ed today)

cliff (klif) *n.* a high, steep face of rock

Cliff

cli·mate (klī′ mət) *n.* the general weather conditions of a place or region (the *climate* in the Pacific Northwest)

cli·max (klī′ maks′) *n.* the high point or part of greatest interest (*climax* of the story)

climb (klīm) *vb.* **1.** to go up or down, especially by using both hands and feet **2.** to rise gradually to a higher point (The airplane took off and *climb*ed to 12,000 feet.) —*n.* the act of climbing (the *climb* up the hill)

cling (kling) *vb.* **clung** (kləng); **cling·ing** **1.** to hold fast to something (*cling* to the rope) **2.** to stay close (she *cling*s to her sister)

clin·ic (klin′ ik) *n.* a place for the study and treatment of outpatients (those who come in only for treatment)

clip (klip) *vb.* **clipped**; **clip·ping** **1.** to fasten with a clip **2.** to cut with scissors or shears (*clip* this thread) **3.** to cut off or trim (*clip* her nails) —*n.* **1.** a device with two blades for clipping (a nail *clip*) **2.** a fastener (a paper *clip*) **3.** a fast pace (at a good *clip*)

clip·per (klip′ ər) *n.* **1.** a device with two blades (a grass *clipper*) **2.** a large, fast sailing vessel

Clipper

cloak (klōk) *n.* **1.** a long loose outer garment that covers other clothing **2.** something that hides or covers (There is a *cloak* of secrecy around his activities.)

clock (kläk) *n.* **1.** a device for keeping the time **2.** an ornamental design on the side of a stocking —*vb.* to time a person as he or she performs something (to *clock* her speed)

close (klōz) *vb.* **closed**; **clos·ing** **1.** to shut (*close* the door) **2.** to make something continuous (to *close* the circle, to *close* the electrical circuit) **3.** to stop or bring to an end (*close* the program) —*adj.* **close** (klōs) **clos·er**; **clos·est** **1.** near (*close* to nine o'clock, *close* to town) **2.** with little space (living in *close* quarters) **3.** careful (take a *close* look) **4.** almost the same (a *close* race)

clos·et (kläz′ ət) *n.* a small room or storage place for clothes and supplies

cloth (klȯth) *n., pl.* **cloths** (klȯthz, klȯths) a woven or a knitted fabric

cloth·ing (klō′ thing) *n.* any kind of clothes

cloud (klaůd) *n.* **1.** a mass of water vapor hanging in the air (The sky is full of *clouds*.) **2.** a mass of smoke or dust that looks like a cloud —*vb.* **1.** to become cloudy (It is *cloud*ing up.) **2.** to make unclear (He *cloud*s the issue with his stories.)

clo·ver (klō′ vər) *n.* a low-growing three-leaved plant with a rounded flower head that grows wild in fields in temperate regions

Clover

clown (klaůn) *n.* **1.** a comedian, as in a circus **2.** a person with poor manners

club (kləb) *n.* **1.** a social group and their meeting place (the beach *club*) **2.** a heavy stick used as a weapon **3.** a stick used in playing golf (a golf *club*) **4.** a suit in playing cards (*clubs* are trumps) —*vb.* **clubbed**; **club·bing** to strike or beat with a club (*club*bed the snake)

clue (klü) *n.* an idea that helps to solve a problem (give me a *clue*)

clum·sy (kləm′ zē) *adj.* **clum·si·er**; **clum·si·est** **1.** awkward (a *clumsy* dancer) **2.** lacking in tact (makes *clumsy* remarks)

clus·ter (kləs′ tər) *n.* a bunch of things together (these flowers grow in *clusters*) —*vb.* to grow or put into a cluster (*cluster*ed the tulip bulbs near the rocks)

clutch (kləch) *vb.* to hold tight (she *clutch*ed her handbag) —*n.* **1.** a tight grasp **2.** the part of a machine that connects the driving and driven portions of the machine (Use the *clutch* when you change gears with a stickshift.)

coach (kōch) *n.* **1.** a person who trains a team (baseball *coach*) or a performer (her acting *coach*) **2.** a railroad car with seats for regular passengers **3.** the rear section of seats in a large passenger plane **4.** a horse-drawn four-wheeled carriage with a raised seat up front for the driver —*vb.* to act as a coach (*coach* her in algebra)

coal (kōl) *n.* **1.** a hard, black fuel that is mined **2.** a glowing piece of burned wood (hot *coal*s in the fireplace) —*vb.* to supply with coal (to *coal* the firebox)

coarse (kōrs) *adj.* **1.** poor in quality **2.** rough in texture (*coarse* sand) **3.** rude (*coarse* language)

coast (kōst) *n.* the land near the sea —*vb.* **1.** to slide downhill **2.** to move along without using power

cock (käk) *n.* **1.** a male bird, a rooster **2.** the hammer of a gun —*vb.* **1.** to draw the hammer of a gun **2.** to turn upward (*cock* your hat)

cock·pit (käk′ pit′) *n.* **1.** the space in an airplane where the pilot sits **2.** the place on a yacht from which a boat is steered

co·coa (kō′ kō) *n.* **1.** a powder made from the ground seeds of the cacao tree **2.** a drink made from cocoa powder

co·co·nut (kō′ kə nət) *n.* **1.** the fruit of the coco palm **2.** the white substance inside the shell of the fruit

code (kōd) *n.* **1.** a system of laws or rules (our *code* of ethics) **2.** a system of signals for sending messages (Morse *code*) **3.** a system of signals with special meaning (secret *code*) —*vb.* to put into the form of a code (*code* the information)

cof·fee (kȯf′ ē) *n.* a drink made from the roasted and ground seeds of the coffee plant

coil (kȯil) *vb.* to wind around and around in a ring —*n.* something that is wound into a coil

coin (kȯin) *n.* money that is made of metal (a pocket full of *coins*)

cold (kōld) *adj.* **1.** low in temperature (there is *cold* juice in the pitcher) **2.** unfriendly (gave us a *cold* look) —*n.* **1.** low temperature (the *cold* makes me shiver) **2.** a feeling of distress with sneezing and coughing (Ann has a *cold.*)

col·lapse (kə laps′) *vb.* **col·lapsed**; **col·laps·ing** **1.** to fall down or cave in (the roof *collapsed*) **2.** to have a physical or mental breakdown (He *collapsed* after he lost his job.)

col·lar (käl′ ər) *n.* a neckband or the part of a garment that surrounds the neckline (The shirt he wore had a button-down *collar.*) —*vb.* to grab by the collar

col·lect (kə lekt′) *vb.* **1.** to gather from different places (*collect* dolls) **2.** to think about something (*collect* one's thoughts) **3.** to ask for money for some purpose (*collect* the rent, *collect* money for the needy)

col·lec·tion (kə lek′ shən) *n.* **1.** the act of gathering together **2.** the things or people gathered together (the coin *collection*) **3.** the soliciting of money for charity (the *collection* for the hot lunch program)

col·lege (käl′ ij) *n.* a school that comes after secondary school, including the equivalent of grades 13-16.

col·lide (kə līd′) *vb.* **col·lid·ed; col·lid·ing** to crash together

col·li·sion (kə lizh′ ən) *n.* an act of crashing together

colo·nel (kərn′ l) *n.* the commander of a regiment in the army

col·o·ny (käl′ ə nē) *n., pl.* **col·o·nies** **1.** people who settle a new land but remain citizens of the country they left **2.** a group of creatures living together (a *colony* of bees)

col·or (kəl′ ər) *n.* **1.** any hue of the rainbow **2.** complexion (Her *color* is good today.) —*vb.* to give color (*Color* it blue.)

colt (kōlt) *n.* a young male horse

col·umn (käl′ əm) *n.* **1.** something tall and thin in shape **2.** a pillar supporting a roof **3.** a section of print in the newspaper (the sports *column*)

comb (kōm) *n.* **1.** a device with teeth for arranging the hair **2.** the fleshy crest on the head of a rooster

com·bat (kəm bat′) *vb.* **com·bat·ed; com·bat·ing** **1.** to fight **2.** to work against (to *combat* hunger) —*n.* (käm′ bat′) a battle (lost in *combat*)

com·bi·na·tion (käm′ bə nā′ shən) *n.* **1.** the act of putting together the separate parts or kinds **2.** a series of numbers that, when dialed, will open a keyless lock

com·bine (kəm bīn′) *vb.* **com·bined; com·bin·ing** **1.** join together (We can *combine* three groups to travel in one bus.) **2.** mix (*Combine* the sugar and beaten eggs.) —*n.* (käm′ bīn′) a big farm machine that harvests and threshes grain

com·bus·tion (kəm bəs′ chən) *n.* the process of burning (Oily rags left in a hot place will cause *combustion.*)

come (kəm) *vb.* **came** (kām); **come**; **com·ing** (kəm′ ing) to move toward or approach

com·e·dy (käm′ ə dē) *n., pl.* **com·e·dies** **1.** a funny event **2.** a funny play that has a happy ending

com·et (käm′ ət) *n.* a heavenly body with a bright, fuzzy head and often a tail pointing away from the sun

com·fort (kəm′ fərt) *n.* **1.** a feeling of ease and well-being **2.** something that makes a person feel more at ease —*vb.* to cheer or console a person

com·ic (käm′ ik) *adj.* funny, amusing (a *comic* book)

com·ma (käm′ ə) *n.* a punctuation mark (,) used to show a slight separation between words, groups of words, or numbers

com·mand (kə mand′) *vb.* to control, take charge, give orders —*n.* **1.** an order (give a *command*) **2.** a state of skill (in *command* of mathematics) **3.** authority (*command* of the unit)

com·ment (käm′ ent′) *n.* a written or spoken opinion or remark —*vb.* to make a remark

com·merce (käm′ ərs) *n.* buying and selling of goods on a large scale (interstate *commerce*)

com·mer·cial (kə mər′ shəl) *adj.* relating to trade that is carried on for a profit

com·mit (kə mit′) *vb.* **com·mit·ted**; **com·mit·ting** **1.** to give over to another person's care **2.** to do something wrong (to *commit* a felony) **3.** to put into custody (*commit* one to a mental institution)

com·mit·tee (kə mit′ ē) *n.* a group of people brought together to perform a certain task or consider a special matter or problem

com·mon (käm′ ən) *adj.* **1.** belonging to or shared by two or more people or by the general public (The bus is a *common* carrier.) **2.** general (She has *common* sense.) —*n.* land owned by the local people (the village *common*)

com·mu·ni·cate (kə myü′ nə kāt′) *vb.* **com·mu·ni·cat·ed; com·mu·ni·cat·ing** to talk together or to send messages back and forth by any means, such as mail, telegram, cable, or computer telecommunication

com·mu·ni·ty (kə myü′ nət ē) *n., pl.* **com·mu·ni·ties** **1.** people living under the same rules or laws **2.** the place where they live

com·pact (kəm pakt′, kam′ pakt′) *adj.* **1.** packed together (in a *compact* arrangement) **2.** made to save space (a *compact* car) —*n.* **1.** a small case for make-up (a *compact*) **2.** a formal agreement

com·pan·ion (kəm pan′ yən) *n.* **1.** a friend or comrade **2.** one of a pair of things made to go together (This sugar bowl is the *companion* to that creamer.)

com·pa·ny (kəm′ pə nē) *n., pl.* **com·pa·nies** **1.** visitors (*Company* is coming.) **2.** a business group (the Electric *Company*) **3.** a group of performers (the opera *company*) **4.** the soldiers led by a captain (*Company* C)

com·pare (kəm paər′) *vb.* **com·pared; com·par·ing** **1.** to look for likenesses and differences **2.** to give the positive, comparative, and superlative forms of an adjective or adverb (*good, better, best,* or *lovely, lovelier, loveliest*)

com·part·ment (kəm pärt′ mənt) *n.* one section that is part of a larger enclosure (the glove *compartment* of the car)

com·pass (kəm′ pəs) *vb.* to walk around —*n.* **1.** a device for telling direction on the earth's surface **2.** a device for drawing circles **3.** a boundary or circumference

Compasses

com·pete (kəm pēt′) *vb.* **com·pet·ed**; **com·pet·ing** to enter into a contest for something such as a prize or a job that others also want

com·plain (kəm plān′) *vb.* **1.** to talk about one's pain, discontent, or trouble (She *complain*ed about the smoke in the room.) **2.** to accuse someone of an injustice

com·ple·ment (käm′ plə mənt) *n.* the number or amount that completes something (The office had its full *complement* of workers.) —*vb.* to act as a complement (Applesauce *complements* roast pork.)

com·plete (kəm plēt′) *adj.* whole, having all its parts —*vb.* **1.** to make whole (I need two more books to *complete* the set.) **2.** to finish something (*Complete* your homework before you go out.)

com·plex (käm pleks′) *adj.* **1.** made up of two or more parts **2.** intricate in some way

com·pli·cate (käm′ plə kāt′) *vb.* **com·pli·cat·ed**; **com·pli·cat·ing** to become confusing or difficult

com·pli·ment (käm′ plə mənt) *n.* a formal expression of approval or courtesy (He gave me a *compliment* on my speech.)

com·pose (kəm pōz′) *vb.* **com·posed**; **com·pos·ing** **1.** to create something new (*compose* a song) **2.** made up of (*compose*d of three layers) **3.** to put in good order (labored to *compose* themselves after the accident)

com·po·si·tion (käm′ pə zish′ ən) *n.* **1.** the act of writing (Read your *composition* before you type it.) **2.** the way that the parts are put together (worried about the *composition* of this project) **3.** an artistic work (his fourth musical *composition*)

com·pound (käm paůnd′) *vb.* to bring together or mix (käm′ paůnd) —*adj.* made up of two or more parts (a *compound* fracture of the leg) —*n.* the substance formed by combining ingredients (a white *compound*)

com·press (kəm pres′) *vb.* to press together —*n.* (käm′ pres′) a soft pad used for applying pressure or medication and often held in place by a bandage

com·pro·mise (käm′ prə mīz′) *n.* an agreement in which each party gives up a little of what he or she had wanted in order to reach a settlement

com·pute (kəm pyüt′) *vb.* **com·put·ed**; **com·put·ing** to calculate or figure out

com·rade (käm′ rad) *n.* companion

con·ceal (kən sēl′) *vb.* **1.** to hide **2.** to keep something secret (*conceal* the truth)

con·ceive (kən sēv′) *vb.* **con·ceived**; **con·ceiv·ing** **1.** to think **2.** to become pregnant

con·cen·trate (kän′ sən trāt′) *vb.* **con·cen·trat·ed**; **con·cen·trat·ing** **1.** to focus attention on one point **2.** to make something smaller in quantity or stronger by removing something such as water (*Concentrate* the juice by boiling it down until it is as thick as syrup.)

con·cept (kän′ sept′) *n.* a general idea

con·cern (kən sərn′) *vb.* to relate to, to be of interest to, or to worry about (*concern*ed about money)

con·cert (kän′ sərt) *n.* a musical performance of singing or orchestra music

con·clude (kən klüd′) *vb.* **con·clud·ed**; **con·clud·ing** **1.** to finish (*conclude* the program) **2.** to make up one's mind (He *concluded* that his brother was right.)

con·crete (kän krēt′) *adj.* **1.** real, specific (Pledging allegiance to the flag is a *concrete* example of patriotism.) **2.** made of concrete —*n.* a hard building material made of cement, sand, and water

con·di·tion (kən dish′ ən) *n.* **1.** something that must be done before another event can occur (I'll go, on the *condition* that you let me drive.) **2.** state of health or fitness (The team is in good *condition.*) —*vb.* to bring to a state of fitness or use

con·duct (kän′ dəkt′) *n.* **1.** a person's behavior **2.** the act of leading or managing (the *conduct* of her business) —*vb.* (kən dəkt′) **1.** to behave (He *conduct*ed himself well.) **2.** to lead or guide (*conduct* the band) **3.** to transmit (*conduct* electricity or radio waves)

cone (kōn) *n.* **1.** a shape that tapers from a circle to a point (ice cream *cone*) **2.** the fruit of certain evergreen trees

Cones

con·fer·ence (kän′ fə rəns) *n.* **1.** a meeting to share ideas on a topic (a *conference* on the importance of reading literature) **2.** an association, as of schools or athletic teams (the Atlantic *Conference* teams)

con·fi·dence (kän′ fə dəns) *n.* **1.** trust (have *confidence* in one's doctor) **2.** assurance (He competes with great *confidence.*) **3.** secret (shared a *confidence* with a friend)

con·fine (kän′ fīn′) *n.* border or limit (within the *confines* of the park) —*vb.* (kən fīn′) **con·fined**; **con·fin·ing** **1.** to stay within limits (*confine* your report to desert plants) **2.** to keep within a boundary (*confined* to your room)

con·firm (kən fərm′) *vb.* **1.** to make something firm or firmer (Her faith in him was *confirm*ed.) **2.** to give proof (Please *confirm* my reservation.)

con·flict (kän′ flikt′) *n.* **1.** a battle **2.** a disagreement —*vb.* (kən flikt′) to clash (Our ideas *conflict* when we talk about managing money.)

con·fuse (kən fyüz′) *vb.* **con·fused**; **con·fus·ing** **1.** to make unclear (That sign *confused* me.) **2.** to mix up (I often *confuse* the twins.)

con·grat·u·late (kən grach′ ə lāt′) *vb.* **con·grat·u·lat·ed**; **con·grat·u·lat·ing** to express joy at someone's good fortune or achievement

con·gress (käng′ grəs) *n.* the senators and representatives acting together as the law-making body of a nation

con·nect (kə nekt′) *vb.* to join together (The bus *connects* with the train at Everett.)

con·nec·tion (kə nek′ shən) *n.* **1.** the act of connecting (Make a good *connection* in the wires.) **2.** relationship (There is a distant *connection* between the two families.)

con·quer (käng′ kər) *vb.* to win by force (to *conquer* the enemy)

con·quest (kän′ kwest′) *n.* **1.** the act of winning the victory (The *conquest* was costly in terms of men and materials.) **2.** the thing that is won (The ships were part of their *conquest.*)

con·scious (kän′ chəs) *adj.* awake and aware of what is going on

con·sec·u·tive (kən sek′ yət iv) *adj.* in a series, one after the other

con·sent (kən sent′) *vb.* to agree (He *consent*ed to sit between you and me.) —*n.* approval (gave his *consent* to their marriage)

con·se·quence (kän′ sə kwens′) *n.* the effect or result (They suffered the *consequence*s of their foolish plan.)

con·ser·va·tion (kän′ sər vā′ shən) *n.* good care and use of resources

con·serve (kən sərv′) *vb.* **con·served**; **con·serv·ing** **1.** to care for and use wisely **2.** to preserve with sugar

con·sid·er (kən sid′ ər) *vb.* to think about (*consider*ed taking a new job)

con·sid·er·a·tion (kən sid′ ə rā′ shən) *n.* **1.** careful thought **2.** regard for others

con·sist (kən sist′) *vb.* to be made (It *consist*s of four ingredients.)

con·so·nant (kän′ sə nənt) *n.* a speech sound made by stopping the breath with the lips, teeth, or tongue

con·stant (kän′ stənt) *adj.* **1.** faithful (*constant* friendship) **2.** continuing without change (*constant* hum of the motor)

con·stel·la·tion (kän′ stə lā′ shən) *n.* a group of stars forming a pattern and having a name

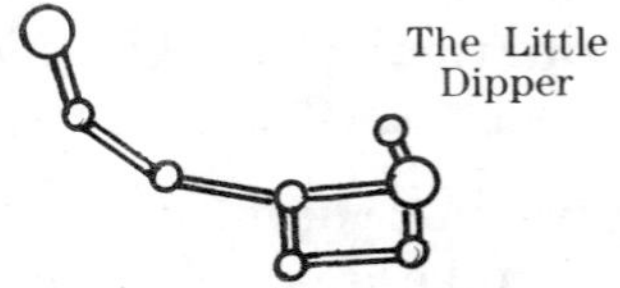

Constellation *Ursa Minor*

con·sti·tu·tion (kän′ stə tü′ shən) *n.* **1.** the structure of a person or thing **2.** the basic laws and principles on which a nation is founded (*Constitution* of the United States)

con·struct (kən strəkt′) *vb.* to build

con·struc·tion (kən strək′ shən) *n.* **1.** the process of building **2.** the structure (They admired the *construction* of the Roman aqueduct.)

con·sult (kən səlt′) *vb.* to ask for advice or information (*consult* a doctor)

con·sume (kən süm′) *vb.* **con·sumed**; **con·sum·ing** **1.** to eat up or drink up **2.** to burn or use up (The fire *consumed* every shred of paper.) **3.** to take all of one's attention (Building the model sailboat *consumed* his attention.)

con·tact (kän′ takt′) *n.* a meeting or a communication with one or more persons —*vb.* **1.** to bring together **2.** to communicate with (*contact* the travel agent about the trip)

con·tain (kən tān′) *vb.* to hold within limits (Will this notebook *contain* all of her notes?)

con·tem·po·rar·y (kən tem′ pə rer′ ē) *adj.* **1.** living or happening at the same time (They are all *contemporary* writers.) **2.** modern —*n., pl.* **con·tem·po·rar·ies** persons living at about the same time (They are my *contemporaries*.)

con·tempt (kən tempt′) *n.* **1.** the act of looking down on or scorning someone **2.** lack of respect for the proceedings in a court (held in *contempt* of court)

con·tent (kən tent′) *adj.* satisfied with what one has —*n.* freedom from worry and care —*n.* (kän′ tent′) everything that is contained

con·test (kən test′) *vb.* to argue or struggle over something —*n.* (kän′ test′) **1.** an athletic competition **2.** a struggle to win (a spelling *contest*)

con·text (kän′ tekst′) *n.* the parts of a passage that influence the meaning of a word or phrase

con·ti·nent (känt′ n ənt) *n.* one of the seven large bodies of land, such as North America or Africa

con·tin·ue (kən tin′ yü) *vb.* **con·tin·ued**; **con·tin·u·ing** **1.** to maintain (*continue* working) **2.** to last (rain *continued*) **3.** to begin again (He *continued* his schooling after serving in the Peace Corps.)

con·tour (kän′ tůr′) *n.* the outline or shape of something

con·tract (kän′ trakt′) *n.* a legal agreement that is binding by law —*vb.* (kən trakt′) **1.** to shorten or shrink (Air expands and *contracts.*) **2.** to catch (*contract* a virus)

con·trac·tion (kən trak′ shən) *n.* a shortened form of a word such as *I'll* for *I will*

con·trar·y (kän′ trer′ ē) *n., pl.* **con·trar·ies** one of two opposite things —*adj.* **1.** completely different (*contrary* opinions) **2.** opposed to one's interests (a *contrary* person)

con·trast (kän′ trast′) *n.* a difference between two things that are related in some way (The *contrast* of red against green is striking.) —*vb.* (kən trast′) to show differences between two things

con·trib·ute (kən trib′ yət) *vb.* **con·trib·ut·ed**; **con·trib·ut·ing** to give a share of what is needed

con·tri·bu·tion (kän′ trə byü′ shən) *n.* **1.** the act of giving toward a common cause **2.** an article written for publication

con·trol (kən trōl′) *vb.* **con·trolled**; **con·trol·ling** to direct, operate, or regulate something (*control* the speed of the car) —*n.* **1.** the power or ability to control (have *control* of the horse) **2.** a device for controlling (in charge of the *controls* on the engine)

con·tro·ver·sy (kän′ trə vər′ sē) *n., pl.* **con·tro·ver·sies** an argument or quarrel

con·ve·nience (kən vē′ nyəns) *n.* **1.** comfort (a rest area for travelers' *convenience*) **2.** suitability (at your *convenience*) **3.** a material advantage (A microwave oven is a modern *convenience.*)

con·ven·tion (kən ven′ chən) *n.* **1.** a formal meeting or conference (an English teachers' *convention*) **2.** a custom or common way of doing things (The ten o'clock coffee break is an American *convention.*)

con·ver·sa·tion (kän′ vər sā′ shən) *n.* informal talk

con·verse (kən vərs′) *vb.* **con·versed**; **con·vers·ing** to talk

con·vert (kən vərt′) *vb.* to change from one thing to another (to *convert* a barn to a house, to *convert* from one religion to another) —*n.* (kän′ vərt′) one who has been converted

con·vey (kən vā′) *vb.* **con·veyed**; **con·vey·ing** to carry or transmit (*convey* by truck or by pipeline, write to *convey* ideas)

con·vict (kən vikt′) *vb.* to find a person guilty of some offense —*n.* (kän′ vikt′) **1.** a person found guilty of a crime **2.** a person in prison for committing a crime

con·vic·tion (kən vik′ shən) *n.* **1.** the act of proving someone guilty of a crime **2.** a strong belief **3.** the state of mind of one who is convinced he is right

con·vince (kən vins′) *vb.* **con·vinced**; **con·vinc·ing** to argue so that a person will agree or believe

cook (ku̇k) *n.* a person who prepares food for eating —*vb.* to get food ready for eating by using heat, as in boiling, baking, broiling, or frying

cook·ie or **cook·y** (kůk′ ē) *n., pl.* **cook·ies** a firm, flat, sweet cake

cool (kül) *adj.* **1.** slightly cold, not warm **2.** not holding heat (a *cool* shirt) **3.** not emotional (a *cool* look on one's face)

co·op·er·ate (kō äp′ ə rāt′) *vb.* **co·op·er·at·ed**; **co·op·er·at·ing** to work together to get something done

co·or·di·nate (kō ȯrd′ n āt′) *vb.* **co·or·di·nat·ed**; **co·or·di·nat·ing** **1.** to work well with others or to get others to work well together **2.** to adjust —*adj.* (kō ȯrd′ n ət) equal in rank or importance

cop·per (käp′ ər) *n.* a tough, reddish metal that is a good conductor of heat and electricity

cop·y (käp′ ē) *n., pl.* **cop·ies** an exact likeness of an original

cor·al (kȯr′ əl) *n.* a hard material formed from the skeletons of masses of tiny sea animals related to the jellyfish (Colorful fish are found near the *coral* reef.)

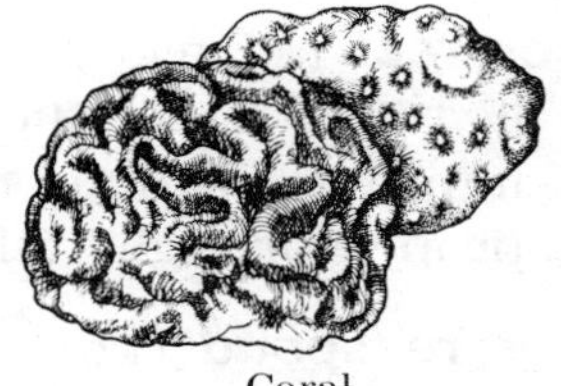
Coral

cord (kȯrd) *n.* **1.** heavy string or thin rope (Tie the package with *cord.*) **2.** a ribbed fabric (blue and white *cord* pants) **3.** an insulated wire cable (Plug in the toaster *cord.*) **4.** a unit of wood cut for fuel equal to 128 cubic feet (Buy a *cord* of wood.)

core (kōr) *n.* the middle part of something such as a fruit (the *core* of the apple) —*vb.* **cored**; **cor·ing** to remove the core

cork (kȯrk) *n.* the light, tough bark of the cork oak tree used for stoppers and other products (a *cork* for the bottle)

corn (kȯrn) *n.* **1.** a plant whose seeds are used for cereal **2.** a thickening of the skin caused by pressure, as on the toe **3.** to preserve with salt (*corn*ed beef)

cor·ner (kȯr′ nər) *n.* **1.** the place where two sides or two streets meet **2.** a place distant from a heavily populated area (a far *corner* of the city, a far *corner* of the earth) **3.** a place with no escape (trapped in a *corner*) —*vb.* to force into a corner (*corner* the villain) —*adj.* at or near a corner (the *corner* store)

cor·po·ra·tion (kȯr′ pə rā′ shən) *n.* a group of persons united under law as one body to run a business or to take part in town government

corps (kōr) *n.*, *pl.* **corps** (kōrz) an organized group of people, a branch of the military forces (Marine *Corps*) or of the government (diplomatic *corps*) or other organized group (*corps* de ballet)

cor·ral (kə ral′) *n.* a pen for horses or cattle —*vb.* **cor·ralled**; **cor·ral·ling** to surround, to capture, to confine in a corral

cor·rect (kə rekt′) *vb.* **1.** to change something to make it right **2.** to show or explain how a thing can be improved or done right (*correct* their grammar) —*adj.* proper or right (the *correct* answer)

cor·re·spond (kȯr′ ə spänd′) *vb.* **1.** to send to and receive letters from someone (*correspond* with a pen pal) **2.** to be similar to or match in some way (Our Congress *corresponds* with the British Parliament.)

cor·ri·dor (kȯr′ ə dər) *n.* a hallway

cos·met·ic (käz met′ ik) *n.* a preparation used to make the skin or hair look more attractive (Lipstick and powder are *cosmetics*.) —*adj.* beautifying (The brisk walk has a *cosmetic* effect on her skin.)

cost (kȯst) *n.* **1.** the price (the *cost* of fruits) **2.** something that is lost in order to do or gain another thing (The *cost* of volunteer work is measured in time and effort, but the rewards are great.) —*vb.* **cost**; **cost·ing** **1.** to cause one to spend (The pen *cost* one dollar.) **2.** to cause one to lose (The fumble *cost* them the championship.)

cos·tume (käs′ tüm′) *n.* a suit or dress typical of a given time, country, or class of people (an 1890's *costume*)

cot·tage (kät′ ij) *n.* **1.** a small house **2.** a summer house, big or little

cot·ton (kät′ n) *n.* **1.** soft, woolly-looking fibers that grow around the seeds of the cotton plant **2.** cloth or thread made of cotton

couch (kaủch) *n.* a sofa or narrow bed for resting or sleeping

cough (kȯf) *vb.* to force air and mucous from the lungs —*n.* a disease that makes one cough (to suffer from a *cough*)

coun·cil (kaủn′ səl) *n.* a group of persons who meet as a body to give advice or to make decisions about important matters (the town *council*)

count (kaủnt) *vb.* **1.** to say a number for each item, one by one, to get the total number (*count* the pencils) **2.** to name the numerals singly or in units such as five or ten up to a certain number (*count* to one hundred by tens) **3.** to rely (*count* on her) —*n.* **1.** the act of counting (the *count* is correct) **2.** the total (*count* of sixty)

count·er (kaủnt′ ər) *n.* **1.** a game piece used to keep the count **2.** a long, narrow surface in a store where articles are displayed or food is served **3.** a work area placed above the drawers and lower cabinets in a kitchen —*vb.* to oppose (to *counter* the attack) —*adv.* in another direction (to go *counter* to the plan) —*adj.* contrary (a *counter* attack)

coun·try (kən′ trē) *n., pl.* **coun·tries** **1.** the land within a nation's boundary **2.** the people of a nation (The whole *country* supported this plan.) **3.** rural area (He lives in the *country*.)

coun·ty (kaủnt′ ē) *n., pl.* **coun·ties** political divisions within a state

cou·ple (kəp′ əl) *vb.* **cou·pled; cou·pling** to join together or to form in pairs —*n.* two persons who are married, engaged, or grouped together for a social function such as a dance

cour·age (kər′ ij) *n.* bravery

cou·ra·geous (kə rā′ jəs) *adj.* showing bravery (the *courageous* deed)

course (kōrs) *n.* **1.** the act of moving on, making progress **2.** the direction or path taken (the moon in its *course* through the sky) **3.** a channel for water or path of a river (the river's *course*) **4.** a planned series of lessons (a *course* in consumer law) **5.** following a common procedure (the usual *course*) —*vb.* **coursed; cours·ing** to run, chase, or move swiftly (His blood *coursed* through his veins.)

court (kōrt) *n.* **1.** a place for playing certain games (tennis *court*) **2.** a place where accused persons are tried by law **3.** the palace of royalty —*vb.* to try to win favors (to *court* those in power)

cour·te·ous (kərt′ ē əs) *adj.* respectful, polite

cour·te·sy (kərt′ ə sē) *n.*, *pl.* **cour·te·sies** **1.** an act of politeness and respect **2.** the granting of a favor as distinguished from a right

cous·in (kəz′ n) *n.* the child of one's uncle or aunt

cov·er (kəv′ ər) *vb.* **1.** to put something over, as a lid **2.** to conceal **3.** to include (the report *covers* these items) —*n.* **1.** something that shelters or hides **2.** an envelope or wrapper for mail (coming to you under separate *cover*)

cov·er·ing (kəv′ ə ring) *n.* something that covers or conceals

cow (kaů) *n.* the full-grown female of any animal for which the male is called a bull, including the ox family, moose, elk, whales, elephants, and seals —*vb.* to subdue with fear (He *cowed* the intruder.)

cow·ard (kaů′ ərd) *n.* a timid, fearful person, lacking in courage

cow·boy (kaů′ bȯi′) *n.* a person who works on a ranch, often riding horseback to care for the cattle on the range

co·zy (kō′ zē) *adj.* **co·zi·er**; **co·zi·est** warm and comfortable —*n., pl.* **co·zies** a padded covering for a teapot to keep the tea hot

crab (krab) *n.* **1.** a sea animal with a broad, flat shell and five pairs of legs **2.** a cranky person —*vb.* **crabbed**; **crab·bing** **1.** to fish for crabs **2.** to complain or find fault

crack (krak) *vb.* **1.** to make a snapping noise **2.** to break on the surface without coming apart **3.** to tell in a funny way (*crack* jokes) **4.** to have a mental breakdown (to *crack* under the pressure) —*n.* **1.** a snapping noise **2.** a narrow opening (open the window a *crack*) **3.** a break in the tone (a *crack* in his voice) —*adj.* excellent in quality or ability (a *crack* engineer)

crack·er (krak′ ər) *n.* a thin crisp biscuit made mainly from flour and water

crack·le (krak′ əl) *vb.* **crack·led**; **crack·ling** **1.** to make snapping noises (the fire *crackled*) **2.** to develop a network of fine cracks —*n.* **1.** a snapping noise **2.** a network of cracks

cra·dle (krād′ l) *n.* **1.** a baby's bed **2.** a place where something began (the *cradle* of democracy) **3.** the support for a telephone receiver (Put the phone back on its *cradle.*) —*vb.* **cra·dled**; **cra·dling** **1.** to place in a cradle **2.** to hold as if in a cradle (*cradle* the baby in one's arms)

craft (kraft) *n.* **1.** artistic skill **2.** skill in getting one's way by tricking someone **3.** a small boat

crane (krān) *n.* **1.** a machine with a long arm for lifting heavy articles **2.** a tall wading bird —*vb.* **craned**; **cran·ing** to stretch the neck to see better

crank (krangk) *n.* **1.** a bent handle used to start an engine in motion **2.** an odd person **3.** a grouch —*vb.* to start by turning a crank

crash (krash) *vb.* **1.** to smash **2.** to make a loud noise —*n.* **1.** a loud burst of noise **2.** failure of a business or the stock market **3.** a collision

crate (krāt) *n.* a large box for shipping goods, often with slats on the sides —*vb.* **crat·ed**; **crat·ing** pack in a crate (*Crate* the fruit for shipment.)

cra·ter (krāt′ ər) *n.* a cup-shaped hole formed around the opening of a volcano or by the impact of a meteorite or the explosion of a bomb

crawl (krȯl) *vb.* **1.** to creep on hands and knees **2.** to move ahead very slowly and carefully (to *crawl* along in heavy traffic) —*n.* **1.** the act of crawling **2.** a swimming stroke **3.** a pen in shallow water for keeping fish or turtles

cray·on (krā′ än, -ən) *n.* a stick of colored wax used for drawing or writing —*vb.* to color with a crayon

cra·zy (krā′ zē) *adj.* **cra·zi·er**; **cra·zi·est** **1.** insane **2.** greatly excited (She is *crazy* about water skiing.)

creak (krēk) *vb.* to make a squeaky sound (The loose board in the floor *creaks.*) —*n.* a squeaky noise

cream (krēm) *n.* **1.** the yellowish butterfat in milk **2.** a dessert made of or having the appearance of cream **3.** a cosmetic used to clean or soften the skin **4.** a pale yellow (*cream*-colored shirt) —*vb.* **1.** to mix until smooth and creamy **2.** to apply cream

crease (krēs) *n.* a line or mark made by folding or by pressing a fold, as in pants —*vb.* **creased**; **creas·ing** to make a crease in

cre·ate (krē āt′) *vb.* **cre·at·ed**; **cre·at·ing** to bring into existence

cre·a·tive (krē āt′ iv) *adj.* having the ability to do new and original things

crea·ture (krē′ chər) *n.* a living person or animal

cred·it (kred′ ət) *n.* **1.** trustworthy **2.** the right to buy now and pay later as in using a *credit* card **3.** the right to receive praise and respect for some act or deed (she deserves *credit*) **4.** units of study completed by a student (nine *credits*) **5.** money remaining in a person's account (a *credit* of sixteen dollars) —*vb.* **1.** to trust **2.** to give credit to (I *credit* my teacher.)

creek (krēk) *n.* a stream that is smaller than a river

creep (krēp) *vb.* **crept** (krept); **creep·ing** **1.** to crawl on hands and knees **2.** to spread along the ground and up nearby walls (Ivy *creeps* up the chimney.) —*n.* the act of crawling

crest (krest) *n.* **1.** a fleshy comb or tuft of feathers on the head of a fowl or bird **2.** the top of anything, as the ridge or summit of a hill (*crest* of the wave) **3.** the plume on a helmet **4.** the upper part of a design on a coat of arms

crew (krü) *n.* **1.** the people who work on a train, ship, or airplane **2.** a gathering of people (a joyful *crew*)

crick·et (krik′ ət) *n.* **1.** an insect known for the chirping sound of the male **2.** a game played on a large field by two teams of eleven players each

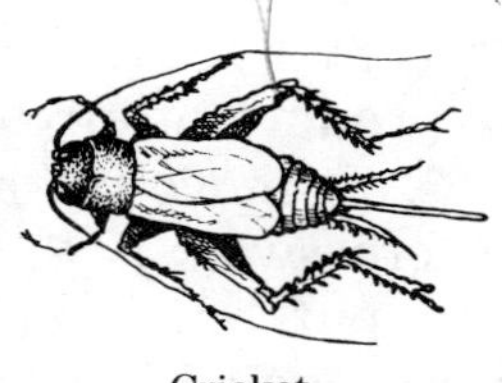

Cricket

crime (krīm) *n.* the act of doing something forbidden by law or not doing something required by law (the *crime* of robbery)

crim·i·nal (krim′ ən l) *n.* a person who commits a crime —*adj.* relating to a serious offense (a *criminal* record)

crip·ple (krip′ əl) *n.* a person or animal that is lame —*vb.* **crip·pled**; **crip·pling** to deprive one of the use of an arm or a leg

cri·sis (krī′ səs) *n., pl.* **cri·ses** (krī′ sēz′) a decisive moment or turning point for better or worse

crisp (krisp) *adj.* **1.** fresh, as in lettuce **2.** flaky, as in pastry **3.** short and clear, as in writing **4.** frosty, as in air —*vb.* to make crisp

crit·ic (krit′ ik) *n.* **1.** a person who is a skillful judge of creative work **2.** someone who finds fault with things

crit·i·cal (krit′ i kəl) *adj.* **1.** inclined to find fault **2.** careful and thoughtful (a *critical* study of a patient) **3.** relating to a crisis (a *critical* point in his recovery)

croc·o·dile (kräk′ ə dīl′) *n.* an animal related to the alligator that lives in warm rivers and marshes (the *crocodiles* in the Nile River)

crook·ed (krük′ əd) *adj.* **1.** bent **2.** dishonest (a *crooked* tax collector)

crop (kräp) *n.* **1.** a harvest (corn *crop*) **2.** the gullet of a bird where food is stored **3.** a short riding whip —*vb.* **cropped**; **crop·ping** **1.** to clip or trim (*Crop* his hair closer to his head.) **2.** to happen unexpectedly (My brother *crops* up once in awhile.)

cross (krȯs) *n.* **1.** an upright bar with a crossbar **2.** the product of mixing two breeds —*vb.* **1.** to form an X **2.** to move to the other side of the street (*Cross* at the crosswalk.) **3.** to draw a line through (*cross* out) **4.** to put one over the other in a different direction (*cross* one's legs) —*adj.* **1.** opposed (We're at *cross* purposes.) **2.** bad-tempered (*cross* this morning)

cross·ing (krȯs′ ing) *n.* **1.** an intersection **2.** where railroad tracks cross a street **3.** a trip across the ocean (Make the Atlantic *crossing.*)

crouch (krau̇ch) *vb.* to stoop low as though sitting on one's heels —*n.* the position of crouching

crow (krō) *n.* a shiny black bird with a harsh cry —*vb.* **1.** to make a shrill sound (to *crow* like a rooster) **2.** to gloat or brag

crowd (kraủd) *vb.* **1.** to press close together (to *crowd* into the bus) **2.** to collect in large numbers (to *crowd* the beaches) —*n.* a large number of people

crown (kraủn) *n.* **1.** a royal headdress **2.** a wreath for the head as a mark of honor **3.** the top part of a head or a hat **4.** the part of a tooth outside the gum —*vb.* **1.** to put a crown on **2.** to bring something to a good ending (*crown* the evening with a song) **3.** to cap a damaged tooth (to *crown* the tooth)

cru·cial (krü′ shəl) *adj.* relating to an important decision point (a *crucial* moment)

crude (krüd) *adj.* **crud·er**; **crud·est** **1.** in a natural state, not refined (*crude* sugar, *crude* oil) **2.** rough or rude in manner (a *crude* remark)

cru·el (krü′ əl) *adj.* **cru·el·er**; **cru·el·est** **1.** brutal, ready to hurt others **2.** painful (*cruel* turn of events)

cru·el·ty (krü′ əl tē) *n., pl.* **cru·el·ties** **1.** an act that hurts people **2.** cruel treatment

cruise (krüz) *vb.* **cruised**; **cruis·ing** **1.** to travel from port to port using the ship as a hotel **2.** to drive at a good operating speed (*cruise* the highway) —*n.* the act of cruising

crumb (krəm) *n.* a small bit of bread or cracker —*vb.* to cover with crumbs

crum·ple (krəm′ pəl) *vb.* **crum·pled**; **crum·pling** **1.** to wrinkle **2.** to collapse (*crumpled* to the floor)

crush (krəsh) *vb.* **1.** to squeeze hard (*crush* her finger **2.** to smash (*crush* stone) **3.** overwhelm (*crush* the enemy)

crust (krəst) *n.* **1.** the browned outer surface of bread **2.** the top and bottom pastry on a pie **3.** the rocky outer shell of the earth

cry (krī) *vb.* **cried; cry·ing** **1.** to shout **2.** to shed tears —*n.* **1.** a loud noise expressing grief or excitement **2.** the act of weeping

crys·tal (krist′ l) *n.* **1.** colorless quartz **2.** high quality glassware **3.** a substance that takes a shape with many flat sides (an ice *crystal*)

cub (kəb) *n.* the young of some animals such as the bear, wolf, and lion

cube (kyüb) *n.* a solid body with six equal square sides

Cube

cul·ti·vate (kəl′ tə vāt′) *vb.* **cul·ti·vat·ed; cul·ti·vat·ing** **1.** to loosen the ground around growing plants **2.** to develop through work or study (*cultivate* his interest in music)

cul·ture (kəl′ chər) *n.* **1.** refinement in taste and manners **2.** a stage or form of civilization (Egyptian *culture*) **3.** the cultivation of crops (wheat *culture*)

cun·ning (kən′ ing) *n.* **1.** skill **2.** slyness —*adj.* **1.** skillful or clever **2.** cute (a *cunning* child) **3.** sly and tricky

cup (kəp) *n.* **1.** a small container to hold liquids for drinking (a *cup* of coffee) **2.** a fancy trophy shaped like a goblet and given as a prize in a contest —*vb.* **cupped; cup·ping** to curve into the shape of a cup

Cup

cup·board (kəb′ ərd) *n.* a small cabinet with shelves for storing dishes or food

curb (kərb) *n.* **1.** a border of stone at the edge of a sidewalk **2.** a check or restraint —*vb.* to control with a restraint

cure (kyůr) *n.* **1.** recovery from a disease **2.** remedy (*cure* for an upset stomach) **3.** a method of medical treatment (a new *cure* for cold sores) —*vb.* **cured; cur·ing** **1.** to heal **2.** to preserve by salting or drying (to *cure* pork)

cu·ri·ous (kyůr′ ē əs) *adj.* **1.** eager to learn new things **2.** different or odd (*curious* stories) **3.** prying (*curious* about our business)

curl (kərl) *vb.* to twist into a ringlet or spiral —*n.* a ringlet or wave, as in the hair

cur·rent (kər′ ənt) *adj.* belonging to the present time (*current* issue of the journal) —*n.* **1.** the flow of air or water (the river *current*) **2.** the flow of electricity (electrical *current*)

cur·tain (kərt′ n) *n.* cloth fitted to cover or decorate a window

curve (kərv) *n.* **1.** a bend (*curve* in the road) **2.** a swerving ball (throw a *curve*) —*vb.* **curved**; **curv·ing** **1.** to make something curve **2.** to proceed from straight to bending (the road *curved*)

cus·tom (kəs′ təm) *n.* **1.** the common practice **2.** *pl.* duties on imported or exported goods

cus·tom·er (kəs′ tə mər) *n.* someone who buys regularly from a store or business

cut (kət) *vb.* **cut**; **cut·ting** **1.** to divide with a sharp edge **2.** to reduce (*cut* the price, *cut* grease) **3.** to stop (*cut* the joking) —*n.* **1.** a piece of something (a good *cut* of meat) **2.** a gash **3.** a path (a *cut* through the woods)

cute (kyüt) *adj.* **cut·er**; **cut·est** **1.** attractive in a youthful way **2.** shrewd at looking out for oneself (that was a *cute* move)

cy·cle (sī′ kəl) *n.* **1.** a regular order of events that repeats itself **2.** a bicycle or tricycle —*vb.* **1.** to move in circles **2.** to ride a bicycle or similar machine

cyl·in·der (sil′ ən dər) *n.* **1.** a long, round body, solid or hollow **2.** the container in which a piston moves back and forth in an engine

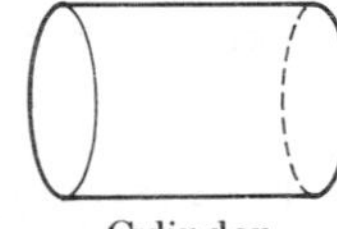
Cylinder

D

dai·ly (dā′ lē) *adj.* **1.** done every day (the *daily* paper) **2.** figured for each day (the *daily* rate at the hotel)

dain·ty (dānt′ ē) *n., pl.* **dain·ties** a delicious tidbit —*adj.* delicate, pretty

dair·y (deər′ ē) *n., pl.* **dair·ies** **1.** a place where milk is stored or processed **2.** a farm that produces milk **3.** a place that sells milk and milk products

dai·sy (dā′ zē) *n., pl.* **dai·sies** a ray flower, usually white, with a central disk of packed flower parts, usually yellow

Daisy

dam (dam) *n.* a barrier across a river or stream to hold back the flow of water

dam·age (dam′ ij) *n.* loss or injury —*vb.* **dam·aged**; **dam·ag·ing** to cause injury or harm

damp (damp) *adj.* moist, slightly wet

dance (dans) *vb.* **danced**; **danc·ing** to move the body, and especially the feet, through a pattern of steps in time to music —*n.* the art of dancing

danc·er (dans′ ər) *n.* one who dances

dan·de·li·on (dan′ də lī′ ən) *n.* a weed related to the daisy with long leaves often eaten as cooked greens

Dancer

dan·ger (dān′ jər) *n.* a situation where death, injury, or other harm is possible

dan·ger·ous (dān′ jə rəs) *adj.* **1.** unsafe (the bridge is *dangerous*) **2.** ready to do harm (a *dangerous* criminal)

dan·gle (dang′ gəl) *vb.* **dan·gled**; **dan·gling** to hang loose (*dangle* feet in the water)

dare (daər) *vb.* **dared**; **dar·ing** **1.** to be bold enough **2.** to have courage —*n.* challenge (took the *dare*)

dark (därk) *adj.* **1.** without light **2.** deep in shade (a *dark* color) **3.** secret or unknown (We're in the *dark* about it.) —*n.* lack of light

dark·en (där′ kən) *vb.* to make darker

dark·ness (därk′ nəs) *n.* the state of being dark (the *darkness* of a moonless night)

dart (därt) *n.* **1.** a small pointed missile **2.** a tapered tuck in clothing —*vb.* to move swiftly

Dart

dash (dash) *vb.* **1.** to smash (*dash* on the rocks) **2.** to move quickly (*dash* around the corner) —*n.* **1.** a splash (a *dash* of lemon juice) **2.** a punctuation mark (—) used to show a break in thought **3.** a shortened form of *dash*board, the control panel in a car or airplane

data (dāt′ ə, dat′ ə) *n., sing.* or *pl.* (*sing.* sometimes **da·tum**) factual information

date (dāt) *n.* **1.** the sweet, brownish fruit of the date palm **2.** the day, month, and year of a happening **3.** an appointment —*vb.* **dat·ed**; **dat·ing** **1.** to write the date on (*date* your letter) **2.** to mark as old-fashioned (His habits *date* him.)

daugh·ter (dȯt′ ər) *n.* a female child

dawn (dȯn) *vb.* **1.** to gradually grow light (The day should *dawn* clear.) **2.** to begin to appear (Civilization *dawn*ed in the Tigris-Euphrates valley.) **3.** to begin to understand (an idea *dawn*ed) —*n.* **1.** early morning **2.** the beginning

day (dā) *n.* **1.** time between sunrise and sunset **2.** a 24-hour period **3.** a period of time (in my grandmother's *day*)

day·break (dā′ brāk′) *n.* dawn

dead (ded) *adj.* **1.** without life (*dead* leaf) **2.** without energy (*dead* battery) **3.** out of date (a *dead* practice) **4.** exact (*dead* shot) —*n.* one of the dead —*adv*, completely (stopped *dead* at the door)

dead·ly (ded′ lē) *adj.* **dead·li·er**; **dead·li·est** fatal, causing death

deaf (def) *adj.* unable to hear, or hard of hearing

deal (dēl) *n.* **1.** action or treatment (a good *deal*, a raw *deal*) **2.** distribution of cards (his *deal*) **3.** quantity (a good *deal* of trouble) —*vb.* to occupy oneself (He *deal*s in wood products.)

deal·er (dēl′ ər) *n.* **1.** one who does business, buying and selling (an automobile *dealer*) **2.** one who deals cards

dear (diər) *adj.* **1.** loved and valued **2.** a form of address in letters (*Dear* Ms. Jones) **3.** high-priced (too *dear* for my pocketbook) —*n.* darling

death (deth) *n.* **1.** the state of being dead **2.** the end (*death* of his ambition)

de·bate (di bāt′) *n.* a discussion with arguments that are presented according to fixed rules —*vb.* **de·bat·ed**; **de·bat·ing** to take part in a debate

de·bris (də brē′) *n.* **1.** remains of anything broken down or destroyed **2.** pieces of tree limbs, rocks, and broken articles collected in one area (*debris* from the flood)

debt (det) *n.* something one owes

dec·ade (dek′ ād′) *n.* **1.** a period of ten years **2.** a set of ten

de·cay (di kā′) *vb.* to rot —*n.* rotting, decomposition

de·cent (dē′ sənt) *adj.* modest, acceptable, in good taste

de·cide (di sīd′) *vb.* **de·cid·ed**; **de·cid·ing** to make up one's mind

dec·i·mal (des′ ə məl) *adj.* based on the number ten —*n.* a proper fraction with a denominator of 10 or a power of ten which is indicated by a decimal point before the numerator (.5=5/10, .05=5/100, .005=5/1000)

de·ci·sion (di sizh′ ən) *n.* the act of making up one's mind, forming an opinion

deck (dek) *n.* **1.** a floor on a ship **2.** a platform that extends from a house for use as outdoor living space **3.** a pack of cards —*vb.* to put on fine clothing or ornaments (*deck*ed out in her fancy clothes)

dec·la·ra·tion (dek′ lə rā′ shən) *n.* an announcement (*Declaration* of Independence)

de·clare (di klaər′) *vb.* **de·clared**; **de·clar·ing** to announce, proclaim, make clear

de·cline (di klīn′) *vb.* **de·clined**; **de·clin·ing** **1.** to bend downward (the path *decline*s) **2.** to fail, come to an end **3.** to refuse (*decline* the offer) —*n.* **1.** a descending slope **2.** a gradual decay or wasting away

dec·o·rate (dek′ ə rāt′) *vb.* **dec·o·rat·ed**; **dec·o·rat·ing** **1.** to make more attractive with ornaments and furnishings **2.** to award a military badge (*decorate* a soldier)

de·crease (di krēs′) *vb.* **de·creased**; **de·creas·ing** to grow, or cause to grow less —*n.* gradual reduction

ded·i·cate (ded′ i kāt′) *vb.* **ded·i·cat·ed**; **ded·i·cat·ing** **1.** to commit something to a sacred or special purpose (*dedicate* a public building to justice and freedom for all) **2.** to devote (*dedicate* one's life to feeding the hungry) **3.** to print an inscription in the front part of a book

deed (dēd) *n.* **1.** an action (a good *deed*) **2.** a record of the buying and selling of real estate —*vb.* to transfer by deed (He'll *deed* the land to me.)

deep (dēp) *adj.* **1.** extending far down from the top (*deep* hole) **2.** extending far back from the front (*deep* woods) **3.** hard to understand (*deep* lecture) **4.** dark (*deep* green) **5.** intense (*deep* sleep) **6.** low (*deep* voice)

deer (diər) *n.*, *pl.* **deer** hoofed mammals, the males of which have antlers

de·feat (di fēt′) *vb.* to win, to overcome —*n.* loss of a contest

de·fend (di fend′) *vb.* **1.** to protect from harm **2.** to uphold one's rights

de·fense (di fens′) *n.* the act of protecting

de·fine (di fīn′) *vb.* **de·fined**; **de·fin·ing** **1.** to state the meaning of **2.** to fix the limits of (*define* the boundaries)

def·i·nite (def′ ə nət) *adj.* **1.** clear **2.** exact **3.** having fixed limits

de·gree (di grē′) *n.* **1.** a step in a series **2.** a unit of temperature (32 *degrees* F) **3.** a unit in measuring angles (90 *degrees*) **4.** a title conferred by a college or university (master's *degree*)

de·lay (di lā′) *n.* **1.** the act of putting something off (*delay* his visit to the dentist) **2.** the time during which something is delayed (There will be a slight *delay.*) —*vb.* **1.** to put off **2.** to move slowly

del·e·gate (del′ i gət) *n.* a person sent with power to act for another or others; a representative —*vb.* (del′ ə gāt′) **del·e·gat·ed**; **del·e·gat·ing** **1.** to send as one's representative **2.** to give over to the care of another (*delegate* authority)

de·lib·er·ate (di lib′ ə rət) *adj.* **1.** giving careful thought **2.** slow in action or in making up one's mind —*vb.* (di lib′ ə rāt′) **de·lib·er·at·ed**; **de·lib·er·at·ing** to consider carefully

del·i·cate (del′ i kət) *adj.* **1.** light, tender, or fragile (*delicate* china) **2.** sensitive (*delicate* instrument) **3.** weak, frail (in *delicate* condition)

de·li·cious (di lish′ əs) *adj.* good in taste or smell

de·light (di līt′) *n.* joy, pleasure —*vb.* to give joy, to take pleasure

de·liv·er (di liv′ ər) *vb.* **1.** to hand over or transfer (*deliver* a package) **2.** to set free (*deliver* from bondage) **3.** to help in childbirth (*deliver* a child)

del·ta (del′ tə) *n.* a triangular or fan-shaped piece of land at the mouth of a river made by mud deposits

de·mand (di mand′) *n.* **1.** the act of claiming that something is due **2.** the need for (*demand* for more housing) —*vb.* **1.** to ask for with authority or force (to *demand* the claim check for the luggage, *demand* to be served) **2.** to need (to *demand* a break from the work)

de·moc·ra·cy (di mäk′ rə sē) *n., pl.* **de·moc·ra·cies** **1.** government by the people **2.** belief that all people are socially equal

dem·on·strate (dem′ ən strāt′) *vb.* **dem·on·strat·ed; dem·on·strat·ing** **1.** to teach by example **2.** to show and explain **3.** to prove by reasoning

den (den) *n.* **1.** the shelter of a wild animal **2.** a hiding place (*den* of thieves) **3.** an informal comfortable room

de·nom·i·na·tor (di näm′ ə nāt′ ər) *n.* the part of the fraction below the line telling the number of equal parts into which a quantity is divided (3 is the *denominator* in 2/3)

de·note (di nōt′) *vb.* **de·not·ed; de·not·ing** **1.** to mark plainly (The signs *denote* town boundaries.) **2.** to indicate (That dial *denote*s air pressure.)

dense (dens) *adj.* **1.** crowded, thick (*dense* crowd) **2.** dull, stupid (*dense* student)

den·si·ty (den′ sət ē) *n., pl.* **den·si·ties** **1.** crowded in space **2.** stupidity

den·tist (dent′ əst) *n.* one who treats and repairs teeth

de·ny (di nī′) *vb.* **de·nied**; **de·ny·ing** **1.** to refuse to believe or admit **2.** to refuse to give (to *deny* him an allowance)

de·part (di part′) *vb.* to go away

de·part·ment (di pärt′ mənt) *n.* a part or division of an organization

de·par·ture (di pär′ chər) *n.* **1.** the act of leaving **2.** setting out on a new venture

de·pend (di pend′) *vb.* **1.** to rely for help or support **2.** to be based on some action or condition (*depends* on the weather)

de·pend·ent (di pen′ dənt) *adj.* **1.** relying on someone else **2.** conditional or subordinate (a *dependent* clause)

de·pos·it (di päz′ ət) *vb.* **1.** to put down **2.** to put money in the bank **3.** to make a part payment on a more expensive item (to *deposit* ten dollars on the radio) **4.** to allow to sink (The river *deposits* mud at the delta.) —*n.* **1.** money put in the bank **2.** money put down in an agreement to purchase **3.** mud carried down by a river **4.** a large amount of something put down by nature (an iron *deposit*)

de·pot (dē′ pō, dep′ ō) *n.* **1.** a railway or bus station **2.** a storehouse

de·pres·sion (di presh′ ən) *n.* **1.** the act of making something lower **2.** a hollow place **3.** sadness **4.** a low period in business activity with many people out of work

de·prive (di prīv′) *vb.* **de·prived**; **de·priv·ing** **1.** to take something away (*deprived* of their freedom) **2.** to stop from having something (*deprive* the prisoners of food)

depth (depth) *n.* **1.** a deep place **2.** distance from front to back, or down **3.** richness (*depth* of color) **4.** abundance (*depth* of knowledge)

de·rive (di rīv′) *vb.* **de·rived**; **de·riv·ing** **1.** to get from a certain source **2.** to trace back to the beginning (to *derive* the history of)

de·scend·ant (di sen′ dənt) *n.* anyone in the line of offspring from a particular ancestor

de·scent (di sent′) *n.* **1.** a downward slope **2.** the act of coming down, as from an ancestor **3.** a sudden attack

de·scribe (di skrīb′) *vb.* **de·scribed**; **de·scrib·ing** **1.** to tell about **2.** to draw a line about (*describe* a triangle)

de·scrip·tion (di skrip′ shən) *n.* telling how something looks or appears to be

des·ert (dez′ ərt) *n.* a large area of sand or dry soil where very little will grow without being watered —*adj.* relating to a desert (a *desert* camp) —*n.* (di zərt′) a just reward or punishment —*vb.* to abandon, to run away from duty (to *desert* the helpless man)

de·serve (di zərv′) *vb.* **de·served**; **de·serv·ing** to be worthy of

de·sign (di zīn′) *vb.* to plan a way of doing something —*n.* purpose or intention

de·sire (di zīr′) *vb.* **de·sired**; **de·sir·ing** **1.** to wish for **2.** to ask for —*n.* a strong wish

desk (desk) *n.* a piece of furniture to use when writing or studying

des·o·late (des′ ə lāt) *vb.* **des·o·lat·ed**; **des·o·lat·ing** to lay waste, abandon —*adj.* (des′ ə lət) **1.** lonely or abandoned **2.** in ruins

de·spair (di spaər′) *vb.* to give up hope —*n.* loss of hope

des·per·ate (des′ pə rət) *adj.* **1.** reckless **2.** frantic **3.** beyond hope

de·spite (di spīt′) *prep.* in spite of

des·sert (di zərt′) *n.* sweets, fruit, or nuts served at the end of a meal

des·ti·na·tion (des′ tə nā′ shən) *n.* the end of a trip

de·stroy (di strȯi′) *vb.* **1.** to ruin **2.** to put an end to

de·struc·tion (di strək′ shən) *n.* **1.** the act of destroying something **2.** ruin

de·tail (di tāl′, dē′ tāl′) *n.* **1.** a small part or item **2.** dealing with every part of something **3.** a small group of soldiers on special assignment —*vb.* to report about every item

de·tect (di tekt′) *vb.* to discover or find out

de·tec·tive (di tek′ tiv) *adj.* relating to the work of detectives —*n.* a person who is hired to solve crimes and catch criminals

de·ter·mi·na·tion (di tər′ mə nā′ shən) *n.* the act of coming to a conclusion

de·ter·mine (di tər′ mən) *vb.* **de·ter·mined**; **de·ter·min·ing** **1.** to make up one's mind **2.** to find out with exactness

de·vel·op (di vel′ əp) *vb.* **1.** to grow gradually **2.** to improve a little at a time

de·vel·op·ment (di vel′ əp mənt) *n.* the act of growing or improving

de·vice (di vīs′) *n.* **1.** a piece of equipment for a special purpose **2.** a clever plan or scheme

dev·il (dev′ əl) *n.* **1.** an evil spirit or demon **2.** a wicked person **3.** a dashing or reckless person

de·vise (di vīz′) *vb.* **de·vised**; **de·vis·ing** to invent or form a plan

de·vo·tion (di vō′ shən) *n.* **1.** deep love or affection **2.** religious worship

dew (dü) *n.* moisture that settles on surfaces at night (*dew* on the grass)

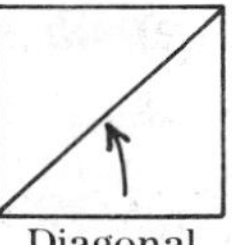
Diagonal

di·ag·o·nal (dī ag′ ən l) *adj.* running in a slanting direction (to the *diagonal* corner) —*n.* a slanted line

di·a·gram (dī′ ə gram′) *n.* a sketch or plan that makes something clearer —*vb.* **di·a·grammed**; **di·a·gram·ming** to show as a sketch or outline

di·al (dī′ əl) *n.* **1.** the face of a watch or clock **2.** the face of any gauge **3.** a knob that can be turned to operate something (radio *dial*) —*vb.* **di·aled**; **di·al·ing** to use a dial to operate or select (*dial* the telephone)

di·a·logue (dī′ ə lȯg′) *n.* **1.** a conversation between two (or more) persons **2.** parts of a book that are written as conversation

di·am·e·ter (dī am′ ət ər) *n.* a straight line through the center that divides a figure in half

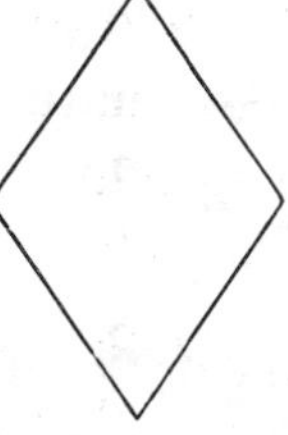
Diamond

di·a·mond (dī′ ə mənd) *n.* **1.** a brilliant precious stone used in jewelry and as a hard cutting edge in industry **2.** a figure with two angles larger and two angles smaller than 90° **3.** one of the four suits in a deck of cards **4.** a baseball infield

di·a·phragm (dī′ ə fram′) *n.* **1.** the muscular wall separating the chest from the abdomen **2.** any thin sheet, as the vibrating disk in a telephone

di·a·ry (dī′ ə rē) *n., pl.* **di·a·ries** **1.** a daily record of experiences **2.** a book for keeping such a record

dic·ta·tor (dik′ tāt′ ər) *n.* **1.** one who has absolute power **2.** one who tells another what to write

dic·tio·nar·y (dik′ shə ner′ ē) *n., pl.* **dic·tio·nar·ies** an alphabetically arranged book giving the pronunciation and meaning of words

die (dī) *vb.* **died**; **dy·ing** **1.** to stop living **2.** to go away gradually (The noise *died* down.) **3.** to long (*dying* to meet you) —*n.* or *n., pl.* **dice** (dīs) **1.** cube with spots on it used in games **2.** *n., pl.* **dies** (dīz) a metal form used in cutting or stamping out material, such as metal

di·et (dī′ ət) *n.* **1.** what a person eats **2.** a special eating plan for better health or weight —*vb.* to eat according to a special plan

dif·fer (dif′ ər) *vb.* **1.** to be unlike **2.** to disagree

dif·fer·ent (dif′ ə rənt) *adj.* not the same

dif·fi·cult (dif′ i kəlt′) *adj.* **1.** hard to do **2.** hard to understand (*difficult* topic)

dig (dig) *vb.* **dug** (dəg); **dig·ging** **1.** to turn over or take out the soil (*dig* a hole) **2.** to uncover (*dig* potatoes) **3.** to find (*dig* up facts) —*n.* **1.** poke (a *dig* in the ribs) **2.** a cutting remark

di·ges·tion (dī jes′ chən) *n.* the ability to take in and assimilate something (Chewing aids *digestion.*)

dig·it (dij′ ət) *n.* **1.** the numerals 0 to 9 **2.** a finger or toe

dig·ni·ty (dig′ nət ē) *n., pl.* **dig·ni·ties** character, stateliness, or high rank

dike (dīk) *n.* a bank of earth heaped up to control water

dim (dim) *adj.* **dim·mer**; **dim·mest** somewhat dark or hard to see

dime (dīm) *n.* a coin worth ten cents (ten pennies)

di·men·sion (də men′ chən) *n.* a measurement of an object's length, width, or depth

din (din) *n.* a loud, confused noise —*vb.* **dinned**; **din·ning** to make a din

din·ner (din′ ər) *n.* **1.** the main meal of the day **2.** a banquet (a *dinner* to honor the governor)

Dinosaur

di·no·saur (dī′ nə sȯr′) *n.* a "terrible lizard," one of the huge reptiles that lived on earth millions of years ago

dip (dip) *vb.* **dipped**; **dip·ping** **1.** to lower for a short time and then raise (*dip* the ring in cleaning fluid) **2.** to go downward (The sun *dipped* behind the horizon.) —*n.* **1.** a plunge into water (go for a *dip* in the ocean) **2.** a drop (a *dip* in prices)

di·rect (də rekt′, dī-) *vb.* **1.** to point out the way (*direct* him to the museum) **2.** to put an address on (*direct* the memo to) —*adj.* straight (a *direct* route)

di·rec·tion (də rek′ shən, dī-) *n.* **1.** the act of leading (under his *direction*) **2.** a line of motion (in that *direction*) **3.** steps to follow (*directions* for making a cake)

dirt (dərt) *n.* **1.** soil or sand **2.** a substance that makes things unclean (as mud) **3.** evil gossip

dis·ap·pear (dis′ ə piər′) *vb.* **1.** to pass out of sight **2.** to become lost

dis·ap·point·ment (dis′ ə pȯint′ mənt) *n.* **1.** a failure to fulfill an expectation **2.** a person or thing that fails to live up to what is expected

di·sas·ter (di zas′ tər) *n.* a sudden misfortune such as a serious accident or flood

dis·card (dis kärd′) *vb.* **1.** to get rid of something useless **2.** to put a playing card on the discard pile —*n.* the act of discarding

dis·ci·pline (dis′ ə plən) *n.* **1.** strict training **2.** punishment **3.** the rules of conduct —*vb.* **dis·ci·plined**; **dis·ci·plin·ing** **1.** to punish **2.** to train in obedience

dis·cour·age (dis kər′ ij) *vb.* **dis·cour·aged**; **dis·cour·ag·ing** to advise against

dis·cov·er (dis kəv′ ər) *vb.* to learn of for the first time

dis·cuss (dis kəs′) *vb.* to talk about openly

dis·ease (diz ēz′) *n.* illness

dis·guise (dis gīz′) *vb.* **dis·guised**; **dis·guis·ing** **1.** to hide one's identity **2.** to change the appearance of —*n.* something put on to hide the identity of

dis·gust (dis gəst′) *n.* a strong dislike —*vb.* to offend the senses of

dish (dish) *n.* **1.** a slightly hollow container for serving food **2.** food served in a dish —*vb.* to put into a dish (*dish* out the spaghetti)

disk or **disc** (disk) *n.* **1.** a round flat object **2.** a phonograph record

dis·may (dis mā′) *vb.* to terrify or cause one to lose courage —*n.* **1.** alarm **2.** a loss of spirit or courage

dis·miss (dis mis′) *vb.* **1.** to send away **2.** to remove from office or employment **3.** to put out of one's mind (*dismiss* the idea)

dis·play (dis plā′) *vb.* to spread out so as to be seen —*n.* a show or exhibition

dis·pose (dis pōz′) *vb.* **dis·posed**; **dis·pos·ing** **1.** to make something fit or ready **2.** to settle **3.** to get rid of

dis·pute (dis pyüt′) *vb.* **dis·put·ed**; **dis·put·ing** to argue or fight about —*n.* a fight

dis·solve (di zälv′) *vb.* **dis·solved**; **dis·solv·ing** **1.** to pass into solution (Water can *dissolve* salt.) **2.** to break up (*dissolve* the partnership)

dis·tance (dis′ təns) *n.* **1.** the length of a straight line between two points **2.** a coolness or reserve in behavior —*vb.* **dis·tanced**; **dis·tanc·ing** to leave far behind

dis·tinct (dis tingkt′) *adj.* **1.** separate **2.** clear

dis·tin·guish (dis ting′ gwish) *vb.* **1.** to clearly tell one from another **2.** to separate from others by a mark of honor

dis·tress (dis tres′) *n.* misery caused by pain, trouble, or danger —*vb.* to cause distress

dis·trib·ute (dis trib′ yət) *vb.* **dis·trib·ut·ed**; **dis·trib·ut·ing** **1.** to deal out **2.** to spread out

dis·trict (dis trikt′) *n.* **1.** a section of a territory marked off for official reasons (a fire *district*) **2.** a region that is known for a particular thing (garment *district*) —*vb.* to divide into district

dis·turb (dis tərb′) *vb.* **1.** to interrupt (to *disturb* his study) **2.** to move (*disturb* the pattern) **3.** to upset

ditch (dich) *n.* a trench dug in the ground —*vb.* **1.** to dig a ditch around **2.** to cause to fall (*ditch*ed his plane in the bay)

dive (dīv) *vb.* **dived** or **dove** (dōv); **div·ing** **1.** to jump head-first into water **2.** to go down at a steep angle —*n.* **1.** the act of diving **2.** a sudden plunge downward **3.** a low-class bar

di·vide (də vīd′) *vb.* **di·vid·ed**; **di·vid·ing** **1.** to separate into parts **2.** to share **3.** to branch (road *divides* here) **4.** to perform a mathematical division —*n.* a mountain ridge that separates two drainage areas (the Continental *Divide*)

di·vi·sion (də vizh′ ən) *n.* **1.** the act of dividing **2.** a part of the whole **3.** a large military unit

do (dü) *vb.* **did** (did); **done** (dən); **do·ing** (dü′ ing); **does** (dəz) **1.** to carry out **2.** to act **3.** to work at **4.** to finish (what he had *done*)

dock (däk) *n.* **1.** a slip for receiving ships **2.** a place in court where a prisoner sits during a trial —*vb.* **1.** to guide to a dock (*dock* a ship) **2.** to take a part away (*dock* a person's wages)

doc·tor (däk′ tər) *n.* **1.** a licensed physician or surgeon **2.** one who holds the highest degree given by a university —*vb.* to practice medicine

doc·u·ment (däk′ yə mənt) *n.* a written or printed paper of importance (A deed is a *document.*) —*vb.* to prove with written evidence

dog (dȯg) *n.* a domestic animal related to wolves and foxes —*vb.* **dogged**; **dog·ging** to track like a hound

doll (däl) *n.* a small human figure used as a toy in child's play

dol·lar (däl′ ər) *n.* paper money equal to 100 cents

dol·phin (däl′ fən) *n.* a water mammal belonging to the same family as whales and sometimes called *porpoise*

do·main (dō mān′) *n.* **1.** land under one's control **2.** field of activity

dome (dōm) *n.* a large cup-shaped section of a roof that rises above the rest of the roof, used mainly on important buildings

Dome

do·mes·tic (də mes′ tik) *adj.* relating to home or family —*n.* a household servant

don·key (däng′ kē) *n., pl.* **don·keys** an ass

door (dōr) *n.* a swinging or sliding barrier at an entry that may be opened or closed

dot (dät) *n.* **1.** a small mark or spot **2.** a signal in the Morse Code —*vb.* **dot·ted**; **dot·ting** to mark with a dot

dou·ble (dəb′ əl) *adj.* **1.** consisting of two parts **2.** folded in two **3.** being twice as much —*n.* a hit in baseball that allows the batter to reach second base

doubt (daůt) *vb.* **1.** to be uncertain **2.** to lack trust

dough (dō) *n.* a soft mass of uncooked bread or pastry that can be rolled out or kneaded

dough·nut (dō′ nət′) *n.* a small cake, usually ring-shaped, fried in fat

dove (dəv) *n.* a small, wild pigeon

down (daůn) *adv.* to a lower position —*adj.* being in a lower position —*prep.* in a downward direction —*vb.* to cause to go down —*n.* **1.** soft feathers **2.** a low point (ups and *downs*)

down·town (daún′ taún′) *adv.* to or toward the business center of a city —*adj.* relating to the business center of a city

doz·en (dəz′ n) *n., pl.* **doz·ens** or **doz·en** twelve things that are alike (a *dozen* eggs)

draft (draft) *n.* **1.** an early copy of written material (a rough *draft* of a report) **2.** an air current (feel a *draft* from the window) —*adj.* used for pulling loads (*draft* animals) —*vb.* **1.** to select for compulsory military service **2.** to do an initial sketch or copy

drag (drag) *n.* something that slows progress —*vb.* **dragged**; **drag·ging** **1.** to move slowly and with difficulty **2.** to trail behind

drag·on (drag′ ən) *n.* an imaginary, long-tailed monster that breathes fire

drain (drān) *vb.* to let all the liquid flow out —*n.* **1.** a pipe or channel used for draining **2.** the act of draining

dra·ma (drä′ mə, dram′ ə) *n.* a serious stage play

draw (dró) *vb.* **drew** (drü); **drawn** (drón); **draw·ing** **1.** to make figures, as with a pencil **2.** to move by pulling **3.** to go by gradually **4.** attract (*draw* attention) **5.** to take (*draw* a breath) —*n.* **1.** the act of drawing **2.** a tie game

draw·er (dró′ ər, drór) *n.* a section of a chest that pulls out (Put socks in the middle *drawer.*)

dread (dred) *vb.* to be afraid to face up to something —*n.* fear of harm —*adj.* causing terror or fear, mixed with respect

dream (drēm) *n.* **1.** thoughts that come during sleep **2.** dream-like thoughts (day*dream*) **3.** something pleasing (The car is a *dream*!) —*vb.* **dreamed**; **dream·ing** **1.** to have a dream **2.** to think of as happening sometime in the future

dress (dres) *vb.* **1.** to put clothes on **2.** to trim a store window **3.** to put a bandage on a wound —*n.* a garment for a female

drift (drift) *n.* **1.** something piled up by the wind (snow-*drift*) **2.** a general idea (*drift* of the conversation) —*vb.* **1.** to be pushed along by the wind or waves **2.** to go along without effort (*drift* through school)

drill (dril) *vb.* **1.** to bore a hole **2.** to practice by repeating something over and over —*n.* **1.** a tool for making holes in hard material **2.** training by repetition

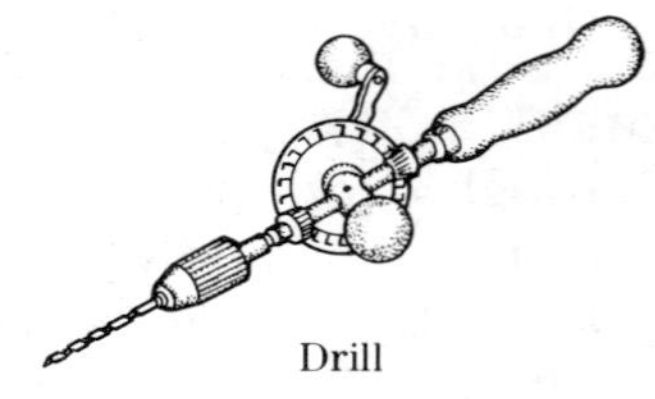
Drill

drink (dringk) *vb.* **drank** (drangk); **drunk** (drəngk); **drink·ing** **1.** to swallow liquid **2.** to take something in (*drink* in the landscape) —*n.* a beverage

drip (drip) *vb.* **dripped**; **drip·ping** to fall in drops —*n.* **1.** the droplets of liquid **2.** the sound of falling drops

drive (drīv) *vb.* **drove** (drōv); **driv·en** (driv′ ən); **driv·ing** (drī′ ving) **1.** to push onward **2.** to go in a vehicle **3.** to keep in motion —*n.* **1.** a trip in a car **2.** a strong effort (a charity *drive*)

drive·way (drīv′ wā′) *n.* a private road from a house to the street

drop (dräp) *n.* anything that holds together like a small liquid mass —*vb.* **dropped**; **drop·ping** **1.** to fall in drops **2.** to let fall **3.** to send **4.** to go suddenly lower (*drop* out of sight)

drought (draůt) *n.* lack of rain

drug (drəg) *n.* **1.** a medicine **2.** a habit-forming substance

drum (drəm) *n.* a musical instrument played by beating with sticks on a tightly-drawn skin on a frame —*vb.* **drummed**; **drum·ming** **1.** to beat a drum **2.** to tap in rhythm

dry (drī) *adj.* **dri·er**; **dri·est** **1.** lacking water (*dry* weather) **2.** lacking freshness (*dry* bread) **3.** lacking in interest (*dry* subject) **4.** lacking sweetness (*dry* wine)

duck (dək) *n.* **1.** a water bird with a flat bill and webbed feet **2.** a cotton fabric similar to canvas —*vb.* **1.** to bob under water briefly **2.** to dodge or evade

duck·ling (dək′ ling) *n.* a young duck

due (dü) *n.* something owed —*adj.* **1.** proper (in *due* time) **2.** as a result (called off *due* to fog) —*adv.* exactly (*due* south)

dull (dəl) *adj.* **1.** not smart (*dull*-witted) **2.** not active (*dull* game) **3.** not clear (*dull* sound or *dull* color) —*vb.* to become dull

dumb (dəm) *adj.* **1.** not able to speak (*dumb* animals) **2.** foolish (a *dumb* thing to do)

dump (dəmp) *vb.* to throw down —*n.* **1.** a place to put trash **2.** a place to store military materials (ammunition *dump*) **3.** a messy, neglected place

dune (dün) *n.* a ridge of sand piled up by the wind

du·pli·cate (dü′ pli kət) *adj.* two exactly alike —*n.* a thing that is exactly like another —*vb.* (dü′ pli kāt′) to make an exact copy

dur·ing (dür′ ing) *prep.* at some time in the course of (*during* the day)

dusk (dəsk) *n.* a state of deepening darkness (hearing the small frogs chirping at *dusk*)

dust (dəst) *n.* fine, dry pieces of earth or other matter

du·ty (düt′ ē) *n., pl.* **du·ties** whatever is required by one's rank or job or relationship

dwell (dwel) *vb.* **dwelt** (dwelt) or **dwelled** (dweld); **dwell·ing** **1.** to live in a place **2.** to stay on a topic (*dwell* on that subject)

dye (dī) *n.* a tint or stain used to color objects —*vb.* **dyed**; **dye·ing** to give a new color by dyeing

E

each (ēch) *adj.* considering each one separately —*pron.* each one —*adv.* apiece

ea·ger (ē′ gər) *adj.* impatient to do or to have

ea·gle (ē′ gəl) *n.* a large bird, related to the hawk, with sharp eyesight and strong flight (the bald or golden *eagle*)

ear (iər) *n.* **1.** the organ of hearing **2.** attentive listening (Give me your *ear.*) **3.** a spike of cereal grass with seeds (*ear* of corn or wheat)

Ear

ear·ly (ər′ lē) *adv.* **ear·li·er**; **ear·li·est** **1.** at or near the beginning of a time period **2.** soon —*adj.* **ear·li·er**; **ear·li·est** near the beginning or before the usual time (an *early* bus)

earn (ərn) *vb.* **1.** to get as pay for work **2.** to deserve (*earn* their loyalty)

ear·nest (ər′ nəst) *adj.* serious (an *earnest* effort)

earn·ings (ər′ ningz) *n., pl.* **1.** money received as pay for work **2.** money received as profit on investments

earth (ərth) *n.* **1.** dirt **2.** land **3.** the planet we live on

earth·quake (ərth′ kwāk′) *n.* a shaking of the ground due to a shifting of the earth's crust

ease (ēz) *n.* **1.** comfort **2.** freedom from difficulty —*vb.* **eased**; **eas·ing** **1.** to make more comfortable **2.** to move very carefully (*Ease* yourself along the tree limb.)

east (ēst) *adv.* to or toward the direction of the sunrise —*adj.* toward or coming from the *east* —*n.* **1.** the point on the compass opposite west **2.** the direction of sunrise

east·ern (ēs′ tərn) *adj.* **1.** toward the east (*eastern* region) **2.** coming from the east (*eastern* customs)

east·ward (ēst′ wərd) *adv.* or *adj.* toward the east —*n.* a direction or part that is toward the east

eas·y (ē′ zē) *adj.* **eas·i·er; eas·i·est** **1.** not hard **2.** free from trouble or worry

eat (ēt) *vb.* **ate** (āt); **eat·en** (ēt′ n); **eat·ing** **1.** to chew food and swallow **2.** to destroy or wear away (The acid *ate* a hole in the rug.)

ech·o (ek′ ō) *n., pl.* **ech·oes** the repetition of a sound caused by the bouncing back of sound waves —*vb.* to repeat

e·clipse (i klips′) *n.* the hiding of a heavenly body when another body passes in front of it —*vb.* **e·clipsed; e·clips·ing** **1.** to cause an eclipse of **2.** to make appear less bright

ec·o·nom·ic (ek′ ə näm′ ik, ē kə-) *adj.* relating to the production, distribution, and consumption of goods and services

e·con·o·my (i kän′ ə mē) *n., pl.* **e·con·o·mies** careful use of money and products

edge (ej) *n.* **1.** the line or border where a surface ends (*edge* of the paper) **2.** the cutting side of a blade —*vb.* **edged; edg·ing** **1.** to sharpen **2.** to move little by little

ed·i·tor (ed′ ət ər) *n.* a person who writes or revises written material for publication

ed·u·cate (ej′ ə kāt′) *vb.* **ed·u·cat·ed; ed·u·cat·ing** **1.** to teach **2.** to provide schooling for

ed·u·ca·tion (ej′ ə kā′ shən) *n.* **1.** developing through instruction and study **2.** knowledge and skill gained by study **3.** the study of the science and art of teaching

eel (ēl) *n.* a long, smooth, snake-like fish

ee·rie (iər′ ē) *adj.* **ee·ri·er; ee·ri·est** **1.** weird **2.** causing fear

ef·fect (i fekt′) *n.* **1.** the result of something **2.** operation (go into *effect*) **3.** influence (*effect* of interest rates) —*vb.* to bring about

ef·fec·tive (i fek′ tiv) *adj.* **1.** producing a definite result **2.** impressive

ef·fi·cient (i fish′ ənt) *adj.* getting something done without waste

ef·fort (ef′ ərt) *n.* **1.** hard work **2.** an attempt (made an *effort* to succeed)

egg (eg) *n.* a hard-shelled oval body produced by a bird and from which it hatches its young —*vb.* to urge

ei·ther (ē′ thər) *adj.* **1.** one or the other **2.** each (parking on *either* street is illegal) —*pron.* the one or the other —*conj.* used in combination with "or" to show different choices (*either* red or blue)

e·lab·o·rate (i lab′ ə rət) *adj.* with great detail and much care —*vb.* (i lab′ ə rāt′) **e·lab·o·rat·ed; e·lab·o·rat·ing** to work out in great detail

e·las·tic (i las′ tik) *adj.* capable of stretching and returning to its original size —*n.* **1.** an elastic fabric **2.** a rubber band

el·bow (el′ bō′) *n.* **1.** the joint of the arm or an animal's forelimb **2.** an object in the shape of a bent arm —*vb.* to push with the elbows (*elbow* her way through the crowd)

el·der (el′ dər) *n.* a shrub related to the honeysuckle —*adj.* older (his *elder* brother) —*n.* one who is older (children who are polite to their *elders*)

e·lect (i lekt′) *adj.* chosen for office but not yet installed (president-*elect*) —*vb.* to choose by vote (*elect* a president)

e·lec·tion (i lek′ shən) *n.* the act of choosing by vote

e·lec·tric (i lek′ trik) or **e·lec·tri·cal** (-tri kəl) *adj.* relating to electricity (*electric* blanket)

e·lec·tric·i·ty (i lek′ tris′ ət ē) *n.* a form of energy produced by chemicals, a dynamo, solar panels, or nuclear energy

e·lec·tron (i lek′ trän) *n.* a tiny particle of negatively charged electricity that forms the outer part of an atom

e·lec·tron·ic (i lek′ trän′ ik) *adj* relating to electrons or the technology based on their use

el·e·ment (el′ ə mənt) *n.* **1.** one simple component of the whole **2.** one of the more than 100 substances that cannot be separated into simpler substances (iron and silver are *elements*)

el·e·men·ta·ry (el′ ə ment′ ə rē) *adj.* relating to what is basic to further study (*elementary* science)

Elephant

el·e·phant (el′ ə fənt) *n.* a huge animal with wrinkled skin, a long trunk, and two ivory tusks

el·e·va·tion (el′ ə vā′ shən) *n.* **1.** a high place, such as a hill or mountain **2.** the height above sea level (an *elevation* of 10,000 feet)

el·e·va·tor (el′ ə vāt′ ər) *n.* **1.** a cage or conveyor for raising or lowering people or goods from one level to another **2.** a storehouse for grain

e·lim·i·nate (i lim′ ə nāt′) *vb.* **e·lim·i·nat·ed**; **e·lim·i·nat·ing** **1.** to remove **2.** to throw out

elk (elk) *n.* a large animal with antlers, a member of the deer family

elm (elm) *n.* a tall, spreading shade tree

Elk

else (els) *adv.* in a different way, place, or time (where *else*) —*adj.* relating to a different person (someone *else*)

else·where (els′ hweər′) *adv.* in or to another place

em·bar·rass (im bar′ əs) *vb.* **1.** to confuse **2.** to make someone lose composure

em·broi·der (im bròid′ ər) *vb.* **1.** to make a design with needle and thread **2.** to add to a story with fanciful details

em·bry·o (em′ brē ō′) *n., pl.* **em·bry·os** anything in its earliest stage of development (the *embryo* of an idea)

e·merge (i mərj′) *vb.* **e·merged**; **e·merg·ing** **1.** to come out of something that has hidden (*emerged* from the darkness) **2.** to become known (the truth may *emerge*)

e·mer·gen·cy (i mər′ jən sē) *n., pl.* **e·mer·gen·cies** a sudden problem needing quick action

e·mo·tion (i mō′ shən) *n.* strong feeling such as love, hate, or fear

em·per·or (em′ pər ər) *n.* the ruler of an empire

em·pha·sis (em′ fə səs) *n., pl.* **em·pha·ses** (-sēz′) extra force or importance given to something

em·pha·size (em′ fə sīz′) *vb.* **em·pha·sized**; **em·pha·siz·ing** to say forcefully

em·pire (em′ pīr′) *n.* a very large nation or a group of nations under one ruler (the British *Empire*)

em·ploy (im plòi′) *vb.* **1.** to use (*employ* yeast in making bread) **2.** to hire (*employ* teenagers for the summer)

em·ploy·ee (im plòi′ ē′) *n.* a person who works for someone else for wages

em·ploy·er (im plòi′ ər) *n.* one who hires others to work for wages

em·ploy·ment (im plȯi′ mənt) *n.* the act of employing or the state of being employed

emp·ty (emp′ tē) *adj.* **emp·ti·er; emp·ti·est** **1.** containing nothing **2.** lacking in sense (*empty* words)

en·a·ble (in ā′ bəl) *vb.* **en·a·bled; en·a·bling** to make possible by giving the means or support (The new schedule *enabled* them to meet the deadline.)

e·nam·el (i nam′ əl) *vb.* **e·nam·eled; e·nam·el·ing** to cover with enamel —*n.* **1.** a hard, glossy paint **2.** a glass-like coating used on the surface of metal and pottery **3.** the hard white coating on teeth

en·close (in klōz′) *vb.* **en·closed; en·clos·ing** **1.** to surround **2.** to insert (to *enclose* a note in the package)

en·coun·ter (in kau̇nt′ ər) *vb.* **1.** to fight **2.** to meet face to face —*n.* **1.** a hostile meeting **2.** an unexpected meeting

en·cour·age (in kər′ ij) *vb.* **en·cour·aged; en·cour·ag·ing** to help by giving courage or confidence

en·cy·clo·pe·di·a (in sī′ klə pēd′ ē ə) *n.* a reference work containing information on all branches of knowledge arranged alphabetically by topic

end (end) *n.* **1.** the part nearest the boundary or limit **2.** death **3.** the final part **4.** an aim or goal **5.** a football player positioned at the *end* of the line —*vb.* to stop

end·less (end′ ləs) *adj.* **1.** without end **2.** continuous (*endless* movement of the tides)

en·dure (in du̇r′) *vb.* **en·dured; en·dur·ing** **1.** to last (*endured* for generations) **2.** to put up with (*endure*s the pain)

en·e·my (en′ ə mē) *n., pl.* **en·e·mies** **1.** one who hates or seeks to attack another **2.** a nation with which another nation is at war

en·er·get·ic (en′ ər jet′ ik) *adj.* active and full of life

en·er·gy (en′ ər jē) *n., pl.* **en·er·gies** strength, power, or ability to be active; the capacity to do work (solar *energy*)

en·force (in fōrs′) *vb.* **en·forced; en·forc·ing 1.** to compel **2.** to put into effect (*enforced* the seat belt law)

en·gage (in gāj′) *vb.* **en·gaged; en·gag·ing 1.** to make a promise or pledge **2.** to make an appointment or reservation (*engaged* an electrician for the work) **3.** to occupy one's time and attention (to be *engaged* in his task)

en·gine (en′ jən) *n.* **1.** a machine for operating something **2.** a locomotive

en·gi·neer (en′ jə niər′) *n.* **1.** a person who studies and practices engineering **2.** a person who runs an engine

en·joy (in jȯi′) *vb.* **1.** to feel pleasure (*enjoy* fishing) **2.** to have the use of (*enjoy* good eyesight)

e·nor·mous (i nȯr′ məs) *adj.* huge

e·nough (i nəf′) *adj.* ample in supply (*enough* flour for a cake) —*n.* a sufficient amount —*adv.* in sufficient degree

en·rich (in rich′) *vb.* to improve by making more beautiful, rich, or fertile

en·ter (ent′ ər) *vb.* **1.** to go in **2.** to join **3.** to take an active part

en·ter·prise (ent′ ər prīz′) *n.* an important activity that involves some risk and requires courage

en·ter·tain (ent′ ər tān′) *vb.* to provide amusement and/or refreshments for guests, usually in one's home

en·thu·si·asm (in thü′ zē az′ əm) *n.* strong feeling

en·tire (in tīr′) *adj.* whole, unbroken

en·trance (en′ trəns) *n.* **1.** the act of going in **2.** a door or other way of going in **3.** permission to go in (*entrance* by ticket only)

en·try (en′ trē) *n., pl.* **en·tries** **1.** the act of going in **2.** a small hall by the door **3.** a record of something written in a book **4.** something recorded in a list (a dictionary *entry*) **5.** a person or thing in a contest

en·ve·lope (en′ və lōp′, än′-) *n.* a cover for a letter or other mailing (a large *envelope* for the insurance forms)

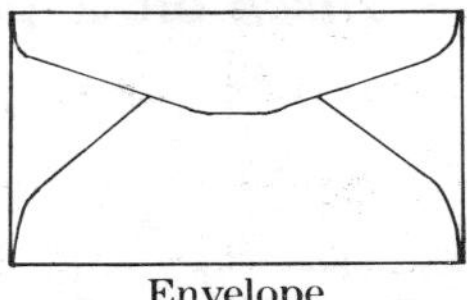
Envelope

en·vi·ron·ment (in vī′ rən mənt) *n.* the surrounding things and influences

en·vy (en′ vē) *n., pl.* **en·vies** a strong desire to have something that another has, accompanied by a feeling of discontent —*vb.* **en·vied**; **en·vy·ing** to feel envy toward

ep·i·sode (ep′ ə sōd′) *n.* one event that is part of a series of events (The story contained three *episodes.*)

e·qual (ē′ kwəl) *adj.* exactly the same in number, degree, quality, or other measure —*n.* one that is equal to another —*vb.* **e·qualed**; **e·qual·ing** to match

e·qual·i·ty (i kwäl′ ət ē) *n., pl.* **e·qual·i·ties** the state of being equal

e·qua·tion (i kwā′ zhən) *n.* in mathematics, a statement of equality between the two sides of the equal sign ($a+b=6$)

e·qua·tor (i kwāt′ ər) *n.* an imaginary line around the earth midpoint between the north and south poles (It is very hot at the *equator.*)

e·quip (i kwip′) *vb.* **e·quipped**; **e·quip·ping** to fit out or supply for a special purpose (*equip* the ship for a rescue effort)

e·quip·ment (i kwip′ mənt) *n.* **1.** the necessary supplies for a special purpose **2.** the act of equipping

e·quiv·a·lent (i kwiv′ ə lənt) *adj.* alike or equal —*n.* a thing that is the same as another in a particular way (*equivalent* in weight)

e·ra (ir′ ə) *n.* an important period in history (an *era* of technological growth)

e·ras·er (i rā′ sər) *n.* a tool for removing marks (the *eraser* on a pencil)

e·rect (i rekt′) *adj.* straight up and down —*vb.* build (*erect* a chimney)

er·ror (er′ ər) *n.* a mistake (make an *error* in spelling)

es·cape (is kāp′) *vb.* **es·caped**; **es·cap·ing** **1.** to get away, flee (to *escape* the intruders) **2.** to avoid (*escape* hard work)

es·pe·cial (is pesh′ əl) *adj.* special or outstanding

es·say (e sā′) *vb.* try —*n.* (es′ ā) a piece of writing dealing with a subject from a personal point of view

es·sen·tial (i sen′ chəl) *adj.* **1.** important and basic to the character of something **2.** necessary

es·tab·lish (is tab′ lish) *vb.* **1.** to set up on a permanent basis (*establish* a scholarship fund) **2.** to prove legally (*establish* that he is heir to the estate)

es·tab·lish·ment (is tab′ lish mənt) *n.* **1.** the act of setting up **2.** something permanently set up as a business

es·tate (is tāt′) *n.* **1.** a fine home on a large piece of property **2.** all of the possessions left by a person when he or she dies

es·ti·mate (es′ tə māt′) *vb.* **es·ti·mat·ed**; **es·ti·mat·ing** to give a general idea of the number, size, or value of something —*n.* (es′ tə mət) a rough idea of the number, size, or cost

e·ter·nal (i tərn′ l) *adj.* without beginning or end

e·val·u·ate (i val′ yə wāt′) *vb.* **e·val·u·at·ed**; **e·val·u·at·ing** to judge the value of

e·vap·o·rate (i vap′ ə rāt′) *vb.* **e·vap·o·rat·ed**; **e·vap·o·rat·ing** **1.** to pass off as a vapor (the water *evaporated*) **2.** to disappear

e·ven (ē′ vən) *adj.* **1.** level (*even* ground) **2.** steady (*even* heart rate) **3.** equal (*even* exchange) **4.** divisible by two (*even* number) —*adv.* **1.** exactly **2.** yet —*vb.* to make equal

eve·ning (ēv′ ning) *n.* late day or early night

e·vent (i vent′) *n.* a happening

ev·er (ev′ ər) *adv.* **1.** always **2.** at any time

ev·er·green (ev′ ər grēn′) *adj.* a tree or plant that stays green throughout the year —*n.* a tree or plant such as spruce or laurel

ev·ery (ev′ rē) *adj.* **1.** each one **2.** all possible (*every* good wish)

ev·ery·bod·y (ev′ rē bäd′ ē) *pron.* every person

ev·ery·day (ev′ rē dā′) *adj.* coming on each day, usual

ev·ery·one (ev′ rē wən) *pron.* every person

ev·ery·thing (ev′ rē thing′) *pron.* all things that exist

ev·ery·where (ev′ rē hweər′) *adv.* in all places

ev·i·dence (ev′ ə dəns) *n.* proof, testimony

ev·i·dent (ev′ ə dənt) *adj.* clear and obvious

e·vil (ē′ vəl) *adj.* **1.** wicked **2.** harmful

ev·o·lu·tion (ev′ ə lü′ shən) *n.* the process of developing from the beginning

e·volve (i välv′) *vb.* **e·volved**; **e·volv·ing** to grow and develop over time

ex·act (ig zakt′) *vb.* demand (*exact* payment) —*adj.* accurate (*exact* copy)

ex·ag·ger·ate (ig zaj′ ə rāt′) *vb.* **ex·ag·ger·at·ed**; **ex·ag·ger·at·ing** to blow up the facts beyond truth or reality (*exaggerated* the size of the fish he caught)

ex·am·i·na·tion (ig zam′ ə nā′ shən) *n.* a test of knowledge, fitness, or ability (history *examination*)

ex·am·ine (ig zam′ ən) *vb.* **ex·am·ined**; **ex·am·in·ing** to look at or question closely

ex·am·ple (ig zam′ pəl) *n.* a pattern, model, sample, or instance to demonstrate what the rest will be like

ex·ceed (ik sēd′) *vb.* **1.** to be greater than **2.** to go beyond the limit (*exceed* the speed limit)

ex·cel·lent (ek′ sə lənt) *adj.* very good, outstanding in quality

ex·cept (ik sept′) *vb.* leave out, omit —*prep.* leaving out (any color *except* red) *conj.* but

ex·cep·tion (ik sep′ shən) *n.* the act of leaving out

ex·cess (ik ses′, ek′ ses′) *n.* more than enough —*adj.* more than the usual amount

ex·ces·sive (ik ses′ iv) *adj.* extreme, beyond the proper limit

ex·change (iks chānj′) *n.* giving one thing in return for another —*vb.* **ex·changed**; **ex·chang·ing** to trade, barter, swap

ex·cite (ik sīt′) *vb.* **ex·cit·ed**; **ex·cit·ing** to stir up interest

ex·claim (iks klām′) *vb.* **ex·claimed**; **ex·claim·ing** to speak out suddenly with strong emotion

ex·cla·ma·tion (eks′ klə mā′ shən) *n.* a sharp cry of surprise, pain, or other strong feeling

ex·clu·sive (iks klü′ siv) *adj.* **1.** shutting out all but the few who have privileges **2.** complete (*exclusive* effort)

ex·cuse (iks kyüz′) *vb.* **ex·cused**; **ex·cus·ing** to pardon or forgive —*n.* (iks kyüs′) **1.** something offered as a reason to be excused **2.** an apology for committing a mistake or neglecting a duty

ex·e·cute (ek′ sə kyüt′) *vb.* **ex·e·cut·ed**; **ex·e·cut·ing** **1.** to put into effect **2.** to put to death by order of the court

ex·ec·u·tive (ig zek′ yət iv) *adj.* **1.** relating to the ability to manage or direct affairs **2.** relating to the branch of government that puts laws into effect (*executive* branch) —*n.* a person who manages and puts laws, rules, policies into effect (The President is the chief *executive.*)

ex·er·cise (ek′ sər sīz′) *n.* **1.** physical exertion **2.** drill and practice work **3.** a program for a special occasion (Veteran's Day *exercises*) —*vb.* **ex·er·cised**; **ex·er·cis·ing** **1.** to use **2.** to exert energy

ex·haust (ig zȯst′) *vb.* **1.** to drain (*exhaust* the supply of water from the well) **2.** to use up entirely (*exhaust* the food supply) **3.** to tire out (*exhaust* one's energy) —*n.* the gases that escape from an engine

ex·hib·it (ig zib′ ət) *vb.* **1.** to show (*exhibit* dismay) **2.** to display (*exhibit* coins) —*n.* **1.** an object or collection put on display **2.** an article used as evidence in court

ex·ist (ig zist′) *vb.* to be, to live

ex·it (eg′ zət) *n.* **1.** the act of going out **2.** a way to go out (take *exit* 12)

ex·ot·ic (ig zät′ ik) *adj.* anything foreign and strange to a place

ex·pand (iks pand′) *vb.* **1.** to spread out **2.** to make bigger **3.** to develop

ex·panse (iks pans′) *n.* a wide stretch (*expanse* of water)

ex·pect (iks pekt′) *vb.* **1.** to look forward to something that is likely to happen (*expect* good weather) **2.** to look forward to agreement (*expect* good behavior)

ex·pe·di·tion (eks′ pə dish′ ən) *n.* **1.** a trip for a special purpose (hunting *expedition*) **2.** the people on the expedition

ex·pense (iks pens′) *n.* cost

ex·pen·sive (iks pen′ siv) *adj.* **1.** costing a lot of money **2.** high priced

ex·pe·ri·ence (iks pir′ ē əns) *n.* **1.** the activities a person takes part in or observes firsthand **2.** the knowledge or skill gained by doing something —*vb.* **ex·pe·ri·enced**; **ex·pe·ri·enc·ing** **1.** to learn by doing **2.** to undergo

ex·per·i·ment (iks per′ ə mənt) *n.* a trial or test made to discover something (an air pressure *experiment*) —*vb.* (iks per′ ə ment′) to do experiments

ex·pert (eks′ pərt′) *adj.* having special knowledge or skill (*expert* mechanic) —*n.* one who has special knowledge or skill (an *expert* on computer programming)

ex·plain (iks plān′) *vb.* **1.** to give a clear account **2.** to give reasons for

ex·plode (iks plōd′) *vb.* **ex·plod·ed**; **ex·plod·ing** **1.** to burst with sudden violence (The fireworks *exploded.*) **2.** to burst forth (*explode* into song) **3.** to disprove (*explode* that old theory)

ex·plo·ra·tion (eks′ plə rā′ shən) *n.* the act of exploring

ex·plore (iks plōr′) *vb.* **ex·plored**; **ex·plor·ing** **1.** to go through carefully to discover important features (Scott *explored* the arctic region.) **2.** to look closely at

ex·plo·sion (iks plō′ zhən) *n.* **1.** a sudden and noisy burst as of gunpowder **2.** a sudden outburst of feeling

ex·port (eks pōrt′) *vb.* to send overseas for sale in foreign countries —*n.* **1.** something that is exported **2.** the act of exporting

ex·pose (iks pōz′) *vb.* **ex·posed**; **ex·pos·ing** **1.** to lay open **2.** to leave without protection **3.** to let light strike photographic film

ex·press (iks pres′) *adj.* send with speed (*express* mail) —*n.* a system for moving people and goods quickly (The next train is an *express.*) —*vb.* to reveal or make known (*express* joy)

ex·tend (iks tend′) *vb.* **1.** to lengthen **2.** to stretch out **3.** to hold out

ex·tent (iks tent′) *n.* the space through which something extends in any dimension (the *extent* of the property)

ex·te·ri·or (eks tir′ ē ər) *adj.* relating to the outside —*n.* the outer surface

ex·ter·nal (eks tərn′ l) *adj.* outside —*n.* the physical appearance

ex·tinct (iks tingkt′) *adj.* **1.** no longer active (an *extinct* volcano) **2.** no longer existing (*extinct* animal)

ex·tra (eks′ trə) *adj.* above and beyond what is expected —*n.* **1.** a person hired for a group scene in a stage show **2.** something additional —*adv.* beyond the ordinary

ex·tract (iks trakt′) *vb.* **1.** to pull out (*extract* a tooth) **2.** to get out (*extract* the juice) **3.** to take out (*extract* an article) —*n.* (eks′ trakt) that which has been drawn out or concentrated (vanilla *extract*)

ex·traor·di·nar·y (iks trȯrd′ n er′ ē) *adj.* **1.** uncommon **2.** remarkable

ex·treme (iks trēm′) *adj.* of the farthest or highest degree (*extreme* cold) —*n.* **1.** the farthest part **2.** the highest degree

eye (ī) *n.* **1.** the organ of sight **2.** watch (an *eye* on the clock) **3.** a hole in something (*eye* of the needle) —*vb.* **eyed**; **ey·ing** to watch closely

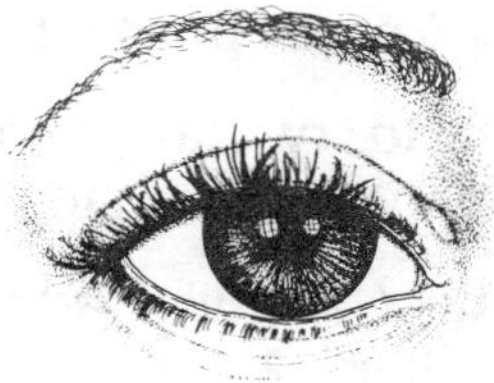

Eye

F

fa·ble (fā′ bəl) *n.* a make-believe story, intended to teach a lesson, in which animals talk and act like people

fab·ric (fab′ rik) *n.* **1.** cloth **2.** framework or structure (*fabric* of our democracy)

fab·u·lous (fab′ yə ləs) *adj.* unreal, resembling a fable

face (fās) *n.* **1.** the front part of the head **2.** surface (*face* of the earth) **3.** presence (in the *face* of danger) —*vb.* **faced**; **fac·ing** **1.** to cover the front (*faced* with brick) **2.** to turn toward (*face* the sun) **3.** to oppose (*face* up to)

fa·cil·i·ty (fə sil′ ət ē) *n., pl.* **fa·cil·i·ties** **1.** ease (handled with *facility*) **2.** strength (*facility* with numbers) **3.** something designed and built for a special purpose (educational *facility*)

fact (fakt) *n.* **1.** a deed, something that actually happened **2.** a true statement about something that happened

fac·tor (fak′ tər) *n.* **1.** something that helps to produce a result **2.** numbers that when multiplied together form a product

fac·to·ry (fak′ tə rē) *n., pl.* **fac·to·ries** a place where goods are made

fade (fād) *vb.* **fad·ed**; **fad·ing** **1.** to lose intensity of color **2.** to lose strength, freshness, or beauty

fail (fāl) *vb.* **failed**; **fail·ing** **1.** to weaken (her voice *failed*) **2.** to stop functioning (the motor *failed*) **3.** to become bankrupt (business *failed*) **4.** to be unsuccessful (*failed* the test) —*n.* failure (We'll be there without *fail.*)

faint (fānt) *adj.* **1.** being weak (feel *faint*) **2.** not clear (a *faint* idea) —*vb.* to lose consciousness (someone *faint*ed) —*n.* an act of fainting

fair (faər) *adj.* **1.** attractive **2.** just **3.** blond **4.** average (did *fair* work) —*adv.* in a fair manner (play *fair*) —*n.* an exhibition of farm products along with entertainment and contests (a county *fair*)

fair·y (faər′ ē) *n., pl.* **fair·ies** a make-believe being with magic powers who has the form of a tiny human being

Fairy

faith (fāth) *n.* belief, confidence, and trust

faith·ful (fāth′ fəl) *adj.* dependable and loyal

fall (fȯl) *vb.* **fell** (fel); **fall·en** (fȯl′ ən); **fall·ing** **1.** to descend freely from a higher to a lower place **2.** to decline or collapse

false (fȯls) *adj.* **fals·er**; **fals·est** **1.** not real **2.** not faithful **3.** not true

fame (fām) *n.* **1.** being known **2.** reputation

fa·mil·iar (fə mil′ yər) *adj.* **1.** well-acquainted **2.** informal (*familiar* manner) **3.** overly intimate (He's being too *familiar*.)

fam·i·ly (fam′ ə lē) *n., pl.* **fam·i·lies** **1.** a group made up of parents and children **2.** a group having common characteristics

fa·mous (fā′ məs) *adj.* widely known, renowned

fan (fan) *n.* **1.** a wedge-shaped object of light-weight material for stirring the air to cool the face **2.** an electrical device with blades for producing an air current **3.** an enthusiastic admirer of a popular individual or group, as in sports or entertainment —*vb.* **fanned; fan·ning** to move the air with a fan

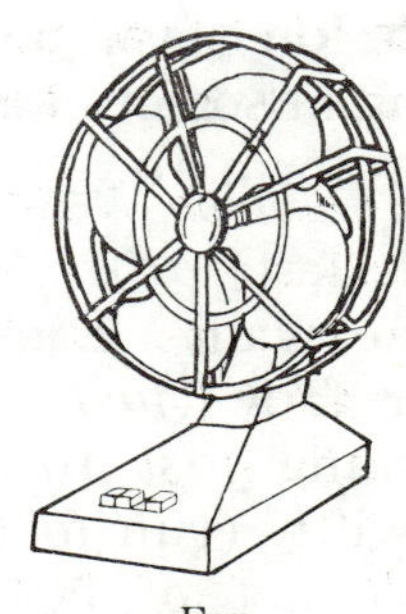
Fan

fan·cy (fan′ sē) *n., pl.* **fan·cies** **1.** imagination (in fact or *fancy*) **2.** liking or inclination (done to her *fancy*) **3.** notion (took a *fancy* to do wood carvings) —*vb.* **fan·cied**; **fan·cy·ing** **1.** to imagine **2.** to have a fondness for —*adj.* **fan·ci·er**; **fan·ci·est** **1.** having decorations (*fancy* shirt) **2.** beyond average worth (*fancy* price)

fan·tas·tic (fan tas′ tik) *adj.* fanciful, hard to believe

far (fär) *adv.* **far·ther** (fär′ thər); **far·thest** (fär′ thest) referring to distance in space; **fur·ther** (fər′-); **fur·thest** **1.** referring to distance in time or degree (*far* nicer) **2.** at a great distance or interval (*far* from school) —*adj.* very distant

far·a·way (far′ ə wā′) *adj.* **1.** distant **2.** dreamy (*far-away* look)

fare (faər) *vb.* **fared**; **far·ing** to go through an experience —*n.* **1.** money paid to travel **2.** a passenger **3.** food (good country *fare*)

fare·well (faər wel′) *n.* good wishes at parting (*farewell* to you) —*adj.* parting (*farewell* hug)

farm (färm) *n.* **1.** land used for raising crops or animals (dairy *farm*) **2.** water where fish are grown (fish *farm*) —*vb.* to operate a farm

fas·ci·nate (fas′ n āt′) *vb.* **fas·ci·nat·ed**; **fas·ci·nat·ing** to charm, hold spellbound

fash·ion (fash′ ən) *n.* **1.** the custom and style of dressing in society **2.** the shape or form —*vb.* to give shape or form to

fast (fast) *adj.* **1.** firmly fixed or attached (a nail *fast* in the wall) **2.** quick (a *fast* airplane) **3.** will not run or fade (*fast* colors) —*adv.* **1.** in a fixed manner (hung *fast* to the rope) **2.** deeply (*fast* asleep) **3.** swiftly (run *fast*) —*vb.* to take little or no food —*n.* the act of fasting

fas·ten (fas′ n) *vb.* to attach or fix securely

fat (fat) *adj.* **fat·ter**; **fat·test** **1.** plump and fleshy **2.** oily, greasy **3.** profitable (a *fat* deal) —*n.* **1.** grease or oil **2.** the best of anything (the *fat* of the land)

fa·tal (fāt′ l) *adj.* causing death

fate (fāt) *n.* **1.** a power beyond a person that is said to control events **2.** fortune or destiny —*vb.* **fat·ed**; **fat·ing** destine, or predestine

fa·ther (fä′ thər) *n.* a male parent

fa·tigue (fə tēg′) *n.* tiredness, physical or mental exhaustion

fault (fȯlt) *n.* **1.** a weakness **2.** a mistake or flaw (a *fault* in the design)

fa·vor (fā′ vər) *n.* **1.** kindness **2.** good will **3.** a small gift given at social functions —*vb.* **1.** to regard kindly **2.** to prefer **3.** to look like

fa·vor·ite (fā′ və rət) *n.* one that is preferred

fawn (fȯn) *vb.* to try to win favor by servile behavior —*n.* a young deer

fear (fiər) *n.* a strong desire to avoid harm —*vb.* **1.** to be afraid of **2.** to regard with terror

feast (fēst) *n.* **1.** a banquet **2.** a meal to celebrate something —*vb.* to eat plentifully

feath·er (feth′ ər) *n.* one of the horny outgrowths that cover a bird —*vb.* to cover with feathers

ea·ture (fē′ chər) *n.* **1.** something noticeable as a part of the face **2.** a main part of something

d·er·al (fed′ ə rəl) *adj.* relating to the United States government and not to the individual states

(fē) *n.* a regular charge for a service, admission, or membership

ble (fē′ bəl) *adj.* **fee·bler** (fē′ blər); **fee·blest** (-bləst) eak, frail, infirm, lacking in vigor

feed (fēd) *vb.* **fed** (fed); **feed·ing** **1.** to give food to **2.** to give nutrients to plants —*n.* food for animals (chicken *feed*)

feel (fēl) *vb.* **felt** (felt); **feel·ing** **1.** to get information through the skin or by sense of touch **2.** to be aware of, to sense

fel·low (fel′ ō) *n.* **1.** a man or boy **2.** an equal in some way —*adj.* a mate, companion, or associate (a *fellow* worker)

felt (felt) *n.* a heavy material made by pressing fibers together, used in making such things as hats, banners, and rug padding

fence (fens) *n.* a barrier to mark a boundary or to prevent entry or escape —*vb.* **1.** to enclose with a fence **2.** to practice the sport of fencing

fend·er (fen′ dər) *n.* **1.** a guard over a wheel on an auto to prevent mud spatter **2.** a device on the front of antique trains to throw off anything on the track

Fender

fern (fərn) *n.* a flowerless plant with large feathery leaves

fer·ry (fer′ ē) *vb.* **fer·ried**; **fer·ry·ing** to carry people and cars across a river, canal, or bay —*n., pl.* **fer·ries** **1.** a boat used for ferrying **2.** a place where one may take a ferry

fer·tile (fərt′ l) *adj.* **1.** producing a rich harvest **2.** capable of reproducing (a *fertile* egg)

fes·ti·val (fes′ tə vəl) *n.* a celebration of an event with cultural or other entertainment

fetch (fech) *vb.* to get something and bring it back (The dog will *fetch* the paper.)

fe·ver (fē′ vər) *n.* a body temperature that is above normal

few (fyü) *pron.* a small number —*adj.* not many —*n.* a small number of people or things

fi·ber (fī′ bər) *n.* a substance that can be separated into threads and spun or woven into yarn (Cotton and hemp plants have *fibers*.)

fic·tion (fik′ shən) *n.* a made-up story

fid·dle (fid′ l) *n.* violin —*vb.* **fid·dled**; **fid·dling** **1.** to play on a fiddle **2.** to tinker with or spend time aimlessly (*fiddle* around, *fiddle* with the cards)

field (fēld) *n.* **1.** a piece of open land, often put to a special use (a *field* of corn, a baseball *field*) **2.** an area of activity or knowledge (the *field* of electronics) —*vb.* in baseball, to play the balls batted to the field —*adj.* relating to a field (*field* games)

fierce (fiərs) *adj.* **fierc·er**; **fierc·est** **1.** violent, savage (a *fierce* fighter) **2.** eager, intense (a *fierce* advocate of a nuclear freeze)

fi·er·y (fī′ ə rē) *adj.* **fi·er·i·er**; **fi·er·i·est** **1.** flaming **2.** very hot **3.** full of zeal (a *fiery* speech)

fig (fig) *n.* the small pear-shaped fruit of a tree related to the mulberry

Figs

fight (fīt) *vb.* **fought** (fȯt); **fight·ing** **1.** to battle or physically struggle against **2.** to oppose (*fight* drugs) —*n.* a physical or verbal battle

fig·ure (fig′ yər) *n.* **1.** a numeral (the *figure* 2) **2.** a well-known person **3.** shape or outline **4.** diagram, pattern, or design —*vb.* **fig·ured**; **fig·ur·ing** **1.** to calculate (*figure* the total) **2.** to work out in one's head

fil·a·ment (fil′ ə mənt) *n.* a fine thread or wire

file (fīl) *n.* **1.** a steel tool with ridges used to smooth out hard surfaces (nail *file*) **2.** a collection of records (the student's *file*) **3.** a device for keeping papers or records, as a folder or a cabinet **4.** a line of persons (come in single *file*) —*vb.* **filed**; **fil·ing** **1.** to smooth with a file by rubbing back and forth **2.** to arrange in order (*file* by topic) **3.** to walk in a line (*file* out the door to the left)

fill (fil) *vb.* **1.** to make full **2.** to occupy completely **3.** to stop up cracks and holes **4.** to supply as directed (*fill* an order)

film (film) *n.* **1.** a thin skin or coating (an oily *film*) **2.** a roll of picture-taking material —*vb.* **1.** to cover with film **2.** to take pictures on a film **3.** to make a motion picture

fil·ter (fil′ tər) *n.* **1.** a material with tiny holes for straining out impurities **2.** a special lens covering to adjust the light for picture-taking

fin (fin) *n.* a winglike part of a fish used to move it through the water

fi·nal (fīn′ l) *adj.* last, often to decide a grade or a contest winner (*final* test) —*n.* **1.** a deciding match or game **2.** a final examination in a course

fi·nan·cial (fə nan′ chəl) *adj.* having to do with money (Banks are *financial* institutions.)

find (fīnd) *vb.* **found** (faůnd); **find·ing** **1.** to discover by chance or by searching **2.** to learn by experience —*n.* something found (a good *find*)

fine (fīn) *n.* money paid as a punishment —*vb.* **fined**; **fin·ing** to demand money as punishment (*fined* for speeding on the highway) —*adj.* **fin·er**; **fin·est** **1.** thin or delicate (*fine* stitches) **2.** worthy (a *fine* person) —*adv.* very well (ran *fine*)

fin·ger (fin′ gər) *n.* **1.** one of the four digits at the end of the hand **2.** the part of a glove made to cover a finger **3.** something that looks like a finger —*vb.* to touch or perform with the fingers

fin·ger·nail (fing′ gər nāl′) *n.* the hard covering at the end of the finger

fin·ish (fin′ ish) *vb.* **1.** to get to the end (*finish* the race) **2.** to use up or eat up (*finish* the ice cream) **3.** to put on a final coat of something, such as paint or varnish on furniture (*finish* the table) —*n.* **1.** the end **2.** the final treatment of the surface (a glossy *finish*)

fir (fər) *n.* a tall evergreen tree related to the pine that is used for lumber

fire (fīr) *n.* **1.** the bright, hot flame produced by burning **2.** excitement (the *fire* of victory in their cheers) —*vb.* **fired**; **fir·ing** **1.** to inflame **2.** to dismiss from a job **3.** to throw (*fire* a rock at the window) **4.** to bake in a kiln (*fire* pottery) **5.** to shoot a gun

fire·man (fīr′ mən) *n., pl.* **fire·men** **1.** a person who is hired to put out fires **2.** a person who tends a fire

fire·place (fīr′ plās′) *n.* an opening in a chimney where a fire can be built

fire·works (fīr′ wərks′) *n., pl.* burning or bursting devices designed to make a display of light and noise for use at celebrations such as the Fourth of July

firm (fərm) *adj.* **1.** hard, stable (*firm* surface) **2.** lasting (*firm* friendship) **3.** fixed (a *firm* date) —*n.* a business partnership

first (fərst) *adj.* or *adv.* before all others —*n.* **1.** number one in a series **2.** something that is first

fish (fish) *n., pl.* **fish** or **fish·es** an animal that lives in the water, is covered with scales, breathes with gills, and reproduces by means of eggs

fish·er·man (fish′ ər mən) *n., pl.* **fish·er·men** a person who fishes for sport or business

fist (fist) *n.* a hand closed tightly with the fingers curled in

fit (fit) *n.* **1.** a sudden attack or convulsion **2.** a sudden impulse or emotion (a *fit* of jealousy) **3.** the way something fits —*adj.* **fit·ter**; **fit·test** healthy —*vb.* **fit·ted**; **fit·ting** **1.** to be suitable (to *fit* the need) **2.** adjusted in size (to *fit* my mother)

fix (fiks) *vb.* **1.** to fasten securely **2.** prepare (I will *fix* lunch.) **3.** repair (*fix* the loose button) —*n.* an awkward situation (in a *fix*)

flag (flag) *n.* **1.** a piece of cloth bearing a design that is used as a symbol of a state or nation **2.** a slab of stone used in paving a walk —*vb.* **flagged**; **flag·ging** **1.** to signal with a flag **2.** to become weak or droopy

flake (flāk) *n.* a thin piece of something (snow*flake*, corn *flake*) —*vb.* **flaked**; **flak·ing** to break into flakes

flame (flām) *n.* blaze

flan·nel (flan′ l) *n.* a soft, loosely woven material of cotton or wool

flap (flap) *vb.* **flapped**; **flap·ping** to move back and forth with a fluttering motion (sheets *flapped* in the wind, birds *flapped* their wings)

flash (flash) *vb.* **1.** to make a sudden bright light or flare **2.** to speed (*flash* by) —*n.* a sudden burst (*flash* of lightning) —*adj.* sudden and of short duration (*flash* flood)

flask (flask) *n.* a narrow-necked container made of glass or metal

flat (flat) *adj.* **flat·ter**; **flat·test** **1.** a smooth, level surface **2.** having little thickness **3.** fixed (a *flat* rate) **4.** dull (a *flat* tone of voice) **5.** lower than the correct musical tone (a *flat* note) —*n.* **1.** an apartment on one floor **2.** a symbol in music **3.** a deflated tire

fla·vor (flā′ vər) *n.* **1.** the taste **2.** something to add to the taste (a lemon *flavor*)

flax (flaks) *n.* the plant having fibers from which linen is made

flea (flē) *n.* a small, wingless, blood-sucking insect that lives as a parasite on warm-blooded animals

flee (flē) *vb.* **fled** (fled); **flee·ing** to run away, as from danger

fleet (flēt) *n.* **1.** all the naval ships of a country **2.** a group of ships under one commanding officer —*adj.* fast

flesh (flesh) *n.* **1.** meat **2.** the edible parts of fruits or animals

flex·i·ble (flek′ sə bəl) *adj.* bendable

flick (flik) *n.* a quick, light stroke —*vb.* to strike lightly as with a fingernail

fli·er (flī′ ər) *n.* an aviator, one who flies

flint (flint) *n.* a very hard stone used for striking with steel to make a spark

flip (flip) *vb.* **flipped**; **flip·ping** **1.** to toss with a quick jerk (*flip* a coin) **2.** to stroke quickly (*flip* a switch) —*n.* an act of flipping

float (flōt) *n.* something that stays on the surface of the water —*vb.* to rest on the surface of a liquid

flock (fläk) *n.* a group of animals such as sheep that are tended together —*vb.* to come together in a crowd

flood (fləd) *n.* a great mass of water overflowing the land —*vb.* to cover with water

floor (flōr) *n.* **1.** the bottom surface of a room **2.** the bottom of the ocean (ocean *floor*) **3.** a story of a building (third *floor*) —*vb.* **1.** to cover with a floor **2.** to knock to the floor

flour (flaůr) *n.* finely ground wheat or other grain

flour·ish (flər′ ish) *vb.* **1.** to grow well **2.** to succeed —*n.* a fancy decoration

flow (flō) *vb.* to run in a stream, as a river —*n.* **1.** the act of flowing **2.** the stream or current

flow·er (flau̇′ ər) *n.* **1.** blossom **2.** the best part —*vb.* **1.** to bloom **2.** to flourish

fluff (fləf) *n.* a very light substance such as down or nap —*vb.* to make something fluffy

flu·id (flü′ əd) *adj.* capable of flowing, as liquid or gas —*n.* a substance that flows and that takes the shape of its container

flush (fləsh) *vb.* **1.** to startle into flight (dogs *flush*ed the quail) **2.** to redden or blush (*flushed* with excitement) **3.** to pour water through (*flushed* the drain) —*n.* the act of flushing —*adj.* even, level, or closely fitted (*flush* with the wall) —*adv.* so as to be flush

flute (flüt) *n.* a tube-shaped woodwind instrument that is played by blowing across a hole near the end and closing the keys and finger-holes

Flute

flut·ist (flüt′ əst) *n.* a flute player

flut·ter (flət′ ər) *vb.* **1.** to move in place with a quick flapping motion **2.** to be active and busy without getting much done

fly (flī) *vb.* **flew** (flü); **flown** (flōn); **fly·ing** **1.** to move along through the air held up by air currents or air pressure **2.** to pilot or travel in an airplane **3.** to float, wave, or soar (*fly* a flag) **4.** to flee, to go fast (to *fly* along the road)

foam (fōm) *n.* a light, bubbly, frothy mass that forms on liquids from shaking or mixing with air —*vb.* to make something form foam

fo·cus (fō′ kəs) *n., pl.* **fo·cus·es** or **fo·ci** (fō′ sī′) **1.** the point at which things come together **2.** the point at which light rays form an image **3.** the main purpose of a discussion or activity

foe (fō) *n.* an enemy

fog (fȯg, fäg) *n.* **1.** a cloud at ground level caused by fine particles of water in the air **2.** a state of confusion —*vb.* **fogged**; **fog·ging** to cover with fog

foil (fȯil) *vb.* to defeat —*n.* **1.** a light, flexible fencing weapon with a blunt point **2.** a very thin sheet of metal (aluminum *foil*)

fold (fōld) *n.* **1.** a bend over itself (the *fold* in the towel) **2.** an enclosure for sheep **3.** a group of people with a common interest (welcome to the *fold*) —*vb.* **1.** to double something over **2.** to clasp or enclose (*fold* her hands)

folk (fōk) *n., pl.* **folk** or **folks** **1.** people in general **2.** a group of people (town *folk*) **3.** close relatives (my *folks*) —*adj.* coming from the common people (*folk* songs)

fol·low (fäl′ ō) *vb.* **1.** to go after or to pursue (*follow* a friend) **2.** to give attention to (*follow* the reports) **3.** to obey

fond (fänd) *adj.* affectionate

food (füd) *n.* solid and liquid material containing protein, carbohydrates, fats, minerals, and vitamins that supply nutrients to the body for growth and functioning

fool (fül) *n.* a person lacking common sense —*vb.* **1.** to waste time (*fool* around) **2.** to tinker with (*fool* with the watch) **3.** to play a trick or a joke (*fool* someone)

foot (fu̇t) *n., pl.* **feet** (fēt) **1.** the end part of the leg **2.** the foundation or base of anything **3.** a unit of measure equal to twelve inches **4.** a group of syllables forming a measure of verse —*vb.* **1.** to go on foot **2.** to pay the bill (to *foot* the bill)

foot·step (fu̇t′ step′) *n.* the sound or imprint of each foot in walking

for (fər, fȯr) *prep.* **1.** as being (mistook him *for* the clerk) **2.** because of (danced *for* joy) **3.** in spite of (lost, *for* all her efforts) **4.** to be ready for **5.** to be used for **6.** in support of —*conj.* **1.** because **2.** since **3.** seeing that

for·bid (fər bid′) *vb.* **for·bade** (-bad′); **for·bid·den** (-bid′ n); **for·bid·ding** to stop by order (*forbid* swimming in the quarry)

force (fōrs) *n.* **1.** strength (*force* of the tide) **2.** effect (rules are still in *force*) **3.** a trained group (air *force*) **4.** violence (taken by *force*) **5.** a physical influence on a body or system producing a change (the *force* of gravity, causing objects that are dropped to fall; centrifugal *force*, one use being to separate cream from milk) —*vb.* **forced**; **forc·ing** **1.** to compel (*force* them into the bus) **2.** to break open (*force* a hole in the defensive line) **3.** to hasten (*force* plants to bloom)

fore (fōr) *adj.* **1.** at or near the front **2.** ahead in time or order —*adv.* toward the front; toward the bow of a ship —*n.* front (come to the *fore*) —*interj.* a warning to persons ahead (*Fore*!)

fore·cast (fōr′ kast′) *vb.* **fore·cast**; **fore·cast·ing** to predict (*forecast* the weather)

fore·finger (fōr′ fing′ gər) *n.* the index finger, the one next to the thumb

for·eign (fȯr′ ən) *adj.* related to a place outside one's own country (*foreign* trade)

fore·man (fōr′ mən) *n., pl.* **fore·men** (-mən) **1.** the chairperson of a jury **2.** the person in charge of a group of workers

for·est (fȯr′ əst) *n.* a large area covered with trees

for·ev·er (fə rev′ ər) *adv.* **1.** always, for time without end **2.** at all times

for·get (fər get′) *vb.* **for·got** (-gät); **for·got·ten** (-gät′ n); **for·get·ting** to fail to recall (*forgot* where she parked her car)

fork (fȯrk) *n.* **1.** a tool usually with four tines, used for eating **2.** a tool for pitching hay **3.** a branch in the road —*vb.* **1.** to lift with a fork **2.** to divide into branches (the road *forks*)

form (fȯrm) *n.* **1.** the shape or appearance of something (seemed in good *form*) **2.** a way of doing something (many *forms* of learning) **3.** a kind or type (*forms* of sea life) **4.** a printed document with blank spaces for recording information —*vb.* **1.** to give shape to (*form* the clay) **2.** develop (*form* ideas)

for · mal (fȯr′ məl) *adj.* following rules or customs

for · ma · tion (fȯr mā′ shən) *n.* **1.** the development or shaping of something **2.** the arrangement of people or objects for some purpose (the birds in vee *formation*) **3.** a structure or process in nature (a rock *formation*)

for · mer (fȯr′ mər) *adj.* coming earlier in time (a *former* teacher)

for · mu · la (fȯr′ myə lə) *n.* **1.** a general rule expressed in symbols **2.** a mixture of milk with other ingredients for feeding a baby

fort (fōrt) *n.* a strong structure built so that it can be defended by the troops occupying it

forth (fōrth) *adv.* forward or onward

for · tress (fȯr′ trəs) *n.* a large place such as a fort or a castle that is permanently strengthened for defense

for · tune (fȯr′ chən) *n.* the good things and bad things that happen to people by chance

for · ward (fȯr′ wərd) *adj.* **1.** near the front (the *forward* deck) **2.** bold and rude (a *forward* person) **3.** moving toward the front —*adv.* onward toward the front (went *forward*) —*n.* a player on a team such as basketball —*vb.* to send or help onward

fos · sil (fäs′ əl) *n.* a trace or image of a plant or animal of long ago pressed into a rock

fos·ter (fos′ tər) *adj.* giving or receiving care although not related by blood or legal adoption (*foster* parents) —*vb.* to bring up and care for as if a parent (to *foster* growth and development)

foul (faủl) *adj.* **1.** offensive to the senses of smell, look, and taste (a *foul* smell) **2.** obscene (*foul* language) **3.** outside the foul lines (*foul* ball) —*n.* breaking the rules in a game —*vb.* **1.** to make something foul **2.** to hit a foul ball **3.** to commit a foul

found (faủnd) *vb.* establish or set up

foun·da·tion (faủn dā′ shən) *n.* **1.** the act of founding **2.** the base or lower part of a structure

foun·tain (faủnt′ n) *n.* a jet of water spouting up from a fixture, often decorative

fowl (faủl) *n., pl.* **fowl** **1.** a bird, especially a rooster or hen **2.** the meat of a full-grown domestic fowl for use as food

fox (fäks) *n.* a wild animal related to the dog

frac·tion (frak′ shən) *n.* **1.** a part of a whole **2.** a number with a numerator and denominator such as 1/2 or 2/3

frag·ile (frag′ əl) *adj.* easily broken

fra·grance (frā′ grəns) *n.* a pleasant smell

frail (frāl) *adj.* delicate, weak

frame (frām) *vb.* **framed**; **fram·ing** **1.** to build a support structure (to *frame* a house) **2.** to enclose in a frame (to *frame* a picture) —*n.* a structure that gives shape or form to something (tall, with a large *frame*) —*adj.* having a frame

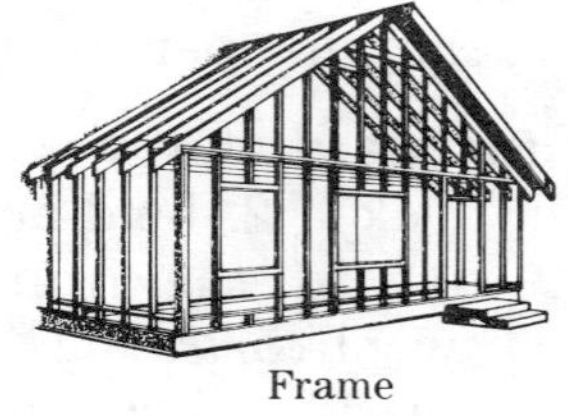
Frame

frame·work (frām′ wərk′) *n.* structure or skeleton to support something

fran·tic (fran′ tik) *adj.* wild with excitement, anxious

free (frē) *adj.* **fre·er** (frē′ ər); **fre·est** (frē′ əst) **1.** able to plan one's own life, not under the control of others **2.** at no cost (*free* sample) **3.** not held back by a burden (*free* from cares) **4.** not blocked up (*free* of all barriers) —*adv.* **free·ly** —*vb.* **freed**; **free·ing** to set free

free·dom (frēd′ əm) *n.* **1.** liberty **2.** openness

freeze (frēz) *vb.* **froze** (frōz); **fro·zen** (frōz′ n); **freez·ing** **1.** to become solid from loss of heat **2.** to kill with frost (the oranges *froze*) —*n.* an act or instance of freezing (The *freeze* surprised everyone.)

freight (frāt) *n.* **1.** goods or cargo carried by train, plane, ship, or truck **2.** the money paid for hauling the goods —*vb.* to send by freight

fren·zy (fren′ zē) *n., pl.* **fren·zies** **1.** wild behavior **2.** intense anxiety

fre·quent (frē′ kwənt) *adj.* happening often

fresh (fresh) *adj.* **1.** in good condition (*fresh* bread) **2.** not preserved (*fresh* fruits and vegetables) **3.** brisk (*fresh* air) **4.** new (a *fresh* start)

fric·tion (frik′ shən) *n.* **1.** the rubbing of two bodies together (*friction* causes wear) **2.** disagreement (*friction* among the leaders)

friend (frend) *n.* **1.** a person who has affection and respect for another (a lifelong *friend*) **2.** a patron and supporter (*friend* of the library)

fright (frīt) *n.* terror, alarm, or panic

fro (frō) *adv.* back to the original position, as in *to and fro*

frog (frȯg or fräg) *n.* **1.** a smooth-skinned tailless animal hatched in the water but able to spend time on land in the adult stage **2.** something in the throat that causes hoarseness **3.** a fancy toggle fastening for a garment

from (frəm) *prep.* out of, followed by the source or starting point (*from* Seattle, *from* a friend, *from* last month)

front (frənt) *n.* **1.** the forward part of anything **2.** the line between air masses (a warm *front*) **3.** a place where there is warfare (at the *front*) —*vb.* stands before (*fronts* the river) —*adj.* related to the front (*front* line)

fron·tier (frən′ tiər′) *n.* **1.** a boundary between countries **2.** the edge of an unsettled region

frost (frȯst) *n.* a fine coating of ice crystals formed when the moisture in the air freezes on a cold surface (*frost* on the field) —*vb.* to cover with something (*frost* a cake)

frown (fraủn) *vb.* to wrinkle the brow in disapproval —*n.* an act of frowning

fruit (früt) *n.* the pulpy part of a plant containing the seed which is usually eaten as dessert

fry (frī) *vb.* **fried**; **fry·ing** to cook in fat or oil in a deep pan or on a griddle —*n., pl.* **fries** (frīz) a dish of fried food (French *fries*)

fu·el (fyü′ əl) *n.* something that can be burned to make heat or energy —*vb.* to take on fuel

ful·crum (fủl′ krəm) *n., pl.* **ful·crums** the support on which a lever turns in moving a body

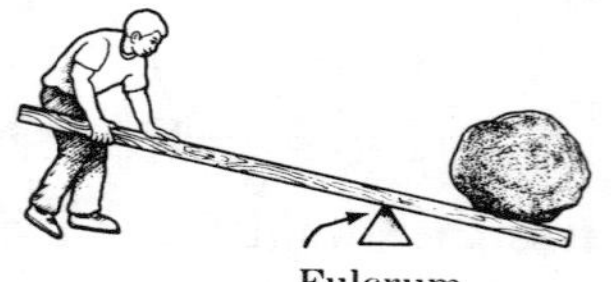
Fulcrum

ful·fill (fủl fill′) *vb.* **ful·filled**; **ful·fill·ing** **1.** to satisfy (*fulfill* their wishes) **2.** to carry out as planned or expected

full (fủl) *adj.* **1.** stuffed to capacity, to the brim **2.** a complete cycle (a *full* year) **3.** rounded, complete (a *full* moon) —*adv.* completely —*n.* the highest measure

fume (fyüm) *n.* vapor or gas (smoke and *fumes*) —*vb.* **1.** to make fumes **2.** to rage in anger (to *fume* at one's enemy)

fun (fən) *n.* amusement or pleasure

func·tion (fəngk′ shən) *n.* **1.** performance or use **2.** a formal ceremony or affair

fund (fənd) *n.* **1.** money set aside for a project **2.** available money (current *funds*) **3.** an ample supply (a *fund* of ideas)

fun·da·men·tal (fən′ də ment′ l) *adj.* basic, primary, essential (a *fundamental* principle)

fu·ner·al (fyü′ nə rəl) *n.* a ceremony for burying the dead

fun·gus (fəng′ gəs) *n., pl.* **fun·gi** (fən′ jī) or **fun·gus·es** plants lacking chlorophyll such as molds and mushrooms that must live on organic matter such as live or decaying plants

fun·nel (fən′ l) *n.* a cone-shaped utensil with a spout at the bottom for pouring liquids or powders into containers with small openings (a *funnel* for filling the gas tank on the lawn mower)

Funnel

fun·ny (fən′ ē) *adj.* **fun·ni·er**; **fun·ni·est** **1.** comical, causing laughter **2.** strange (The stillness gave him a *funny* feeling.)

fur (fər) *n.* **1.** a treated pelt of an animal **2.** a coat, jacket, or stole made with fur **3.** the thick hairy coat of a mammal

fu·ri·ous (fyůr′ ē əs) *adj.* violently angry

fur·nace (fər′ nəs) *n.* a large, enclosed burner where fuel is burned for heating or other purposes

fur·nish (fər′ nish) *vb.* to provide what is needed

fur·ni·ture (fər′ ni chər) *n.* the movable articles such as beds, tables, and chairs used to furnish a home for convenience and ornamentation

fur·ther (fər′ t͟hər) *adv.* to a greater distance in time or degree (The heat went up *further.*) —*adj.* going beyond (*further* thought) —*vb.* to promote or advance (to *further* the cause of peace)

fuse (fyüz) *n.* **1.** a cord that will burn easily, used to set off fireworks or explosives **2.** a device that breaks an electric circuit when the current becomes too strong —*vb.* **fused**; **fus·ing** to join by melting together (*fused* the two metals)

fuss (fəs) *n.* a bustle or commotion over a trivial matter

fu·ture (fyü′ chər) *adj.* relating to time yet to come

G

gadg·et (gaj′ ət) *n.* an interesting device, often one for which the name is not known (one of those *gadgets* that loosens the peel of an orange)

gai·ly (gā′ lē) *adv.* in a lively or bright manner

gain (gān) *n.* **1.** profit (reported *gains* to the Internal Revenue Service) **2.** increase (a *gain* in weight) —*vb.* **1.** get (*gain* valuable experience) **2.** win or achieve (*gain* the gold medal)

gal·ax·y (gal′ ək sē) *n., pl.* **gal·ax·ies** one of the many systems of stars that makes up the universe (the Milky Way *galaxy*)

gale (gāl) *n.* **1.** a strong wind measuring between 32 and 63 miles per hour **2.** a noisy outburst (*gales* of laughter)

gal·lon (gal′ ən) *n.* a unit of liquid measure equal to four quarts

gal·lop (gal′ əp) *vb.* to run rapidly by leaps as a horse does —*n.* the springing leap of a four-footed animal, especially a horse

game (gām) *n.* **1.** a sport, contest, or activity played for amusement and won by skill, strength, or luck **2.** animals hunted for sport or for food —*adj.* **gam·er**; **gam·est** **1.** having courage **2.** relating to animals that are hunted (*game* laws)

gang (gang) *n.* **1.** a group of persons working or acting together **2.** a lawless group (a street *gang*)

gap (gap) *n.* **1.** an opening or separation (a *gap* in the fence) **2.** a mountain pass

ga·rage (gə räzh′) *n.* **1.** a shelter for an automobile **2.** a repair shop for an automobile

gar·bage (gär′ bij) *n.* waste food from a kitchen or a market

gar·den (gärd′ n) *n.* **1.** a plowed area where vegetables or flowers are grown **2.** an enclosure where plants are exhibited (a botanical *garden*)

gar·ment (gär′ mənt) *n.* any article of clothing

gas (gas) *n., pl.* **gas·es** **1.** an airlike substance having the tendency to expand to fill its container **2.** a gas or mixture of gases used as fuel or as an anesthetic (He was given *gas* when he had his tooth pulled.) **3.** short for gasoline (*gas* for the car) —*vb.* **gassed**; **gas·sing**; **gas·ses** **1.** to supply with gas **2.** to poison with gas

gas·o·line (gas′ ə lēn′) *n.* a highly flammable liquid obtained from petroleum and used as a fuel for cars, motor boats, airplanes, and other internal combustion engines

gasp (gasp) *vb.* to breathe with difficulty (to *gasp* for breath) —*n.* catching of the breath with difficulty

gate (gāt) *n.* a door or frame used to open and close the entrance in a fence or wall

gath·er (ga<u>th</u>′ ər) *vb.* **1.** to bring together (*gather* the family) **2.** to collect (*gather* berries) **3.** to increase (*gather* speed) **4.** to stimulate (*gather* ideas) —*n.* a shirring for fullness in a garment

gauge (gāj) *n.* **1.** an instrument for measuring (a pressure *gauge*) **2.** a standard of measurement, as the capacity of a barrel —*vb.* **gauged**; **gaug·ing** **1.** to measure exactly with an instrument **2.** to estimate (How thick would you *gauge* this to be?)

gaunt (gȯnt) *adj.* **1.** bony and thin (looked *gaunt* from her long illness) **2.** grim and bare (the *gaunt* look of the empty house)

gay (gā) *adj.* **gay·er**; **gay·est** **1.** bright and showy **2.** relating to homosexuals —*n.* a homosexual

gaze (gāz) *vb.* **gazed**; **gaz·ing** to look at with interest or wonder —*n.* a long, intent look

Gears

gear (giər) *n.* **1.** equipment (pack your *gear*) **2.** a wheel with teeth that transfers motion —*vb.* to adjust (*gear* the lesson to student needs)

gee (jē) *interj.* **1.** used to express surprise or enthusiasm **2.** used to command a horse or ox to turn to the right

gem (jem) *n.* **1.** a stone used in jewelry **2.** a small rare object

gene (jēn) *n.* the part of the cell nucleus that carries the traits of the parents to the offspring

gen·er·al (jen′ ə rəl) *adj.* not specific, dealing with the broad topic —*n.* a commissioned high-ranking officer in the army or air force

gen·er·a·tion (jen′ ə rā′ shən) *n.* one step in the natural descent of a family, usually a period of 25 to 30 years (the younger *generation*)

gen·er·a·tor (jen′ ə rāt′ ər) *n.* a machine that changes one kind of power to another; for example, water power or nuclear power to electricity

gen·er·ous (jen′ ə rəs) *adj.* free in giving, unselfish

ge·nius (jē′ nyəs) *n.* a great natural ability in some important aspect of life

gen·tle (jent′ l) *adj.* **gen·tler**; **gen·tlest** **1.** kindly, peaceful, caring **2.** moderate (*gentle* horse)

gen·tle·man (jent′ l mən) *n., pl.* **gen·tle·men** (-mən) **1.** a well-mannered man **2.** a term of politeness (Give the *gentleman* this letter.)

gen·tly (jent′ lē) *adv.* in a gentle manner

gen·u·ine (jen′ yə wən) *adj.* real, truly what it seems to be

ge·nus (jē′ nəs) *n., pl.* **gen·er·a** (jen′ ə rə) **1.** a classification of animals and plants that comes between family and species **2.** a class of things made up of two or more lower classes (The *genus* Felis includes the tiger and the cat.)

ge·og·ra·phy (jē äg′ rə fē) *n.* a science that deals with the surface of the earth, including climate, plant and animal life, where people live, products, and other natural features

ge·ol·o·gy (jē äl′ ə jē) *n.* a science that deals with the history of the earth as recorded in rocks

ge·om·e·try (jē äm′ ə trē) *n.* a branch of mathematics that treats the properties, measurements, and relations of lines, angles, surfaces, and solids

germ (jərm) *n.* **1.** the basic element of a plant or animal **2.** a microbe, especially one causing disease

ges·ture (jes′ chər) *n.* a bodily motion used to help express an idea —*vb.* **ges·tured**; **ges·tur·ing** to make a gesture

get (get) *vb.* **got** (gät); **got** or **got·ten** (gät′ n); **get·ting** (get′ ing) **1.** to gain or obtain (*get* some tea) **2.** arrive (*get* home) **3.** go (*get* away) **4.** catch (*get* a cold) **5.** manage (*get* along)

ghost (gōst) *n.* **1.** supposedly the spirit of a dead person **2.** the soul **3.** something partial or shadowy (*ghost* of a smile)

gi·ant (jī′ ənt) *n.* **1.** a fictional character of great size and strength **2.** a person who has a large body or great mental powers (a *giant* among statesmen)

gift (gift) *n.* **1.** a present **2.** a special talent or natural ability

gi·gan·tic (jī gant′ ik) *adj.* huge, or like a giant in some way

gill (gil) *n.* an organ in a fish used for taking oxygen out of water —*n.* (jil) a unit of liquid measure equal to one-fourth pint

gin (jin) *n.* **1.** a machine to separate seeds from cotton **2.** a distilled alcoholic beverage —*vb.* **ginned**; **gin·ning** to separate seeds from cotton

gin·ger (jin′ jər) *n.* a spice obtained from the sharply fragrant root of the ginger plant

gin·ger·bread (jin′ jər bred′) *n.* a molasses cake flavored with ginger

gi·raffe (jə raf′) *n.* a cud-chewing spotted mammal from Africa, easily recognized by its very long legs and neck

girl (gərl) *n.* **1.** a female child or young woman **2.** a female servant

give (giv) *vb.* **gave** (gāv); **giv·en** (giv′ ən); **giv·ing** **1.** to turn over to another's possession, bestow **2.** to utter **3.** to provide **4.** to cause **5.** to grant or yield (*give* permission)

gla·cier (glā′ shər) *n.* a large body of ice, covering a great expanse of land, moving slowly down to the sea

glad (glad) *adj.* **glad·der**; **glad·dest** happy

glance (glans) *vb.* **glanced**; **glanc·ing** **1.** to hit a surface at an angle and fly off to the other side **2.** to give a quick look —*n.* a quick look

gland (gland) *n.* an organ producing a secretion needed in the functioning of the body

glare (glaər) *vb.* **glared**; **glar·ing** **1.** to shine with a brilliant light **2.** to give a fierce look —*n.* **1.** a brilliant light **2.** a fierce look

glass (glas) *n.* **1.** a hard, brittle substance made from silica found in sand, and mixed with other minerals **2.** an article such as a drinking glass, window pane, or mirror made from glass

gleam (glēm) *n.* a flash or glimmer of light

glide (glīd) *vb.* **glid·ed**; **glid·ing** to move noiselessly with a smooth motion —*n.* the act of sliding along smoothly

glid·er (glīd′ ər) *n.* **1.** an aircraft shaped somewhat like an airplane but without an engine **2.** a porch seat that swings from a frame

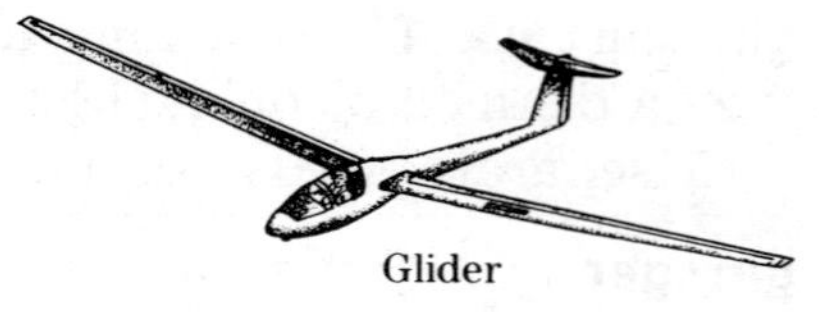
Glider

glimpse (glimps) *vb.* **glimpsed**; **glimps·ing** to get a quick passing look —*n.* a short, hurried look

glis·ten (glis′ n) *vb.* to shine with a sparkling light

globe (glōb) *n.* **1.** a round object such as a ball or sphere **2.** the earth **3.** a model of the earth

gloom (glüm) *n.* **1.** partial or total darkness **2.** sadness or a depressing condition

glo·ri·ous (glōr′ ē əs) *adj.* **1.** full of honor (*glorious* deeds) **2.** magnificent (*glorious* view)

glo·ry (glōr′ ē) *n., pl.* **glo·ries** praise and honor —*vb.* **glo·ried**; **glo·ry·ing** to rejoice, feel proud

glove (gləv) *n.* a leather or fabric cover for the hand with a separate tubelike place for each finger —*vb.* to cover with a glove

glow (glō) *vb.* **1.** to give off heat and light without flame **2.** to look warm and flushed —*n.* **1.** light that comes from hot coals **2.** light that comes from the early morning and late afternoon sun

glue (glü) *n.* a substance that makes things stick together —*vb.* **glued**; **glu·ing** to stick with glue

gnaw (nȯ) *vb.* **gnawed**; **gnaw·ing** to eat away a little at a time (The dog *gnawed* the old shoe.)

go (gō) *vb.* **went** (went); **gone** (gȯn); **go·ing** (gō′ ing) **goes** **1.** to move from one place to another **2.** to run (the clock *goes*) **3.** to disappear (candy *goes* fast here) **4.** belong (This shirt and tie *go* together.)

goal (gōl) *n.* **1.** a point or post aimed at in a game **2.** an aim or purpose in work or in life

goat (gōt) *n.* a horned mammal more nimble than sheep and used as a source of milk in many countries

god (gäd) *n.* a being believed to possess more than human powers (Ancient people worshipped many *gods.*)

god·dess (gäd′ əs) *n.* a female god

gold (gōld) *n.* a precious metal valuable for its beautiful color, freedom from tarnish, and ease in shaping, used in fine jewelry and ornaments

golf (gälf) *n.* a game played on a grassy course with nine or eighteen holes, followed in a sequence, in which a small golf ball is hit with a selected club having a wooden or metal head

gong (gäng) *n.* a metal disk that makes a loud ringing sound when struck

Gong

good (gu̇d) *adj.* **bet·ter** (bet′ ər); **best** (best) *adj.* **1.** suitable (a *good* time to study) **2.** complete (It will take a *good* week.) **3.** honest and reliable (a *good* worker) **4.** loving and kind (a *good* family) —*n.* **1.** something good **2.** *pl.* manufactured goods **3.** *pl.* personal property **4.** *pl.* yard goods

good·bye (gu̇d bī′) *n.* farewell, often used as an interjection

good·ness (gu̇d′ nəs) *n.* the state of being good, having virtue and worth

goose (güs) *n., pl.* **geese** (gēs) **1.** a large, web-footed, flat-billed water bird, in size, between a swan and a duck **2.** the flesh of a goose for use as food **3.** a silly person (a silly *goose*)

gov·ern (gəv′ ərn) *vb.* **1.** to rule **2.** to exercise authority **3.** to administer or execute the law

gov·ern·ment (gəv′ ərn mənt) *n.* **1.** an established system of administering political affairs **2.** the persons making up the governing body

gov·er·nor (gəv′ ər nər) *n.* **1.** the highest executive official in the state **2.** any person or thing that controls or governs (A *governor* controlled the speed of the engine.)

gown (gaůn) *n.* **1.** a woman's dress, especially one for a dressy occasion **2.** a loose outer garment **3.** a robe worn by university professors and graduates (a cap and *gown*)

grab (grab) *vb.* **grabbed**; **grab·bing** to seize suddenly, snatch —*n.* the act of grabbing

grace (grās) *n.* **1.** behavior that is marked by attractiveness, kindness, and ease of manner **2.** a short prayer before or after a meal —*vb.* **graced**; **grac·ing** **1.** to honor or dignify **2.** to adorn or decorate

grace·ful (grās′ fəl) *adj.* showing beauty in form or action

gra·cious (grā′ shəs) *adj.* full of grace and kindness

grade (grād) *n.* **1.** a year's work in school **2.** a mark or rating on a test (a *grade* of 80) **3.** the slope of a road (a steep *grade*) —*vb.* **grad·ed**; **grad·ing** **1.** to sort (*grade* the fruit) **2.** to give a grade to

grad·u·al (graj′ ə wəl) *adj.* going step by step (a *gradual* decline in absences)

grad·u·ate (graj′ ə wət) *n.* a person who has received a degree or diploma —*vb.* (graj′ ə wāt′) **grad·u·ated**; **grad·u·at·ing** to finish a course of study

grain (grān) *n.* **1.** the seedlike fruit of cereal grasses such as wheat, corn, or oats **2.** cereal grasses or plants **3.** a tiny bit of something (a *grain* of sand)

gram (gram) *n.* a unit of weight in the metric system equal to 1/1,000 kilogram

gram·mar (gram′ ər) *n.* science that deals with classes of words, their uses, and relations in the sentence

grand (grand) *adj.* above others in the same class (*grand* prize, *grand* total)

grand·fa·ther (grand′ fä′ th̲ər) *n.* a father's or mother's father

grand·moth·er (grand′ məth̲′ ər) *n.* a father's or mother's mother

grand·stand (grand′ stand′) *n.* the principal stand (on an athletic field) for people who watch the game

gran·ite (gran′ ət) *n.* a very hard crystalline rock used for building

grant (grant) *vb.* **1.** to give to (*grant* a request) **2.** to admit to something not yet proved (*grant* that it is correct) —*n.* **1.** the act of granting **2.** a gift (a study *grant*)

grape (grāp) *n.* a smooth green, red, or purple berry which grows in clusters on a grapevine

graph (graf) *n.* a diagram that shows the relationship between two changing measures through a system of lines

grasp (grasp) *vb.* **1.** to grab and hold with the hand **2.** to grab onto with the mind (*grasp* an understanding) —*n.* **1.** the act of grasping **2.** possession (The diploma is within his *grasp.*) **3.** understanding (Her *grasp* of the subject is excellent.)

grass (gras) *n.* green plants eaten by grazing animals

grass·hop·per (gras′ häp ər) *n.* **1.** a leaping insect very harmful to plants **2.** a locust (A swarm of *grasshoppers* will eat a field bare.)

grate (grāt) *n.* a frame of iron bars for holding fuel —*vb.* **grat·ed; grat·ing** to make into small pieces (*grate* the orange peel)

grate·ful (grāt′ fəl) *adj.* thankful (The parent was *grateful* for the help.)

grave (grāv) *n.* a place to bury a dead person —*adj.* **grav·er; grav·est** important, solemn, needing serious consideration (a *grave* problem)

grav·el (grav′ əl) *n.* a coarse mixture of sand, pebbles, and pieces of rock

grave·yard (grāv′ yärd) *n.* cemetery, a burial place

grav·i·ty (grav′ ət ē) *n., pl.* **grav·i·ties** **1.** the attraction of the earth on bodies at the surface **2.** the condition of being grave or serious (The *gravity* of the situation worried them.)

gra·vy (grā′ vē) *n., pl.* **gra·vies** a sauce for meat, fish, or vegetables often made from the juice that drips from meat while cooking

gray (grā) *adj.* **1.** related to the color gray **2.** having gray hair **3.** dull and dreary —*n.* **1.** something gray in color **2.** a neutral color made by mixing black and white

graze (grāz) *vb.* **grazed**; **graz·ing** **1.** to eat grass and weeds from a pasture **2.** to touch lightly in passing **3.** to scratch slightly by rubbing against something —*n.* a scrape or rubbed place made by grazing

grease (grēs) *n.* **1.** soft animal fat **2.** a thick lubricant for machinery made from petroleum —*vb.* **greased**; **greas·ing** to smear or lubricate with grease

great (grāt) *adj.* **1.** large in size, number, weight, or other measure (a *great* flock of Canada geese) **2.** important or remarkable (a *great* cellist)

greed·y (grēd′ ē) *adj.* **greed·i·er**; **greed·i·est** **1.** being too eager for food and drink **2.** having a selfish longing for things

green (grēn) *adj.* **1.** having the color of grass **2.** consisting of or covered with green plants **3.** not ripe (*green* tomatoes) **4.** having little experience (*green* workers) **5.** not treated (*green* firewood) — *n.* **1.** a color between blue and yellow **2.** the parts of a golf course around each hole **3.** evergreen foliage cut for decorations (Christmas *greens*)

greet (grēt) *vb.* to welcome in a friendly way

greet·ing (grēt′ ing) *n.* a friendly expression on meeting someone

grid (grid) *n.* **1.** a network of vertical and horizontal lines, as on a map, for locating places **2.** a gridiron used for broiling over a flame

grief (grēf) *n.* a deep sadness

grim (grim) *adj.* **grim·mer**; **grim·mest** **1.** fierce (a *grim* temper) **2.** harsh and surly (a *grim* look on his face)

grime (grīm) *vb.* **grimed**; **grim·ing** to smear with dirt or soot —*n.* dirt rubbed into the surface (hands are covered with *grime*)

grin (grin) *vb.* **grinned**; **grin·ning** to show the teeth in a wide smile —*n.* the act of showing the teeth in a broad smile of pleasure

grind (grīnd) *vb.* **ground** (graủnd); **grind·ing** **1.** to make into powder or meal by crushing or rubbing over a rough surface as a grindstone (*grind* the wheat into flour) **2.** to rub together with a grating noise (*grind* the teeth) **3.** to force through a knife-like cutter (*grind* the meat) **4.** to operate with a crank

grind·er (grīn′ dər) *n.* **1.** a device that grinds **2.** a person who turns the crank to make a machine work (the organ *grinder*)

grip (grip) *vb.* **gripped**; **grip·ping** **1.** to grasp tightly **2.** to hold the interest of —*n.* a firm grasp

griz·zly (griz′ lē) *adj.* **griz·zli·er**; **griz·zli·est** **1.** grayish **2.** streaked or mixed with gray

groan (grōn) *vb.* **1.** to make a low moaning sound as if in pain **2.** to creak under a strain (Then the wagon *groan*ed under the load.) —*n.* a deep moaning sound of pain or ridicule (His suggestion was greeted with *groans* and hisses.)

gro·cer·y (grō′ sə rē) *n.*, *pl.* **gro·cer·ies** **1.** a store that sells food **2.** *pl.* the foods sold at a grocery

groom (grüm) *n.* **1.** a person who takes care of horses **2.** an officer of the English royal household **3.** a man who is getting married —*vb.* **1.** to make neat and attractive as by cleaning and brushing (*groom* the dog) **2.** to make fit, especially in appearance and behavior (to *groom* a candidate for office)

groove (grüv) *n.* **1.** a long, narrow channel **2.** a regular habit —*vb.* **grooved**; **groov·ing** to form a groove in

gross (grōs) *adj.* **1.** complete, entire (*gross* profit) **2.** vulgar and indecent (*gross* humor) **3.** extreme (*gross* injustice) **4.** thick, dense (*gross* vegetation) **5.** huge, flabby (*gross* appearance) —*n., pl.* **gross** **1.** twelve dozen **2.** the entire amount

ground (graůnd) *n.* **1.** the land **2.** the soil **3.** an area (camping *ground*) **4.** coffee sediment (coffee *grounds*) **5.** a basic argument (*grounds* for complaint) —*vb.* to force to the ground (planes *grounded* by weather; boats *grounded* by the storm)

group (grüp) *n.* a number of persons acting together —*vb.* to combine into a group

grove (grōv) *n.* a small stand of trees

grow (grō) *vb.* **grew** (grü); **grown** (grōn); **grow·ing** **1.** to sprout and develop to maturity, as in plants **2.** to be able to develop in a particular environment (Apples *grow* in the temperate region.) **3.** to expand (The population is *growing.*)

growl (graůl) *vb.* **1.** to make a deep, throaty sound (The dog *growled.*) **2.** to grumble and find fault (The tenant *growled* about the furnace.)

growth (grōth) *n.* **1.** the act or process of growing **2.** a gradual increase (*growth* of industry) **3.** something produced by growing (A *growth* of moss covered the rock.)

grum·ble (grəm′ bəl) *vb.* **grum·bled**; **grum·bling** to mutter in complaint (*grumble* about the rainy weekend) —*n.* the act of grumbling

grunt (grənt) *n.* a sound made deep in the throat (the *grunt* of a hog) —*vb.* to make a guttural, throaty sound

guar·an·tee (gar′ ən tē′) *n.* **1.** a statement saying who is responsible for repair or replacement **2.** a promise to answer for the debt or duty of another —*vb.* **guar·an·teed**; **guar·an·tee·ing** to make oneself responsible for (to *guarantee* a loan)

guard (gärd) *n.* **1.** a position of defense (Her *guard* is up.) **2.** the duty of keeping watch (on *guard*) **3.** a device giving protection (The boys on the soccer team wore shin *guards*.) **4.** a football lineman next to the center —*vb.* protect, watch over

guess (ges) *vb.* to decide without having enough information —*n.* an opinion formed by guessing

guest (gest) *n.* **1.** a visitor in one's house or at one's table **2.** a patron at a hotel, inn, or restaurant

guid·ance (gīd′ ns) *n.* the process of being helped or given direction

guide (gīd) *n.* **1.** one who leads or directs another **2.** one who influences or provides counsel **3.** a standard used as a measure of correctness **4.** a device used to control the operation of a machine —*vb.* **guid·ed**; **guid·ing** **1.** to direct **2.** to show the way

guilt (gilt) *n.* **1.** the state of a person who has committed a crime **2.** a feeling of responsibility for wrongdoing (*guilt* for the way he treated his mother)

gui·tar (gə tär′) *n.* a six-stringed musical instrument played by plucking the strings and strumming

Guitar

gulf (gəlf) *n.* **1.** a part of the ocean or sea that curves into the land (the *Gulf* of Mexico) **2.** a wide separation as in age, interests, or beliefs (The *gulf* between them widened.)

gull (gəl) *n.* **1.** a web-footed water bird usually white with blue-gray wings and a thick bill **2.** one who is easily tricked or duped —*vb.* to trick or dupe someone

Gull

gum (gəm) *n.* **1.** the flesh covering the jawbone around the roots of the teeth **2.** a substance that drips from certain plants and trees as India rubber **3.** a substance prepared for chewing (chewing *gum*) —*vb.* **gummed**; **gum·ming** to stick or stiffen, as if with gum

gun (gən) *n.* **1.** a cannon (a big *gun*) **2.** a small firearm —*vb.* **gunned**; **gun·ning** to hunt with a gun

gun·pow·der (gən′ paůd′ ər) *n.* an explosive substance

gup·py (gəp′ ē) *n., pl.* **gup·pies** a small fresh-water fish about one and one-half inches long

gust (gəst) *n.* **1.** a sudden rush of wind or burst of fire or smoke **2.** a sudden outburst of deep feeling

guy (gī) *n.* **1.** a rope, chain, rod, or wire attached to something to steady it **2.** a fellow —*vb.* to guide or steady with guys (The steel beams being hauled up were steadied with *guys*.)

gym (jim) *n.* short for gymnasium

gym·na·si·um (jim nā′ zē əm) *n.* a place or building for athletic exercises

H

hab·it (hab′ ət) *n.* **1.** clothing (riding *habit*) **2.** a usual routine or way of behaving

hab·i·tat (hab′ ə tat′) *n.* the natural setting in which a plant or animal grows

hail (hāl) *n.* small chunks of ice that sometimes fall from the clouds especially during thunderstorms —*vb.* **1.** to fall as hail **2.** to greet or attract the attention of (*hail* a cab) —*interj.* used to express enthusiastic approval (*Hail! Hail!*) —*n.* an exclamation of greeting, approval, or praise

hair (haər) *n.* a threadlike filament growing out of the skin of people and many animals

half (haf, håf) *n., pl.* **halves** (havz, håvz) one of two equal parts (a *half* of an orange) —*adj.* being one of two equal parts —*adv.* to the extent of half (*half* empty)

hall (hȯl) *n.* **1.** a large building used as a center for city or town government (city *hall*) **2.** a building set apart for a special purpose as at a college (music *hall*) **3.** a corridor (wait in the *hall*)

halt (hȯlt) *adj.* lame or crippled (help the blind and the *halt*) —*vb.* **1.** to limp **2.** to hesitate **3.** to stop —*n.* a stop (call a *halt*)

ham (ham) *n.* **1.** cured pork **2.** a showy performer **3.** an amateur radio operator

ham·burg·er (ham′ bər′ gər) *n.* **1.** ground beef, called hamburger **2.** a sandwich made of a ground beef patty on a split bun

ham·mer (ham′ ər) *n.* **1.** a tool with a steel head fitted crosswise on a handle, used to pound nails **2.** a heavy metal ball thrown for distance in a track-and-field contest (*hammer* throw) —*vb.* **1.** to hit with a hammer **2.** to give something repeated blows

hand (hand) *n.* **1.** the structure at the end of the arm useful for fingering, grasping, and holding **2.** a hand-like structure on animals, such as a paw, a claw, or a pincer **3.** something that points as a hand on a dial **4.** skill (try one's *hand* at the harmonica) —*vb.* to pass with the hand (*Hand* me the wrench.)

hand·i·cap (han′ di kap′) *n.* **1.** an advantage given to one less skilled in a contest **2.** a disadvantage that makes progress difficult **3.** a disadvantage given in a contest —*vb.* **hand·i·capped**; **hand·i·cap·ping** **1.** to give a handicap **2.** to put at a disadvantage

hand·ker·chief (hang′ kər chif) *n., pl.* **hand·ker·chiefs** a small square cloth used for wiping the eyes, nose, or mouth

han·dle (han′ dəl) *n.* a part of a tool intended to be grasped or held —*vb.* **han·dled**; **han·dling** **1.** to touch or hold with the hand **2.** to deal with (*handle* the problem) **3.** to sell or buy (Does that store *handle* pianos?)

hand·some (han′ səm) *adj.* **hand·som·er**; **hand·som·est** **1.** pleasing to look at **2.** generous (a *handsome* tip)

hand·writ·ing (hand′ rīt′ ing) *n.* **1.** material written by hand **2.** a person's style of penmanship

hand·y (han′ dē) *adj.* **hand·i·er**; **hand·i·est** **1.** nearby (a *handy* convenience store) **2.** easy to manage (a *handy* tool) **3.** skillful in handwork (a *handy* person)

hang (hang) *vb.* **hung** (həng) also **hanged**; **hang·ing** **1.** to suspend or support from above (*Hang* a plant from the ceiling.) **2.** to be put to death by hanging with a rope or wire —*n.* **1.** the manner in which something hangs (Check the *hang* of these curtains.) **2.** knack (get the *hang* of it)

hap·pen (hap′ ən) *vb.* **1.** to come about by chance (Nothing will *happen* to you.) **2.** to take place (Beautiful sunsets *happen* often here.)

hap·py (hap′ ē) *adj.* **hap·pi·er; hap·pi·est** **1.** suitable (*happy* solution to the problem) **2.** lucky (*happy* choice) **3.** pleased

har·bor (här′ bər) *n.* **1.** a protected port for ships **2.** a place of safety and refuge —*vb.* **1.** to give shelter **2.** to hold a thought or feeling (to *harbor* a grudge)

hard (härd) *adj.* **1.** not easy to cut or break (*hard* wood) **2.** not easy to do (*hard* work) —*adv.* **1.** with great effort (tried *hard*) **2.** with pain (took his failure *hard*)

hard·ship (härd′ ship′) *n.* something that causes pain

hard·ware (härd′ waər′) *n.* things made of metal, such as tools and machine parts

harm (härm) *n.* damage —*vb.* to hurt or injure

har·mo·ny (här′ mə nē) *n.* **1.** pleasing musical sounds **2.** peace and friendship

har·ness (här′ nəs) *n.* straps put on an animal to control it —*vb.* to gain control of something

harp (härp) *n.* a musical instrument played by plucking strings set on a triangular frame

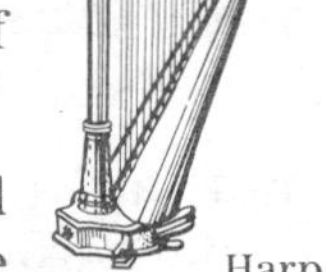
Harp

har·poon (här′ pün) *n.* a spear used for hunting large aquatic mammals such as whales —*vb.* to spear with a harpoon

harsh (härsh) *adj.* unpleasant to hear, touch, or endure (a *harsh* winter)

har·vest (här′ vəst) *n.* **1.** the crop or yield of a growing season **2.** the time for gathering the crop —*vb.* to gather in, as a food crop

hash (hash) *n.* chopped food such as meat and potatoes —*vb.* **1.** to chop into pieces **2.** to talk about in detail (*hash* it out)

haste (hāst) *n.* speed of action

hat (hat) *n.* an article of clothing made to be worn on the head

hatch (hach) *n.* a small door, usually in the floor (escape *hatch*) —*vb.* to produce from an egg

hate (hāt) *n.* a very strong dislike —*vb.* **hat·ed**; **hat·ing** to feel ill will toward

haul (hȯl) *vb.* **1.** to pull **2.** to move something in a vehicle —*n.* the amount brought in

haunt (hȯnt) *vb.* **1.** to come to mind frequently (The song *haunt*ed him.) **2.** to visit as a ghost —*n.* a place often visited

have (hav) *vb.* **had**; **hav·ing**; **has** **1.** to own or possess **2.** to feel obligated (*have* to work) **3.** to feel (*have* pity) **4.** to eat (*have* lunch)

hawk (hȯk) *n.* a bird of prey with a hooked bill and sharp claws —*vb.* to try to sell something by calling out in the street (*hawk*ing peanuts)

hay (hā) *n.* grass that is cut and dried as food for animals

haz·ard (haz′ ərd) *n.* danger —*vb.* to risk something dangerous

haze (hāz) *vb.* **hazed**; **haz·ing** to become cloudy —*n.* fine particles of dust and water in the air

he (hē) *pron.* the male person; that man

head (hed) *n.* **1.** the part of the body above the neck **2.** the mind **3.** the front side of a coin **4.** the leader or director —*adj.* **1.** relating to the one in charge **2.** coming from the front (*head* wind) —*vb.* **1.** to be in charge of **2.** to be in front of

head·line (hed′ līn′) *n.* a title in large type over a story in a newspaper or magazine

head·long (hed′ lȯng′) *adv.* **1.** headfirst (fell *headlong*) **2.** too quickly —*adj.* rash or reckless

head·quar·ters (hed′ kwȯrt′ ərz) *n.* the place from which the head person directs or commands

health (helth) *n.* **1.** freedom from illness **2.** a person's physical condition

health·y (hel′ thē) *adj.* **health·i·er**; **health·i·est** **1.** in good physical condition **2.** free from illness

heap (hēp) *n.* a pile —*vb.* to put into a pile

hear (hiər) *vb.* **heard** (hərd); **hear·ing** (hiər′ ing) to take in through the ear

heart (härt) *n.* **1.** the organ that pumps blood through the body **2.** the central or most important part of something **3.** a kindly feeling

hearth (härth) *n.* the floor in front of a fireplace

heat (hēt) *vb.* to warm something —*n.* **1.** warmth **2.** strong feeling **3.** a race to qualify for the final race

heave (hēv) *vb.* **heaved**; **heav·ing** **1.** to lift or throw with effort **2.** to breathe with effort —*n.* a strong upward motion used to lift or throw something heavy or to breathe when tired or depressed

heav·en (hev′ ən) *n.* **1.** the sky (*heavens* above) **2.** dwelling place of God **3.** a place of peace and happiness

heav·y (hev′ ē) *adj.* **heav·i·er**; **heav·i·est** **1.** having great weight **2.** burdensome

hedge (hej) *n.* a row of bushes that forms a fence —*vb.* **hedged**; **hedg·ing** **1.** to fence off with a hedge **2.** to avoid giving a definite answer

heed (hēd) *vb.* to pay attention —*n.* attention (pay *heed* to the message)

heel (hēl) *n.* **1.** the back of the foot behind the arch **2.** the part of a shoe, sock, or stocking that covers the heel **3.** the end of a crusty loaf of bread —*vb.* to lean to one side

height (hīt) *n.* the distance from the bottom to the highest point

heir (aər) *n.* **1.** the person who legally gets property after the death of its owner **2.** the person who legally gets a title or throne upon the death of the person holding it

hel·i·cop·ter (hel′ ə käp′ tər) *n.* an aircraft lifted vertically and moved in any direction by large blades mounted atop the vehicle

he·li·um (hē′ lē əm) *n.* a very light gas that will not burn

hell (hel) *n.* **1.** a place for evil souls after death **2.** misery

hel·lo (hə lō′) *interj.* a greeting

hel·met (hel′ mət) *n.* a covering to protect the head

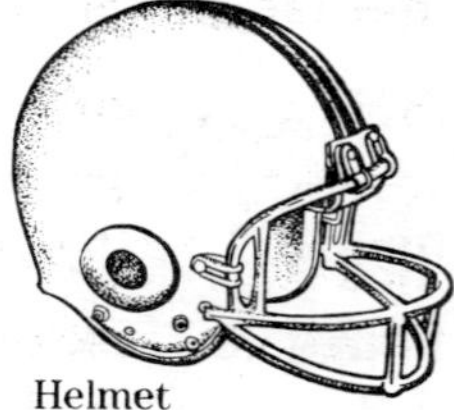
Helmet

help (help) *vb.* **1.** to assist in an activity **2.** to relieve someone in pain **3.** to rescue someone in danger —*n.* **1.** a group of hired workers **2.** assistance

help·less (help′ ləs) *adj.* unable to help oneself

hem·i·sphere (hem′ ə sfiər′) *n.* **1.** one of the halves of the earth, either divided by the equator into northern and southern hemispheres or by a meridian into eastern and western hemispheres **2.** one-half of a sphere

hen (hen) *n.* a female bird or domestic fowl

hence (hens) *adv.* **1.** from this time **2.** from this place **3.** therefore

her (hər) *adj.* relating to a certain woman or girl (*her* paint brush) —*pron.* objective case of SHE

herb (ərb, hərb) *n.* a plant or plant part used as a medicine or a seasoning

herd (hərd) *n.* a group of animals of one kind kept together (*herd* of cattle)

here (hiər) *adv.* in, at, or to this place —*n.* this place

her·i·tage (her′ ət ij) *n.* what is passed down from our ancestors within a family, a culture, or a nation

he·ro (hē′ rō) *n.*, *pl.* **he·roes** **1.** a person who is remembered for his or her great deeds **2.** a person who shows courage **3.** the leading male character in a story or play

her·ring (her′ ing) *n.* a North Atlantic fish used for food

hers (hərz) *pron.* one or more things belonging to her

her·self (hər self′) *pron.* her own self

hes·i·ta·tion (hez′ ə tā′ shən) *n.* a pause, often due to being forgetful or uncertain

hey (hā) *interj.* **1.** a call for someone's attention **2.** an expression of surprise

hi (hī) *interj.* an informal greeting

hide (hīd) *vb.* **hid** (hid); **hid·den** (hid′ n) or **hid**; **hid·ing** **1.** to keep out of sight **2.** to block from view —*n.* the skin of an animal

high (hī) *adj.* **1.** tall **2.** very important (*high* position) **3.** strong (*high* wind) **4.** above the middle in pitch (*high* note) —*adv.* at or to a high place —*n.* **1.** an elevated place **2.** geared for top speed

high·land (hī′ lənd) *n.* mountainous land or a high plateau

high·way (hi′ wā′) *n.* a main public road

hike (hīk) *vb.* **hiked**; **hik·ing** to take a long walk —*n.* a long walk

hill (hil) *n.* **1.** a natural elevation of land smaller than a mountain **2.** a mound of earth (an ant *hill*)

hill·side (hil′ sīd′) *n.* the slope between the top and bottom of the hill

him (him) *pron.* objective case of HE

him·self (him self′) *pron.* his own self

hind (hīnd) *adj.* placed at the back (the dog's *hind* legs) —*n.* a female of the red deer

hint (hint) *n.* an indirect suggestion or clue —*vb.* to suggest

hip (hip) *n.* the wide part of the body just below the waist

hip·po·pot·a·mus (hip′ ə pät′ ə məs) *n., pl.* **hip·po·pot·a·mus·es** or **hip·po·pot·a·mi** a large plant-eating animal with thick hairless skin that lives in African rivers

hire (hīr) *n.* money paid for wages or rent —*vb.* **hired**; **hir·ing** to employ for pay

his (hiz) *adj.* of or relating to him (*his* sweater)

his·to·ry (his′ tə rē) *n., pl.* **his·to·ries** a written account of what happened in the past

hit (hit) *vb.* **hit**; **hit·ting** **1.** to strike a blow **2.** to reach (*hit* the top) **3.** to discover by chance (*hit* upon a cure) —*n.* **1.** a blow **2.** a bit of luck (made a *hit*)

hitch (hich) *vb.* to fasten —*n.* **1.** a jerky movement (gave his jacket a *hitch*) **2.** an unexpected problem (finished the work without a *hitch*) **3.** a kind of knot in a rope

hith·er·to (hi<u>th</u>′ ər tü′) *adv.* up to this time

hive (hīv) *n.* **1.** a place where honeybees live **2.** a place where there is a lot of activity

ho (hō) *interj.* a word to attract attention or express surprise

hoarse (hors) *adj.* **hoars·er**; **hoars·est** a rough, grating voice

hob·by (häb′ ē) *n., pl.* **hob·bies** an activity engaged in for pleasure or interest

hoe (hō) *n.* a tool with a thin blade and long handle used for weeding a garden —*vb.* to weed or loosen the soil around plants

hog (hȯg, häg) *n.* an adult domestic swine —*vb.* **hogged**; **hog·ging** to take more than one's share

hoist (hȯist) *vb.* to raise up especially by using a pulley —*n.* **1.** a lift **2.** mechanical equipment for lifting

hold (hōld) *vb.* **held** (held); **hold·ing** **1.** to keep under one's control **2.** to support **3.** to contain (*holds* a quart) **4.** to keep something together (the knot *held*) —*n.* **1.** a grip on something **2.** the cargo compartment below deck in a ship or airplane

hole (hōl) *n.* **1.** an opening through something (a *hole* in my coat) **2.** a hollowed out place (a *hole* in the ground)

hol·i·day (häl′ ə dā′) *n.* a day out of work or school, usually to celebrate an event

hol·low (häl′ ō) *adj.* **1.** empty inside **2.** sunken (*hollow* cheeks) —*n.* an empty space inside something —*vb.* to dig out or make hollow

hol·ly (häl′ ē) *n.*, *pl.* **hol·lies** an evergreen tree or bush with dark green shiny leaves and red berries used widely as a Christmas decoration

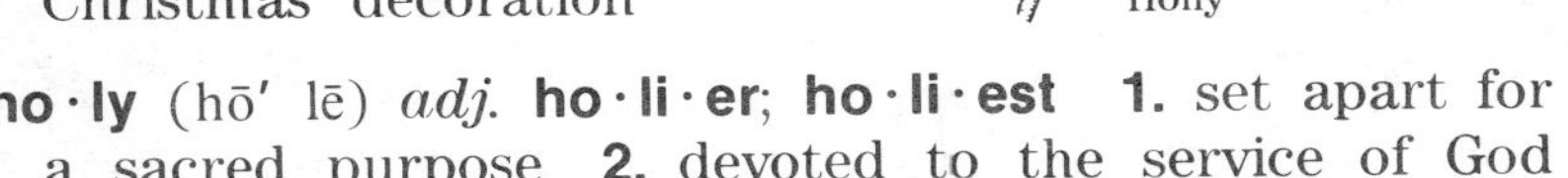

Holly

ho·ly (hō′ lē) *adj.* **ho·li·er**; **ho·li·est** **1.** set apart for a sacred purpose **2.** devoted to the service of God

home (hōm) *n.* **1.** the house in which one lives **2.** a place for the care of disabled persons —*adv.* to or at home

home·land (hōm′ land′) *n.* native land

home·made (hōm′ mād′) *adj.* made at home

home·ward (hōm′ wərd) or **home·wards** (-wərdz) *adv.* or *adj.* toward home

home·work (hōm′ wərk′) *n.* work such as school assignments to be done outside the classroom

hom·o·nym (häm′ ə nim′) *n.* a word that is the same as another in spelling and sound but different in meaning such as *compass*, an instrument for drawing circles or an instrument which points north

hon·est (än′ əst) *adj.* fair and truthful

hon·ey (hən′ ē) *n.* a sweet substance made by bees from nectar gathered from flowers

hon·or (än′ ər) *n.* recognition and respect —*vb.* **1.** to treat with respect **2.** to live up to an agreement (to be on one's *honor*)

hon·or·a·ble (än′ ə rə bəl) *adj.* worthy of honor

hood (hůd) *n.* **1.** a flexible head covering that is often attached to the neck of an outer garment such as a cape or jacket **2.** a cover for certain types of machinery such as the engine of a car

hoof (hůf, hüf) *n., pl.* **hooves** (hůvz, hüvz) or **hoofs** the horn covering that protects the toes of some animals such as horses, oxen, and swine

hook (hůk) *n.* a curved metal device used to fasten a door or to grasp something to pull it along —*vb.* to catch or fasten with a hook

hoop (hůp, hüp) *n.* a ring-shaped strip, usually of metal (the *hoops* on the barrel)

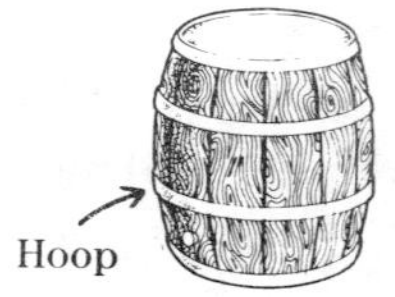

Hoop

hop (häp) *vb.* **hopped**; **hop·ping** **1.** to jump along on one foot **2.** to take a short trip especially by airplane **3.** to get a free ride (*hopped* a ride to the fair)

hope (hōp) *vb.* **hoped**; **hop·ing** to feel that your wish may come true —*n.* belief that something desired will happen

hop·per (häp′ ər) *n.* **1.** one that hops **2.** a funnel-shaped container that can be filled through the top and emptied through the bottom (The *hoppers* on the freight train are carrying grain.)

ho·ri·zon (hə rīz′ n) *n.* **1.** the line where the sky and earth appear to come together **2.** the boundary around a person's interests and expectations

hor·i·zon·tal (hȯr′ ə zänt′ l) *adj.* parallel to the floor or level ground —*n.* something that is horizontal

horn (hȯrn) *n.* **1.** one of the hard bony growths on the head of hoofed animals such as cattle or goats **2.** something shaped like a horn, such as a wind instrument (a trumpet)

hor·ri·ble (hȯr′ ə bəl) *adj.* full of pain, fear, or dismay

hor·rid (hȯr′ əd) *adj.* extremely unpleasant (*horrid* weather)

hor·ror (hȯr′ ər) *n.* something dreadful, revolting, and shocking (the *horrors* of war)

horse (hȯrs) *n.* **1.** a large, hoofed, grass-eating mammal used for riding or pulling loads **2.** a frame that supports something, as a sawhorse **3.** a piece of equipment used for vaulting

horse·back (hȯrs′ bak′) *adv.* on the back of a horse

hose (hōz) *n., pl.* **hose** or **hos·es** **1.** stocking or sock **2.** a flexible tube for carrying fluid —*vb.* **hosed**; **hos·ing** to water or wash with a hose

hos·pi·tal (häs′ pit′ l) *n.* a place where sick and injured people are given medical and surgical care

host (hōst) *n.* **1.** a huge crowd **2.** a person who entertains guests **3.** the bread used in the Eucharist

hos·tile (häst′ l) *adj.* **1.** very unfriendly **2.** relating to an enemy

hot (hät) *adj.* **hot·ter**; **hot·test** **1.** having a high temperature (*hot* weather) **2.** quick to get angry (a *hot* temper) **3.** sharp tasting (*hot* mustard)

ho·tel (hō tel′) *n.* a place where travelers may rent a room for one or more nights

hound (håund) *n.* a dog, usually one of a hunting breed, that follows game by the sense of smell —*vb.* to hunt or go after someone or something as a hound does

hour (aůr) *n.* **1.** one twenty-fourth part of a day **2.** the time of day

house (haůs) *n., pl.* **hous·es** (haů zəz) **1.** a place where people live **2.** a small building to shelter a dog or tools (dog*house*, tool*house*) **3.** family (the *house* of Tudor) **4.** a body of persons who makes laws (*houses* of Congress)

house·hold (haůs′ hōld′) *n.* all the persons who live as one family in a house

house·wife (haůs′ wīf′) *n., pl.* **house·wives** (-wīvz′) a married woman in charge of a household

how (haů) *adv.* **1.** in what way or manner **2.** by what means (*How* do airplanes fly?) **3.** in what state or condition (*How* is Grandpa?) **4.** to what degree or amount (*How* much do you need it?) **5.** what do you think of (*How* about this?)

how·ev·er (haů ev′ ər) *adv.* **1.** nevertheless; on the other hand; yet; in spite of that **2.** to whatever extent or degree (*however* long you stay)

howl (haůl) *vb.* **1.** to wail like a dog or a wolf **2.** to let out a long sad cry as in pain or grief —*n.* a cry or wail

hub (həb) *n.* **1.** the center of a wheel, propeller, or fan **2.** a center of activity (Every airline has one city as a *hub.*)

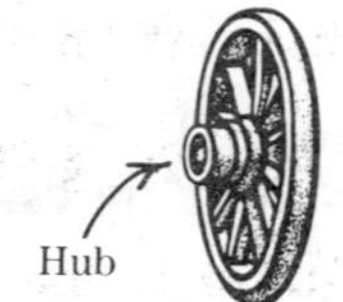

hud·dle (həd′ l) *vb.* **hud·dled**; **hud·dling** **1.** to crowd together (*huddled* under the umbrella) **2.** to come together to talk (The football team *huddled* to plan the next play.) **3.** to curl up (*huddle* by the fire) —*n.* **1.** a closely packed group **2.** a conference

hug (həg) *vb.* **hugged**; **hug·ging** **1.** to hold in one's arms, to embrace **2.** to keep close to (*hug* the curb) —*n.* an embrace

huge (hyüj) *adj.* very large, enormous

hull (həl) *n.* **1.** the covering of a fruit or seed **2.** the frame or body of a ship or airship

hum (həm) *vb.* **hummed; hum·ming** **1.** to make a continuing *m-m-m-m-m-m* sound with the mouth closed **2.** to be active and busy (The bus station *hummed* with activity.) —*n.* the act of humming

hu·man (hyü′ mən) *adj.* **1.** relating to a man or woman **2.** having the form or qualities of people in general

hu·man·i·ty (hyü man′ ət ē) *n., pl.* **hu·man·i·ties** **1.** the human race **2.** human qualities such as sympathy and kindness **3.** *pl.* cultural subjects such as literature

hum·ble (həm′ bəl) *adj.* **hum·bler; hum·blest** **1.** not proud or bold; modest **2.** lowly (in a *humble* cottage) —*vb.* **hum·bled; hum·bling** **1.** to make humble **2.** to take away someone's power or independence (*humbled* the enemy)

hu·mid (hyü′ məd) *adj.* damp (*humid* weather)

hu·mid·i·ty (hyü mid′ ət ē) *n., pl.* **hu·mid·i·ties** the moisture in the air

hum·ming·bird (həm′ ing bərd′) *n.* a small, brightly colored bird whose wings beat rapidly in flight making a humming sound

hu·mor (hyü′ mər) *n.* **1.** mood or state of mind (in good *humor*) **2.** something that is amusing (the *humor* in the story)

hump (həmp) *n.* **1.** a lump or bulge as on the back of a camel **2.** a difficult part

hun·dred (hən′ drəd) *n.* **1.** ten times ten **2.** a large number (*hundreds* of times)

hun·ger (həng′ gər) *n.* **1.** a need for food **2.** a strong desire (a *hunger* for an education) —*vb.* **1.** to feel hunger **2.** to have a strong desire

hun·gry (həng′ grē) *adj.* **hun·gri·er; hun·gri·est** **1.** feeling a need for food **2.** having a strong desire

hunt (hənt) *vb.* **1.** to pursue wild animals in order to capture or kill them for sport or food **2.** to search —*n.* an act of hunting

hurl (hərl) *vb.* to throw with force

hur·rah (hə rȯ′, -rä) *interj.* an expression of joy and triumph

hur·ri·cane (hər′ ə kān′) *n.* a violent storm that begins over the sea in warm climates and has winds of seventy-three miles per hour or greater

hur·ry (hər′ ē) *vb.* **hur·ried; hur·ry·ing** to act with haste —*n., pl.* **hur·ries** a state of great haste

hurt (hərt) *vb.* **hurt; hurt·ing** **1.** to feel pain **2.** to do harm to —*n.* **1.** an injury or wound **2.** suffering **3.** harm

hus·band (həz′ bənd) *n.* a married man —*vb.* to manage carefully

hush (həsh) *vb.* to make quiet or calm (*hush* the puppy) —*n.* stillness

hut (hət) *n.* a small, simple shelter

hy·dro·e·lec·tric (hī′ drō i lek′ trik) *adj.* relating to the making of electricity by water power

hy·dro·gen (hī′ drə jən) *n.* a colorless, odorless, and tasteless flammable gas that is the lightest of the chemical elements

hymn (him) *n.* a song of praise, usually to God

hy·poth·e·sis (hī päth′ ə səs) *n., pl.* **hy·poth·e·ses** (-ə sēz′) something not proved but assumed to be true for purposes of argument or further investigation

I

ice (īs) *n.* **1.** frozen water **2.** a frozen dessert —*vb.* **iced**; **ic·ing** **1.** to chill or coat with ice **2.** to cover with icing

ice·berg (īs′ bərg′) *n.* a large mass of ice that has been detached from a glacier and is floating in the sea

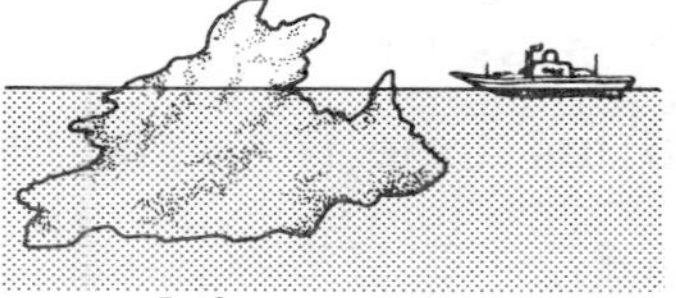
Iceberg

ice·box (īs′ bäks′) *n.* a storage box with ice in it for preserving food; a refrigerator

i·de·a (ī dē′ ə) *n.* a thought or notion

i·de·al (ī dē′ əl) *adj.* **1.** perfect **2.** existing only in the mind —*n.* a standard of excellence

i·den·ti·cal (ī dent′ i kəl) *adj.* just the same

i·den·ti·fi·ca·tion (ī dent′ ə fə kā′ shən) *n.* something that tells who a person is (She carries *identification* in her billfold.)

i·den·ti·fy (ī dent′ ə fī′) *vb.* **i·den·ti·fied**; **i·den·ti·fy·ing** **1.** to find the identity of **2.** to become the same as (to *identify* Tom as the leader)

i·den·ti·ty (ī dent′ ət ē) *n., pl.* **i·den·ti·ties** the same as something described (establish *identity* from dental records)

i·dle (īd′ l) *adj.* **i·dler** (īd′ ler); **i·dlest** (īd ləst) **1.** lacking a basis in fact (*idle* rumor) **2.** not working (*idle* people) **3.** lazy, avoiding work

if (if) *conj.* **1.** in case that (*if* it snows) **2.** whether (see *if* she is ready)

ig·no·rance (ig′ nə rəns) *n.* the state of not having much knowledge

ig·nore (ig nōr′) *vb.* **ig·nored**; **ig·nor·ing** to pay no attention to

ill (il) *adj.* **worse** (wərs); **worst** (wərst) **1.** in poor health (an *ill* person) **2.** hostile (an *ill* feeling) —*n.* evil

il·lit·er·ate (i lit′ ə rət) *adj.* unable to read or write well enough to function in daily life —*n.* an uneducated person

ill·ness (il′ nəs) *n.* sickness

il·lus·trate (il′ əs trāt′) *vb.* **il·lus·trat·ed**; **il·lus·trat·ing** **1.** to make clear with examples or pictures **2.** to decorate

il·lus·tra·tion (il′ əs trā′ shən) *n.* **1.** an example to make something clear **2.** a picture or diagram that explains or decorates

im·age (im′ ij) *n.* a likeness of a person or thing (the *image* in the mirror) —*vb.* to picture something in the mind

i·mag·i·na·tion (i maj′ ə nā′ shən) *n.* the ability to bring to mind images and thoughts of things never before seen or experienced

i·mag·ine (i maj′ ən) *vb.* **i·mag·ined**; **i·mag·in·ing** **1.** to form a mental image of something not present **2.** to think, plan, suppose

im·i·tate (im′ ə tāt′) *vb.* **im·i·tat·ed**; **im·i·tat·ing** to copy or follow a pattern

im·me·di·ate (i mēd′ ē ət) *adj.* **1.** coming next without delay (*immediate* future) **2.** next in line (*immediate* successor)

im·mense (i mens′) *adj.* huge, boundless (an *immense* forest)

im·mi·grant (im′ i grənt) *n.* a person who enters another country to live permanently

im·pact (im′ pakt′) *n.* one body striking another, a collision

im·pa·tient (im pā′ shənt) *adj.* **1.** restless **2.** eager (*impatient* for her turn to come)

im·port (im pōrt′) *vb.* to bring goods into a country (to *import* bananas) (im′ pōrt) —*n.* **1.** something imported **2.** importance (His age was of little *import.*)

im·por·tant (im pȯrt′ nt) *adj.* **1.** in need of attention **2.** worthy of consideration **3.** of great influence or authority (an *important* position)

im·pose (im pōz′) *vb.* **im·posed**; **im·pos·ing** **1.** to require (*impose* a tax) **2.** to take advantage of (*impose* on his hospitality)

im·pos·si·ble (im päs′ ə bəl) *adj.* **1.** not able to exist or occur **2.** hopeless

im·press (im pres′) *vb.* **1.** to stamp or mark by applying pressure **2.** to influence strongly —*n.* (im′ pres) a distinctive mark or effect

im·pres·sion (im presh′ ən) *n.* **1.** a mark produced by pressure **2.** an image produced in the mind by some external influence **3.** an unclear remembrance or belief (I have the *impression* that Ann changed jobs recently.)

im·pris·on (im priz′ n) *vb.* to put in prison

im·prove (im prüv′) *vb.* **im·proved**; **im·prov·ing** to make something greater or better

im·pulse (im pəls′) *n.* **1.** a sudden drive forward producing motion **2.** a sudden tendency to do something (a sudden *impulse* to give apples to the children) **3.** a wave of energy through the nerve fibers affecting movement

in (in) *prep.* **1.** within (walk *in* the park) **2.** into (dove *in* the lake) **3.** during (*in* the night) —*adv.* **1.** toward the inside (jumped *in*) **2.** toward a place (flew *in* this morning —*adj.* going inward (the *in* door)

inch (inch) *n.* a unit of length equal to 1/36 yard or 2.54 centimeters

in·ci·dent (in′ sə dənt) *n.* a happening or event

in·cline (in klīn′) *vb.* **in·clined**; **in·clin·ing** to lean or tilt —*n.* (in′ klīn) slope

in·clined (in klīnd′) *adj.* **1.** leaning or sloping **2.** having a willingness to do something (*inclined* to finish the work)

in·clude (in klüd′) *vb.* **in·clud·ed**; **in·clud·ing** to take as part of the whole (*included* a poem by Carl Sandburg)

in·come (in′ kəm′) *n.* money that comes in from work or business activity

in·com·plete (in′ kəm plēt′) *adj.* not finished

in·cor·rect (in′ kə rekt′) *adj.* **1.** not true **2.** not right **3.** not proper

in·crease (in krēs′) *vb.* **in·creased**; **in·creas·ing** **1.** to become larger **2.** to become greater in number —*n.* (in′ krēs′) the growth

in·cred·i·ble (in kred′ ə bəl) *adj.* so unusual as to seem impossible or unbelievable (The story of the rescue was *incredible.*)

in·deed (in dēd′) *adv.* truly, without question

in·def·i·nite (in def′ ə nət) *adj.* having no exact description or limits (He was *indefinite* about where the picnic would be.)

in·de·pend·ence (in′ də pen′ dəns) *n.* the state of being separate, not under the control or support of another

in·dex (in′ deks′) *n., pl.* **in·dex·es** or **in·di·ces** (in′ də sēz′) **1.** a list of names or topics and where in a book they may be found, given in alphabetical order **2.** a pointer or sign —*vb.* to list in an index —*n.* the finger next to the thumb (*index* finger)

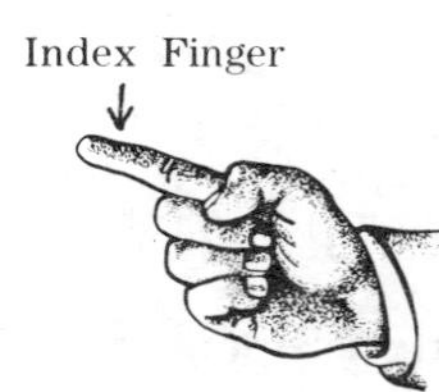

in·di·cate (in′ də kāt′) *vb.* **in·di·cat·ed**; **in·di·cat·ing** **1.** to point out **2.** to say briefly

in·dif·fer·ent (in dif′ ə rənt) *adj.* having no bias or preference one way or the other

in·di·rect (in′ də rekt′) *adj.* **1.** not straight or short (an *indirect* way home) **2.** not straight to the point (answered in an *indirect* manner)

in·di·vid·u·al (in′ də vij′ ə wəl) *adj.* **1.** intended for one person (*individual* serving of fish) **2.** different from others (each has *individual* markings) —*n.* **1.** a person **2.** a single member of a class or species

in·door (in′ dōr′) *adj.* relating to the inside of a building

in·doors (in′ dōrz′) *adv.* in or into a building (stay *indoors*)

in·duce (in düs′) *vb.* **in·duced**; **in·duc·ing** **1.** to persuade **2.** to cause (*induced* a chemical reaction with the substances) **3.** to come to a conclusion from the facts given (*induced* the answer after a careful reading)

in·dus·tri·al (in dəs′ trē əl) *adj.* relating to industry, especially manufacturing

in·dus·try (in′ dəs trē) *n., pl.* **in·dus·tries** **1.** care and effort in working **2.** a branch of business or manufacturing (the shoe *industry*)

in·ev·i·ta·ble (in ev′ ət ə bəl) *adj.* impossible to avoid

in·ex·pen·sive (in′ iks pen′ siv) *adj.* cheap

in·fant (in′ fənt) *n.* a very young child —*adj.* **1.** relating to very young children **2.** intended for young children (*infant* car seat)

in·fect (in fekt′) *vb.* **1.** to pass on a germ, virus, or bacteria causing disease **2.** to sway a person's beliefs by sharing one's feelings

in·fec·tion (in fek′ shən) *n.* **1.** the state of being infected **2.** an infectious disease

in·fi·nite (in′ fə nət) *adj.* being or seeming to be without limits

in·flu·ence (in′ flü′ əns) *n.* **1.** the power to cause an effect without using authority **2.** corrupt interference with authority for personal gain —*vb.* to sway or modify

in·form (in fȯrm′) *vb.* to tell someone something

in·for·ma·tion (in′ fər mā′ shən) *n.* knowledge

in·gre·di·ent (in grēd′ ē ənt) *n.* one of the substances that makes up a mixture (The cake requires six *ingredients.*)

in·hab·it (in hab′ ət) *vb.* to live in

in·hab·it·ant (in hab′ ət ənt) *n.* a person or animal who lives permanently in a place

i·ni·tial (i nish′ əl) *adj.* the first or earliest

in·jure (in′ jər) *vb.* **in·jured**; **in·jur·ing** to hurt or damage

in·ju·ry (in′ jə rē) *n.*, *pl.* **in·ju·ries** **1.** the act that damages **2.** the hurt or damage suffered or sustained

ink (ingk) *n.* a usually liquid, colored material used for writing and printing —*vb.* to put ink on

in·land (in′ land′) *n.* the part of a country away from the shore and toward the interior —*adj.* relating to the interior of a country

inn (in) *n.* a public house where travelers may eat and sleep

in·ner (in′ ər) *adj.* **1.** situated far in, near a center **2.** relating to the mind or spirit

in·ning (in′ ing) *n.* a part of a baseball game consisting of a turn at bat for each team

in·no·cent (in′ ə sənt) *adj.* free from guilt or blame

in·nu·mer·a·ble (i nü′ mə rə bəl) *adj.* too many to be counted

in·quire (in kwīr′) *vb.* **in·quired**; **in·quir·ing** **1.** to ask about **2.** to investigate

in·sect (in′ sekt′) *n.* **1.** a very small animal with no backbone, having a body divided into three parts (head, thorax, and abdomen), three pairs of legs, and usually one or two pairs of wings **2.** an animal such as a spider similar to a true insect

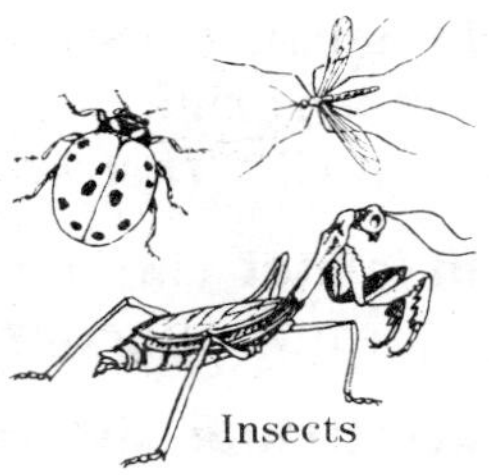
Insects

in·sert (in sərt′) *vb.* to set in (*insert* the piece in the puzzle) —*n.* (in′ sərt) a part that is inserted or provided for insertion (a graph provided as an *insert* in the notebook)

in·side (in sīd′) *n.* the inner surface (The *inside* of the box was lined with satin.) —*adj.* relating to the inside (an *inside* door) —*prep.* to or on the inside (*inside* the barn)

in·sight (in′ sīt′) *n.* understanding

in·sist (in sist′) *vb.* to take a strong stand (*insist* that we do the dishes)

in·spect (in spekt′) *vb.* to look at or examine closely (*inspect* the new paint job)

in·spec·tion (in spek′ shən) *n.* the act of examining closely

in·spi·ra·tion (in′ spə rā′ shən) *n.* **1.** the act of taking in a breath of air **2.** the act of being moved mentally or emotionally by some uplifting influence

in·spire (in spīr′) *vb.* **in·spired**; **in·spir·ing** **1.** to have an uplifting influence on **2.** to inhale

in·stall (in stȯl′) *vb.* **1.** to place in office (*install* the new president) **2.** to put in place for use (*install* the air conditioner)

in·stance (in′ stəns) *n.* an example (for *instance*)

in·stant (in′ stənt) *n.* moment (the *instant* it happened) —*adj.* made to be quick and easy to use (*instant* hot cereal)

in·stead (in sted′) *adv.* **1.** in place of (Use oil *instead* of margarine for frying.) **2.** as a substitute (go to the movies *instead*)

in·stinct (in′ stingkt′) *n.* a natural reaction that is performed unconsciously

in·sti·tute (in′ stə tüt′) *vb.* **in·sti·tut·ed; in·sti·tut·ing** to set up and get something started —*n.* an organization, usually for the promotion of education or welfare (an *institute* for the deaf)

in·sti·tu·tion (in′ stə tü′ shən) *n.* **1.** the establishment (*institution* of the new rules) **2.** an established organization or custom

in·struc·tion (in strək′ shən) *n.* **1.** the practice of teaching **2.** the knowledge imparted by a teacher

in·stru·ment (in′ strə mənt) *n.* **1.** the means for getting something done **2.** a tool or device **3.** a device used to produce music (a piano is an *instrument)* **4.** a legal document such as a will

in·su·la·tion (in′ sə lā′ shən) *n.* the act of covering something with a material that is a poor conductor (Electric wires are covered with *insulation.*)

in·sult (in səlt′) *vb.* to treat badly so as to offend —*n.* (in′ səlt) an act or statement showing disrespect

in·sur·ance (in shu̇r′ əns) *n.* **1.** the act of insuring **2.** coverage by a contract in which one party guarantees another against loss for a sum of money

in·take (in′ tāk′) *n.* **1.** an opening through which fluid is taken in **2.** the act of taking in

in·tel·lec·tu·al (int′ l ek′ chə wəl) *adj.* relating to the power and capacity for thinking (Study is *intellectual* work.)

in·tel·li·gence (in tel′ ə jəns) *n.* the ability to learn, reason, and understand (has the *intelligence* to go to college)

in·tend (in tend′) *vb.* to have in mind as an aim or goal

in·tense (in tens′) *adj.* **1.** present to an extreme degree (*intense* heat) **2.** straining to the utmost (*intense* effort) **3.** showing strong feeling (*intense* anger)

in·tent (in tent′) *n.* **1.** the act of meaning to do something **2.** the state of mind with which an act was done —*adj.* showing eager attention

in·ter·est (in′ trəst, int′ ə rəst) *n.* **1.** a legal share in something (inherited an *interest* in the business) **2.** money paid by a borrower for the borrowed money **3.** a feeling of attention and curiosity toward a subject (an *interest* in American history)

in·ter·fere (int′ ər fiər′) *vb.* **in·ter·fered; in·ter·fer·ing** to meddle in the concerns of others

in·te·ri·or (in tir′ ē ər) *adj.* enclosed or operating within the boundaries —*n.* the inner part of something

in·ter·me·di·ate (int′ ər mē′ dē ət) *adj.* situated in the middle between extremes —*n.* something that is in a middle position

in·ter·nal (in tərn′ l) *adj.* **1.** situated inside **2.** relating to the inside of the body **3.** having to do with the domestic affairs of a country

in·ter·na·tion·al (int′ ər nash′ ən l) *adj.* involving two or more nations

in·ter·pret (in tər′ prət) *vb.* **1.** to explain the meaning of **2.** to translate the meaning into an art form

in·ter·pre·ta·tion (in ter′ prə tā′ shən) *n.* **1.** an explanation of the meaning **2.** the imparting of meaning through drama, music, or art

in·ter·rupt (int′ ə rəpt′) *vb.* to break in on a process or course of action

in·ter·sect (int′ ər sekt′) *vb.* **1.** to meet and cross at a given place (the roads *intersect*) **2.** overlap

in·ter·state (int′ ər stāt′) *adj.* involving two or more states (*interstate* traffic)

in·ter·val (int′ ər vəl) *n.* the time or space between two things or events (*interval* between classes)

in·ter·view (int′ ər vyü′) *n.* **1.** a meeting in which a reporter obtains information from a person for use by the media **2.** a meeting in which a job applicant is questioned to determine his or her background for the job —*vb.* to seek information from

in·tes·tine (in tes′ tən) *n.* tubes in the lower part of the digestive system where most of the food is digested and absorbed

in·ti·mate (int′ ə māt′) *vb.* **in·ti·mat·ed**; **in·ti·mat·ing** to hint at or suggest —*adj.* (int′ ə mət) **1.** deeply personal (*intimate* papers) **2.** involving warm friendship

in·to (in′ tə, -tü) *prep.* **1.** to the inside (*into* the box) **2.** to the state (got *into* mischief)

in·tri·cate (in′ tri kət) *adj.* complicated, hard to understand

in·tro·duce (in′ trə düs′) *vb.* **in·tro·duced**; **in·tro·duc·ing** **1.** to present one person to another for the purpose of making them acquainted **2.** to begin something or put it into practice for the first time

in·vade (in vād′) *vb.* **in·vad·ed**; **in·vad·ing** **1.** to go in using force (*invade* enemy territory) **2.** to use another person's property without permission (*invade* the person's privacy)

in·va·sion (in vā′ zhən) *n.* an act of going beyond one's own boundaries or limits, thus encroaching on the rights of others

in·vent (in vent′) *vb.* to create something new and useful

in·ven·tor (in vent′ ər) *n.* one who invents

in·vest (in vest′) *vb.* **1.** to place in a position of honor or authority **2.** to place money in an account to earn financial gains

in·ves·ti·gate (in ves′ tə gāt′) *vb.* **in·ves·ti·gat·ed**; **in·ves·ti·gat·ing** to carefully examine an unclear situation

in·ves·ti·ga·tion (in ves′ tə gā′ shən) *n.* the act or the process of looking into a situation in which the facts are unclear

in·vest·ment (in vest′ mənt) *n.* **1.** the act of placing someone officially in office **2.** the placement of money in an account for income or profit

in·vis·i·ble (in viz′ ə bəl) *adj.* **1.** not able to be seen (*invisible* gas) **2.** out of sight (*invisible* to the naked eye)

in·vi·ta·tion (in′ və tā′ shən) *n.* the act of requesting someone to come to an event (an *invitation* to a party)

in·vite (in vīt′) *vb.* **in·vit·ed**; **in·vit·ing** to ask someone to be present or to participate

in·vol·un·tar·y (in väl′ ən ter′ ē) *adj.* **1.** done without having any choice **2.** a compulsory action **3.** a reflex action

in·volve (in välv′) *vb.* **in·volved**; **in·volv·ing** **1.** to bring someone in as a participant **2.** to include within a topic or situation

in·ward (in′ wərd) *adj.* toward the inside —*adv.* **in·ward** or **in·wards** (-wərdz) toward the inside or center (move *inward*)

i·o·dine (ī′ ə dīn′, ī′ əd n) *n.* a nonmetallic element found in the sea and used in medicine, especially as an antiseptic and in the treatment of the thyroid gland

i·on (ī′ ən, ī′ än′) *n.* an atom or group of atoms that carries an electric charge formed by losing or gaining one or more electrons

i·ron (ī′ ərn) *n.* a heavy metal that rusts easily and is strongly attracted to magnets

ir·reg·u·lar (i reg′ yə lər) *adj.* **1.** having an uneven shape or an informal arrangement (*irregular* pattern) **2.** having no guiding rule, method, rate, or custom (*irregular* hours)

ir·ri·gate (ir′ ə gāt′) *vb.* **ir·ri·gat·ed**; **ir·ri·gat·ing** **1.** to supply water to dry land for raising crops **2.** to keep something moist

is (iz) present tense, third person singular of BE

is·land (ī′ lənd) *n.* a piece of land smaller than a continent that is surrounded by water

isle (īl) *n.* a small island

i·so·late (ī′ sə lāt′) *vb.* **i·so·lat·ed**; **i·so·lat·ing** to separate from others

is·sue (ish′ ü) *n.* **1.** the topic of an argument **2.** the flow of people, things, or a liquid (the *issue* of supplies from the warehouse; the *issue* of oil from the pipe)

it (it) *pron.* the person or thing mentioned before to which "it" refers

i·tal·ic (i tal′ ik) *adj.* relating to a type style with slanted letters —*n.* an italic character or type

i·tem (īt′ əm) *n.* **1.** one article in a list of things **2.** one piece of news

its (its) *adj.* relating to it or itself (lost *its* attraction)

it·self (it self′) *pron.* its own self

i·vo·ry (ī′ və rē) *n., pl.* **i·vo·ries** **1.** the substance that makes up the tusks of an elephant **2.** a creamy-yellowish-white color

J

jack (jak) *n.* **1.** a playing card that bears a picture of a young man **2.** a device for raising something heavy such as a car **3.** one of the small six-pointed metal objects used in a child's game of jacks.

jack·et (jak′ ət) *n.* **1.** a short coat **2.** a wrapper for a book or set of papers (a book *jacket*)

jag·ged (jag′ əd) *adj.* rough-edged (The paper had a *jagged* edge.)

jail (jāl) *n.* prison —*vb.* to hold in custody or to put in jail

jam (jam) *vb.* **jammed**; **jam·ming** **1.** to push into a small space **2.** to press together so tightly as to be unworkable (the machinery is *jammed*) **3.** to send out conflicting messages that cannot be understood (*jam* the airwaves)

jar (jär) *vb.* **jarred**; **jar·ring** **1.** to shake (The passing truck *jarred* the windows.) **2.** to have a disagreeable effect (The roller skating *jarred* my nerves.) —*n.* **1.** a grating sound **2.** an unexpected shake **3.** a broad-mouthed container (a *jar* of jam)

jaw (jȯ) *n.* **1.** the bony parts of the mouth that bear teeth **2.** one of a pair of moving parts that open and close for holding, pulling, crushing, and the like (*jaws* of an alligator)

jel·ly (jel′ ē) *n., pl.* **jel·lies** a sweet spread for bread or cake made by boiling fruit juice and sugar until it reaches a jelling point

jel·ly·fish (jel′ ē fish′) *n.* an invertebrate marine animal with a nearly transparent saucer-shaped body and tentacles with stinging cells

jerk (jərk) *n.* a quick pull or thrust —*vb.* to give a quick sudden pull

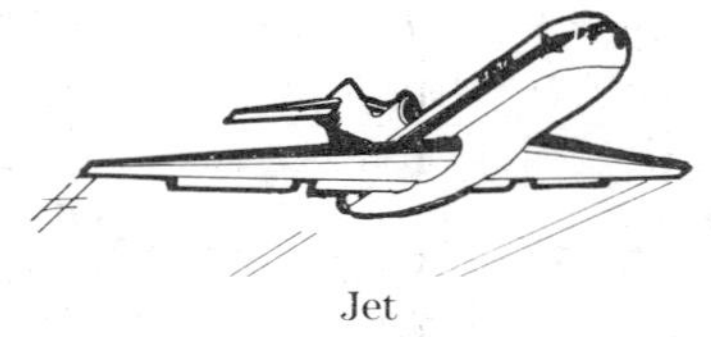
Jet

jet (jet) *n.* **1.** a black, shiny mineral often used for jewelry **2.** a rush of liquid or gas through a small opening (a gas *jet*) **3.** an engine that produces forward motion as a result of the rearward discharge of a jet of heated air and gases through the exhaust nozzles (*jet* engine) **4.** a jet-propelled airplane

jew·el (jü′ əl) *n.* an ornament of precious stones set in metal and worn as a decoration

jew·el·ry (jü′ əl rē) *n.* rings, necklaces, bracelets, or earrings worn as ornaments

job (jäb) *n.* **1.** a piece of work or a duty that one must do **2.** work for which one receives pay (the *job* of mail carrier)

join (jȯin) *vb.* **1.** to bring two or more things together and fasten them **2.** to bring people together for a special action (The labor organizations *join*ed in lobbying.) **3.** to become a member (He'll *join* the soccer team.) **4.** to take part with a group (*join* in the singing)

joint (jȯint) *n.* **1.** a place in a body where two bones come together (elbow *joint*) **2.** the place where two things are connected (*joint* in the pipe)

joke (jōk) *n.* something said or done to cause laughter

jol·ly (jäl′ ē) *adj.* **jol·li·er**; **jol·li·est** cheerful and merry —*adv.* very (a *jolly* nice day)

jour·nal (jərn′ l) *n.* **1.** a daily record of events, as a diary **2.** a daily record of business transactions **3.** a newspaper or magazine dealing with current news

jour·ney (jər′ nē) *n., pl.* **jour·neys** travel from one place to another —*vb.* **jour·neyed**; **jour·ney·ing** to travel

joy (jȯi) *n.* a happy feeling

joy·ous (jȯi′ əs) *adj.* filled with joy

judge (jəj) *vb.* **judged; judg·ing** to form a decision after much study and thought —*n.* a public official who decides questions brought before the court

judg·ment or **judge·ment** (jəj′ mənt) *n.* a formal decision or opinion of the court after hearing the case

Jug

jug (jəg) *n.* a deep container with a handle and narrow mouth usually holding a gallon of liquid

juice (jüs) *n.* a natural fluid of a living body (apple *juice*)

juic·y (jü′ sē) *adj.* **juic·i·er; juic·i·est** having a lot of juice (The oranges are *juicy*.)

jump (jəmp) *vb.* **1.** to leap into the air or across a barrier **2.** to go up (prices *jump*ed) —*n.* **1.** a leap **2.** a sudden upward movement

jun·gle (jəng′ gəl) *n.* a dense growth of trees and plants

ju·nior (jü′ nyər) *n.* **1.** a son with the same name as his father **2.** a member of the class in its next-to-last year in high school or college —*adj.* younger or lower in rank (a *junior* executive)

Junk

junk (jəngk) *n.* **1.** rubbish **2.** a poorly made product **3.** a Chinese sailing ship

ju·ry (jůr′ ē) *n., pl.* **ju·ries** **1.** persons sworn in to hear a case in court and give a verdict **2.** a group that judges and gives prizes at a contest

just (jəst) *adj.* good, reasonable, and based on standards —*adv.* **1.** exactly (*just* right) **2.** barely (*just* made it) **3.** only (*just* this once)

jus·tice (jəs′ təs) *n.* **1.** just and lawful action **2.** a judge

K

kan·ga·roo (kang′ gə rü′) *n., pl.* **kan·ga·roos** a leaping animal native to Australia with strong hind legs and a thick tail used as a support, and, in the female, a pouch on the stomach in which the young are carried

Kangaroo

keel (kēl) *n.* a timber or plate running lengthwise on the bottom of a ship and extending usually to provide stability —*vb.* **1.** to turn over **2.** to fall as in a faint

keen (kēn) *adj.* **1.** having a sharp edge (a *keen* blade) **2.** mentally quick and eager (a *keen* mind)

keep (kēp) *vb.* **kept** (kept); **keep·ing** **1.** to carry out faithfully (*keep* a promise) **2.** to take actions in a fitting and proper way (*keep* house; *keep* silence; *keep* food)

ken·nel (ken′ l) *n.* **1.** a shelter for a dog **2.** a place where dogs are bred or boarded

ker·nel (kərn′ l) *n.* **1.** the whole seed or grain of a cereal **2.** the inner part of a fruit stone or nut

ker·o·sene (ker′ ə sēn′) *n.* a mixture of hydrocarbons distilled from petroleum, used chiefly as lamp fuel and as a solvent for cleaning

ket·tle (ket′ l) *n.* a container for cooking food or boiling water

key (kē) *n.* **1.** a device for turning the bolt in a lock **2.** any of the levers to be pressed in operating the keyboard of a typewriter or piano **3.** the principal tonality of a musical composition (*key* of G) **4.** a low island or reef (the Florida *Keys*) —*adj.* of basic importance (the *key* topic)

key·board (kē′ bōrd′) *n.* a set of keys, as on a computer

kick (kik) *vb.* **1.** to hit with the foot **2.** to complain —*n.* **1.** a blow with the foot **2.** the act of kicking, as in football

kid (kid) *n.* **1.** a young goat **2.** the flesh, fur, or skin of a kid **3.** a child —*vb.* **kid·ded**; **kid·ding** to tease

kid·ney (kid′ nē) *n., pl.* **kid·neys** either of the organs near the backbone which filter blood and excrete urine

kill (kil) *vb.* **1.** to put to death **2.** destroy (*kill* the weeds) **3.** to make useless (*kill* time) **4.** to defeat (*kill* a bill in the legislature) —*n.* an animal shot in a hunt

kin (kin) *n.* a person's relatives

kind (kīnd) *n.* a group with similar traits or interests (*kinds* of water birds) —*adj.* having a good and loving nature (a *kind* old man)

kin·der·gar·ten (kin′ dər gärt′ n) *n.* a school or class for young children who are not yet ready to enter Grade 1

kind·ness (kīnd′ nəs) *n.* **1.** the quality of being kind **2.** a kind act

king (king) *n.* **1.** a male ruler of a country who inherits his kingdom and rules for life **2.** a playing card marked with a picture of a king

king·dom (king′ dəm) *n.* **1.** a country ruled by a king or queen **2.** one of the three divisions of natural objects (animal *kingdom*, plant *kingdom*, and mineral *kingdom*)

kiss (kis) *vb.* to touch with the lips in greeting or affection —*n.* **1.** the act of kissing **2.** a small meringue cookie **3.** a foil-wrapped chocolate candy

kit (kit) *n.* **1.** a small case with an assortment of toiletries (a travel *kit*) **2.** a set of parts to assemble (model airplane *kit*) **3.** any of several packaged sets of related objects or materials (first-aid *kit*)

kitch·en (kich′ ən) *n.* a room for food preparation

kite (kīt) *n.* a light, covered frame with a tail designed to be flown at the end of a long string

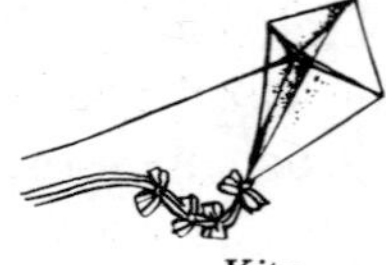
Kite

kit·ten (kit′ n) *n.* a young cat

knee (nē) *n.* **1.** the joint between the thigh and lower leg **2.** the part of a garment that covers the knee (tore the *knee* of her jeans)

kneel (nēl) *vb.* **knelt** (nelt) or **kneeled** (nēld); **kneel·ing** to position oneself on the knees using the toes to maintain balance

knife (nīf) *n., pl.* **knives** (nīvz) a cutting blade with a handle (a paring *knife*) —*vb.* **knifed**; **knif·ing** to cut or wound with a knife

knight (nīt) *n.* **1.** a mounted soldier who served under a feudal lord in medieval times **2.** a man given the title of knight by a sovereign because of his merit or service to his country

knit (nit) *vb.* **knit** or **knit·ted**; **knit·ting** **1.** to grow together (his broken bone *knit* slowly) **2.** to make a fabric of looped stitches by threading yarn over a needle in a series of stitches

knob (näb) *n.* the round handle on a door

knock (näk) *vb.* **1.** to rap on a hard surface such as a door **2.** to use a door knocker —*n.* **1.** a sharp blow **2.** a misfortune (a hard *knock*) **3.** a pounding noise (*knock* in the engine)

knot (nät) *n.* a twining and looping of string or cord to make a firm lump —*vb.* **knot·ted**; **knot·ting** **1.** to tie with a knot **2.** to form knots

know (nō) *vb.* **knew** (nü); **known** (nōn); **know·ing** **1.** to understand (*know* the rules) **2.** to recognize (*know* that person)

knowl·edge (näl′ ij) *n.* **1.** a body of information **2.** concepts and understanding gained from experience

L

la·bel (lā′ bəl) *n.* a tag attached to an article giving information such as contents or washing instructions —*vb.* **la·beled** or **la·belled**; **la·bel·ing** or **la·bel·ling** **1.** to attach a label **2.** to classify something

la·bor (lā′ bər) *n.* **1.** work that requires physical or mental effort **2.** workers as a class (*Labor* was represented at the meeting.) **3.** the process of giving birth to offspring

lab·o·ra·to·ry (lab′ rə tōr′ ē, lab′ ə rə-) *n., pl.* **lab·o·ra·to·ries** **1.** one or more rooms set up for conducting tests and scientific experiments **2.** a class period for trying out what was learned in class lectures

lace (lās) *n.* **1.** a cord used to thread through eyelets on the instep of a shoe to draw them together **2.** a fancy openwork fabric

lack (lak) *n.* the absence of something needed —*vb.* to need or to have a shortage

lad (lad) *n.* boy, youth

lad·der (lad′ ər) *n.* a device for climbing, having two parallel supports joined together with horizontal rungs about twelve inches apart

lad·en (lād′ n) *adj.* heavily loaded

la·dy (lād′ ē) *n., pl.* **la·dies** woman

lag (lag) *vb.* **lagged**; **lag·ging** to move slowly so as to fall behind —*n.* **1.** the amount of time or distance the lagging one is behind **2.** the interval between two activities (the *lag* between events)

lake (lāk) *n.* a large inland body of water fed by springs or melting snow

lamb (lam) *n.* a sheep less than one year old —*vb.* to bring forth a lamb

lame (lām) *adj.* **lam·er; lam·est** having a disability that causes walking to be painful, limping, or halting

lamp (lamp) *n.* any of various devices that produce artificial light by burning oil or gas, or using electricity

lance (lans) *n.* **1.** a weapon with a long shaft and sharp metal head which was used by soldiers on horseback **2.** a spear used for killing whales

land (land) *n.* **1.** the solid part of the earth's surface **2.** the portion owned by an individual (taxes on his *land* and buildings) **3.** a nation (the *land* of Italy)

land·ing (lan′ ding) *n.* **1.** the act of coming to land (fasten your seatbelts in preparation for *landing*) **2.** a place for passengers to get on and off (tie the boat to the *landing*) **3.** a level part of a staircase (stop at the *landing* to rest a minute)

land·mark (land′ märk′) *n.* **1.** an object used as a guide **2.** a very important event which may serve as a guide to the future

land·scape (land′ skāp′) *n.* **1.** a view of the area from one place **2.** a picture of natural scenery

lane (lān) *n.* **1.** a narrow but easily followed passageway not wide enough to be a road **2.** one strip of road wide enough for a single line of cars (This road has four *lanes*.) **3.** a sea channel for ships **4.** a bowling alley

lan·guage (lang′ gwij) *n.* **1.** human speech **2.** the form of speech used in common by the people of a nation or culture (the English *language*) **3.** the technical words associated with an area of study (the *language* of the computer)

lan·tern (lant′ ərn) *n.* a portable lamp with a protective cover

lap (lap) *n.* **1.** the front part of the thighs when seated (sit on my *lap*) **2.** the part of a garment that folds over another part (This wrap skirt has a generous *lap.*) —*vb.* **lapped; lap·ping** **1.** to overlap or cover another part **2.** to take in food or drink with the tongue

large (lärj) *adj.* **larg·er; larg·est** bigger than average

lark (lärk) *n.* a small brownish bird that lives on the ground

lar·va (lär′ və) *n., pl.* **lar·vae** (-vē) a young, wingless often wormlike form of an insect when it first hatches from the egg

lash (lash) *vb.* **1.** to strike with a whip **2.** a sudden verbal attack (He may *lash* out at them for being so noisy.) **3.** to tie with a rope, cord, or chain —*n.* **1.** something used for whipping **2.** an eyelash

last (last) *adj.* **late; lat·er; last 1.** after all the rest **2.** the recent past (*last* Monday) —*vb.* to go on in time, continue —*adv.* **1.** at the end **2.** most recently

late (lāt) *adj.* **lat·er; last 1.** coming after the usual time (a *late* dinner) **2.** toward the end of the day (a *late* phone call)

lat·er·al (lat′ ə rəl) *adj.* related or directed to the side (a *lateral* pass)

lat·i·tude (lat′ ə tüd′) *n.* **1.** distance north or south of the equator **2.** freedom from restrictions (gave them *latitude* in what they would study)

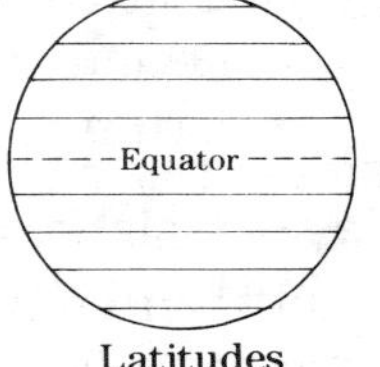

Latitudes

lat·ter (lat′ ər) *adj.* relating to the more recent of two things (as for the *latter* example)

laugh (laf) *vb.* to express amusement, mirth, or at times, scorn, by smiling accompanied by one of a range of sounds from a loud *ha-ha* to a soft chuckle —*n.* the act or sound of laughing

laugh·ter (laf′ tər) *n.* the sound of laughing

launch (lȯnch) *vb.* **1.** to set a small boat or newly built ship into the water (*launch* the new submarine) **2.** to send upward with great force (*launch* a rocket) **3.** to set in motion —*n.* **1.** an open or half-decked boat propelled by oars or an engine **2.** a utility boat carried by a warship

laun·dry (lȯn′ drē) *n., pl.* **laun·dries** the clothes or linens in the process of being laundered

la·va (läv′ ə) *n.* **1.** the melted rock that flows from a volcano or crack in the earth's surface **2.** the volcanic flow that has solidified

law (lȯ) *n.* **1.** a rule of conduct recognized as binding and enforced by authority **2.** the collection of such rules (*law* of the land) **3.** a rule of nature that always works the same way (*law* of inertia)

lawn (lȯn) *n.* **1.** a grass-covered area around a house **2.** a sheer linen or cotton material

law·yer (lȯ′ yər) *n.* a member of the profession that conducts lawsuits for clients and advises them of their legal rights and responsibilities

lay (lā) *vb.* **laid** (lād); **lay·ing** **1.** to put, place, or set down on a horizontal surface or at rest (*lay* the book on the desk) **2.** to lay forcefully, to fell (trees *laid* over by the storm) **3.** to produce an egg **4.** to place so as to cover a surface or area (*lay* a sidewalk, *lay* carpeting, *lay* a foundation) —*n.* the relationship of one thing to another (the *lay* of the land)

lay·er (lā′ ər) *n.* **1.** one who lays (a brick*layer*) **2.** one horizontal thickness (a *layer* of sandstone in the rock) —*vb.* to put things in layers

la·zy (lā′ zē) *adj.* **la·zi·er**; **la·zi·est** **1.** not ambitious **2.** having a dislike for work or activity

lead (lēd) *vb.* **led** (led); **lead·ing** **1.** to go at the head to show the way **2.** to be first in the class, usually in achievement **3.** to conduct (*lead* the campaign) **4.** to direct (*lead* a horse to water)

lead·er (lēd′ ər) *n.* one who guides or directs

leaf (lēf) *n., pl.* **leaves** (lēvz) **1.** one unit of foliage growing from a stem that functions in the production of food by photosynthesis **2.** one layer in a book having a page on each side **3.** a piece of a tabletop that can be added or removed to adjust the size of the table —*vb.* to produce leaves

leaf·y (lē′ fē) *adj.* **leaf·i·er**; **leaf·i·est** **1.** like a leaf **2.** covered with leaves

league (lēg) *n.* an alliance for a common purpose (the *League* of Women Voters; the Little *League*)

leak (lēk) *vb.* **1.** to pass through an opening that should not be there (Rain will *leak* through the roof. Gas fumes may *leak*.) **2.** to become known (The story *leak*ed to the media.) —*n.* **1.** the hole or the person through which the leaked material passes **2.** the act of leaking

lean (lēn) *vb.* **1.** to tilt or bend from a straight position **2.** to depend on (His mother *lean*s on him for help.) —*adj.* **1.** having little or no fat **2.** lacking in richness (a *lean* year)

leap (lēp) *vb.* **leaped** or **leapt** (lēpt); **leap·ing** (lē′ ping) **1.** to jump or spring from a surface **2.** to act quickly (*leap* to conclusions) —*n.* **1.** the act of jumping **2.** the distance jumped

learn (lərn) *vb.* **learned** (lernd); **learn·ing** **1.** to gain knowledge or skill by study or experience **2.** to memorize

leath·er (le<u>th</u>′ ər) *n.* the tanned hide of an animal

leave (lēv) *vb.* **left** (left); **leav·ing** **1.** to depart from a place **2.** to let something remain as it is (*Leave* the cat alone.) **3.** to disregard or omit (*leave* out that reference; some information *left* out)

lec·ture (lek′ chər) *n.* a speech or talk given before a group —*vb.* **lec·tured**; **lec·tur·ing** **1.** to deliver a talk **2.** to scold

ledge (lej) *n.* something like a shelf jutting out, as from a wall (the window *ledge*; the *ledge* of rock)

left (left) *adj.* when facing north, it is the part of the body to the west —*n.* the part on the left side —*vb.* past of LEAVE

leg (leg) *n.* **1.** one of the limbs used in walking **2.** the part of a garment that covers the leg (the pants *leg*) **3.** something like a leg (chair *leg*) **4.** stage of a long trip (first *leg*)

le·gal (lē′ gəl) *adj.* pertaining to the law

leg·end (lej′ ənd) *n.* a story handed down from olden times and generally accepted to be true but having no verifiable base

leg·end·ar·y (lej′ ən der′ ē) *adj.* relating to a legend

leg·is·la·tion (lej′ əs lā′ shən) *n.* **1.** the process of making laws **2.** the laws that are made

length (length) *n.* **1.** the distance end to end on the long side of an object **2.** the duration of time (*length* of the class)

length·wise (length′ wīz′) *adv.* in the direction of the length (fold it *lengthwise*) —*adj.* placed or directed lengthwise (a *lengthwise* crease in the paper)

length·y (leng′ thē) *adj.* **length·i·er**; **length·i·est** very long

lens (lenz) *n.* a curved layer of glass ground to change the direction of the rays of light passing through it so they will come together to form a clear image

less (les) *adj.* **1.** smaller in size or amount **2.** lower in rank —*adv.* to a lesser extent —*prep.* minus —*n.* a smaller amount

les·son (les′ n) *n.* **1.** something to be learned **2.** a reading from Scripture

lest (lest) *conj.* for fear that

let (let) *vb.* **let**; **let·ting** to allow (*let* it be known, *let* me pass)

let·ter (let′ ər) *n.* **1.** one character of the alphabet **2.** a communication sent through the mail **3.** the strict meaning in every detail (the *letter* of the law) **4.** the profession of literature (men and women of *letters*)

lev·el (lev′ əl) *n.* **1.** a device used to determine if an object is on a true horizontal plane **2.** a horizontal position **3.** one step or stage in rank (went up one *level*) —*vb.* **lev·eled**; **lev·el·ing** to make flat and level

lev·er (lev′ ər, lē′ vər) *n.* **1.** a bar such as a crowbar used for prying **2.** a handle such as a gearshift that sticks out of machinery and by which it is operated

lib·er·al (lib′ ə rəl) *adj.* **1.** generous **2.** allowing freedom

lib·er·ty (lib′ ərt ē) *n., pl.* **lib·er·ties** **1.** independence **2.** freedom from control in one's personal life

li·brar·y (lī′ brer′ ē) *n., pl.* **li·brar·ies** a place where literary, artistic, and reference materials are stored and catalogued for the use of its patrons

li·cense (līs′ ns) *n.* **1.** permission to do something that is granted by an authority **2.** liberty of action that is carried too far —*vb.* **li·censed**; **li·cens·ing** to grant a permit

lick (lik) *vb.* **1.** to stroke with the tongue **2.** to pass over like a tongue (flames *lick*ed the curtains) **3.** to defeat (*lick* the other team) —*n.* **1.** the act of licking **2.** a small amount (not a *lick* of work)

lid (lid) *n.* **1.** a movable cover, separate or hinged (the *lid* on the hamper) **2.** eyelid

lie (lī) *vb.* **lay** (lā); **lain** (lān); **ly·ing** (lī′ ing) **1.** to stretch out flat as on a bed **2.** to be located (Rhode Island *lies* in southeastern New England.)

lie (lī) *vb.* **lied**; **ly·ing** to make an untrue statement with the intent of being believed —*n.* something said with the intention of deceiving

lieu·ten·ant (lü ten′ ənt) *n.* **1.** a commissioned officer in the army who ranks next below a captain **2.** a commissioned officer in the navy who ranks next below a lieutenant commander

life (līf) *n., pl.* **lives** (livz) **1.** the quality that sets animals and plants apart from rocks, earth, and water and which they lose when they die **2.** the sequence of physical and mental experiences that constitute a person's existence **3.** a biography of a person **4.** a manner of living

life·less (līf′ ləs) *adj.* without life

life·time (līf′ tīm′) *n.* the length of one's life

lift (lift) *vb.* **1.** to move upward to a higher position **2.** to remove (*lift* the ban on travel) **3.** to raise up (*lift* the box, *lift* your voices) —*n.* **1.** the act of lifting **2.** a layer in the heel of a shoe **3.** the upward force that keeps an airplane in the air

light (līt) *n.* **1.** the illumination that makes it possible to see things **2.** a glow within a person's eyes —*adj.* having brightness —*vb.* **light·ed** or **lit** (lit); **light·ing** **1.** to set to burning, as a candle **2.** to flip a switch for an electric light

light (līt) *vb.* **light·ed** or **lit** (lit); **light·ing** **1.** to get down from a horse **2.** to come to rest (*light* on a branch) —*adv.* without much baggage (travel *light*) —*adj.* **1.** not heavy or hard to bear (*light* housework) **2.** agile (*light*-footed) **3.** not serious or hard to understand (*light* reading)

light·house (līt′ haůs′) *n.* a tower near the shore with a powerful light to guide sailors

light·ing (līt′ ing) *n.* **1.** the act of lighting **2.** the arrangement of lights **3.** the way light falls on a person or object (special *lighting* for the photograph)

light·ning (līt′ ning) *n.* the light associated with a discharge of electricity between two clouds or between a cloud and the earth during a thunderstorm

like (līk) *vb.* **liked**; **lik·ing** to enjoy or feel an attraction to —*n.* liking —*adj.* similar (he was child*like* in behavior) —*prep.* similar to (*like* her mother) —*conj.* as if (It looks *like* the sun will come out.)

like·wise (līk′ wīz′) *adv.* **1.** moreover **2.** in like manner

lil·y (lil′ ē) *n., pl.* **lil·ies** a plant that grows from a bulb with a leafy stem and showy funnel-shaped flowers (the tiger *lily*)

limb (lim) *n.* **1.** an animal's wings or legs that are used in moving around **2.** a large branch of a tree

lime (līm) *n.* **1.** a white substance made from calcium carbonate, limestone, or shells and used in manufacturing and on lawns and gardens **2.** a small greenish citrus fruit related to the lemon

lime·stone (līm′ stōn′) *n.* a rock originally formed from shells in a similar manner as coral

lim·it (lim′ ət) *n.* a boundary line (the town *limits*)

lim·i·ta·tion (lim′ ə tā′ shən) *n.* **1.** the act of limiting **2.** a boundary or limit

limp (limp) *vb.* to walk lamely —*n.* a faltering walk —*adj.* lacking stiffness

line (līn) *vb.* **lined**; **lin·ing** to cover the inner surface (*line* the jacket with silk) —*n.* **1.** rope, thread, or cord **2.** the boundary marker (state *line*) **3.** wire for carrying telephone or telegraph signals **4.** a row of things (a *line* of stores)

lin·en (lin′ ən) *n.* cloth made from flax

lin·er (lī′ nər) *n.* a large ship or airplane used for public transportation —*n.* **1.** a person who lines things **2.** a material used for lining

lin·ger (ling′ gər) *vb.* to stay on longer than usual as though hesitant or reluctant to leave

link (lingk) *n.* **1.** a single ring of a chain **2.** something that unites —*vb.* **1.** to join with links **2.** to make a good joint

li·on (lī′ ən) *n.* a large tan animal of the cat family with a tufted tail, the male of which has a mane

lip (lip) *n.* **1.** either of the two fleshy folds that surround the mouth opening **2.** a flaring edge on a hollow vessel

liq·uid (lik′ wəd) *n.* **1.** any substance that flows like water and can be poured from one container to another **2.** a fluid —*adj.* relating to a fluid substance that flows like water

list (list) *n.* **1.** an enumeration of items **2.** a tilt to one side —*vb.* **1.** to put on a list **2.** to lean or tilt to one side

lis·ten (lis′ n) *vb.* to pay attention for the purpose of hearing

lit·er·al (lit′ ə rəl) *adj.* confined to what the words say without interpretation

lit·er·ar·y (lit′ ə rer′ ē) *adj.* relating to literature

lit·er·a·ture (lit′ ə rə chůr′) *n.* **1.** the body of written works judged to be excellent in form of expression and to deal with ideas of permanent or universal interest **2.** printed matter

lit·ter (lit′ ər) *n.* **1.** a stretcher for carrying a sick or injured person **2.** the number of young born at one time (*litter* of puppies) **3.** objects or rubbish scattered about —*vb.* to cover with litter

lit·tle (lit′ l) *adj.* **lit·tler** (lit′ lər) or **less** (les); **lit·tlest** (lit′ ləst) or **least** (lēst) **1.** small in size, quantity, or importance **2.** short in duration **3.** narrow-minded or mean —*adv.* **less** (les); **least** (lēst) to a very small degree —*n.* something small in amount (I'd like a *little.*)

live (liv) *vb.* **lived**; **liv·ing** to be or to stay alive —*adj.* (līv) **1.** existing **2.** workable **3.** charged with energy (a *live* wire)

live·ly (līv′ lē) *adj.* active, animated, and full of life

liv·er (liv′ ər) *n.* a large glandular organ with five lobes, active in secretion of bile to aid digestion and in helping to keep the chemical balance in the blood

live·stock (līv′ stäk′) *n.* animals raised on a farm for profit

Lizard

liz·ard (liz′ ərd) *n.* a small, slim reptile with external ears, two pairs of limbs, and a long, tapering tail

load (lōd) *n.* **1.** something that is heavy to carry **2.** something that is mentally hard to bear —*vb.* **1.** to put a load on something (*load* the freight car) **2.** to oppress (*load*ed down with worry) **3.** to fill

loaf (lōf) *n., pl.* **loaves** (lōvz) **1.** a rectangular shaped mass of bread **2.** any food baked in a rectangular shape (meat *loaf*) —*vb.* to stay idle

loan (lōn) *n.* **1.** money that is given to a borrower to be returned at a given time with interest **2.** any article given to a borrower for temporary use —*vb.* lend

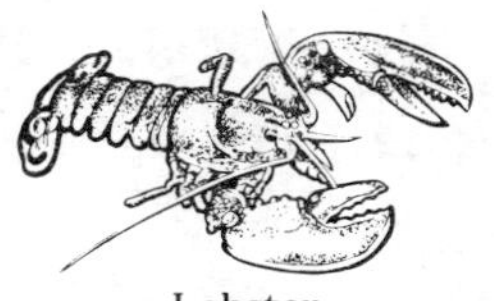
Lobster

lob·ster (läb′ stər) *n.* a large sea crustacean used for food

lo·cal (lō′ kəl) *adj.* **1.** confined to a particular place (*local* news) **2.** stopping at all of the stations along a route (a *local* train)

lo·cate (lō′ kāt′) *vb.* **lo·cat·ed; lo·cat·ing** **1.** to find the exact place **2.** to settle in a particular spot

lo·ca·tion (lō kā′ shən) *n.* **1.** the act of locating **2.** a place where something is situated (The business has a new *location*.)

lock (läk) *n.* **1.** a device for fastening a door **2.** a section of a canal bound by gates at each end and used to raise or lower a boat as it passes from one level to another **3.** a small portion of hair —*vb.* to fasten with a lock

lo·co·mo·tive (lō′ kə mōt′ iv) *n.* an engine for pulling trains that runs under its own power —*adj.* related to a self-propelled engine

lodge (läj) *vb.* **lodged**; **lodg·ing** **1.** to provide with a temporary shelter or dwelling **2.** to settle or become fixed in place (The pearl became *lodged* in the crevice.) —*n.* a house set apart for special use (a hunting *lodge*)

loft (lȯft) *n.* an area under a sloping roof, such as an attic, a choir loft, or a hayloft

loft·y (lȯf′ tē) *adj.* **loft·i·er**; **loft·i·est** **1.** towering high (a *lofty* steeple) **2.** of high rank (in a *lofty* position)

log (lȯg; läg) *n.* **1.** a piece of tree trunk with branches removed **2.** the daily record kept on a ship or airplane —*vb.* **logged**; **log·ging** **1.** to cut down trees, trim the branches, and ship the logs **2.** to enter a record in a log

log·ic (läj′ ik) *n.* a science that deals with the rules for good reasoning

log·i·cal (läj′ i kəl) *adj.* **1.** having to do with logic **2.** reasonable and sound (*logical* thinking)

lone (lōn) *adj.* being alone, separated from other people or things (the *lone* animal left in the field)

lone·some (lōn′ səm) *adj.* **1.** wanting the company of others (*lonesome* for her family) **2.** in a remote area (traveled a *lonesome* road)

long (lȯng) *adj.* **long·er** (lȯng′ gər); **long·est** (lȯng′ gəst) **1.** extending a greater than average time or distance **2.** reaching a given measure (ten feet *long*; five minutes *long*) **3.** having a long vowel sound: ā, ē, ī, ō, ū —*adv.* for a long time —*n.* a long time —*vb.* to strongly desire

lon·gi·tude (län′ jə tüd′) *n.* the distance in degrees east or west of the 0° meridian

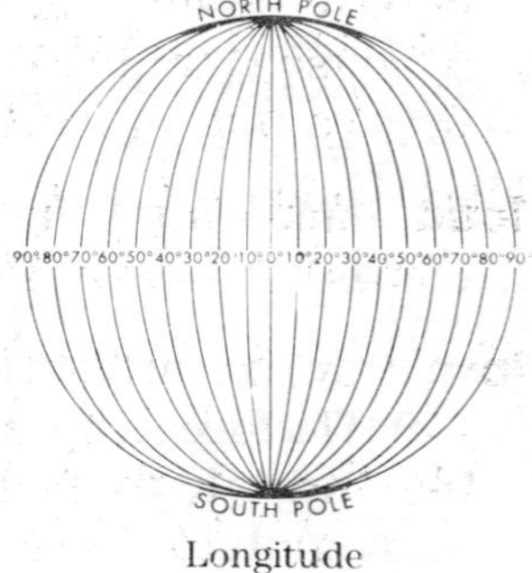

Longitude

look (lu̇k) *vb.* **1.** to see **2.** to appear (*looks* healthy) —*n.* **1.** an act of looking (Take a *look* at this.) **2.** appearance (a tired *look*)

look·out (lu̇k′ au̇t′) *n.* **1.** a tower-like structure for observing a wide area **2.** a person keeping watch **3.** the act of watching (on the *lookout*)

loom (lüm) *n.* a frame for weaving —*vb.* to appear in a hazy, larger-than-natural form

loop (lüp) *n.* **1.** a rounded shape formed when a section of string folds back over itself **2.** a loop-shaped object —*vb.* to make a loop

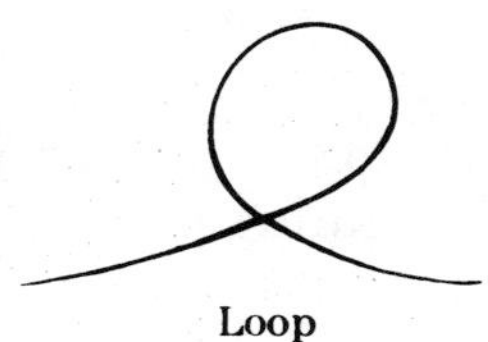
Loop

loose (lüs) *adj.* **loos·er**; **loos·est** **1.** not attached (a *loose* board) **2.** not tightly fitted (a *loose* shirt) **3.** lacking a binding or packaging (*loose* peanuts) —*vb.* **loosed**; **loos·ing** to make loose —*adv.* loosely

lord (lȯrd) *n.* a person who has authority over people or property —*vb.* to act like a lord toward others

lose (lüz) *vb.* **lost** (lȯst); **los·ing** (lü′ zing) **1.** to be unable to find (to *lose* a ring) **2.** to fail to win (to *lose* the race) **3.** to have something slip away (*lose* time)

loss (lȯs) *n.* **1.** the act of losing something **2.** failure to win

lost (lȯst) *adj.* **1.** being away from the intended route **2.** no longer to be found **3.** not used to good advantage (*lost* opportunities)

lot (lät) *n.* **1.** something that represents a chance (to choose by *lot*) **2.** a piece of land sufficient for building a house (build two houses on that *lot*) **3.** a large number (a *lot* of friends)

loud (lau̇d) *adj.* **1.** noisy **2.** vivid or intense (*loud* colors) —*adv.* loudly

love (ləv) *n.* attraction to a person in varying degrees from fondness to an affectionate devotion —*vb.* **loved**; **lov·ing** **1.** to feel warm affection **2.** to enjoy or be attracted to (*love* sports)

low (lō) *vb.* to moo like a cow —*n.* the act of mooing —*adj.* **1.** less than an average height **2.** below average on a variety of measures, such as loudness, energy, temperature, or pressure —*n.* something that is low —*adv.* at or to a low level

low·land (lō′ lənd) *n.* a low, level area of land

loy·al (lȯi′ əl) *adj.* **1.** faithful to those who deserve that commitment **2.** having allegiance to one's country **3.** binding oneself to principles of conduct

loy·al·ty (lȯi′ əl tē) *n., pl.* **loy·al·ties** **1.** faithfulness **2.** allegiance (*loyalty* to the flag)

luck (lək) *n.* the good or bad fortune that comes to a person by chance

lum·ber (ləm′ bər) *n.* timber, especially when cut into boards —*vb.* **1.** to cut logs into lumber **2.** to move clumsily because of bulk **3.** to rumble along (The truck *lumber*ed down the dirt road.)

lu·mi·nous (lü′ mə nəs) *adj.* bright and clear

lump (ləmp) *n.* **1.** a chunk, a shapeless mass (*lump* of clay) **2.** a swelling (*lump* on her head)

lu·nar (lü′ nər) *adj.* of or relating to the moon (a *lunar* eclipse)

lunch (lənch) *n.* **1.** the midday meal **2.** any light meal —*vb.* to eat lunch

lun·cheon (lən′ chən) *n.* a formal lunch

lung (ləng) *n.* either of the two saclike organs in the chest used for breathing

lus·ter (ləs′ tər) *n.* a shine caused by reflecting light

lux·u·ry (lək′ shə rē) *n., pl.* **lux·u·ries** **1.** an article that is costly, elegant, and associated with pleasurable living **2.** something that adds to but is not necessary for a good life (the *luxury* of a fur coat)

M

mac·a·ro·ni (mak′ ə rō′ nē) *n., pl.* **mac·a·ro·nies** a pasta made from wheat flour and dried in the form of tubes

ma·chine (mə shēn′) *n.* a piece of mechanical apparatus that transmits force or motion to do work (a washing *machine*) —*adj.* related to the use of machines (a *machine* shop) —*vb.* **ma·chined**; **ma·chin·ing** to make by using machines (to *machine* the metal plates to exact measurements)

ma·chin·er·y (mə shē′ nə rē) *n.* the parts of a machine

mad (mad) *adj.* **mad·der**; **mad·dest** **1.** having a mental disorder causing insanity **2.** angry (in a *mad* state) **3.** enthusiastic (a *mad* collector of pop records)

mad·am (mad′ əm) *n.* a polite way to address a woman (*Madam*, may I help you?)

ma·dame (mə däm′) *n., pl.* **mes·dames** (mā däm′) a title like Mrs. for a woman who is not English-speaking (*Madame* Bovary)

mag·a·zine (mag′ ə zēn′) *n.* **1.** a storage place for military supplies (the gunpowder *magazine*) **2.** a publication, containing articles and stories, that is issued periodically; for example, weekly, monthly, or quarterly

mag·ic (maj′ ik) *n.* **1.** the belief that charms have a supernatural power over nature **2.** the use of "sleight-of-hand" tricks where the hand is quicker than the eye **3.** anything that charms people, such as a lilting voice —*adj.* relating to magic

ma·gi·cian (mə jish′ ən) *n.* a "sleight-of-hand" performer

mag·ma (mag′ mə) *n.* melted rock under the earth's crust

mag·ne·si·um (mag nē′ zē əm) *n.* a light-weight, silvery element that burns with a dazzling light; used in flashbulbs, fireworks, and in the production of light metals

mag·net (mag′ nət) *n.* **1.** a piece of iron that possesses the power to attract certain other metals **2.** a lodestone

mag·ne·tism (mag′ nə tiz′ əm) *n.* the power to attract certain objects that is possessed by magnets

mag·nif·i·cent (mag nif′ ə sənt) *adj.* having beauty and splendor (*magnificent* silk robes)

mag·ni·fy (mag′ mə fī′) *vb.* **mag·ni·fied; mag·ni·fy·ing** **1.** to make an object appear larger **2.** to exaggerate in importance (to *magnify* the story of the accident)

mag·ni·tude (mag′ nə tüd′) *n.* greatness in size, number, effort, influence, or other characteristic (the *magnitude* of the plan)

maid (mād) *n.* **1.** a female servant **2.** an unmarried girl

maid·en (mād′ n) *adj.* **1.** first (the ship on its *maiden* voyage) **2.** unmarried woman (*maiden* aunt)

mail (māl) *n.* **1.** the public system of transporting and delivering letters and packages **2.** letters and packages received through the mail

main (mān) *n.* **1.** a pipeline (water *main*) **2.** the high seas (over the bounding *main*) **3.** strength (with might and *main*) —*adj.* most important (*main* office)

main·land (mān′ land′) *n.* part of a continent (They could see the *mainland* from the offshore island.)

main·tain (mān tān′) *vb.* **1.** to preserve in a certain condition **2.** to provide support for (*maintain* her parents) **3.** to continue to support a point of view (He *maintain*ed it was the right thing to do.)

main·te·nance (mānt′ n əns) *n.* the act of maintaining

ma·jor (mā′ jər) *adj.* **1.** greater in size, number, or quantity (*major* expense) **2.** an army officer ranking next below a lieutenant colonel

ma·jor·i·ty (mə jȯr′ ət ē) *n., pl.* **ma·jor·i·ties** **1.** the age of acquiring full civil rights **2.** the group that includes more than one-half of the total **3.** the amount by which the larger group exceeds the smaller group (The larger group won by a *majority* of five.)

make (māk) *vb.* **made** (mād); **mak·ing** **1.** to bring into existence **2.** to assemble **3.** to cause to become (to *make* her the treasurer) **4.** to perform (to *make* a figure-eight on the ice)

ma·lar·i·a (mə ler′ ē ə) *n.* a disease marked by fever, chills, and sweating caused by the bite of certain mosquitoes that carry a parasite which attacks the red blood corpuscles

male (māl) *adj.* relating to a boy or man —*n.* one that is male

mam·mal (mam′ əl) *n.* a warm-blooded animal with a backbone that has two pairs of limbs, some body hair, nourishes its young with the milk of the female, and gives birth to live young rather than eggs (except for the lower orders of mammals)

man (man) *n., pl.* **men** (men) **1.** a human person **2.** an adult male —*vb.* **manned; man·ning** to supply with men (*man* the equipment)

man·age (man′ ij) *vb.* **man·aged; man·ag·ing** to control, conduct, direct (*manage* the business)

man·age·ment (man′ ij mənt) *n.* **1.** control, direction **2.** the group of executive officers of a business (This was *management*'s decision.)

mane (mān) *n.* the long hair on the neck or shoulders of an animal, as on a horse or male lion

man·ger (man′ jər) *n.* an open container holding food for farm animals

man·kind (man′ kīnd′) *n.* the human race

man·ner (man′ ər) *n.* **1.** way (in a kind *manner*) **2.** *pl.* behavior (Those boys have good *manners.*)

man·sion (man′ chən) *n.* a fine, large house

man·tle (mant′ l) *n.* **1.** a loose cape **2.** something that covers (a *mantle* of snow) **3.** the part of the earth between the core and the crust (The earth's *mantle* is about 1,800 miles thick.) —*vb.* **man·tled**; **man·tling** to cover as if with a mantle

man·u·al (man′ yə wəl) *adj.* relating to the hands (She traded in her *manual* typewriter for an electric one.) —*n.* handbook (a teacher's *manual*)

man·u·fac·ture (man′ yə fak′ chər) *n.* the making of goods by manual labor or by machinery —*vb.* **man·u·fac·tured**; **man·u·fac·tur·ing** to make goods from raw materials, especially on a large scale

man·u·script (man′ yə skript′) *n.* a handwritten or typewritten copy of a document to be published

man·y (men′ ē) *adj.* **more** (mōr); **most** (mōst) referring to a large number (*many* songbirds) —*pron.* a large number (*many* of them) —*n.* a large number

map (map) *n.* **1.** a picture or representation of a part of the earth's surface **2.** a picture or chart of the sky showing the heavenly bodies —*vb.* **mapped**; **map·ping** **1.** to make a map **2.** to plan in detail

ma·ple (mā′ pəl) *n.* any of several kinds of trees with deeply notched leaves grown for their hard wood or sweet sap

mar·ble (mär′ bəl) *n.* **1.** a type of crystallized limestone capable of taking a high polish, used in sculpture and architecture **2.** a little ball, usually of glass, used in a children's game —*adj.* made of or looking like marble

march (märch) *vb.* **1.** to walk with an even stride in step with others (to *march* with the band) **2.** to make progress (time *march*es on) —*n.* **1.** the act of marching **2.** a piece of music written in march time (a popular *march*)

mare (maər) *n.* an adult female of the horse or other equine animal

mar·gin (mär′ jən) *n.* **1.** a border or edge **2.** the clear space around a printed or written page **3.** an extra amount kept as spare (a *margin* of safety, a *margin* of error)

ma·rine (mə rēn′) *adj.* relating to the sea (*marine* forecast) —*n.* **1.** the ships of a country (the merchant *marine*) **2.** a member of the U.S. Marine Corps

mark (märk) *n.* **1.** an indicator (high water *mark*) **2.** a target (hit the *mark*) **3.** a score (good *mark* in algebra) **4.** a blemish (a *mark* on the table) —*vb.* **1.** to make a mark **2.** to put a tag on (*mark* the merchandise) **3.** to grade (*mark* the test)

mar·ket (mär′ kət) *n.* **1.** a store where foods are sold **2.** a place where people gather to buy and sell goods (flea *market*) —*vb.* to buy or sell in a market

mar·riage (mar′ ij) *n.* a legal commitment to live as man and wife

mar·ry (mar′ ē) *vb.* **mar·ried**; **mar·ry·ing** **1.** to take as husband or wife **2.** to join in wedlock

marsh (märsh) *n.* a soft, wetland area overgrown with grasses and sedge

mar·vel·ous (mär′ və ləs) *adj.* causing wonder and admiration (a *marvelous* performance)

mask (mask) *n.* **1.** a cover for the face, as a disguise (Halloween *mask*) **2.** a protection for the face (a catcher's *mask*) —*vb.* conceal

mass (mas) *n.* **1.** an amount of matter of no definite shape or size but of some bulk (a *mass* of ice) **2.** a large number (a *mass* of sunbathers) —*vb.* to gather into a mass

mas·sive (mas′ iv) *adj.* large, heavy, and bulky

mast (mast) *n.* a tall pole on a sailboat that supports the sails and rigging

mas·ter (mas′ tər) *n.* **1.** an artist of great skill **2.** a male teacher **3.** one having authority —*vb.* **1.** to rule or direct **2.** to control or subdue

mat (mat) *n.* **1.** a heavy, coarse fabric used as a floor covering or at a door to wipe one's shoes on **2.** a piece of material to use under one place setting of dishes at the table (a place *mat*) **3.** a thick pad or cushion used on the floor for tumbling or wrestling —*vb.* **mat·ted**; **mat·ting** to crush or tangle fibers together with pressure or wear

match (mach) *n.* **1.** one person or thing that resembles another (They make a good *match.*) **2.** a contest held between two parties or teams (a golf *match*) **3.** an object for lighting a fire that is chemically treated to light when scratched —*vb.* to choose something that goes with another (*match* her dress)

mate (māt) *n.* **1.** either member of a married couple **2.** one of a pair (the *mate* to this shoe) —*vb.* **mat·ed**; **mat·ing** to marry

ma·te·ri·al (mə tir′ ē əl) *adj.* **1.** relating to matter or substance (A car is a *material* thing.) **2.** having to do with physical as opposed to spiritual needs —*n.* **1.** the stuff from which something is made **2.** objects related to a task (gather *material* for the report)

mat·ter (mat′ ər) *n.* **1.** something that occupies space in the form of a solid, liquid, or gas **2.** something to be dealt with —*vb.* to make a difference (It does not *matter.*)

mat·tress (mat′ rəs) *n.* the top layer of a bed, covering the spring or box spring and forming a flexible support for the sleeper

ma·ture (mə tür′) *adj.* **1.** to be fully grown physically or mentally (*mature* person) **2.** ripe (*mature* fruit) —*vb.* **ma·tured**; **ma·tur·ing** to bring to full growth

ma·tu·ri·ty (mə tür′ ət ē) full growth

max·i·mum (mak′ sə məm) *n., pl.* **max·i·mums** or **max·i·ma** (-sə mə) the largest size or amount (The boy has reached *maximum* growth.) —*adj.* the greatest possible

may (mā) *helping verb, past* **might** (mīt); *pres. sing.* and *pl.* **may** **1.** to have permission (They *may* come tomorrow.) **2.** to be somewhat likely (That *may* be correct.) **3.** to wish or pray (*May* you have a safe journey.)

may·be (mā′ bē) *adv.* perhaps

may·or (mā′ ər) *n.* the chief elected official of a city or town

me (mē) *pron.* objective case of I

mead·ow (med′ ō) *n.* a grassland used as a pasture or hayfield

meal (mēl) *n.* **1.** all the food prepared to be eaten for breakfast, lunch, or dinner **2.** the act of eating —*n.* coarsely ground corn or other seed (corn *meal*)

mean (mēn) *adj.* **1.** ordinary or humble (*mean* surroundings) **2.** stingy, nasty, malicious, or humiliating (a *mean* disposition) —*vb.* **meant** (ment); **mean·ing** (mē′ ning) **1.** to intend (I *mean* to go.) **2.** to denote (What does this word *mean*?) —*n.* **1.** the average (a *mean* score) **2.** method (use every *means* to get it) **3.** wealth (people of *means*)

mean·ing (mē′ ning) *n.* the intention or purpose

mean·while (mēn′ hwīl′) *n.* meantime, or the time between two events —*adv.* during the time between two events

mea·sles (mē′ zəlz) *n., sing.* or *pl.* an acute, contagious disease marked by fever and a red rash

mea·sure (mezh′ ər) *n.* **1.** the means of determining the dimensions of something **2.** the amount, extent, capacity, or degree of something **3.** a system of measuring (linear *measure*) —*vb.* **mea·sured**; **mea·sur·ing** to find the dimensions based on an accepted standard or system of measuring

mea·sure·ment (mezh′ ər mənt) *n.* the act of measuring

meat (mēt) *n.* **1.** animal tissue prepared for food (buying chicken as the *meat* for dinner) **2.** the edible part of food (nut *meats*)

me·chan·ic (mi kan′ ik) *n.* a person who works with his or her hands making repairs on machines

med·al (med′ l) *n.* an award made of metal, stamped with a design and message, and given to commemorate a special achievement or event

med·i·cal (med′ i kəl) *adj.* relating to the science or practice of medicine (*medical* history)

med·i·cine (med′ ə sən) *n.* **1.** a substance used in treating illness **2.** the science or art of treating disease and of restoring or maintaining health

me·di·e·val (mēd′ ē ē′ vəl) *adj.* relating to the Middle Ages

me·di·um (mēd′ ē əm) *n., pl.* **me·di·ums** or **me·di·a** (-ē ə) **1.** the middle condition, or the mean **2.** the means (This currency is the *medium* of exchange.)

meet (mēt) *vb.* **met** (met); **meet·ing** **1.** to encounter or to notice in passing **2.** to go to a place where a person will be by appointment (*meet* at the library) **3.** to be introduced to some new people (to *meet* new friends) **4.** experience (*meet* misfortune) —*n.* an event for sports competition (track *meet*)

mel·an·chol·y (mel′ ən käl′ ē) *n.* depression or a gloomy mood

mel·o·dy (mel′ ə dē) *n., pl.* **mel·o·dies** a pleasing series of musical tones

melt (melt) *vb.* **1.** to change from a solid to a liquid (Butter *melts*.) **2.** to grow less (The fog *melt*ed away.)

mem·ber (mem′ bər) *n.* **1.** one part of a person, animal, or plant **2.** one individual in a group

mem·ber·ship (mem′ bər ship′) *n.* the state of being a member, as of a club

mem·brane (mem′ brān′) *n.* a thin, soft, flexible layer of plant or animal tissue

mem·o·ra·ble (mem′ ə rə bəl) *adj.* worth remembering

me·mo·ri·al (mə mōr′ ē əl) *adj.* **1.** preserving the memory of a person or thing **2.** something intended to keep the memory of a person or event alive (the Jefferson *Memorial*)

mem·o·rize (mem′ ə rīz′) *vb.* **mem·o·rized**; **mem·o·riz·ing** to learn by heart

mem·o·ry (mem′ ə rē) *n., pl.* **mem·o·ries** **1.** the act or process of remembering **2.** the store of all the ideas and experiences learned and retained (Tell it all from *memory.*)

mend (mend) *vb.* **1.** improve or correct (*mend* your ways) **2.** restore (*mend* clothes) —*n.* **1.** the process of improving **2.** a place that is mended

men·tal (ment′ l) *adj.* **1.** relating to the mind **2.** carried on in the mind **3.** having a disorder of the mind (a *mental* problem)

men·tion (men′ chən) *n.* a quick passing remark about something (He did make *mention* of it.) —*vb.* to refer to or speak about briefly in passing

men·u (men′ yü) *n.* a list of dishes that can be served at a meal and from which the customer chooses

mer·chant (mər′ chənt) *n.* a person who carries on a large business as a trader or storekeeper

mer·cu·ry (mər′ kyə rē) *n., pl.* **mer·cu·ries** **1.** a heavy, silver-white metallic element that is liquid at ordinary temperatures and is sometimes called *quicksilver* **2.** the silver column of liquid in a mercury thermometer or barometer **Mer·cu·ry** *n.* the smallest planet in the solar system and the closest to the sun

mer·cy (mər′ sē) *n., pl.* **mer·cies** sympathetic treatment or gentle forbearance shown toward someone who is an offender, opponent, or object of some misfortune (The judge showed *mercy* in giving the man a light sentence.)

mere (miər) *adj., superlative* **mer·est** nothing more than (a *mere* taste of sweetness)

me·rid·i·an (mə rid′ ē ən) *n.* an imaginary line on the earth reaching from the North Pole to the South Pole and numbered according to the number of degrees east or west of the 0° meridian which passes through Greenwich, England (The *meridian* passing through Pittsburgh, Pennsylvania is located at 80° west longitude.)

mer·it (mer′ ət) *n.* **1.** the state of deserving recognition, usually good **2.** an act of worth or excellence that entitles one to a reward or sign of approval (The plan had *merit.*)

mer·ry (mer′ ē) *adj.* **mer·ri·er**; **mer·ri·est** full of joy and good spirit (We wish you a *merry* holiday.)

mess (mes) *n.* **1.** a dirty or littered condition **2.** a state of confusion **3.** the meal eaten by an organized group such as military personnel who eat together regularly (The soldiers went to *mess* in the mess hall.) —*vb.* **1.** to litter or make dirty (*mess* the place up) **2.** to make things confused (*mess* up the plan) **3.** to take meals at a mess

mes·sage (mes′ ij) *n.* a communication

met·al (met′ l) *n.* an element that, with the exception of mercury, is solid at ordinary temperatures, conducts heat and electricity to a greater or lesser extent, often has a luster, and can usually be hammered into a sheet or formed into wire (Copper is the best conductor of electricity of the common *metals.*)

me·tal·lic (mə tal′ ik) *adj.* **1.** related to metal **2.** containing metal (bookends with a *metallic* luster)

me·te·or (mēt′ ē ər) *n.* **1.** a small particle in space that begins to burn when it enters the earth's atmosphere, and which rarely hits the earth (A *meteor* that falls to earth is known as a meteorite.) **2.** a "shooting star"

me·ter (mēṭ′ ər) *n.* **1.** a pattern or rhythm in poetry (The *meter* of this poem is iambic tetrameter.) **2.** in the metric system of measure, a length equal to 39.37 inches **3.** an instrument for measuring a substance that passes through it (water *meter*)

meth·od (meth′ əd) *n.* **1.** an orderly way of doing something (a *method* for teaching spelling) **2.** an orderly arrangement

met·ric (met′ rik) *adj.* relating to the metric system in particular or to measurement in general

met·ro·pol·i·tan (met′ rə päl′ ət n) *adj.* relating to a metropolis or large city (*metropolitan* police)

mi·crobe (mī′ krōb′) *n.* a microscopic plant or animal, especially one that causes disease such as a germ

mi·cro·phone (mī′ krə fōn′) *n.* an instrument that can convert sound waves into an electrical current for the purpose of sending it to a receiver or recording it

mi·cro·scope (mī′ krə skōp′) *n.* an instrument with a lens used in making very small objects appear large for detailed study

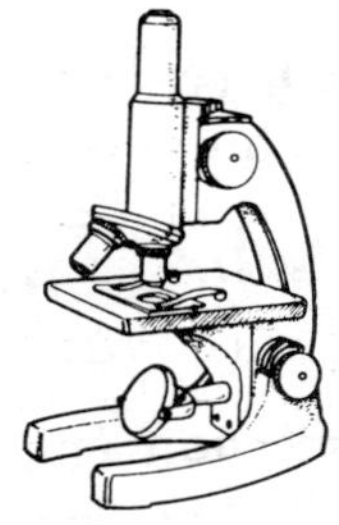

Microscope

mid·day (mid′ dā′) *n.* noon

mid·dle (mid′ l) *adj.* **1.** equally distant from the ends or outer limits **2.** in size, halfway between small and large

mid·night (mid′ nīt′) *n.* **1.** the middle of the night **2.** twelve o'clock at night

mid·way (mid′ wā′) *adv.* halfway between the beginning and the end

might (mīt) *vb. past* of MAY—used as a helping verb to express remote possibility (She *might* come, but I doubt it.) —*n.* power to do something (He hurled the baseball with all his *might.*)

mi·grate (mī′ grāt′) *vb.* **mi·grat·ed**; **mi·grat·ing** **1.** to leave one country in order to go to live in another (They *migrated* from Portugal to the United States.) **2.** to travel on a regular schedule from one region to another (Birds *migrate* to the north in the spring.)

mild (mīld) *adj.* **1.** gentle to others **2.** weak (a *mild* reaction to the shot)

mile (mīl) *n.* **1.** a measure of distance on land (One statute *mile* equals 5,280 feet.) **2.** a measure of distance at sea (A nautical *mile* equals about 6,076 feet.)

mil·i·tar·y (mil′ ə ter′ ē) *adj.* relating to soldiers, the army, or war (a *military* uniform) —*n., pl.* members of the armed forces

milk (milk) *n.* **1.** a white liquid secreted by the breasts or udder of a female mammal for feeding her young **2.** a liquid resembling milk secreted by certain plants such as milkweed —*vb.* to draw the milk (to *milk* a cow)

mill (mil) *n.* **1.** a building containing the machinery and equipment to perform manufacturing operations (a steel *mill*) **2.** a machine for crushing or grinding (a coffee *mill*) —*vb.* to wander around in a mass (The crowd was *mill*ing around.)

mil·lion (mil′ yən) *n.* a very large number (*millions* of fleas) —*adj.* 1,000,000

mind (mīnd) *n.* **1.** the part of a human being that senses, reasons, wills, and remembers (the processes of the *mind*) **2.** a way of thinking (change his *mind*) **3.** memory (He called to *mind* an earlier visit.) —*vb.* **1.** to obey (*mind* your parents) **2.** to be careful or concerned (*mind* what you're doing)

mine (mīn) *pron.* the one or ones belonging to me (The pencils are *mine.*) —*n.* **1.** a shaft and tunnels in the earth from which minerals are taken **2.** an explosive buried in the ground to hinder the enemy **3.** an explosive placed in a body of water to sink enemy ships —*vb.* **mined**; **min·ing** **1.** to get minerals from a mine **2.** to lay military mines (*mine* the harbor)

min·er·al (min′ ə rəl) *n.* **1.** an inorganic substance that is neither animal nor vegetable and that contains no carbon **2.** a usually crystalline substance —*adj.* relating to a mineral (*mineral* oil)

min·gle (ming′ gəl) *vb.* **min·gled**; **min·gling** to come together as a group (to *mingle* with the guests)

min·i·a·ture (min′ ē ə chür′) *n.* a very small copy of something —*adj.* very small (*miniature* chocolates)

min·i·mum (min′ ə məm) *n., pl.* **min·i·mums** or **min·i·ma** (-mə) the least possible amount —*adj.* lowest or least possible (*minimum* size)

min·is·ter (min′ əs tər) *n.* **1.** a person authorized to conduct religious services as a clergyman or pastor **2.** a person who represents the government in a foreign country (a foreign *minister*) —*vb.* to give service or attend to wants and needs (*minister* to the needy)

mi·nor (mī′ nər) *adj.* less in extent or importance (a *minor* mishap) —*n.* **1.** a person under the legal age **2.** an area of study in which fewer credits than required in a major are taken

mi·nor·i·ty (mə nȯr′ ət ē) *n., pl.* **mi·nor·i·ties** fewer than one-half of the total number (Women legislators are in the *minority.*)

mint (mint) *n.* **1.** a place where coins are made (visiting the *mint* in Philadelphia) **2.** a plant of the mint family with a tangy taste and smell used in the making of confections such as peppermints

mi·nus (mī′ nəs) *prep.* **1.** decreased by (eight *minus* three) **2.** lacking (the belt *minus* its buckle) —*adj.* having a negative quality (a grade of B *minus*)

min·ute (min′ ət) *n.* **1.** sixty seconds or one-sixtieth part of an hour **2.** a brief period of time (Just a *minute*!) —*adj.* **mi·nute** (mī nüt′) **mi·nut·er; mi·nut·est** very small (every *minute* detail)

mir·a·cle (mir′ ə kəl) *n.* **1.** an event which seems to go beyond what can be done by human or natural law **2.** something rare that is judged to be the work of God **3.** a wonderful example of something (The microwave oven is a *miracle* of technology.)

mir·ror (mir′ ər) *n.* **1.** a piece of glass with a silvery backing that reflects images **2.** something that reflects like a mirror —*vb.* to reflect

mis·chief (mis′ chəf) *n.* **1.** damage done by one or more persons intending to tease or irritate **2.** behavior that causes trouble

mis·er·a·ble (miz′ ə rə bəl) *adj.* terribly unhappy or uncomfortable

mis·er·y (miz′ ə rē) *n.*, *pl.* **mis·er·ies** unhappiness

mis·for·tune (mis fôr′ chən) *n.* bad luck

miss (mis) *vb.* **1.** to fail to do something (*miss* the bus) **2.** to feel the absence or loss of (*miss* her friend) —*n.* a title for an unmarried woman (*Miss* Jones)

mis·sile (mis′ əl) *n.* an object or weapon that can be thrown or shot

mis·sion (mish′ ən) *n.* **1.** a place where missionaries work **2.** a group of persons sent out to complete a special task

mis·sion·ar·y (mish′ ə ner′ ē) *adj.* relating to a mission —*n.* a person sent out by a church to spread a religious faith

mis·spell (mis spel′) *vb.* to spell incorrectly

mist (mist) *n.* particles of moisture in the air falling like fine rain or drizzle —*vb.* to become misty

mis·take (mə stāk′) *vb.* **mis·took** (mə stůk′); **mis·tak·en** (mə stā′ kən); **mis·tak·ing** **1.** to misunderstand (to *mistake* his intentions) **2.** to fail to identify correctly (*mistook* him for his brother) —*n.* an error

mis·tress (mis′ trəs) *n.* the female head of a household

mit·ten (mit′ n) *n.* a warm covering for the hand with no separation for the four fingers, but only the thumb

mix (miks) *vb.* to stir different ingredients together

mix·ture (miks′ chər) *n.* **1.** the act of mixing **2.** the substance mixed

moan (mōn) *n.* a low wailing sound as if in pain or grief —*vb.* to utter a grieving sound

mo·bile (mō′ bəl) *adj.* capable of moving or being moved easily (*mobile* home)

moc·ca·sin (mäk′ ə sən) *n.* **1.** a heelless shoe made of soft leather such as deerskin in a style similar to that worn by the American Indian **2.** a shoe of similar style to the true moccasin **3.** a poisonous snake

mode (mōd) *n.* **1.** a style **2.** a way of doing something **3.** the score achieved by the largest number of students

mod·el (mäd′ l) *n.* **1.** a finished example of something to serve as a guide for making others **2.** an exact copy of something in miniature size **3.** a person who poses for an artist

mod·er·ate (mäd′ ə rət) *adj.* reasonable, ordinary, near the middle on any scale such as temperature or behavior —*vb.* (mäd′ ə rāt′); **mod·er·at·ed**; **mod·er·at·ing** to make less severe or extreme (*moderate* your voices)

mod·ern (mäd′ ərn) *adj.* relating to the present time and current technology

mod·est (mäd′ əst) *adj.* **1.** showing humility about one's merits **2.** showing moderation in thought, dress, and actions

mod·i·fy (mäd′ ə fī′) *vb.* **mod·i·fied**; **mod·i·fy·ing** **1.** to change something by bringing it closer to a moderate position **2.** to qualify something by the use of descriptive words

moist (mȯist) *adj.* damp

mois·ture (mȯis′ chər) *n.* **1.** dampness **2.** a small quantity of liquid, enough to make something moist

mo·las·ses (mə las′ əz) *n.* a thick, dark syrup produced when refining sugar

mold (mōld) *n.* **1.** a hollow form used to give shape to something (a gelatin *mold*) **2.** a fungus growth on decaying matter —*vb.* **1.** to press or pour into a shape (*mold* pottery) **2.** to become moldy

mole (mōl) *n.* **1.** a birthmark on the human skin that is usually brown and sometimes raised and hairy **2.** a small burrowing animal with strong forefeet, velvety fur, and very small eyes

Mole

mol·e·cule (mäl′ i kyül′) *n.* the smallest possible piece of an element that retains its characteristics

mol·ten (mōlt′ n) *adj.* melted by high heat (He poured *molten* metal into a mold.)

mo·ment (mō′ mənt) *n.* **1.** a brief period of time, such as an instant (Please stop a *moment.*) **2.** importance (a concern of some *moment*)

mo·men·tum (mō ment′ əm) *n.* the force of a moving body due to its weight and speed (The *momentum* is equal to the weight of the moving body times its speed.)

mon·arch (män′ ərk) *n.* **1.** a lifetime ruler of a kingdom or empire **2.** a large orange and black butterfly

Monarch

mon·ey (mən′ ē) *n., pl.* **mon·ies** (mən′ ēz) coins or paper money issued for buying and selling in a particular country (United States *money*)

mon·key (məng′ kē) *n., pl.* **mon·keys** **1.** one of the primates excluding man, especially one of the longer-tailed forms as distinguished from apes **2.** a child filled with mischief —*vb.* **mon·keyed**; **mon·key·ing** to fool with

mon·ster (män′ stər) *n.* **1.** a fictitious storybook animal that frightens people **2.** a wicked and cruel person

month (mənth) *n.* one-twelfth of a year

mon·u·ment (män′ yə mənt) *n.* a statue, stone, building, or other object erected in the memory of some person or event

mood (müd) *n.* **1.** a feeling or state of mind **2.** forms of the verb that give added meaning to the sentence

moon (mün) *n.* a satellite of a planet that shines by the sun's reflected light —*vb.* to behave in a dreamy way

moon·light (mün′ līt′) *n.* the light of the moon

moose (müs) *n.* a large animal of the deer family, the male of which has huge flattened antlers

Moose

mor·al (mȯr′ əl) *n.* the lesson to be learned from a fable or an experience —*adj.* concerned with good behavior and the distinction between right and wrong

more (mōr) *adj.* in greater quantity or degree (*more* work than we had yesterday) —*adv.* **1.** in addition **2.** to a greater degree (*more* excited)

more·o·ver (mōr ō′ vər) *adv.* **1.** further **2.** besides

morn·ing (mȯr′ ning) *n.* the first half of the day, sunrise to noon

mor·pheme (mȯr′ fēm′) *n.* the smallest meaningful unit in a word

mor·tal (mȯrt′ l) *adj.* **1.** capable of causing death (in *mortal* danger) **2.** deadly (in a *mortal* struggle) —*n.* a human being (these *mortals*)

mor·tar (mȯrt′ ər) *n.* a small, heavy bowl in which herbs, seeds, and other substances may be ground with a pestle by pounding and rubbing —*n.* a building material that is spread between bricks and stones to hold them together

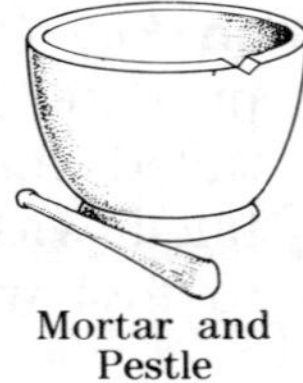
Mortar and Pestle

mos·qui·to (məs kēt′ ō) *n., pl.* **mos·qui·toes** an insect, the female of which sucks blood, and, in certain species, transmits diseases such as malaria

moss (mȯs) *n.* a leafless plant that often grows in velvety patches on damp rocks, bark, or ground

most (mōst) *adj.* **1.** the majority (*most* farmers) **2.** the greatest (the *most* success) —*adv.* to the greatest degree (*most* careful)

mo·tel (mō tel′) *n.* a building similar in use to a hotel, but in which each room has an entrance from the outside with a nearby parking area provided

moth (mȯth) *n., pl.* **moths** (mȯ<u>th</u>z, mȯths) a night-flying insect with duller coloring than the butterfly and feathery antennae

moth·er (mə<u>th</u>′ ər) *n.* a female parent —*adj.* having to do with a mother (a *mother* hen) —*vb.* to act as a mother (*mother*ed her sister's children)

mo·tion (mō′ shən) *n.* **1.** the act of moving **2.** a proposal of action made before a formal assembly (a *motion* to accept the report as read)

mo·tive (mōt′ iv) *n.* something that moves a person to take an action (His *motive* was to be helpful.) —*adj.* pertaining to motion

mo·tor (mōt′ ər) *n.* a small engine that changes electrical energy into motion or power to do work —*adj.* causing motion —*vb.* to travel by automobile (to *motor* through the mountains)

mound (maůnd) *n.* a small hill or pile of dirt such as the raised ground for the pitcher's mound in baseball

mount (maůnt) *n.* a high hill or mountain (*Mount* McKinley) —*vb.* **1.** climb (*mount* the stairs) **2.** to prepare a chart, graph, or other visual for display by putting it on a firm backing (*mount*ed on poster board)

moun·tain (maůnt′ n) *n.* a mass of earth that rises much higher than a hill

mourn·ful (mōrn′ fəl) *adj.* showing or feeling sorrow or grief

mouse (maůs) *n., pl.* **mice** (mis) a small furry, gnawing rodent, smaller than a rat, to which it is related

mouth (maůth) *n., pl.* **mouths** (maůt͟hz, maůths) the opening through which a person or animal takes food and makes sounds for expression and communication

move (müv) *vb.* **moved**; **mov·ing** to change from one position to another or pass from one place to another

mov·ie (mü′ vē) *n.* motion picture

mow (maů) *n.* a place in a barn where hay is stored (hay (*mow*) —*vb.* (mō) **mowed**; **mowed** or **mown** (mōn); **mow·ing** **1.** to cut grass with a mower or a scythe **2.** to cut down in large numbers (*Mow* down the enemy.)

much (məch) *adj.* **more** (mōr); **most** (mōst) great in amount or extent —*adv.* more, most (*much* sooner) —*n.* a great quantity or degree (gave them *much*)

mud (məd) *n.* **1.** a slimy, sticky mixture of solid material and water **2.** wet dirt

muf·fle (məf′ əl) *vb.* **muf·fled**; **muf·fling** **1.** to wrap closely in a coat or shawl to protect the head and neck from the cold **2.** to put a thick layer of material over something noisy to deaden the sound

mule (myül) *n.* an animal that is a cross between a horse and a donkey

mul·ti·pli·ca·tion (məl′ tə plə kā′ shən) *n.* **1.** the process of multiplying **2.** a short way of adding one number to itself the number of times indicated by another number

mul·ti·ply (məl′ tə plī′) *vb.* **1.** to become larger in number **2.** to use multiplication to find the product of two numbers

mul·ti·tude (məl′ tə tüd) *n.* a large number of persons or things

mum·ble (məm′ bəl) *vb.* **mum·bled**; **mum·bling** to run words together so as to be hard to understand

mur·der (mərd′ ər) *n.* the intentional and unlawful killing of a human being —*vb.* to commit murder

mur·mur (mər′ mər) *n.* **1.** a soft, low, indistinct sound that goes on and on, such as the quiet babbling of a brook or the sound of a heart heard through a stethoscope when there is an abnormal flow of blood through the valves **2.** a sound of voices that is low and indistinct —*vb.* to mumble softly

mus·cle (məs′ əl) *n.* tissue of the body made up of long cells that can contract (pull up shorter) when stimulated to produce motion or organ function

mu·se·um (myu̇ zē′ əm) *n.* **1.** a building designed for the display of collections of objects **2.** an institution organized to acquire, display, and care for objects of lasting value and interest as representative of a culture or stage of progress of a civilization

mush·room (məsh′ rüm) *n.* a soft, fleshy part of a fungus that is shaped like a little umbrella, many of which are poisonous

Mushroom

mu·sic (myü′ zik) *n.* **1.** the art and science of combining sounds into a work that includes rhythm, melody, harmony, and color **2.** the written score of a musical composition (three pieces of *music* on the stand)

mu·si·cian (myü zish′ ən) *n.* a person who plays music as a profession

mus·ket (məs′ kət) *n.* a gun formerly carried by infantry soldiers

must (məst) *helping verb* **1.** is obliged or commanded (You *must* come.) **2.** is required by the body (You *must* take in liquids to live.) **3.** is required by law or custom (You *must* obey the traffic signals.)

mus·tache or **mous·tache** (məs′ tash′) *n.* **1.** the hair allowed to grow on a man's upper lip **2.** hair growing around the mouth of an animal

mus·tard (məs′ tərd) *n.* the sharp-smelling and tasting seeds of the mustard plant which are ground into powder and used as a condiment or seasoning

mut·ter (mət′ ər) *vb.* **1.** to talk in a low voice with lips partly closed so as to be hard to hear **2.** to grumble in discontent

mu·tu·al (myü′ chə wəl) *adj.* having something in common or in exchange, each with the other (*mutual* benefits, *mutual* enemies)

muz·zle (məz′ əl) *n.* **1.** the projecting jaws and nose of an animal **2.** a casing made of leather straps to cover the jaws of an animal to prevent biting **3.** the end of a gun that discharges **4.** any implement with a jawlike opening —*vb.* **1.** to put a muzzle on **2.** to restrain freedom to speak

my (mī) *adj.* relating or belonging to me (*my* arm)

mys·ter·y (mis′ tə rē) *n., pl.* **mys·ter·ies** **1.** something not understood or explained (the *mysteries* of space, the *mystery* of his disappearance) **2.** a story that keeps the reader in suspense

myth (mith) *n.* legendary stories handed down from primitive times, often containing references to gods and goddesses, that attempt to explain the creation of the world, the forces of nature, and man's relationship with other human beings and with the supernatural

N

nail (nāl) *n.* **1.** a horny cover protecting the upper end of each finger and toe **2.** a thin, pointed piece of metal driven through materials such as wood to fasten pieces together —*vb.* to fasten with a nail

na·ked (nā′ kəd) *adj.* **1.** without clothing **2.** having no covering

name (nām) *n.* one or more words by which a person or thing is designated (The *name* of this object is "toaster.") —*vb.* **named**; **nam·ing** **1.** to give a name to or call (They call him Ozzie, but his *name* is Oswald.) **2.** mention (*Name* one advantage.)

nap (nap) *vb.* **napped**; **nap·ping** **1.** to sleep briefly **2.** to doze —*n.* **1.** a short sleep especially during the day **2.** a soft, fuzzy surface on material

nap·kin (nap′ kən) *n.* a square of cloth or paper used while eating to protect clothing and wipe the mouth and fingers

nar·ra·tive (nar′ ət iv) *n.* something that is told in the form of a story —*adj.* relating to a narrative

nar·row (nar′ ō) *adj.* **1.** thinner than average **2.** limited in width or scope —*n.* a narrow passage between two bodies of water, usually used in the plural (the *narrows*)

na·tion (nā′ shən) *n.* a large territory under one government with a common language

na·tion·al (nash′ ən l) *adj.* relating to a nation —*n.* a citizen of a nation

na·tive (nāt′ iv) *adj.* **1.** being the place where one was born (*native* land) **2.** having from birth (*native* ability) **3.** grown in the vicinity (*native* corn) —*n.* a person who was born in that place

nat·u·ral (nach′ ə rəl) *adj.* **1.** born with the tendency (a *natural* teacher) **2.** produced by nature (*natural* wonders)

nat·u·ral·ist (nach′ ə rə ləst) *n.* a person who shows interest in and studies about plants and animals, often finding work in a national park or forest preserve

na·ture (nā′ chər) *n.* **1.** the individual character of a person or thing (a woman's *nature*) **2.** a person's natural disposition (his *nature*) **3.** the physical universe (the laws of *nature*)

nau·ti·cal (nȯt′ i kəl) *adj.* relating to sailors, ships, or things of the sea

na·val (nā′ vəl) *adj.* of or relating to a navy or its ships (*naval* warship)

nav·i·ga·tion (nav′ ə gā′ shən) *n.* the science of planning and directing the route of a ship or airplane

na·vy (nā′ vē) *n., pl.* **na·vies** **1.** the total naval establishment of a country including personnel, ships, port facilities, and support functions **2.** a dark blue color

near (niər) *adv.* close or within a short distance —*prep.* close to —*adj.* **1.** closely related (a *near* relative) **2.** being closer (the *near* end of the street) —*vb.* to come near (as we *near* the site of the disaster)

near·by (niər bī′) *adv.* or *adj.* not far away

neat (nēt) *adj.* clean, tidy, in good taste

nec·es·sar·y (nes′ ə ser′ ē) *adj.* being absolutely required —*n., pl.* **nec·es·sar·ies** something that is required

neck (nek) *n.* **1.** the narrow part connecting the head to the shoulders **2.** something like a neck in shape (the *neck* of the jug)

neck·lace (nek′ ləs) *n.* a string of beads or other objects worn about the neck

nec·tar (nek′ tər) *n.* **1.** a sweet liquid which bees take from plants in order to make honey **2.** in mythology, the drink of the Greek and Roman gods

need (nēd) *n.* **1.** something one should do (the *need* to do one's homework) **2.** the lack of something necessary (a family in *need*)

nee·dle (nēd′ l) *n.* **1.** a very thin, pointed steel rod used in sewing or knitting **2.** a pointer on a dial **3.** a thin tube for giving shots of medication

neg·a·tive (neg′ ət iv) *adj.* **1.** making a denial or refusal (She made a *negative* response.) **2.** less than zero (a *negative* number) **3.** relating to the electron in electricity (a *negative* charge) —*n.* a refusal (answered in the *negative*)

ne·glect (ni glekt′) *vb.* to give little attention or respect to something —*n.* **1.** an instance of failure to pay attention to something **2.** the condition caused by neglect

neigh·bor (nā′ bər) *n.* one living close by another —*vb.* to be near to or border on

nei·ther (nē′ t͟hər, nī′ t͟hər) *n.* not one of them —*conj.* **1.** not either (*neither* hard nor soft) **2.** nor (*neither* did he) —*adj.* not either

nerve (nərv) *n.* **1.** a strand of nerve fiber that joins the brain to a part of the body and carries nerve impulses enabling it to function **2.** control (*nerves* of steel) **3.** gall (the *nerve* to be so impudent)

ner·vous (nər′ vəs) *adj.* **1.** relating to a nerve (*nervous* tissue) **2.** relating to the system of nerves (*nervous* system) **3.** shy or fearful (*nervous* reaction)

nest (nest) *n.* **1.** a place prepared by a bird to lay its eggs **2.** a snug home or apartment —*vb.* **1.** to build a nest **2.** to fit one in the other (*nest*ed the boxes)

net (net) *n.* **1.** a fabric made in a loose mesh pattern **2.** something for trapping fish or butterflies —*vb.* **1.** to catch, as in a net **2.** to gain as profit after costs are subtracted —*adj.* free from charges (*net* profit)

net·work (net′ wərk′) *n.* a group of connected people or stations that work together for improved communication or other function (the television *network*)

neu·tral (nü′ trəl) *adj.* **1.** not favoring or taking either side **2.** having a soft basic coloration, such as gray or beige —*n.* **1.** a person who is neutral on an issue **2.** the condition in which the gears in the transmission of an engine are not in contact, preventing movement

neu·tron (nü′ trän′) *n.* an uncharged particle that has a mass slightly greater than that of a proton and which is present in all atomic nuclei except that of the hydrogen atom

nev·er (nev′ ər) *adv.* **1.** not ever **2.** not in any way

nev·er·the·less (nev′ ər t͟hə les′) *adv.* **1.** however **2.** in spite of that

new (nü) *adj.* **1.** recent or modern (*new* ideas) **2.** different from the former (*new* job) **3.** recently discovered or enrolled —*adv.* newly

new·born (nü′ bȯrn′) *adj.* recently born or renewed (*newborn* effort)

new·com·er (nü′ kəm′ ər) *n.* a new arrival (The *newcomer* arrived yesterday.)

news·pa·per (nüz′ pā pər) *n.* a paper usually containing news, articles, features, and advertising that is published regularly

next (nekst) *adj.* the one on either side —*adv.* the one to follow that is nearest in time, place, or order

nib·ble (nib′ əl) *vb.* **nib·bled**; **nib·bling** to take gently in tiny bites —*n.* an act of nibbling

nice (nīs) *adj.* having good manners and a pleasant attitude

nick·el (nik′ əl) *n.* a hard, workable, metallic element, silver-white in color, resistant to corrosion, taking a high polish and used, in combination with copper, in the U.S. five-cent coin

nick·name (nik′ nām′) *n.* a familiar form of a name used mainly by friends and acquaintances (Dwight D. Eisenhower's *nickname* was Ike.)

night (nīt) *n.* the period from dusk to dawn when no natural light can be seen

night·fall (nīt′ fȯl′) *n.* the coming of night with the disappearance of the last rays of the sun

ni·tro·gen (nī′ trə jən) *n.* a colorless, odorless, gaseous element that makes up seventy-eight percent of the atmosphere by volume and is present in combined form in all animal and vegetable tissue, especially in proteins

no (nō) *adv.* **1.** not any (*no* sweeter) **2.** not so (*No,* I'm not tired.) —*adj.* **1.** not any (have *no* money) **2.** hardly any (with *no* effort) **3.** not a (He's *no* singer.)

no·bil·i·ty (nō bil′ ət ē) *n., pl.* **no·bil·i·ties** the quality or state of being noble

no·ble (nō′ bəl) *adj.* **no·bler**; **no·blest** **1.** famous **2.** of high birth or rank —*n.* a person of noble birth or rank (The *noble*s entered.)

no·bod·y (nō′ bäd′ ē) *pron.* no person

nod (näd) *vb.* **nod·ded**; **nod·ding** **1.** to dip the head forward quickly as a greeting or a sign of agreement **2.** to bend up and down (The children's heads *nodded* as they grew weary.) —*n.* the act of nodding

noise (noiz) *n.* a loud sound that is unexpected or interferes with present activities —*vb.* **noised**; **nois·ing** to spread a rumor

nois·y (nȯi′ zē) *adj.* **nois·i·er**; **nois·i·est** full of noises (a *noisy* crowd in the bleachers)

no·mad (nō′ mad′) *n.* **1.** one of a group that has no regular home but wanders from place to place, often caring for a herd of animals **2.** one living like a nomad —*adj.* wandering, nomadic

nom·i·nate (näm′ ə nāt′) *vb.* **nom·i·nat·ed; nom·i·nat·ing** to choose as a candidate

none (nən) *pron.* **1.** not one **2.** not any —*adv.* **1.** not at all (*none* too early) **2.** by no means

non·sense (nän′ sens′) *n.* something lacking in sense such as foolish actions or words

noon (nün) *n.* twelve o'clock in the daytime

nor (nər, nȯr) *conj.* and not; used in negative phrases after neither (neither food *nor* drink)

nor·mal (nȯr′ məl) *adj.* **1.** regular, average, or usual **2.** mentally of average intelligence and sane —*n.* one that is normal or average

north (nȯrth) *adv.* to or toward the north (The nomads traveled *north.*) —*adj.* positioned near or coming from the north (*north* wind) —*n.* regions north of a stated point (the *North*)

north·east (nȯrth ēst′) *adv.* to or toward the northeast —*n.* **1.** the direction between north and east **2.** the regions north and east of a stated point (the *North*east) —*adj.* situated toward or coming from the northeast

north·ern (nȯr′ th̲ərn) *adj.* lying toward or coming from the north (the *northern* island)

north·ward (nȯrth′ wərd) *adv.* or *adj.* toward the north —*n.* a northern direction, part, or point

north·west (nȯrth west′) *adv.* to or toward the northwest —*n.* **1.** the direction between north and west **2.** regions northwest of a specified point (traveled to the *North*west)

north·west·ern (nȯrth wes′ tərn) *adj.* **1.** relating to the northwest **2.** lying toward or coming from the northwest

nose (nōz) *n.* **1.** the part of the face that contains the nostrils for breathing or smelling **2.** a part of an object that looks like a nose (the *nose* of the airplane)

nos·tril (näs′ trəl) *n.* either of the openings at the end of the nose through which one breathes

not (nät) *adv.* used to express a negative (They are *not* here.), a denial (That's *not* what I did.), or a refusal (I will *not* do that.)

no·ta·tion (nō tā′ shən) *n.* **1.** the act of writing down a brief note or notes **2.** a system of notes for specific usage (mathematical *notation*)

notch (näch) *n.* **1.** a V-shaped cut or indentation **2.** a narrow gap between mountains (Franconia *Notch*) —*vb.* to cut a notch in

note (nōt) *vb.* **not·ed**; **not·ing** **1.** to notice carefully **2.** to write notes **3.** to remark —*n.* **1.** a musical sound or the symbol for that sound **2.** a short letter **3.** a memorandum

note·book (nōt′ bu̇k′) *n.* a cover containing paper, usually ruled, for writing notes

noth·ing (nəth′ ing) *pron.* **1.** not anything (They have *nothing.*) **2.** one of no interest or value (She's *nothing* to me.) —*adv.* not at all (It was *nothing* like that.)

no·tice (nōt′ əs) *n.* **1.** an announcement or notification **2.** attention (brought to my *notice*) —*vb.* **no·ticed**; **no·tic·ing** to observe or make mention of (He *noticed* a deer in the field.)

no·tion (nō′ shən) *n.* **1.** idea or opinion **2.** small articles such as buttons or thread

noun (nau̇n) *n.* a word that names a person, place, or thing

nov·el (näv′ əl) *adj.* new, different, or striking in appearance —*n.* a book containing a story that is usually fictitious

now (naů) *adv.* **1.** at the present or within a few minutes of the present (I will go *now.*) **2.** sometimes (The children are coming to visit, first one and *now* another.) —*conj.* since —*n.* the present time —*adj.* relating to the present

now·a·days (naů′ ə dāz′) *adv.* of or at the present time (Things are different *nowadays.*)

no·where (nō′ hweər) *adv.* **1.** not in or at any place **2.** to no place (They said they are going *nowhere.*) —*n.* a place that does not exist (a trip to *nowhere*)

nu·cle·ar (nü′ klē ər) *adj.* **1.** relating to the nucleus of a cell **2.** relating to atomic energy or atomic weapons (*nuclear* energy; *nuclear* warfare)

nu·cle·us (nü′ klē əs) *n., pl.* **nu·cle·i** (-klē ī) **1.** the central part of a cell containing chromosomes and genes essential to vital functions and heredity **2.** the central part of an atom consisting of protons and neutrons, with the exception of hydrogen which has only one proton and no neutrons

nudge (nəj) *vb.* **nudged**; **nudg·ing** to poke gently to attract attention —*n.* a slight poke or touch

nui·sance (nüs′ ns) *n.* an annoying pest or unpleasant person

numb (nəm) *adj.* **1.** having no feeling or sensation (He complained of *numb* fingers.) **2.** showing no signs of emotion —*vb.* to make or become numb

num·ber (nəm′ bər) *n.* **1.** the total amount **2.** numeral (the *number* 7) **3.** many (a *number* of phone calls) —*vb.* **1.** to list the numerals (*Number* your paper.) **2.** to include (were *number*ed among the winners)

nu·mer·al (nü′ mə rəl) *n.* a symbol or symbols representing a number

nu·mer·a·tor (nü′ mə rāt′ ər) *n.* the part of the fraction that is above the line (Four is the *numerator* of the fraction 4/5.)

nu·mer·ous (nü′ mə rəs) *adj.* relating to a large number (*numerous* trips)

nurse (nərs) *n.* a person who is trained to care for the sick —*vb.* **nursed**; **nurs·ing** **1.** to feed at the breast **2.** to care for the sick

nurs·er·y (nər′ sə rē) *n., pl.* **nurs·er·ies** **1.** a room furnished for the needs of small children **2.** a place where young trees and plants are raised and sold

nut (nət) *n.* **1.** a dry fruit or seed with a firm edible kernel enclosed in a woody or leathery shell (Crack the *nut* to get the meat.) **2.** a piece of metal with a hole in it that threads onto a bolt (Tighten the *nut* on the bolt.)

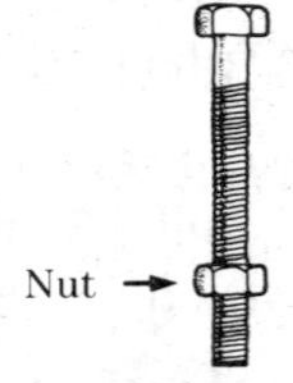

nu·tri·ent (nü′ trē ənt) *n.* a chemical substance in food that makes a specific contribution to the health of the body (Proteins, vitamins, iron, and calcium are examples of *nutrients*.)

ny·lon (nī′ län′) *n.* a man-made material used in carpets, upholstery, yarn, stockings, bristles for brushes, and other articles where strength and durability are important

nymph (nimf) *n.* **1.** an immature insect that is smaller but similar to the adult **2.** in mythology, a minor goddess living in a beautiful, natural setting

O

oak (ōk) *n.* a tree bearing the acorn as fruit, and having hard wood used in furniture and home-building

oar (ōr) *n.* a long, thin, wooden shaft with a broad blade at one end used for rowing or steering a boat

o·a·sis (ō ā′ səs) *n., pl.* **o·a·ses** (-sēz′) a small, fertile green spot in the desert usually having a spring or well for irrigation

oath (ōth) *n. pl.* **oaths** (ōt͟hz) a solemn appeal to God or to some revered person to bear witness to the truth of one's word or to the sacredness of a promise (testified under *oath* to tell the truth)

o·be·di·ence (ō bēd′ ē əns) *n.* the act of obeying

o·bey (ō bā′) *vb.* **o·beyed**; **o·bey·ing** **1.** to act in accordance with another's wishes or commands (*Obey* those in authority.) **2.** to conform to a guiding principle (*Obey* your conscience.)

ob·ject (äb′ jikt) *n.* **1.** something that can be seen or touched (A desk is an *object.*) **2.** something that makes an impression on the mind (They are the *object* of much curiosity.) **3.** the noun or noun equivalent that receives the action of the verb **4.** the noun or the noun equivalent that completes a prepositional phrase —*vb.* (əb jekt′) to oppose something (*object* to the change in schedule)

ob·jec·tive (əb jek′ tiv) *adj.* **1.** existing in the real world **2.** dealing with facts without any personal bias —*n.* an aim or goal

ob·scure (äb skyu̇r′) *adj.* **1.** unclear, difficult to see or understand **2.** remote, far from public notice and worldly affairs —*vb.* **ob·scured**; **ob·scur·ing** to make obscure

ob·ser·va·tion (äb′ sər vā′ shən) *n.* **1.** the act of noticing or watching something **2.** the gathering of information (*observations* of plant growth)

ob·serve (əb zərv′) *vb.* **ob·served**; **ob·serv·ing** **1.** to watch or notice **2.** to watch with close attention so as to learn (*Observe* the procedure.) **3.** to obey (*Observe* the rules.) **4.** to celebrate (*Observe* the holiday.) **5.** to remark (*observed* that it looked like it might rain)

ob·sta·cle (äb′ stə kəl) *n.* something that obstructs progress

ob·tain (əb tān′) *vb.* to get by request or through effort (*obtain* a copy of a rare book)

ob·vi·ous (äb′ vē əs) *adj.* being easy to see or understand

oc·ca·sion (ə kā′ zhən) *n.* **1.** a favorable time or circumstance (on two *occasions*) **2.** a ceremony or celebration (a happy *occasion*)

oc·cu·pant (äk′ yə pənt) *n.* **1.** a person or family group that lives in or occupies **2.** a person who takes possession

oc·cu·pa·tion (äk′ yə pā′ shən) *n.* **1.** one's regular work or business **2.** the possession and control of an area

oc·cu·py (äk′ yə pī′) *vb.* **oc·cu·pied**; **oc·cu·py·ing** **1.** to fill up (*occupy* her time) **2.** to take possession and control (*occupy* the territory)

oc·cur (ə kər′) *vb.* **oc·curred**; **oc·cur·ring** **1.** to happen (A freak storm *occurred.*) **2.** to come to mind (It *occurred* to me.) **3.** appears (Heart disease *occurs* more frequently among men.)

o·cean (ō′ shən) *n.* the vast body of salt water covering nearly three-fourths of the earth's surface

o' clock (ə kläk′) *adv.* according to or on the clock

oc·tave (äk′ tiv) *n.* **1.** a musical interval of eight degrees or steps **2.** the tone on the eighth step from a given tone

oc·to·pus (äk′ tə pəs) *n., pl.* **oc·to·pus·es** or **oc·to·pi** (-pī′) a sea mollusk without a shell having a rounded body and eight arms with suckers for holding on to something such as its prey

odd (äd) *adj.* **1.** different from ordinary (an *odd* story) **2.** without a mate (an *odd* sock) **3.** not divisible by two (an *odd* number) **4.** not regular (*odd* times of the day)

o·dor (ōd′ ər) *n.* a scent, whether agreeable or disagreeable

of (əv) *prep.* **1.** proceeding from (*of* good family) **2.** by reason of (tired *of* hardship) **3.** belonging to (the top *of* the dresser) **4.** by (the television scripts *of* Rod Serling) **5.** made from (a crown *of* gold) **6.** an amount (a pound *of* candy) **7.** containing (a basket *of* apples) **8.** that is (the state *of* Alaska) **9.** about (stories *of* courage) **10.** before (ten minutes *of* two)

off (ȯf) *adv.* **1.** from a place (walked *off*) **2.** so as to be no longer supported or attached (fell *off*) **3.** aside (turned *off* at the exit ramp) **4.** so as to stop or finish (shut *off* the engine, finish it *off*) **5.** away from work (took some time *off*)

of·fend (ə fend′) *vb.* **1.** to insult **2.** to hurt **3.** to cause resentment

of·fense (ə fens′) *n.* **1.** the act of offending **2.** a violation of the law (a criminal *offense*)

of·fen·sive (ə fen′ siv) *adj.* **1.** relating to attack or insult (*offensive* remarks) **2.** causing displeasure (an *offensive* odor) —*n.* the state of one who is making an attack (to take the *offensive*)

of·fer (ȯf′ ər) *vb.* **1.** to present for acceptance or rejection (*Offer* her a peach.) **2.** to suggest (to *offer* an idea) **3.** to make available (He *offer*ed his television set for a good price.)

of·fice (ȯf′ əs) *n.* **1.** a special duty or position (held the *office* of general treasurer) **2.** a place where business is done (the lawyer's *office*) **3.** a place where a service is supplied (Call the housekeeping *office*.)

of·fi·cer (ȯf′ ə sər) *n.* **1.** a person charged with law enforcement (police *officer*) **2.** a person who holds office **3.** one who holds a commission in the armed forces

of·fi·cial (ə fish′ əl) *n.* an officer —*adj.* **1.** relating to an office (*official* reply to your memo) **2.** holding an office **3.** authorized and approved (*official* uniform)

off·shore (ȯf′ shōr′) *adv.* at a distance from the shore (fishing *offshore*) —*adj.* (ȯf′ shōr′) **1.** moving away from the shore (*offshore* winds) **2.** located off the shore (*offshore* oil rig)

off·spring (ȯf′ spring′) *n., pl.* **off·spring** **1.** the young of a person or animal **2.** descendants of one set of parents (The old woman beamed at her *offspring.*)

of·ten (ȯf′ ən) *adv.* frequently, many times

oh (ō) *interj.* an exclamation of surprise or pain

oil (ȯil) *n.* **1.** a greasy, flammable liquid from plant, animal, or mineral sources that cannot be dissolved in water and is important as a food, fuel, or lubricant, depending upon its composition **2.** artist's paint (He painted in *oils.*)

old (ōld) *adj.* **1.** ancient (an *old* story) **2.** lasting from an earlier time (an *old* bridge partner) **3.** belonging to an earlier period (*old* model) **4.** having existed for a certain time (just turned twenty years *old*) —*n.* an earlier time (days of *old*)

ol·ive (äl′ iv) *n.* a tree of the Mediterranean region, having beautiful wood and fruit that is used as a relish or for making olive oil

o·men (ō′ mən) *n.* an event thought to predict either something good or evil happening in the future (an *omen* of peace)

om·i·nous (äm′ ə nəs) *adj.* foretelling evil or harm (an *ominous* yellow-green sky)

o·mit (ō mit′) *vb.* **o·mit·ted; o·mit·ting** **1.** to leave out (*Omit* one name on the list.) **2.** fail to do (*omitted* picking up the mail)

on (ȯn) *prep.* **1.** touching the top (*on* the desk) **2.** against (*on* the screen) **3.** in or near (*on* the lake) **4.** during (*on* Sunday) **5.** in process (*on* fire) **6.** to put into action (Turn the engine *on.*)

once (wəns) *adv.* **1.** one single time (We went to see it *once.*) **2.** some one time formerly (*once* upon a time) —*n.* **1.** one single time **2.** this time (at *once*)

on·ion (ən′ yən) *n.* the strong-smelling bulb of a plant related to the lilies that is used as a seasoning for foods and as a vegetable

on·ly (ōn′ lē) *adj.* **1.** the very best (the *only* one for me) **2.** alone in its class (the *only* one left) —*adv.* **1.** merely (*only* an ounce) **2.** solely (made it *only* for her use) **3.** as recently as (*only* yesterday) —*conj.* except that (I would go, *only* I have homework to do.)

on·to (ȯn′ tə) *prep.* **1.** to a position on **2.** to a state of awareness about (I'm *onto* your tricks.)

on·ward (ȯn′ wərd) also **on·wards** (-wərdz) *adv.* toward a forward position in space or time (Let's push *onward.*)

o·paque (ō pāk′) *adj.* **1.** not letting light pass through (dark, *opaque* glass) **2.** hard to understand (The topic was too *opaque* for them.)

o·pen (ō′ pən) *adj.* **1.** having no barriers (an *open* pasture) **2.** having the barrier in a position to allow passage (*open* doors and windows) **3.** having no lid (*open* box) **4.** planned to provide public knowledge (an *open* meeting) **5.** accessible to anyone (an *open* beach area)

o·per·a (äp′ ə rə) *n.* a play in which the speaking parts are sung

op·er·ate (äp′ ə rāt′) *vb.* **op·er·ated; op·er·at·ing** **1.** to work or function, as a machine **2.** to manage (*operate* a business) **3.** to perform surgery

op·er·a·tion (äp′ ə rā′ shən) *n.* **1.** the act, process, or method of functioning **2.** a procedure used by a surgeon to correct a disorder **3.** a process as in mathematics **4.** a military or naval action (naval *operation*)

op·er·a·tor (äp′ ə rāt′ ər) *n.* one that operates (telephone *operator*)

o·pin·ion (ə pin′ yən) *n.* **1.** a personal view **2.** an appraisal that rests on insufficient knowledge and is therefore not certain **3.** a formal statement by an expert

op·po·nent (ə pō′ nənt) *n.* a rival or foe

op·por·tu·ni·ty (äp′ ər tü′ nət ē) *n., pl.* **op·por·tu·ni·ties** **1.** a favorable time and circumstance **2.** a chance to attain a goal

op·pose (ə pōz′) *vb.* **op·posed**; **op·pos·ing** **1.** to offer resistance (*oppose* the decision) **2.** to relate for the purpose of comparison or contrast (the benefits, as *opposed* to the liabilities or drawbacks)

op·po·site (äp′ ə zət) *n.* one that is opposite or contrary (Day is the *opposite* of night.) —*adj.* **1.** at the other end or side (*opposite* end of town) **2.** being in conflict (an *opposite* position) —*adv.* on opposite sides —*prep.* facing or across from (sat *opposite* me)

op·po·si·tion (äp′ ə zish′ ən) *n.* **1.** the act of opposing (His team played in *opposition* to mine in the playoffs.) **2.** a group of people who oppose someone or something (The people in the new development are the *opposition*.)

op·tic (äp′ tik) *adj.* relating to the eye or sight (the *optic* nerve)

or (ȯr) *conj.* used between words or phrases that express alternatives (eggs *or* cereal)

o·ral (ōr′ əl) *adj.* spoken (an *oral* examination)

or·ange (ȯr′ inj) *n.* **1.** a juicy, sweet-tasting fruit with an orange rind, growing on an evergreen tree with shiny leaves and fragrant white flowers **2.** the color made by mixing red and yellow

or·bit (ȯr′ bət) *n.* **1.** the elliptical path followed by a planet around the sun **2.** the bony socket that contains the eye —*vb.* to revolve in orbit

or·chard (ȯr′ chərd) *n.* a place where fruit trees are grown

or·ches·tra (ȯr′ kəs trə) *n.* a company of musical performers playing several different instruments including strings and brass

or·deal (ȯr dēl′) *n.* any severe or trying test or experience

or·der (ȯrd′ ər) *n.* **1.** a command or a mandate **2.** things bought or sold (an *order* of onion rings) **3.** the sequence of months or seasons (in a time *order*) **4.** a group of people who have chosen to live under the same rule (fraternal *order*s, religious *order*s) —*vb.* to give an order for (*order* some boots)

or·der·ly (ȯrd′ ər lē) *adj.* **1.** tidy and in good order (an *orderly* study area) **2.** having good behavior (an *orderly* class) —*n., pl.* **or·der·lies** **1.** a soldier who carries messages for an officer **2.** an attendant in a hospital

or·di·nal (ȯrd′ n əl) *n.* ordinal number; any number used to indicate order in a series (second, ninth, twenty-fifth)

or·di·nar·y (ȯrd′ n er′ ē) *n.* regular, average, or customary —*adj.* normal, usual, or as expected (an *ordinary* meal)

ore (ōr) *n.* a mineral substance or rock that contains a metal or chemical for which it is mined

or·gan (ȯr′ gən) *n.* **1.** a musical instrument played on one or more keyboards while the sound produced travels through one or more sets of pipes by means of compressed air **2.** a structure in the body composed of cells and tissues and performing a specific function (The heart is an *organ* that acts like a pump to maintain the circulation of the blood.)

or·gan·ism (ȯr′ gə niz′ əm) *n.* **1.** a living person, animal, or plant **2.** a living being composed of mutually dependent parts that maintain the vital processes

or·ga·ni·za·tion (ȯr′ gə nə zā′ shən) *n.* **1.** the process of organizing **2.** the state of being organized **3.** a group of people united for a common cause

or·ga·nize (ȯr′ gə nīz′) *vb.* **or·ga·nized**; **or·ga·niz·ing** to join separate parts into a united whole

o·ri·ent (ōr′ ē ent′) *vb.* **1.** to adjust in relation to surroundings especially to the points of the compass **2.** to familiarize with an existing situation or environment

or·i·gin (ȯr′ ə jən) *n.* **1.** the source from which something arises **2.** one's parentage and ancestry **3.** the first stage of existence (the *origin* of written language)

o·rig·i·nal (ə rij′ ən l) *n.* something from which a copy or reproduction is made (The *original* is in the museum.) —*adj.* **1.** relating to the beginning (*original* settlers) **2.** doing things in novel, creative ways (an *original* thinker)

Ostrich

os·trich (äs′ trich) *n.* a two-toed, swift-footed bird, the largest of living birds, native to Africa and Arabia, and raised for its beautiful feathers

oth·er (ət͟h′ ər) *adj.* **1.** being the remaining one out of two or more **2.** additional (he and one *other* person) **3.** alternate (every *other* day) —*pron.* **1.** remaining one (Read one book and then the *other*.) **2.** another thing (something or *other*)

oth·er·wise (ət͟h′ ər wīz′) *adv.* **1.** differently (cannot play it *otherwise*) **2.** in different circumstances **3.** in other respects (an *otherwise* pleasant person)

ot·ter (ät′ ər) *n.* a web-footed, fish-eating animal with a long, slightly flattened tail, related to the minks and valued for its dense, dark-brown fur

ought (ȯt) *helping verb* used to express moral obligation (*ought* to do your work)

ounce (aủns) *n.* **1.** a unit of weight equal to 1/16 pound **2.** a unit of liquid equal to 1/16 pint

our (aủr) *adj.* relating to us (*our* books)

our·selves (aủr selvz′) *pron.* our own selves

out (aủt) *adv.* **1.** away from the inside or the usual place or state (went *out* in the sun) **2.** away from home or one's work place (went *out* for coffee) **3.** to a point of exhaustion (Our supply of milk ran *out.*) **4.** aloud (called *out* to the umpire)

out·break (aủt′ brāk′) *n.* a breaking out or outburst (an *outbreak* of chicken pox)

out·come (aủt′ kəm′) *n.* result

out·door (aủt′ dōr′) *adj.* relating to the outdoors (an *outdoor* barbecue)

out·doors (aủt dōrz′) *adv.* out of doors in the open air (My dogs like to stay *outdoors.*) —*n.* the open air (The *outdoors* is bright in the moonlight.)

out·fit (aủt′ fit′) *n.* the equipment for a special purpose (his soccer *outfit*) —*vb.* **out·fit·ted**; **out·fit·ting** to furnish with an outfit (to *outfit* the band)

out·law (aủt′ lȯ′) *n.* **1.** a person or group excluded from the benefits and protection of the law **2.** a lawless person **3.** a fugitive from the law

out·let (aủt′ let′) *n.* **1.** a place or opening where something comes out **2.** a means of letting out an emotion (found an *outlet* for his anger) **3.** a place for plugging in an appliance (Where is the electrical *outlet*?)

out·line (aủt′ līn′) *n.* **1.** a line that traces along the outer edge of an object **2.** a brief statement or sketch (the *outline* of a report)

out·look (au̇t′ lu̇k′) *n.* **1.** a way of looking at a situation (She had a strange *outlook* on life.) **2.** a view toward the future (*outlook* for next year)

out·side (au̇t′ sīd′) *n.* **1.** the place beyond an enclosure **2.** an outer surface —*adj.* relating to the outside —*adv.* outdoors —*prep.* beyond the limits of (just *outside* Chicago)

out·skirts (au̇t′ skərts′) *n.,pl.* the outlying district or part near the edge of town

out·stand·ing (au̇t stan′ ding) *adj.* **1.** unpaid (several debts *outstanding*) **2.** standing out from a group **3.** distinguished (an *outstanding* actress)

out·ward (au̇t′ wərd) *adj.* away from the center toward the outside —*adv.* toward the outside

o·val (ō′ vəl) *adj.* having the shape of a hen's egg —*n.* an oval figure

ov·en (əv′ ən) *n.* a heated compartment, as in a stove, for baking, heating, or drying

o·ver (ō′ vər) *adv.* **1.** across a barrier **2.** in a downward direction (bend *over*) —*prep.* **1.** higher than **2.** above in power or value —*adj.* **1.** being more than needed **2.** finished, ended

o·ver·all (ō′ vər ȯl′) *adv.* considering everything (The repairs looked good *overall.*) —*adj.* covering everything (the *overall* cost of the paint job)

o·ver·board (ō′ vər bōrd′) *adv.* over the side of the ship (washed *overboard*)

o·ver·come (ō′ vər kəm′) *vb.* **o·ver·came** (-kām); **o·ver·come**; **o·ver·com·ing** **1.** to win or conquer (*overcame* the opponent) **2.** to make weak or disabled (*overcome* by the drug)

o·ver·flow (ō′ vər flō′) *vb.* to spread over, as water, beyond its usual limits (The river *overflow*ed its banks.)

o·ver·head (ō′ vər hed′) *adv.* above one's head —*adj.* (ō′ vər hed′) passing or operating above the head (an *overhead* sprinkler system) —*n.* ongoing business expenses such as rent, heat, and lighting

o·ver·lap (ō′ vər lap′) *vb.* **o·ver·lapped**; **o·ver·lap·ping** to arrange two layers of material so that one partly covers the other (The wrap-skirt has a deep *overlap*.)

o·ver·look (ō′ vər lu̇k′) *vb.* **1.** to look at the surrounding area from above (The deck *overlooks* a garden.) **2.** to look at without noticing something (In reading the report, he *overlook*ed the error.) **3.** to purposely pass over without notice (She *overlook*ed his handwriting until his arm healed.)

o·ver·night (ō′ vər nīt′) *adv.* for or during the night (She stayed *overnight* at a resort.) —*adj.* (ō vər nīt′) lasting through the night (an *overnight* flight to Europe)

o·ver·pow·er (ō′ vər pau̇′ ər) *vb.* **1.** to overcome by superior force **2.** to affect a person physically or mentally (He had a vibrant, *overpowering* personality.)

o·ver·throw (ō′ vər thrō′) *vb.* **o·ver·threw** (-thrü); **o·ver·thrown** (-thrōn′); **o·ver·throw·ing** **1.** to remove from a position of power (*overthrow* the dictator) **2.** to defeat or overcome —*n.* (ō′ vər thrō′) **1.** the act of overthrowing **2.** defeat (The *overthrow* of the challenger won their team the trophy.)

o·ver·whelm (ō′ vər hwelm′) *vb.* to overpower completely, to crush, or to oppress (The small boat was *overwhelm*ed by the wave.)

owe (ō) *vb.* **owed**; **ow·ing** **1.** to be in debt to (*owe* the paper carrier for the newspapers) **2.** to take as a duty (We *owe* allegiance to our country.)

owl (au̇l) *n.* a night bird of prey with large head and eyes and short hooked beak, that lives on mice, rats, small birds, and insects

Owl

own (ōn) *adj.* belonging to oneself or itself (has her *own* notebook) —*vb.* **1.** to have property (*own* a house) **2.** to admit (*own* up to the mistake)

own·er·ship (ō′ nər ship′) *n.* the state of being an owner (He has *ownership* of the parking lot.)

ox (äks) *n., pl.* **ox·en** (äk′ sən) the adult castrated male of cattle used as food and as a beast of burden (The *ox* pulled a heavy load.)

ox·ide (äk′ sīd′) *n.* a compound of oxygen with one or more additional elements

ox·y·gen (äk′ si jən) *n.* a colorless, odorless, tasteless gas, essential to life and the burning process, making up about twenty percent of the atmosphere and present in nature in various compounds

oys·ter (ȯis′ tər) *n.* a soft, gray edible shellfish found in shallow seawater adhering to rocks

P

pace (pās) *n.* **1.** rate of walking (at a fast *pace*) **2.** a horse's gait, in which the legs on the same side move at the same time —*vb.* **paced**; **pac·ing** **1.** to walk at a certain rate (They *paced* themselves to arrive at 11:00 A.M.) **2.** to move at a pace (a *pacing* horse)

pa·cif·ic (pə sif′ ik) *adj.* calm and peaceful

pack (pak) *n.* **1.** a large bundle tied up for carrying, especially on the back of a person or animal **2.** a group of people, animals, or things (a *pack* of thieves; a *pack* of wolves; a *pack* of cards) —*vb.* **1.** to put things into a container for storage or transport **2.** to put clothes into a suitcase for traveling **3.** to make full (*pack* the gymnasium with spectators)

pack·age (pak′ ij) *n.* a bundle of goods made up for shipping to another place

pack·et (pak′ ət) *n.* a small package

pad (pad) *n.* **1.** a layer of soft material that has some thickness (a mattress *pad*, an ink *pad*) **2.** the soft cushions under the toes of some animals **3.** a stack of paper glued together at one end —*vb.* **pad·ded**; **pad·ding** **1.** to walk with quiet steps (He *padded* around in slippers.) **2.** to stuff with soft material (He *padded* the arms of the chair.)

pad·dle (pad′ l) *n.* **1.** an implement having a flat blade at the end of a long handle used for moving and steering a canoe **2.** one of the broad fins on a waterwheel **3.** an implement for stirring or mixing —*vb.* **pad·dled**; **pad·dling** **1.** to move or stir by a paddle **2.** to spank as if by a paddle **3.** to play in shallow water

page (pāj) *n.* **1.** a person hired to deliver messages **2.** one side of a leaf of a printed document —*vb.* **paged**; **pag·ing** **1.** to act as a page **2.** to summon by calling out a person's name **3.** to mark or number the pages

pail (pāl) *n.* a round container or bucket for carrying liquids

pain (pān) *n.* **1.** physical discomfort such as a burning, aching, or throbbing sensation **2.** mental discomfort due to grief or other emotional difficulty —*vb.* **1.** to cause pain **2.** to experience pain

paint (pānt) *vb.* **1.** to cover a surface with paint (*paint* a wall) **2.** to make a picture with paint **3.** to put on a layer of liquid as if painting —*n.* a mixture that dries to form a thin coating when spread on a surface

paint·er (pānt′ ər) *n.* one who paints

paint·ing (pānt′ ing) *n.* a picture or other work produced through the art of painting

pair (paər) *n., pl.* **pairs** also **pair** **1.** two matched objects (a *pair* of gloves) **2.** a thing made by connecting two similar parts (a *pair* of tongs) **3.** a mated couple **4.** two comrades with the same work or interests —*vb.* **1.** to form a pair **2.** to arrange in pairs

pa·ja·mas (pə jä′ məz) *n., pl.* a two-piece, loose-fitting suit for sleeping or lounging

pal (pal) *n.* a close friend or companion

pal·ace (pal′ əs) *n.* the home of the royal family or other high-ranking person

pale (pāl) *adj.* **pal·er**; **pal·est** **1.** being a light, almost white, color **2.** lacking the warm color of a healthy person —*vb.* **paled**; **pal·ing** to turn an ashy white

palm (päm) *n.* **1.** a tropical tree with a tall trunk topped with large fan-shaped leaves **2.** the under part of the hand excluding the fingers —*vb.* to get rid of by trickery (to *palm* off the radio as a higher-priced model)

pan (pan) *n.* an implement to hold food that is being cooked by boiling, baking, or frying —*vb.* **panned**; **pan·ning** to wash earthy material to locate bits of metal such as gold

pan·cake (pan′ kāk′) *n.* a flat cake made by frying batter on a fry pan or griddle

pane (pān) *n.* a single sheet of glass in a window frame

pan·el (pan′ l) *n.* **1.** a group of persons gathered to discuss or judge something **2.** a rectangular piece of material the edges of which are grooved, framed, or bordered in some manner as to make the piece identifiable when set onto a larger surface (a wall *panel*, a colored *panel* on the skirt) **3.** a board on which instruments or controls are mounted (control *panel*)

pan·ic (pan′ ik) *n.* a sudden fear that causes people to lose control and behave wildly

pan·ther (pan′ thər) *n.* a large wild cat such as the puma, cougar, mountain lion, leopard, or jaguar

pan·try (pan′ trē) *n., pl.* **pan·tries** a small room where dishes and food are kept

pa·per (pā′ pər) *n.* **1.** material made from shredded fibers of wood, rags, or straw, and rolled into thin, flexible sheets **2.** a newspaper **3.** an essay or term paper **4.** a fancy wall covering (wall*paper*) **5.** stationery (letter *paper*) —*vb.* to cover with paper (*paper* the room) —*adj.* made of paper

par·a·chute (par′ ə shüt′) *n.* an umbrella-shaped device of thin, strong cloth fastened with cords to a harness which is worn by a person to make a safe descent from an airplane in emergencies, test flights, or as a sport

Parachute

pa·rade (pə rād′) *n.* **1.** a procession through the streets of bands and organized groups in celebration of some event **2.** a formation and marching of troops before an officer for inspection **3.** a procession of animals and circus performers (circus *parade*) —*vb.* **pa·rad·ed**; **pa·rad·ing** **1.** to march in procession **2.** to show off in a public place (*parade* down Fifth Avenue on Easter)

par·a·dise (par′ ə dīs′) *n.* **1.** the Garden of Eden **2.** heaven **3.** a place of beauty and complete happiness

par·a·graph (par′ ə graf′) *n.* a section of a piece of writing, containing one or more sentences, that deals with only one main topic or gives the words of one speaker —*vb.* to divide into paragraphs

par·al·lel (par′ ə lel′) *adj.* two straight lines the same distance from each other at all points (Railroad tracks are *parallel.*) —*n.* one of the imaginary lines equally distant from the equator at all points that indicates latitude (The horse latitudes are located approximately at the 30° *parallels* north and south of the equator.) —*vb.* to run equally distant from another line (The road runs *parallel* to the river.)

par·a·lyze (par′ ə līz′) *vb.* **par·a·lyzed**; **par·a·lyz·ing** **1.** to lose the power to move or the sense of touch **2.** to make someone helpless **3.** to cause all activity to stop (The loss of electricity *paralyzed* the factory.)

par·cel (pär′ səl) *n.* **1.** a package **2.** a piece of land —*vb.* **par·celed**; **par·cel·ing** **1.** to wrap into a bundle **2.** to divide something and pass it out (*parceled* out the candy)

par·don (pärd′ n) *n.* **1.** forgiveness **2.** a politeness (I beg your *pardon.*) **3.** an official notice that a person is freed from punishment —*vb.* **1.** to free from punishment for a crime **2.** to forgive

par·ent (par′ ənt) *n.* **1.** a mother or father **2.** an animal or plant that produces offspring

pa·ren·the·sis (pə ren′ thə səs) *n., pl.* **pa·ren·the·ses** (-sēz′) one of a pair of marks ( ) used in writing to mark off words set into the passage to explain or modify, to set off a group of mathematical terms to be treated as a unit, or to separate enumeration from the text that follows as *1)* or *a)*

park (pärk) *n.* **1.** a piece of land set aside for the enjoyment of the public **2.** a field for ball games —*vb.* to stop a vehicle in an appropriate place with the intention of not using it for awhile

par·lia·ment (pär′ lə mənt) *n.* the legislature of certain countries such as Great Britain (In Great Britain, *Parliament* makes the laws and sees that they are enforced.)

par·lor (pär′ lər) *n.* **1.** a comfortable room for conversation **2.** a shop with some accommodation for comfort and convenience (a beauty *parlor*)

par·rot (par′ ət) *n.* a hook-billed bird with brilliantly colored feathers, amusing to people because of its ability to mimic speech —*vb.* to teach or to be taught to repeat words from memory without understanding them

Parrot

part (pärt) *n.* **1.** a piece of something but less than a whole **2.** a spare piece of machinery that can be used to replace a worn piece **3.** a dividing line on the head from which hair is combed in different directions **4.** one of the characters in a play **5.** the lines and actions of the character —*vb.* **1.** to depart from someone **2.** to separate or break a thing into parts **3.** to break or tear apart

par·tial (pär′ shəl) *adj.* **1.** biased in favor of one side of a question or topic **2.** relating to one part only (a *partial* paralysis)

par·tic·i·pa·tion (pär tis′ ə pā′ shən) *n.* the act of sharing in some action with others

par·ti·ci·ple (pärt′ ə sip′ əl) *n.* a word that functions partly as an adjective and partly as a verb

par·tic·u·lar (pər tik′ yə lər) *adj.* **1.** relating to one part rather than the whole **2.** special (a show of *particular* talent) **3.** fussy (She is *particular* about her clothes.) —*n.* a detail (in every *particular*)

part·ly (pärt′ lē) *adv.* to some extent, but not wholly (The fog was *partly* to blame.)

part·ner (pärt′ nər) *n.* **1.** one who shares with another in some action or endeavor (*partners* in business) **2.** either one of a married couple **3.** each of those who play on the same side in a game (tennis *partner*)

part·ner·ship (pärt′ nər ship′) *n.* **1.** the state of being a partner **2.** the association of business partners

pass (pas) *vb.* **1.** to go by (*pass* the store) **2.** to successfully complete requirements (*Pass* to the next grade.) —*n.* **1.** a gap in the mountains (Go through the *pass.*) **2.** the act of passing **3.** a written permit allowing free admission or passage (a railroad *pass*)

pas·sage (pas′ ij) *n.* **1.** the act of passing (the *passage* of time) **2.** a hall or corridor for passing **3.** a section of a written document

pas·sen·ger (pas′ n jər) *n.* a person who is carried from one place to another in a vehicle

pas·sion (pash′ ən) *n.* **1.** any strong emotion **2.** strong attachment for an activity (a *passion* for sailing) **3.** the suffering of Christ between the night of the Last Supper and his death

past (past) *adj.* **1.** relating to a time that has gone by (for the *past* two days) **2.** no longer in office (*past* president) —*prep.* **1.** beyond in time **2.** after —*n.* the time gone by —*adv.* **1.** by **2.** so as to pass by (The monkey ran *past.*)

paste (pāst) *n.* **1.** a mixture of flour and starch with water for sticking things together **2.** any food that is chopped fine and mixed with liquid to make a paste-like texture (sardine *paste*)

pas·ture (pas′ chər) *n.* a field where animals graze —*vb.* **pas·tured**; **pas·tur·ing** **1.** to graze **2.** to lead animals to a pasture

pat (pat) *n.* **1.** a light tap with the hand **2.** one serving of butter —*vb.* **pat·ted**; **pat·ting** to tap gently with the open hand —*adj.* **pat·ter**; **pat·test** good and timely (a *pat* answer)

patch (pach) *n.* **1.** a piece of material attached to a garment to cover a worn or torn place **2.** a plot of land planted with a crop that is different from the surrounding area (a cabbage *patch*) —*vb.* **1.** to mend **2.** to repair (*patch* up a quarrel)

pat·ent (pat′ nt) *adj.* **1.** protected by an official document **2.** obvious (a *patent* lie) — sometimes pronounced (pāt′ ənt) —*vb.* to take out a patent

path (path) *n., pl.* **paths** (pathz) **1.** a track made by the frequent passage of people or animals **2.** the track in which something moves (the *path* of the moon around the earth)

pa·tience (pā′ shəns) *n.* the state of being patient

pa·tient (pā′ shənt) *adj.* **1.** bearing misfortune, hardship, and pain without complaining **2.** behaving in a calm, controlled way —*n.* a person under a doctor's care

pa·tri·ot (pā′ trē ət) *n.* a person who loves, supports, and defends his or her country

pa·tri·ot·ic (pā′ trē ät′ ik) *adj.* **1.** behaving like a patriot **2.** showing love of country

pa·tri·ot·ism (pā′ trē ə tiz′ əm) *n.* love, support, and defense of one's country and loyalty to its principles

pa·trol (pə trōl′) *n.* **1.** walking a specified area to maintain order and security **2.** a person or group on guard duty —*vb.* **pa·trolled**; **pa·trol·ling** to walk an area to watch and protect

pat·tern (pat′ ərn) *n.* **1.** something to be copied as a model or guide (*pattern* for a birdhouse) **2.** a design used in decorating —*vb.* to make something according to a pattern

pause (pȯz) *n.* a short stop or rest —*vb.* **paused**; **paus·ing** to stop for a short while

pave (pāv) *vb.* **paved**; **pav·ing** **1.** to put a hard surface on a road, walk, or parking area (*pave* the driveway) **2.** to make something easy by doing some work or planning in advance (*pave* the way)

pave·ment (pāv′ mənt) *n.* **1.** the material used for paving **2.** a paved surface

paw (pȯ) *n.* the foot of a four-footed animal with claws —*vb.* **1.** to tap or scrape with the forefoot (to *paw* the ground) **2.** to touch clumsily (to *paw* things over)

pay (pā) *vb.* **paid** (pād); **pay·ing** **1.** to give money in exchange for goods, work, or services **2.** to give money that is due (*pay* rent) **3.** to offer or give freely (*pay* attention) **4.** to be profitable (It will *pay* you to study hard.) —*n.* **1.** the act of paying **2.** the money paid

pay·ment (pā′ mənt) *n.* **1.** the act of paying **2.** the amount paid

pea (pē) *n., pl.* **peas** (pēz) a green vegetable that is the round seed found in the pods of a garden plant

peace (pēs) *n.* **1.** freedom from war **2.** a state of calmness and harmony among people **3.** an agreement to end a war **4.** freedom of the mind from worry or disturbing thoughts

peace·ful (pēs′ fəl) *adj.* **1.** free from war, violence, and commotion **2.** inclined toward finding reasonable ways to solve problems **3.** not easily led into an argument

peach (pēch) *n.* a pale-yellow fruit with a sweet pulp, a hairy skin, and a very rough stone

pea·cock (pē′ käk′) *n.* the male bird of the peafowl, noted for its long, shimmering, iridescent tail feathers marked with eyelike spots which it can raise in a fan shape —*vb.* to walk in a vain manner

Peacock

peak (pēk) *n.* **1.** the top of a hill or mountain **2.** the maximum point of anything (The noise reaches its *peak* in the afternoon.) **3.** the high point of a person's career

pea·nut (pē′ nət′) *n.* **1.** a plant related to the peas, grown for its underground pods of oily, nutlike seeds which are used in making peanut oil and peanut butter **2.** any small person or thing, especially a small amount of money (working for *peanuts*)

pear (paər) *n.* the fleshy, edible fruit of an orchard tree related to the apple that is larger at the base than it is at the stem end

Pear

pearl (pərl) *n.* **1.** a usually white or near-white, smooth, round bead with a soft luster formed within the shell of some mollusk such as the pearl oyster and used in necklaces, rings, or other jewelry **2.** mother-of-pearl: the lustrous lining of some shells such as the abalone

peas·ant (pez′ nt) *n.* a poor farmer or farm laborer in rural areas of Europe

peat (pēt) *n.* a dark-brown, earthy substance, made up of plants that rotted in a wet area, which is dug up, dried, and used for food

peb·ble (peb′ əl) *n.* a small stone with rounded edges

peck (pek) *n.* **1.** equal to one-fourth of a bushel in dry measure (bought a *peck* of apples) **2.** a large amount (a *peck* of nonsense) **3.** the act of pecking —*vb.* **1.** to dig or pick up with the bill (The birds *peck*ed at the seeds.) **2.** to nick with a sharp tool

pe·cu·liar (pi kyül′ yər) *adj.* **1.** different from what is expected (a *peculiar*-looking chair) **2.** common only to a particular person or place (a *peculiar* habit)

ped·al (ped′ l) *n.* a small metal bar or lever pressed by the foot to operate a machine or instrument (the gas *pedal* in a car; the volume *pedal* on a piano) —*adj.* relating to the foot or feet (a *pedal* reflector on the bicycle) —*vb.* **ped·aled**; **ped·al·ing** to work the pedal (*pedal* a bicycle)

ped·dle (ped′ l) *vb.* **ped·dled**; **ped·dling** to sell goods from door to door

ped·dler (ped′ lər) *n.* a person who peddles goods from door to door

pe·des·tri·an (pə des′ trē ən) *n.* **1.** a person who travels on foot (Drivers watch out for *pedestrians*.) **2.** dull, lacking in imagination (a *pedestrian* plan)

peel (pēl) *vb.* to take off the outer covering (*peel* the apple) —*n.* a skin or rind of fruits or vegetables (the orange *peel*, the potato *peel*)

peer (piər) *n.* **1.** a person who is equal to another in the eyes of the law (tried before one's *peers*) **2.** a person belonging to one of the five ranks of British peerage, as duke, marquis, earl, viscount, or baron —*vb.* to look with searching eyes

peg (peg) *n.* **1.** a short stick, pointed usually at one end, used to fasten things together **2.** a piece of wood sticking out from a wall for hanging things (Hang your jacket on the *peg*.) **3.** a stick driven into the ground to mark a boundary or hold a tent rope —*vb.* to pin or mark with a peg

pen (pen) *n.* **1.** an instrument used for writing with ink **2.** a fenced-in yard for farm animals (pig*pen*) —*vb.* **1.** to put in a pen **2.** to write (*pen* a note)

pen·al·ty (pen′ l tē) *n.*, *pl.* **pen·al·ties** **1.** punishment such as a fine or jail term for breaking the law **2.** a disadvantage given to one side of a sports contest for breaking a rule **3.** mental suffering for some act committed

pen·cil (pen′ səl) *n.* an instrument used for writing, usually in black lead but sometimes in a colored, chalk-like material —*vb.* to write or mark with a pencil

pen·du·lum (pen′ jə ləm) *n.* a body suspended on a cord or chain so as to swing according to the law of gravity

pen·e·trate (pen′ ə trāt′) *vb.* **pen·e·trat·ed; pen·e·trat·ing** **1.** to go through (*penetrate* the skin) **2.** to affect one's understanding and feelings

pen·guin (pen′ gwən) *n.* a large antarctic seabird that uses its wings for swimming rather than flying

pen·in·su·la (pə nin′ sə lə) *n.* a piece of land attached to the mainland at one point and surrounded by water on the other three sides

pen·ny (pen′ ē) *n., pl.* **pen·nies** (pen′ ēz) a cent or one one-hundredth of a dollar in United States and Canadian money

peo·ple (pē′ pəl) *n., pl.* **people** or **peo·ples** **1.** persons (Five *people* were there.) **2.** the individuals who make up a group, a nation, or a race (the *people* of the United States) **3.** the public (*people* want peace) —*vb.* **peo·pled; peo·pling** **1.** to supply with people **2.** to establish communities (*peopled* the colonies)

pep·per (pep′ ər) *n.* **1.** the tangy dried and ground fruit of the East Indian pepper plant, called black pepper **2.** the ground, ripened seed of the East Indian pepper plant, called white pepper **3.** a garden plant with fruit that is sharp and red when ripe (hot *pepper*s) **4.** a garden plant with fruit used as a vegetable (sweet *peppers*) —*vb.* to season with pepper

per·ceive (pər sēv′) *vb.* **per·ceived; per·ceiv·ing** to see or hear and grasp the meaning (*perceived* disappointment in her voice)

per·cent (pər sent′) *adv.* or *adj.* figured on the basis of the number of units per hundred (Eighteen *percent* is eighteen per hundred.) —*n.* percentage (What *percent* of the group will go?)

per·cent·age (pər sent′ ij) *n.* **1.** a part of the whole given in hundredths **2.** a part of the whole assigned to profit, taxes, commission, or other division of the total

per·cep·tion (pər sep′ shən) *n.* **1.** the ability to perceive **2.** a formulation of what one perceives

perch (pərch) *n.* **1.** a small, freshwater fish **2.** a branch or pole on which a bird sits **3.** a seat that has been raised —*vb.* to sit on a high rod, branch, or seat

per·cus·sion (pər kəsh′ ən) *n.* **1.** a bang or blow **2.** an instrument played by striking as a drum **3.** the perception of sound waves striking the eardrum

per·fect (pər′ fikt) *adj.* **1.** complete and having no defects **2.** of excellent quality —*vb.* (pər fekt′) to make perfect through improvement

per·fec·tion (pər fek′ shən) *n.* a completeness and quality that cannot be improved

per·form (pər fȯrm′) *vb.* **1.** to do or carry out some action **2.** to act or accomplish something requiring talent or skill (*perform*ed with the orchestra)

per·form·ance (pər fȯr′ məns) *n.* **1.** the carrying out of actions **2.** the presentation of one's talent (the *performance* of a stage play)

per·fume (pər′ fyüm′) *n.* a fragrance such as that of flowers to be worn on the skin —*vb.* to make pleasing by adding perfume

per·haps (pər haps′) *adv.* maybe

per·il (per′ əl) *n.* the state of being in danger or at risk

pe·rim·e·ter (pə rim′ ət ər) *n.* **1.** the outline or boundary of an area **2.** in mathematics, the sum of the lengths of all sides of an area

pe·ri·od (pir′ ē əd) *n.* **1.** a punctuation mark (.) used at the end of a declarative sentence or an abbreviation **2.** a length of time, as a period in history or a class period

per·ma·nent (pər′ mə nənt) *adj.* relating to something that is lasting, not intended to change

per·mis·sion (pər mish′ ən) *n.* **1.** the act of allowing **2.** the consent of someone in charge

per·mit (pər mit′) *vb.* **per·mit·ted; per·mit·ting** to agree to or allow —*n.* (pər′ mit) a license, pass, or other statement of consent

per·pen·dic·u·lar (per′ pən dik′ yə lər) *adj.* **1.** at right angles to another line or surface **2.** upright or vertical, at a 90° angle from the ground (The wall is *perpendicular* to the floor.) —*n.* something such as a line or structure that is at right angles to another line or base

per·sist (pər sist′) *vb.* to continue to do or endure beyond a normal time period (The noise *persist*ed.)

per·sist·ent (pər sis′ tənt) *adj.* continuing to act or exist beyond a normal time period (a *persistent* heat wave)

per·son (pərs′ n) *n.* **1.** human being **2.** one's individual self or personality (one's *person*) **3.** appearance or presence (She was there in *person.*)

per·son·al (pərs′ n əl) *adj.* relating or belonging to a person

per·son·al·i·ty (pərs′ n al′ ət ē) *n., pl.* **per·son·al·i·ties** **1.** the qualities of a person that make him or her different from everyone else **2.** one's individuality (a pleasing *personality*)

per·son·nel (pərs′ n el′) *n.* all of the persons employed in a business, a service, or other organization

per·spec·tive (pər spek′ tiv) *n.* **1.** the art of drawing on a flat surface so that objects appear to have depth and distance from the viewer **2.** the ability to see things in an appropriate relationship

per·spi·ra·tion (pər′ spə rā′ shən) *n.* the act of giving off perspiration or sweat from glands in the skin

per·suade (pər swād′) *vb.* **per·suad·ed; per·suad·ing** to convince someone by a presentation of arguments to agree to or support a particular point of view

pest (pest) *n.* **1.** a disease or pestilence that spreads quickly and causes many deaths **2.** a troublesome or destructive person, animal, or thing (a plant *pest*)

pet (pet) *n.* **1.** a domesticated animal that is kept for pleasure and companionship **2.** a favored person who is treated with affection —*adj.* favorite —*vb.* **pet·ted**; **pet·ting** to stroke gently, or caress

pet·al (pet′ l) *n.* one of the delicate colored leaves that form the showy part of a flower

Petals

pe·ti·tion (pə tish′ ən) *n.* **1.** a paper containing a formal request addressed to a higher authority and often containing a number of signatures of supporters **2.** a prayer that a favor will be granted —*vb.* to make a petition or request

pe·tro·le·um (pə tro′ lē əm) *n.* the dark, crude oil that is brought up from the earth by drilling into the pockets where it is found and pumping it out

phase (fāz) *n.* **1.** any one step in the development or performance of an action (the planning *phase*) **2.** one of the changes in appearance of the moon (the new moon *phase*)

phi·los·o·pher (fə läs′ ə fər) *n.* **1.** a person who studies philosophy **2.** a thoughtful person who seeks goodness and truth

phi·los·o·phy (fə läs′ ə fē) *n., pl.* **phi·los·o·phies** the thoughtful study of the truths and principles of existence, knowledge, and conduct

phone (fōn) *n.* short for telephone

pho·no·graph (fō′ nə graf′) *n.* an instrument that reproduces sounds recorded on disks or cylinders

pho·to (fōt′ ō) *n.* short for photograph

pho·to·graph (fōt′ ə graf′) *n.* a picture made by a chemical process through the use of a camera —*vb.* to take a picture using a camera

pho·tog·ra·phy (fə täg′ rə fē) *n.* the making of pictures on light-sensitive film through the use of a camera, and making prints from the film

pho·to·syn·the·sis (fōt′ ə sin′ thə səs) *n.* the process by which plants form sugars and starches from carbon dioxide and water in the presence of light

phrase (frāz) *n.* **1.** two or more words in a sentence acting as a grammatical unit (prepositional *phrase*) **2.** in music, a part of a melody, usually four to eight measures **3.** a brief, common expression —*vb.* **phrased**; **phras·ing** to put into words

phys·i·cal (fiz′ i kəl) *adj.* **1.** relating to the body (a *physical* examination) **2.** relating to the real world (*physical* map) **3.** relating to physics

phy·si·cian (fə zish′ ən) *n.* **1.** a doctor of medicine **2.** a person who is licensed to heal human disease

phys·i·cist (fiz′ ə səst) *n.* a specialist in the science of physics, which deals with matter and energy in terms of motion and force

phys·ics (fiz′ iks) *n.* a science that treats matter and energy, under topics such as mechanics, heat, sound, light, electricity, and atomic energy

pi·an·o (pē an′ ō) *n., pl.* **pi·an·os** a large percussion instrument having steel strings that sound when struck by hammers which are operated by the fingers on a keyboard

pick (pik) *vb.* **1.** to choose (*pick* a ripe plum) **2.** to eat just a little (*pick* at her food) **3.** to gather one by one (*pick* strawberries) **4.** to chip away with a pointed tool **5.** to steal the contents of (*pick* a pocket) **6.** to irk somone (*pick* a fight) —*n.* **1.** pickax **2.** the act of choosing **3.** the best ones (the *pick* of the litter)

pic·nic (pik′ nik′) *n.* an outing by a group bringing its own food —*vb.* **pic·nicked**; **pic·nick·ing** to take part in a picnic

pic·ture (pik′ chər) *n.* **1.** a painting, drawing, photograph, or engraving representing a real-life person or scene, or an imaginary one **2.** a colorful description

3. a motion picture **4.** a television image —*vb.* **pic·tured**; **pic·tur·ing** **1.** to make a picture by any method **2.** to describe so as to create an image

pie (pī) *n.* a food generally made by baking a filling in a pastry crust

piece (pēs) *n.* **1.** a separate portion of something (*piece* of cake, *piece* of marble) **2.** one of a group **3.** a section that is marked off (a *piece* of farm land) **4.** a finished article (a *piece* of jewelry) —*vb.* **pieced**; **piec·ing** to put pieces together to make a whole (*pieced* together a quilt)

pier (piər) *n.* **1.** a column or large block of concrete that supports an arch of a bridge **2.** a structure built out into the water as a place to tie up boats or to stand while fishing

pig (pig) *n.* a young swine raised for its meat

pi·geon (pij′ ən) *n.* a strong-flying, grain-eating bird that is found in many parts of the world and is recognized by its stocky body, short legs, and smooth feathers

pile (pīl) *n.* **1.** a large stake or post driven into the ground to strengthen the base for a building **2.** a furry or fuzzy surface on material —*vb.* **piled**; **pil·ing** to make a stack or a heap

pil·grim (pil′ grəm) *n.* **1.** one of the early settlers who came to form the Plymouth Colony in 1620 **2.** a person who goes on a pilgrimage to a holy place

pil·lar (pil′ ər) *n.* **1.** a column supporting a part of a roof **2.** someone who supports (a *pillar* of the community)

pil·low (pil′ ō) *n.* a sack of feathers or foam used under the head for comfort while sleeping —*vb.* to serve as a comfortable support for

pi·lot (pī′ lət) *n.* **1.** a person who is qualified to guide a ship where navigation is difficult **2.** one who is qualified to guide an airplane or other airship to its destination —*vb.* to direct the course of a vessel or airship

pin (pin) *n.* **1.** a smooth, slender, pointed piece of wire used to fasten things together **2.** an ornament that is attached to a pin and worn as a decoration **3.** one of ten pieces set up to be knocked down in bowling —*vb.* **pinned**; **pin·ning** to fasten with a pin

pinch (pinch) *vb.* **1.** to squeeze between the thumb and forefinger or something similar that closes (*pinch*ed her finger in the door) **2.** to look pale and thin (*pinch*ed with worry) —*n.* **1.** the act of pinching **2.** a time of need (in a *pinch*)

pine (pīn) *vb.* **pined**; **pin·ing** **1.** to lose one's health due to grief **2.** to long for —*n.* a cone-bearing evergreen tree with needles instead of leaves and wood that is important in building

pine·ap·ple (pīn′ ap′ əl) *n.* a tropical plant with cone-shaped fruit and hard, spiny leaves

Pineapple

pink (pingk) *vb.* to cut fabric with special shears to give it a saw-toothed edge —*n.* plants with thick, jointed stems, thin leaves, and pleasant-smelling flowers—a color between white and light-red —*adj.* of the color pink

pint (pīnt) *n.* a unit equal to one-half quart or sixteen ounces

pi·o·neer (pī′ ə niər′) *n.* one of the first settlers to enter a region and prepare the way for others —*vb.* to explore or take part in early development

pipe (pīp) *n.* **1.** a tube with a bowl at the end for smoking tobacco or blowing bubbles **2.** a long, hollow tube for conducting a liquid or gas —*vb.* **piped**; **pip·ing** **1.** to install pipes **2.** to speak in a high voice

pi·rate (pī′ rət) *n.* **1.** a lawless robber on the high seas **2.** someone who behaves like a robber or commits piracy

pis·tol (pist′ l) *n.* a small, short gun made to be held and fired in one hand

pit (pit) *n.* **1.** a deep hole (The animal was trapped in the *pit.*) **2.** an indentation on the skin —*vb.* **pit·ted**; **pit·ting** **1.** to put in a pit **2.** to mark with small hollows or holes **3.** to match the strength of one against another (*pit* one against another)

pitch (pich) *n.* **1.** a sticky substance from pine trees **2.** the act of pitching **3.** the slope of a roof **4.** the highness or lowness of tone —*vb.* **1.** to set up (*pitch* a tent) **2.** toss (*pitch* hay) **3.** to throw a baseball **4.** to adjust the highness of tone of a tune (*pitch* it a little lower)

pitch·er (pich′ ər) *n.* **1.** a container with a handle and a lip for holding and pouring liquids **2.** a baseball player who pitches

pit·y (pit′ ē) *n.* sympathy for the problems of others —*vb.* **pit·ied**; **pit·y·ing** to have pity for

piv·ot (piv′ ət) *n.* a point on which something turns (She *pivots* on one toe.) —*vb.* to turn on a pivot

place (plās) *n.* **1.** a space or spot (a *place* to study) **2.** a duty (It is my *place* to wash dishes today.) **3.** position in the rank order (in last *place*) **4.** the position of a numeral in relation to others (*place* value) —*vb.* **placed**; **plac·ing** **1.** to put in place **2.** to find a job

plague (plāg) *n.* **1.** an epidemic disease **2.** something troublesome —*vb.* **plagued**; **plagu·ing** **1.** to make miserable due to disease **2.** to torment

plain (plān) *adj.* **1.** open, smooth, clear to the eyes (in *plain* sight) **2.** obvious, clear to the mind (in *plain* language) **3.** simple, ordinary, common (*plain* people, *plain* food) **4.** simple weave, solid color, without decoration (*plain* dress) —*n.* a wide stretch of level grassland (Cattle feed on the *plains.*) —*adv.* simply, openly, clearly

plan (plan) *n.* **1.** diagram or outline (floor *plan* of the house) **2.** a list of actions in sequence, a procedure (travel *plans*) —*vb.* **planned**; **plan·ning** to make a plan (*plan* a sports center)

plane (plān) *vb.* **planed**; **plan·ing** to make something smooth and even with a plane —*n.* **1.** a carpenter's tool for stripping off thin layers of wood **2.** a flat, even surface **3.** airplane —*adj.* flat, level

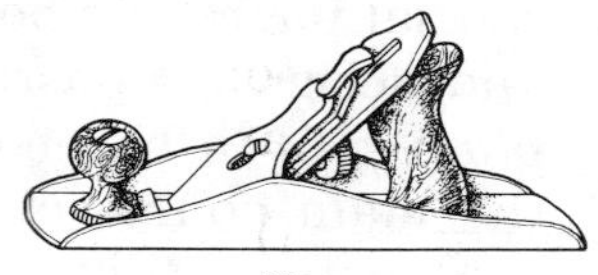

Plane

plan·et (plan′ ət) *n.* a heavenly body that revolves around the sun and shines by reflected light

plank (plangk) *n.* **1.** a thick piece of sawed timber **2.** an item in a party platform on which political candidates run for election

plank·ton (plangk′ tən) *n.* the microscopic plant and animal life that is freely floating or weakly swimming on the surface of the ocean

plant (plant) *vb.* **1.** to place in soil to grow (*plant* tomatoes) **2.** to found or settle (*plant* a colony) —*n.* **1.** any living thing with cellulose cell walls but without sensation or the ability to move **2.** the buildings, tools, machinery, and fixtures of an industry or institution (the school's physical *plant*)

plan·ta·tion (plan tā′ shən) *n.* **1.** an estate which includes a large planted area cultivated by laborers **2.** any large planted area (coffee *plantation*)

plant·er (plant′ ər) *n.* **1.** the owner or cultivator of a plantation **2.** a person or machine that plants seeds **3.** a container for planting decorative plants

plas·ter (plas′ tər) *n.* a material for coating walls and ceilings —*vb.* to cover with plaster

plas·tic (plas′ tik) *adj.* **1.** made of plastic **2.** capable of being molded or shaped —*n.* a material that can be molded or formed into films, fibers, and substitutes for wood, glass, leather, and other materials

plate (plāt) *n.* **1.** thin, rigid material (steel *plate*) **2.** a shallow dish (china *plate*) **3.** a piece of metal on which something is printed or engraved (license *plate*) **4.** a sheet of metal engraved with pictures or text for making special pages in a book **5.** a seal with the owner's name and design for pasting inside the cover of a book (book-*plate*) **6.** in baseball, the home base (home *plate*) **7.** the main course of a meal —*vb.* **plat·ed**; **plat·ing** to coat with a thin layer of metal, often gold or silver

pla·teau (pla tō′) *n., pl.* **pla·teaus** a high land that is broad and flat

plat·form (plat′ fȯrm′) *n.* **1.** a raised surface, as a stage or railroad platform **2.** a statement of the principles and policies of a political party

plat·i·num (plat′ n əm) *n.* a rare, heavy, grayish-white metallic element used widely for chemical utensils and expensive jewelry

play (plā) *n.* **1.** the amusement and experimentation of children as they interact with others and with objects **2.** the activity in games and other active recreation (his turn at *play*) **3.** the stage presentation of a story (a *play*) **4.** quick movements (the *play* of light through the trees) —*vb.* **1.** to take part in a sport or activity **2.** to amuse oneself **3.** to perform on an instrument **4.** to move swiftly, as a light flickers

play·ful (plā′ fəl) *adj.* full of jest or humor

play·ground (plā′ graůnd) *n.* an area set aside for games and recreation

plead (plēd) *vb.* **plead·ed** or **pled**; **plead·ing** **1.** to beg or pray (*plead* for mercy) **2.** to argue for or against a charge before the court **3.** to answer "guilty" or "not guilty"

pleas·ant (plez′ nt) *adj.* pleasing and agreeable

please (plēz) *vb.* **pleased**; **pleas·ing** **1.** to give enjoyment **2.** to be willing (if you *please*)

plea·sure (plezh′ ər) *n.* **1.** a joyous feeling **2.** wish or preference (I await your *pleasure.*)

pledge (plej) *n.* **1.** a binding promise **2.** something given as security for one's word —*vb.* **pledged**; **pledg·ing** **1.** to promise **2.** to give as a guarantee **3.** to drink a toast to one's health

plen·ti·ful (plent′ i fəl) *adj.* yielding or existing in abundance

plen·ty (plent′ ē) *n.* a full supply or as much as one might need

plot (plät) *n.* **1.** a small piece of ground **2.** the story line of a novel, short story, or play **3.** a devilish scheme

plow (plau̇) *n.* **1.** a farm implement for turning up the soil in preparation for planting **2.** an attachment for the front of a truck for use in scraping snow from a roadway —*vb.* **1.** to break up **2.** to break into and forge ahead (*plow* into her work)

pluck (plək) *vb.* **1.** to pick (*pluck* apples) **2.** to remove (*pluck* feathers) **3.** to pull a string and let go (*pluck* a harp) —*n.* **1.** a pull or tug **2.** courage, self-confidence, bravery

plug (pləg) *n.* **1.** something, as of rubber or metal, used to fill a hole **2.** a device on the end of a cord designed to make an electrical connection —*vb.* **plugged**; **plug·ging** **1.** to stop a leak **2.** to work steadily (*plug* along) **3.** to connect to an electrical outlet

plum (pləm) *n.* **1.** a smooth, oval, edible fruit related to the peach and often red or purple in color **2.** a dark, reddish-purple color **3.** something choice or desirable

plum·age (plü′ mij) *n.* a bird's feathers

plume (plüm) *n.* a long, beautiful feather (the *plume* of a peacock) —*vb.* **1.** to adjust and preen (The bird *plumes* itself.) **2.** to pride or feel proud **3.** to beautify with feathers

plump (pləmp) *adj.* well filled out —*vb.* **1.** to make something plump **2.** to fall heavily (*plumped* down on the chair)

plunge (plənj) *vb.* **plunged**; **plung·ing** **1.** to dive or jump (*plunge* into the water) **2.** to go headlong into something (*plunged* into his work) —*n.* **1.** a sudden leap **2.** a reckless investment

plu·ral (plůr′ əl) *adj.* relating to a word form meaning more than one (*plural* noun)

plus (pləs) *prep.* increased by (three *plus* two) —*adj.* **1.** more than zero (a *plus* number) **2.** indicating addition (the *plus* sign) **3.** relating to positive electricity (the *plus* terminal)

ply·wood (plī′ wůd′) *n.* a building material made by gluing thin layers of wood together, usually at right angles for strength, and applying heat and pressure

pneu·mo·nia (nů mō′ nyə) *n.* a disease causing inflammation of the lungs

pock·et (päk′ ət) *n.* **1.** a pouch stitched into or onto a garment for carrying small things **2.** a pocket-shaped place or thing **3.** a space in a wall for receiving a sliding door **4.** an air space where there is a sudden change of density, causing airplanes to drop (an air *pocket*) —*vb.* **1.** to put in a pocket (to *pocket* the money) **2.** to act without showing (to *pocket* one's feelings)

po·em (pō′ əm) *n.* a written message in verse

po·et (pō′ ət) *n.* one who writes poems

po·et·ic (pō et′ ik) *adj.* relating to poets or poetry

po·et·ry (pō′ ə trē) *n.* **1.** poems **2.** writing in verse with rhythm and meter, usually expressing lofty thoughts

point (pȯint) *n.* **1.** an item or detail **2.** the important topic (main *point*) **3.** a dot, which has position but no dimension **4.** the sharp end of something, as a pin —*vb.* **1.** to sharpen (put a *point* on) **2.** to indicate position or direction with the extended forefinger **3.** to separate whole numbers from decimals (*point* off two places) **4.** to head in a direction (*point* east)

poise (pȯiz) *vb.* **poised**; **pois·ing** **1.** to balance **2.** to hang suspended, to hover (*poised* for a strike)

poi·son (pȯiz′ n) *n.* a substance which causes death, usually by chemical action, when introduced into the body —*vb.* **1.** to kill or injure with poison **2.** to corrupt or contaminate (*poison*ed their minds)

poi·son·ous (pȯiz′ n əs) *adj.* **1.** having the effect of poison **2.** deadly

poke (pōk) *n.* **1.** a bag or sack (a pig in a *poke*) **2.** a common herb with white flowers and purple berries, also called pokeweed or pigeon berry **3.** a thrust or push **4.** *slang:* a slow person —*vb.* **1.** to push against or prod **2.** to thrust in or out

po·lar (pō′ lər) *adj.* **1.** relating to the earth's north pole or south pole **2.** relating to a pole of a magnet

pole (pōl) *n.* **1.** either end of the earth's axis **2.** one terminal of an electrical cell **3.** a long, slim staff or rod (a fishing *pole*) —*vb.* to push with a long pole

po·lice (pə lēs′) *n., pl.* **police** the part of the government that enforces the law, prevents and detects crime, and keeps order —*vb.* **po·liced**; **po·lic·ing** to watch and keep order

po·lice·man (pə lēs′ mən) or **po·lice·wom·an** (pə lēs′ wu̇m′ ən) *n., pl.* **po·lice·men**; **po·lice·wom·en** a member of the police force

pol·i·cy (päl′ ə sē) *n., pl.* **pol·i·cies** **1.** a course of action adopted as a basis for making decisions (Our *policy* is not to pay for employee travel.) **2.** a document telling what an insurance company will do in exchange for the premium paid

po·li·o (pō′ lē ō) *n.* poliomyelitis

po·li·o·my·e·li·tis (pō′ lē ō′ mī′ ə līt′ əs) *n.* an infectious disease, more common in children, causing inflammation of the nerve cells and resulting in paralysis often followed by a wasting away of affected muscles

pol·ish (päl′ ish) *vb.* **1.** to give a shine or luster to a surface or piece of furniture, especially when made of wood **2.** to teach someone good manners —*n.* **1.** a product used to make something shine **2.** a shiny surface **3.** good manners

po·lite (pə līt′) *adj.* **po·lit·er**; **po·lit·est** **1.** related to the traits of a well-educated person **2.** showing courtesy

po·lit·i·cal (pə lit′ i kəl) *adj.* pertaining to politics or government

pol·i·ti·cian (päl′ ə tish′ ən) *n.* **1.** one who is involved in party politics **2.** a seeker or holder of public office **3.** one who is skilled in the science of government **4.** a statesman **5.** sometimes, one who seeks power and favors

pol·i·tics (päl′ ə tiks′) *n., sing.* or *pl.* the science and art of government

pol·len (päl′ ən) *n.* **1.** the dustlike powder in the center of flowers which fertilizes the seeds **2.** this material, mainly in ragweed, that causes hay fever

pol·lute (pə lüt′) *vb.* **pol·lut·ed**; **pol·lut·ing** to make foul or impure (*pollute* the river)

pol·lu·tion (pə lü′ shən) *n.* **1.** the act of making unclean **2.** the state of being unclean **3.** contamination

pond (pänd) *n.* a small body of water

po·ny (pō′ nē) *n., pl.* **po·nies** a small breed of horse, usually not more than fourteen hands high at the shoulder, or 56 inches, one "hand" being equal to 4 inches

pool (pül) *n.* **1.** a small body of water, often rather deep (swimming *pool*) **2.** a game like billiards played on a table with six pockets **3.** the money collected by bettors or investors

poor (pür) *adj.* **1.** lacking in money and goods **2.** not good in quality **3.** feeble (*poor* condition)

pop (päp) *vb.* **popped**; **pop·ping** **1.** to burst with a noise (*pop* the balloon) **2.** to open wide (His eyes *popped* out.) —*n.* **1.** an explosive sound **2.** a carbonated drink or soda **3.** a gunshot

pop·corn (päp′ kȯrn′) *n.* a variety of corn with small kernels that, when heated, burst with a popping noise into puffy, white nuggets; usually served with salt and melted butter

pop·py (päp′ ē) *n., pl.* **pop·pies** **1.** a hairy-stemmed plant with attractive flowers, usually red, but may be yellow or white in some species **2.** an artificial flower given in return for a contribution to a fund for disabled war veterans

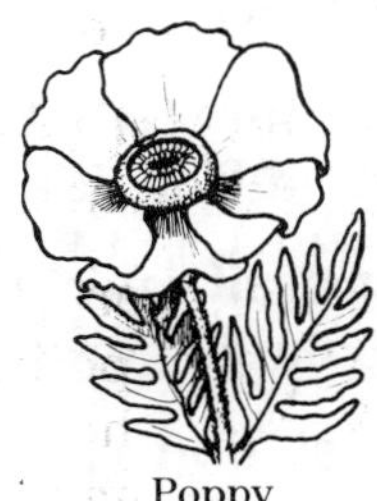
Poppy

pop·u·lar (päp′ yə lər) *adj.* **1.** relating to all the people (*popular* vote) **2.** appealing to most people (*popular* music) **3.** easy to understand (*popular* psychology)

pop·u·la·tion (päp′ yə lā′ shən) *n.* the total number of people living in a state, region, or nation

porch (pōrch) *n.* a covered platform or veranda built out from the main wall of a house and forming an approach to the entrance door, a piazza

por·cu·pine (pȯr′ kyə pīn′) *n.* a gnawing rodent having barbed spines or quills mixed in its hairy coat

pork (pōrk) *n.* the fresh or salted flesh of a pig prepared as food

po·rous (pōr′ əs) *adj.* **1.** full of tiny holes **2.** capable of absorbing liquids (*porous* sponge)

por·poise (pȯr′ pəs) *n.* **1.** a small, gregarious marine mammal, five to eight feet long, usually blackish on the back and pale beneath, and having a blunt, rounded snout **2.** a cetacean related to the whales and dolphins

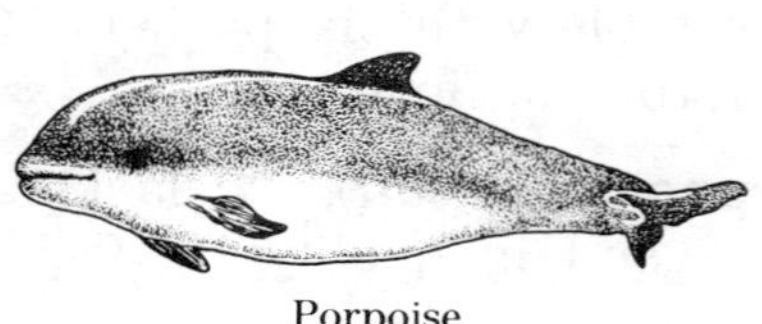

Porpoise

por·ridge (pȯr′ ij) *n.* a food made by boiling the meal of a grain in water until it thickens (oatmeal *porridge*)

port (pōrt) *n.* **1.** a harbor where ships arrive and depart **2.** an airport **3.** the left side of a ship or airplane, when looking forward —*adj.* on the left side of a ship (a *port* cabin)

por·tion (pōr′ shən) *n.* a piece or part of something —*vb.* to divide into shares and distribute

por·trait (por′ trət, -trāt′) *n.* a picture of a person drawn, painted, or photographed from real life

po·si·tion (pə zish′ ən) *n.* **1.** the location or situation (*position* of the water tower) **2.** the condition (in an awkward *position*) **3.** work, employment (found a *position*) **4.** social standing (person of high *position*)

pos·i·tive (päz′ ət iv) *adj.* **1.** definitely and carefully stated (a *positive* statement of confidence) **2.** based on fact or experience (*positive* proof) **3.** confident and certain (*positive* he will win) **4.** more than zero (a *positive* number) **5.** a plus (+) terminal of a battery (*positive* pole) **6.** showing the presence of what was tested for (The test for scarlet fever was *positive.*)

pos·sess (pə zes′) *vb.* **1.** to own **2.** to have in one's control (*possess*ed the power to free them)

pos·ses·sion (pə zesh′ ən) *n.* **1.** ownership (wanted *possession* of the cabin near the lake) **2.** something owned (lost his *possession*s in the flood) **3.** control (The team had *possession* of the football.)

pos·ses·sive (pə zes′ iv) *adj.* **1.** showing the desire to own or keep **2.** being a form of a noun or pronoun that shows possession —*n.* a form of a word that shows possession (girl's)

pos·si·bil·i·ty (päs′ ə bil′ ət ē) *n., pl.* **pos·si·bil·i·ties** **1.** the condition of being able to happen **2.** something that may happen

post (pōst) *n.* **1.** a strong, upright length of metal or timber used to support or hold something (fence *post,* lamp*post*) **2.** a pole on a race track indicating the start or finish line of a race **3.** a place where troops are stationed (army *post*) —*vb.* **1.** to pin up a notice (*post* the notice) **2.** to send by mail (*post* a letter) **3.** to assign someone to watch (*post* a guard)

post·age (pōs′ tij) *n.* the amount charged for sending by mail

post·er (pōs′ tər) *n.* a large advertisement intended to be posted in a public place

pos·ture (päs′ chər) *n.* the way one holds the body in sitting, standing, or walking —*vb.* **pos·tured**; **pos·tur·ing** to get into a particular position or pose

pot (pät) *n.* **1.** a deep container, usually metal, used in the kitchen for cooking **2.** a clay or plastic container for growing plants —*vb.* **pot·ted**; **pot·ting** to put or keep in a pot

po·ta·to (pə tāt′ ō) *n., pl.* **po·ta·toes** a thick, underground tuber that is widely grown and eaten

po·ten·tial (pə ten′ chəl) *adj.* possible

pot·ter·y (pät′ ə rē) *n., pl.* **pot·ter·ies** a place where wet clay is shaped into dishes, vases, or other containers and hardened by baking in a kiln at high temperatures

pouch (pau̇ch) *n.* **1.** a bag or sack for carrying something (mail *pouch*) **2.** a fold of skin for carrying the young, as on a kangaroo —*vb.* to put into a pouch

poul·try (pōl′ trē) *n.* domestic fowls, such as turkeys, chickens, ducks, and geese, raised to provide meat and eggs for food

pound (paůnd) *n.* **1.** sixteen ounces in avoirdupois (an English and American system of weights) weight **2.** the basic unit of money in Great Britain as the dollar is in the United States **3.** a fenced-in area where stray dogs are kept —*vb.* to hit hard, over and over again

pour (pōr) *vb.* **1.** to cause to flow out freely (*pour*ed milk into the glass) **2.** to rain hard (*pour*ed all morning) **3.** to let out feelings and thoughts (*pour*ed out his problems)

pov·er·ty (päv′ ərt ē) *n.* **1.** the state of being poor or in need **2.** lack of something (They faced the *poverty* of their emergency supplies.)

pow·der (paůd′ ər) *n.* **1.** fine particles of something (talcum *powder*) **2.** an explosive used in blasting or gunnery (gun*powder*) —*vb.* **1.** to grind to a powder **2.** to sprinkle with powder

pow·er (paů′ ər) *n.* **1.** the ability and the authority to do something **2.** control (in the *power* of the authorities) **3.** the person or group in a position of influence (The United States is a world *power*.) **4.** force or energy (nuclear *power*) —*adj.* **1.** relating to power (*power* play) **2.** using power (*power* drill) —*vb.* to supply with power (Propane gas *power*s the torch.)

pow·er·ful (paů′ ər fəl) *adj.* strong; full of power

prac·ti·cal (prak′ ti kəl) *adj.* **1.** relating to experience and practice (*practical* knowledge) **2.** relating to action and usefulness rather than thought (*practical* person)

prac·tice (prak′ təs) *vb.* **prac·ticed**; **prac·tic·ing** **1.** to do frequently or as a rule (*practice* neatness) **2.** to do exercises as a means of learning (*practice* the guitar) **3.** to work in a profession (*practice* law) —*n.* **1.** habit (the *practice* of jogging daily) **2.** exercise to gain skill

prai·rie (preər′ ē) *n.* a large area of fairly level grassland

praise (prāz) *vb.* **praised**; **prais·ing** **1.** to applaud or show approval (*praise* her workmanship) **2.** to worship or glorify (*praise* the Lord) —*n.* **1.** an act of praising **2.** worship

pray (prā) *vb.* **1.** to beg or petition (*pray* to be excused) **2.** to speak to God (*pray* for her father's health)

prayer (praər) *n.* **1.** the act of praying **2.** a particular set of words (the Lord's *Prayer*) **3.** words of praise, thanksgiving, or petition to God (a *prayer* for suitable employment) **4.** a service that is mostly prayer

pre·cau·tion (pri kȯ′ shən) *n.* **1.** an advance plan to avoid problems **2.** positive steps taken in advance to prevent evil and bring good results

pre·cede (pri sēd′) *vb.* **pre·ced·ed**; **pre·ced·ing** to go before in time, place, rank, or importance

pre·cious (presh′ əs) *adj.* **1.** of high price (*precious* stones) **2.** highly valued (*precious* memories) **3.** dearly loved (*precious* person)

pre·cise (pri sīs′) *adj.* **1.** exact and definite (*precise* orders) **2.** accurate and distinct (*precise* words)

pre·ci·sion (pri sizh′ ən) *n.* accuracy and exactness (the *precision* of the instrument)

pred·i·cate (pred′ i kət) *n.* the part of a sentence that tells something about the subject; the verb and its modifiers

pre·dict (pri dikt′) *vb.* to tell in advance or forecast (*predict* a change in the weather)

pre·dic·tion (pri dik′ shən) *n.* a forecast or prophecy

pre·fer (pri fər′) *vb.* **pre·ferred**; **pre·fer·ring** to desire or choose something else (I *prefer* red to blue.)

pre·fix (prē′ fiks′) *vb.* to add at the beginning (to *prefix* the word "cover" with "dis" to make "discover") —*n.* a meaningful unit attached to the beginning of a word which changes its meaning

pre·his·tor·ic (prē′ his tȯr′ ik) *adj.* relating to a time before written records were kept (*prehistoric* animals)

prej·u·dice (prej′ ə dəs) *n.* a personal bias that causes one to make a judgment without considering facts or reason —*vb.* **prej·u·diced**; **prej·u·dic·ing** to damage or injure with an unfair opinion

pre·lim·i·nar·y (pri lim′ ə ner′ ē) *n., pl.* **pre·lim·i·nar·ies** something that is done before the main part of the action or process —*adj.* preparatory or introductory

prep·a·ra·tion (prep′ ə rā′ shən) *n.* **1.** the act of getting ready (the *preparations* for the senior play) **2.** the things that have been made ready (The class lists and other *preparations* are completed.)

pre·pare (pri paər′) *vb.* **pre·pared**; **pre·par·ing** to make ready (*prepare* for the trip)

prep·o·si·tion (prep′ ə zish′ ən) *n.* a word that shows the relationship of the noun or pronoun that follows it to some other word in the sentence

pre·scribe (pri skrīb′) *vb.* **pre·scribed**; **pre·scrib·ing** **1.** to set down a rule of action (to *prescribe* limits to coffee breaks) **2.** to advise the use of a medication or treatment (The doctor *prescribed* aspirin and bed rest.)

pres·ence (prez′ ns) *n.* **1.** the fact of being in a particular place (His *presence* went unnoticed.) **2.** the state of being nearby (Her *presence* surprised them.) **3.** a person's appearance (a person of dignified *presence*)

pres·ent (prez′ nt) *n.* a gift —*vb.* (pri zent′) **1.** to introduce (*present* a friend) **2.** to bring into view (*present* before the court) **3.** to put on for the audience (*present* a play) **4.** to give as a gift (to *present* a token of appreciation)

pres·er·va·tion (prez′ ər vā′ shən) *n.* the act of keeping from harm or loss

pre·serve (pri zərv′) *vb.* **pre·served**; **pre·serv·ing** **1.** to protect from loss or injury **2.** to prepare to keep without spoiling (*preserve* tomatoes) **3.** to maintain (to *preserve* peace) —*n.* **1.** an area where game or fish are protected (a game *preserve*) **2.** *pl.* fruits and vegetables prepared for winter storage by cooking or freezing

pres·i·dent (prez′ ə dənt) *n.* **1.** the chief of state of a modern republic **2.** a person who presides over a meeting **3.** the chief officer of a corporation, university, or society

press (pres) *n.* **1.** a machine for putting pressure on something to flatten or stamp it **2.** the news media (the *press*) **3.** a closet for clothing (clothes*press*) **4.** a printing machine (a printing *press*) —*vb.* **1.** to put pressure on in order to squeeze or flatten **2.** to strongly urge

pres·sure (presh′ ər) *n.* **1.** the act of pushing or squeezing **2.** the use of influence or authority (political *pressure*) **3.** the distress of conflicts in schedule (*pressure* of daily life)

pres·tige (pres tēzh′) *n.* the importance one has due to reputation and achievement

pre·tend (pri tend′) *vb.* **1.** to make believe **2.** to make a false show (to *pretend* interest when the story bored her)

pret·ty (prit′ ē) *adj.* **pret·ti·er**; **pret·ti·est** pleasing or attractive in a feminine way —*adv.* fairly or moderately (*pretty* old)

pre·vail (pri vāl′) *vb.* **1.** to exist generally (Silence *prevailed* in the library.) **2.** to gain the advantage or to prove to be better (Their friendship *prevail*ed through the hard times.) **3.** to persuade (*prevail*ed upon him to come)

pre·vent (pri vent′) *vb.* to stop or keep from happening (*prevent* forest fires)

pre·vi·ous (prē′ vē əs) *adj.* coming before in time, earlier (received my letter *previous* to yours)

prey (prā) *n.* **1.** an animal hunted by another for food (Mice fall *prey* to the hawks.) **2.** a helpless person **3.** the act of hunting animals for food (birds of *prey*) —*vb.* **1.** to seize and eat (The dogs *prey* upon the rabbits in the area.) **2.** to have a bad effect (His guilt *prey*ed upon him.)

price (prīs) *n.* the cost of something (The *price* is low.) —*vb.* **priced**; **pric·ing** **1.** to put a price on something **2.** to ask the cost of something (*price*d the videotape)

prick·ly (prik′ lē) *adj.* **prick·li·er**; **prick·li·est** **1.** having thorns or spines **2.** stinging (a *prickly* feeling)

pride (prīd) *n.* **1.** a boastful attitude **2.** too high an opinion of one's importance **3.** a feeling of dignity and self-respect **4.** something one is proud of (His wonderful children were his *pride.*) —*vb.* **prid·ed**; **prid·ing** to have a feeling of pride

priest (prēst) *n.* one who has been ordained to preside at religious services

pri·mar·y (prī′ mer′ ē) *adj.* **1.** first in the order of things (the *primary* grades) **2.** first in importance (our *primary* aim) **3.** basic (The *primary* colors are red, yellow, and blue.) —*n., pl.* **pri·mar·ies** an election in which members of political parties choose their candidates for office

prime (prīm) *n.* the first or best part of something —*adj.* first in time or importance —*vb.* **primed**; **prim·ing** to get something or someone ready to work or operate

prim·i·tive (prim′ ət iv) *adj.* **1.** relating to the first or earliest **2.** simple and crude

prince (prins) *n.* the son of a king or emperor, in line to be king

prin·cess (prin′ səs) *n.* **1.** the daughter of a king or emperor **2.** the wife of a prince

prin·ci·pal (prin′ sə pəl) *adj.* the first or highest in rank —*n.* **1.** the person who plays the most important part **2.** the head of a school

prin·ci·ple (prin′ sə pəl) *n.* **1.** a rule of action **2.** a foundation or underlying truth (the *principle*s of education)

print (print) *n.* **1.** a mark made by pressure (thumb*print*) **2.** something that has been printed (large *print*) **3.** cloth stamped with a design (The cloth had a Liberty of London *print* on it.) —*vb.* **1.** to stamp or press (*print* the designs) **2.** to publish (*print* the newspaper) **3.** to write in letters like type (*print* your name) **4.** to make a picture from a negative (*print* extra copies)

print·er (print′ ər) *n.* **1.** a person whose trade is printing books or other matter **2.** a machine that prints

pri·or (prī′ ər) *adj.* coming before in time, order, or importance —*n.* a religious officer at the head of a priory of monks

prism (priz′ əm) *n.* a transparent, three-sided bar used to separate light into the colors of the rainbow

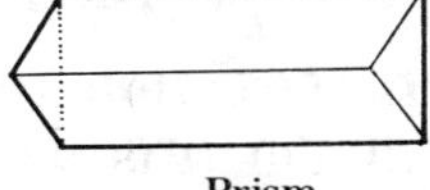
Prism

pris·on (priz′ n) *n.* jail, a place where prisoners may be held

pris·on·er (priz′ n ər) *n.* **1.** a person serving a sentence in prison **2.** an enemy soldier captured during warfare

pri·vate (prī′ vət) *adj.* **1.** relating to an individual or an organized group (*private* business) **2.** not holding a public office or position (a *private* citizen) —*n.* an enlisted man in the army, a common soldier

priv·i·lege (priv′ ə lij) *n.* a special right enjoyed by some but not others

prize (prīz) *n.* **1.** a reward for a contest winner **2.** something of value worth trying for **3.** something taken from an enemy during war, such as a ship —*vb.* to value something

prob·a·ble (präb′ ə bəl) *adj.* likely but not certain

prob·a·bly (präb′ ə blē) *adv.* very likely

probe (prōb) *n.* **1.** a close examination **2.** a thin instrument for checking a small cavity —*vb.* **probed**; **prob·ing** to examine, investigate

prob·lem (präb′ ləm) *n.* **1.** a matter involving difficulty or uncertainty **2.** a question posed for discussion **3.** in mathematics, an exercise to be worked out

pro·ce·dure (prə sē′ jər) *n.* the way something is done

pro·ceed (prō sēd′) *vb.* **1.** to go onward (*Proceed* with your work after lunch.) **2.** to come out of (A big crowd *proceed*ed from the pep rally.)

pro·cess (präs′ es′) *n.* **1.** a series of steps in an operation (Building a house is a difficult *process.*) **2.** the slow changes that take place over time (the *process* of growing older) —*vb.* to put something through a process (to *process* the apples for cider)

pro·ces·sion (prə sesh′ ən) *n.* the act of moving forward in an orderly way (the funeral *procession*)

pro·claim (prō klām′) *vb.* to make an official announcement (to *proclaim* today as literacy day)

pro·duce (prə düs′) *vb.* **pro·duced**; **pro·duc·ing** **1.** to do, to gather, to show (to *produce* more evidence) **2.** to put on, as a play (*produce* a stage show) **3.** to yield (This tree *produce*s cherries.) **4.** to manufacture (The factory *produce*s electronic devices.) —*n.* (präd′ üs, prōd′ üs) fresh fruits and vegetables

prod·uct (präd′ əkt) *n.* **1.** anything that is made whether by physical labor or mental labor (The idea came as a *product* of his experience.) **2.** the answer in multiplication (The *product* of 2×3 is 6.)

pro·duc·tion (prə dək′ shən) *n.* **1.** the act of producing (the *production* of cameras) **2.** something produced (the stage *production*)

pro·fes·sion (prə fesh′ ən) *n.* **1.** an occupation that requires an extended period of learning and that is mental rather than physical in nature, such as teaching, law, and medicine **2.** a declaration of one's beliefs or actions (a *profession* of religious faith or friendship)

pro·fes·sor (prə fes′ ər) *n.* a teacher of the highest rank at a college or university

prof·it (präf′ ət) *n.* **1.** monetary gain, which is income less expenses **2.** benefit or advantage (There is *profit* in taking clear notes.) —*vb.* to benefit (to *profit* from the deal)

prof·it·a·ble (präf′ ət ə bəl) *adj.* yielding a gain or benefit (*profitable* business)

pro·gram (prō′ gram, -grəm) *n.* **1.** a brief outline or list of the things to be presented **2.** a plan of action for a project **3.** a performance (a radio *program*)

prog·ress (präg′ rəs) *n.* **1.** a movement forward **2.** growth or development (*progress* of the class) —*vb.* (prə gres′) **1.** to go forward **2.** to improve, grow, or develop (to *progress* in age and wisdom)

pro·gres·sion (prə gresh′ ən) *n.* the act of going forward or moving through stages of development

proj·ect (präj′ ekt′) *n.* **1.** a plan or scheme **2.** in school, an assignment that requires planning and the use of talent and energy to carry it out **3.** a large-scale effort that requires many resources (a housing *project*)

pro·jec·tion (prə jek′ shən) *n.* **1.** something that juts out **2.** a way of representing the earth's surface on paper, as in a map (a polar *projection*, a Mercator *projection*) **3.** an estimate of changes that may occur in the future (a *projection* of population growth)

prom·i·nent (präm′ ə nənt) *adj.* **1.** noticeable (a *prominent* nose) **2.** distinguished (a *prominent* person in the community)

prom·ise (präm′ əs) *n.* **1.** a formal agreement to do something (a *promise* to deliver an article on time) **2.** an indication of the future (This student shows *promise.*) —*vb.* **prom·ised**; **prom·is·ing** to make a promise

pro·mote (prə mōt′) *vb.* **pro·mot·ed**; **pro·mot·ing** **1.** to move up in rank or position (*promoted* to the job of supervisor) **2.** to help something to flourish or improve (*promote* the welfare of the elderly)

pro·mo·tion (prə mō′ shən) *n.* **1.** advancement in position or rank **2.** the act of helping something to grow (the *promotion* of peace)

prompt (prämpt) *vb.* **1.** to rouse to action (*prompt* her to do it) **2.** to remind of something not remembered (*prompt* an actress)

pro·noun (prō′ naůn′) *n.* a word such as *she* that is used as a substitute for a noun

pro·nounce (prə naůns′) *vb.* **pro·nounced**; **pro·nounc·ing** **1.** to declare (They *pronounced* him free to leave.) **2.** to speak clearly (*Pronounce* these words.)

pro·nun·ci·a·tion (prə nən′ sē ā′ shən) *n.* the act or manner of saying a word

proof (prüf) *n.* **1.** evidence that something is true **2.** the facts or tests that prove something —*adj.* capable of resisting (water*proof* coat)

proof·read (prüf′ rēd′) *vb.* **proof·read** (-red′); **proof·read·ing** (-rēd′ ing) to read in order to make corrections

prop (präp) *n.* something that supports something else (They put another *prop* under the tree house.) —*vb.* **propped**; **prop·ping** to support by placing something under or against (They *propped* a sagging wall.)

prop·a·gan·da (präp′ ə gan′ də) *n.* the deliberate spreading of ideas to help or harm a person or cause

pro·pel (prə pel′) *vb.* **pro·pelled**; **pro·pel·ling** to drive onward (*propel* the bicycle)

pro·pel·ler (prə pel′ ər) *n.* a device with blades for cutting through air or water causing an airplane or ship to move forward

Propeller

prop·er (präp′ ər) *adj.* **1.** suitable, fitting (That's not a *proper* outfit to wear.) **2.** appropriate to some persons or things (*proper* in their culture) **3.** specific to one place (the population of Dallas *proper*)

prop·er·ty (präp′ ərt ē) *n., pl.* **prop·er·ties** **1.** a characteristic or trait (Coldness is a *property* of ice.) **2.** something that is owned (The house is her *property.*)

proph·e·cy (präf′ ə sē) *n., pl.* **proph·e·cies** **1.** a prediction of something to come **2.** the sayings of a prophet

pro·por·tion (prə pōr′ shən) *n.* **1.** the relation of size, number, and degree of one thing to another (In sports, the *proportion* of boys to girls is three to one in this school.) **2.** a good balance of all parts (The bookcase has good *proportions.*) —*vb.* to make the parts suitable to each other in size or shape

pro·pos·al (prə pō′ zəl) *n.* **1.** the act of offering something for consideration **2.** an offer of marriage

pro·pose (prə pōz′) *vb.* **pro·posed**; **pro·pos·ing** **1.** to suggest or offer for consideration **2.** to make an offer of marriage

prop·o·si·tion (präp′ ə zish′ ən) *n.* **1.** a proposal **2.** a statement of a topic to be discussed **3.** in math, the statement of a theorem to be demonstrated or a problem to be solved

pro·pul·sion (prə pəl′ shən) *n.* **1.** the act of driving forward **2.** the propelling force (The engine gives it *propulsion.*)

prose (prōz) *n.* **1.** the ordinary way people speak and write **2.** not poetry

pros·pect (präs′ pekt′) *n.* **1.** the view when looking out and ahead **2.** looking ahead in anticipation (This job has good *prospects* for next year.) **3.** a person who might want one's services (He's a good *prospect* for buying insurance.) —*vb.* to explore for mineral deposits (*prospect* for gold)

pros·per·i·ty (präs per′ ət ē) *n.* the state of being successful, with money enough for a good living

pros·per·ous (präs′ pə rəs) *adj.* having success and good fortune

pro·tag·o·nist (prō tag′ ə nist) *n.* **1.** the important or central character in a story or drama **2.** the chief supporter of a cause or movement

pro·tect (prə tekt′) *vb.* to guard and keep safe

pro·tec·tion (prə tek′ shən) *n.* **1.** the act of protecting **2.** the person or thing that keeps something safe, a defense (This shelter offers some *protection.*)

pro·tec·tive (prə tek′ tiv) *adj.* giving or intended to give protection

pro·tein (prō′ tēn′) *n.* a food nutrient containing nitrogen that is formed by animals and plants and is needed by humans and animals to maintain life processes

pro·test (prō′ test′) *n.* a formal statement objecting to something —*vb.* **1.** to plead and present reasons in complaint against a decision or action **2.** to demonstrate against

pro·ton (prō′ tän′) *n.* a very tiny particle carrying a positive electrical charge that is present in the nucleus of every atom and equal in magnitude to the electron, the number being different for each element

pro·tract (prō trakt′) *vb.* **1.** to make longer in time or space **2.** to map by means of a scale **3.** to extend using a protractor

pro·trac·tor (prō trak′ tər) *n.* an instrument for measuring and figuring angles on paper

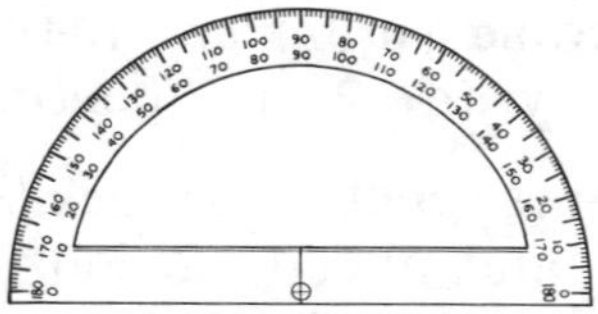

Protractor

pro·trude (prō trüd′) *vb.* **pro·trud·ed**; **pro·trud·ing** to stick out or project (The long handle *protrudes* from the toolbox.)

proud (praůd) *adj.* **1.** being too satisfied with oneself **2.** feeling satisfaction or pleasure (*proud* of his daughter's success) **3.** having appropriate self-respect (too *proud* to ask for anything he didn't really need)

prove (prüv) *vb.* **proved**; **prov·ing** **1.** to provide good reasons or evidence **2.** to check by means of arithmetic

prov·erb (präv′ ərb′) *n.* a short saying expressing a well-known truth such as "A penny saved is a penny earned."

pro·vide (prə vīd′) *vb.* **pro·vid·ed**; **pro·vid·ing** **1.** to prepare or get ready in advance (*provide* for his retirement) **2.** to equip or supply (*provide* them with uniforms) **3.** to make as a requirement (You may go, *provide*d your homework is done.)

prov·ince (präv′ əns) *n.* a division of a country having a government of its own as in Canada (*Province* of Quebec)

pry (prī) *vb.* **pried**; **pry·ing** **1.** to look closely at, especially another person's business **2.** to remove a tight cover (*pry* open the lid)

psy·chi·a·trist (sī kī′ ə trist) *n.* a doctor who treats mental disorders

psy·chol·o·gist (sī käl′ ə jəst) *n.* a specialist in psychology

psy·chol·o·gy (sī käl′ ə jē) *n.* the science of human nature and behavior that deals with a person's mental states and processes

pub·lic (pəb′ lik) *n.* the people as a whole (The *public* is invited to attend.) —*adj.* **1.** relating to the people as a whole (*public* property) **2.** open to general use (a *public* beach) **3.** well-known (*public* figure)

pub·lic·i·ty (pəb′ lis′ ət ē) *n.* **1.** the process and business of getting public attention **2.** advertising (The campaign had radio and television *publicity.*)

pub·lish (pəb′ lish) *vb.* to print and offer for sale, especially a book or magazine (Her book was *publish*ed.)

pud·ding (pu̇d′ ing) *n.* a soft, creamy dessert usually made with milk, eggs, flavoring, and other ingredients (chocolate *pudding*)

pud·dle (pəd′ l) *n.* a small pool of dirty water (He got his shoes wet walking in *puddles*.)

pu·eb·lo (pü eb′ lō) *n., pl.* **pu·eb·los** a village of agricultural Indian people of the Southwest living in multiple dwelling adobe houses often built into cliff walls and entered by ladders, such as Montezuma's Castle in Arizona, now a national monument

puff (pəf) *n.* **1.** a short blast of air (*puffs* of smoke from the locomotive) **2.** a light, air-filled pastry (cream *puff*) **3.** a quilted bed covering —*vb.* **1.** to blow in little blasts **2.** to breathe hard from exercise **3.** to swell up

pull (pu̇l) *vb.* **1.** to exert force toward oneself (*pull* the wagon) **2.** to stretch (*pull* on the elastic band) **3.** to take out or off (*pull* a tooth) —*n.* **1.** the act of pulling (the *pull* on the cord) **2.** a force that moves something (*pull* of gravity)

pul·ley (pu̇l′ ē) *n., pl.* **pul·leys** **1.** a grooved wheel around which runs a belt or rope used for lifting something on one end of the rope by pulling down on the other, increasing the pulling force **2.** one of the simple machines

Pulley

pulp (pəlp) *n.* **1.** the soft fleshy part of a fruit or vegetable **2.** the soft mass of ground wood, cotton, or linen of which paper is made **3.** a low class of magazine printed on cheap paper (the *pulps*)

pulse (pəls) *n.* **1.** a beating or throbbing, as in an artery **2.** the beating of the arteries, caused by the regular contractions of the heart, which can be felt with fingertips next to the bone inside the wrist

pump (pəmp) *n.* a device for moving liquids —*vb.* **1.** to move fluids by raising, drawing, or forcing them, as with a pump **2.** to question (*pump* him for information)

pump·kin (pəmp′ kin) *n.* a yellow-orange fruit used as a vegetable and as a fall decoration

punch (pənch) *n.* **1.** a blow with the fist **2.** a tool for making holes **3.** a drink mixed with several ingredients, often including fruit juices —*vb.* to poke, prod, strike, or pierce (to *punch* cattle; to *punch* a hole)

punc·tu·a·tion (pəngk′ chə wā′ shən) *n.* the practice of using marks such as periods and commas in writing to make the meaning clear

pun·ish (pən′ ish) *vb.* to cause someone to suffer pain, the payment of a fine, jail, or even death for an offense or crime

pun·ish·ment (pən′ ish mənt) *n.* **1.** the act of punishing or state of being punished **2.** the penalty for a fault or crime (He had to do extra chores as *punishment.*)

pup (pəp) *n.* a young dog, a puppy

pu·pil (pyü′ pəl) *n.* **1.** anyone who is receiving lessons from a teacher, a student **2.** the dark center in the iris, or colored part, of the eye

pup·pet (pəp′ ət) *n.* **1.** a doll-like figure hanging on strings and moved from above in a sort of drama **2.** a person under the control of another person

Puppet

pup·py (pəp′ ē) *n., pl.* **pup·pies** a young dog

pur·chase (pər′ chəs) *vb.* **pur·chased**; **pur·chas·ing** to buy —*n.* **1.** the act of buying (the *purchase* of a set of tools) **2.** something bought (a necessary *purchase*)

pure (pyür) *adj.* **pur·er**; **pur·est** **1.** clear or clean **2.** free from anything else (*pure* gold) **3.** absolute (*pure* nonsense)

pur·ple (pər′ pəl) *n.* a mixture of red and blue —*adj.* a reddish-blue color

pur·pose (pər′ pəs) *n.* **1.** a reason **2.** an aim or intention

purse (pərs) *n.* **1.** a small bag for carrying money **2.** a woman's handbag **3.** money offered as a prize (The *purse* was $5,000.)

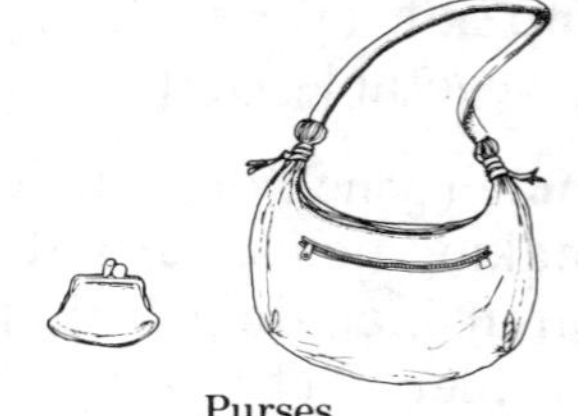
Purses

pur·sue (pər sü′) *vb.* **pur·sued**; **pur·su·ing** **1.** to chase with an effort to overtake or catch **2.** to continue with an effort to reach a goal (*pursue* business courses)

pur·suit (pər süt′) *n.* **1.** the act of chasing (in *pursuit* of the rabbit) **2.** an effort to reach a goal (the *pursuit* of freedom) **3.** an occupation or hobby that engages a person (her artistic *pursuits*)

push (pu̇sh) *vb.* **1.** to press against with force, with the intent of moving something (*Push* your chairs back quietly.) **2.** to thrust (*push* her way to the platform) **3.** to press oneself to try (*push* to get my work done)

put (pu̇t) *vb.* **put**; **put·ting** **1.** to move or place (I *put* the cup on the table.) **2.** to push or thrust (He *put* the ball through the hoop.) **3.** to express or translate (He *put* his notes into Spanish.) **4.** to bring to a certain condition (*Put* the fur in cold storage.) **5.** to attach (She *put* faith in their friendship.)

puz·zle (pəz′ əl) *vb.* **puz·zled**; **puz·zling** **1.** to confuse or baffle (The ad *puzzled* him.) **2.** to think about or weigh carefully (to *puzzle* over her car expenses) —*n.* **1.** a toy or word game that causes deep thought **2.** something that causes confusion or deep thought

pyr·a·mid (pir′ ə mid′) *n.* a huge structure with a square base and four triangular sides that meet in a point at the top, many of which were built in ancient Egypt as tombs for the pharaohs

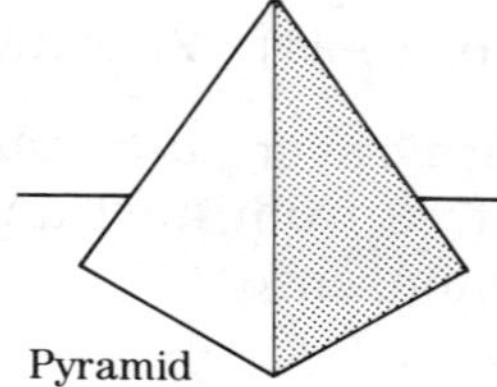
Pyramid

Q

quack (kwak) *vb.* to utter the throaty cry of a duck —*n.* **1.** the cry of a duck **2.** a person who falsely claims to have medical skill **3.** a person who falsely claims to have knowledge in any field —*adj.* relating to a quack (*quack* medicine)

quail (kwāl) *n., pl.* **quail** or **quails** a stocky game bird such as the bobwhite

quaint (kwānt) *adj.* having an old-fashioned attractiveness (a *quaint* little basket)

qual·i·fi·ca·tion (kwäl′ ə fə kā′ shən) *n.* **1.** the act of meeting standards of performance (the *qualifications* for a driver's license) **2.** the placing of limitations on something (The treatment will continue, with *qualifications*.)

qual·i·ty (kwäl′ ət ē) *n., pl.* **qual·i·ties** **1.** the nature or character of something (Loyalty was her outstanding *quality*.) **2.** high grade, superiority (His inner *quality* showed.)

quan·ti·ty (kwänt′ ət ē) *n., pl.* **quan·ti·ties** **1.** amount (a *quantity* of grain) **2.** number (a *quantity* of pumpkins)

quar·rel (kwȯr′ əl) *n.* a disagreement or angry dispute (They had a *quarrel* about money.) —*vb.* **quar·reled**; **quar·rel·ing** to find fault or disagree angrily

quar·ry (kwȯr′ ē) *n., pl.* **quar·ries** **1.** a large open hole from which blocks of stone are removed by cutting or blasting **2.** a hunted bird or animal (The dog picked up the scent of the *quarry*.) **3.** a square stone or tile

quart (kwȯrt) *n.* a measure of capacity equal to two pints or one-fourth gallon

quar·ter (kwȯrt′ ər) *n.* **1.** one-fourth of a whole **2.** a coin worth one-fourth of a dollar or twenty-five cents

3. one leg with the surrounding parts of an animal carcass (a hind*quarter* of beef) —*vb.* **1.** to divide into four equal parts **2.** to furnish with food and lodging —*adj.* relating to a quarter (a *quarter* past the hour)

quar·ter·back (kwȯrt′ ər bak′) *n.* in football, the back who directs the offense of the team and calls the plays

quartz (kwȯrts) *n.* one of the commonest minerals, silicon dioxide, the chief component of sand, found in masses such as agate or jasper, or crystals such as rock crystal and amethyst, and used in crystal form to control the frequencies of radio transmitters

queen (kwēn) *n.* **1.** a female monarch (Elizabeth, *Queen* of England) **2.** the wife or widow of a king **3.** a playing card with a picture of a queen **4.** a fertile female ant, bee, termite, or wasp **5.** a woman who is best in some category (a movie *queen*; a beauty *queen*)

queer (kwiər) *adj.* or *adv.* **1.** strange, different from normal **2.** questionable or suspicious (something *queer* about the deal he made) —*vb.* to spoil (*queer*ed their chances of going)

quest (kwest) *n.* search (their *quest* for riches) —*vb.* to seek

ques·tion (kwes′ chən) *n.* **1.** something asked **2.** a problem for discussion **3.** an objection (follow the rules without *question*)

quick (kwik) *adj.* or *adv.* **1.** fast (a *quick* learner) **2.** impatient (a *quick* nature) —*n.* the flesh under a fingernail or toenail (down to the *quick*)

quick·en (kwik′ ən) *vb.* to make faster or livelier

qui·et (kwī′ ət) *n.* the state of being quiet or tranquil —*adj.* calm, mild, peaceful, or still —*adv.* quietly —*vb.* to make or become quiet

quill (kwil) *n.* **1.** a large feather from the wing or tail of a bird **2.** a pen made from a feather

quilt (kwilt) *n.* a bed cover made of two layers of cloth, often pieced into a pattern, with a layer of cotton, wool, or down in between and stitched in channels or patterns to keep the filling from shifting —*vb.* to make a quilt

quit (kwit) *vb.* **quit**; **quit·ting** **1.** to stop, especially before the work is done **2.** to leave (*quit* the area)

quite (kwīt) *adv.* **1.** entirely (not *quite* finished) **2.** to a great extent (*quite* hungry)

quiv·er (kwiv′ ər) *n.* **1.** a light case for arrows **2.** the act of shaking or shivering —*vb.* to shake or shiver

quiz (kwiz) *n., pl.* **quiz·zes** a short test, oral or written, usually requiring short answers —*vb.* **quizzed**; **quiz·zing** **1.** to question in detail **2.** to give a short test

quo·ta·tion (kwō tā′ shən) *n.* **1.** something that is quoted (The *quotation* was taken from one of Edith Wharton's books.) **2.** the words that are quoted

quote (kwōt) *vb.* **quot·ed**; **quot·ing** **1.** to copy a passage from another's speech or writing, giving the source **2.** to repeat the words of another

quo·tient (kwō′ shənt) *n.* the answer in division, or the number of times one number goes into another (In the problem 10 ÷ 2, the *quotient* is 5.)

R

rab·bit (rab′ ət) *n.* a small, burrowing, long-eared mammal such as the cottontail, similar to a hare, but smaller

ra·bies (rā′ bēz) *n.* a serious, often fatal disease of mammals that is caught by humans if bitten by an infected animal, and for which treatment must be given immediately

rac·coon (ra kün′) *n.* a small tree-dwelling animal that hunts mostly at night, is related to the bear, and has a gray coat with a black mask around the eyes and rings on the tail

race (rās) *n.* **1.** a contest of speed as in driving or running **2.** any contest (the *race* for election to the student council) **3.** a swift current of water (the mill *race*) **4.** a great division of mankind made up of people descended from common stock and similar in appearance (Mongoloid *race*, Caucasian *race*, Negro *race*) —*vb.* **raced**; **rac·ing** **1.** to go at top speed **2.** to take part in a race

ra·cial (rā′ shəl) *adj.* related to a division of people based on race

rack (rak) *n.* **1.** a frame on which articles are hung, attached, or arranged for display or storage (towel *rack*) **2.** destruction (*rack* and ruin) —*vb.* **1.** to stretch or strain **2.** to cause to suffer (*rack*ed with pain)

rack·et (rak′ ət) *n.* **1.** a lot of noise, gaiety, or commotion **2.** a paddle-shaped bat with the oval part strung to form a firm mesh, used in tennis and other games

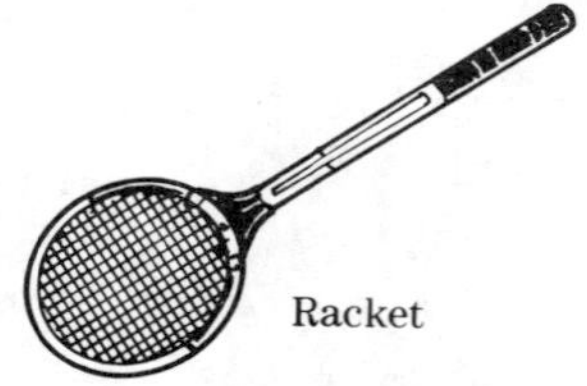

Racket

ra·dar (rā′ där′) *n.* **1.** a word devised from the first letters of *ra*dio *d*etecting *a*nd *r*anging **2.** a device for finding large masses such as airplanes and ships coming from a distance

ra·di·ant (rād′ ē ənt) *adj.* glowing or shining (*radiant* with happiness)

ra·di·a·tion (rād′ ē ā′ shən) *n.* **1.** the act of radiating outward from a center **2.** radiant energy moving out in the form of waves

ra·di·a·tor (rād′ ē āt′ ər) *n.* **1.** a device to heat a room **2.** a device to cool an engine

rad·i·cal (rad′ i kəl) *adj.* **1.** fundamental, relating to the root (a *radical* change) **2.** different from what is common or basic, extreme (a *radical* person) —*n.* a person who wants to do away with tradition and make many changes

ra·di·o (rād′ ē ō′) *n., pl.* **ra·di·os** **1.** the sending or receiving of messages by sound waves without a wire **2.** a device for receiving radio messages —*adj.* relating to radio —*vb.* to send a message by radio

ra·di·o·ac·tive (rād′ ē ō ak′ tiv) *adj.* having the property of sending out rays which consist either of electrified particles, alpha and beta rays, or of radiant energy of high frequency gamma rays

rad·ish (rad′ ish) *n.* a garden plant in the mustard family with a fleshy, hot-tasting root that is eaten raw

ra·di·us (rād′ ē əs) *n., pl.* **ra·di·i** (rād′ ē ī′) **1.** a straight line from the center of a circle to the circumference **2.** a somewhat circular area with a specified radius (The bell could be heard within a *radius* of a mile.)

raft (raft) *n.* **1.** a floating frame of logs or boards on which one can travel by water **2.** a large number (a *raft* of tourists) —*vb.* to carry or travel on a raft

rag (rag) *n.* **1.** a worn or torn piece of cloth that is worthless **2.** torn or worn clothing (wearing *rags*)

rage (rāj) *n.* **1.** violent anger (in a *rage*) **2.** violence or fury (the *rage* of disease) —*vb.* **raged**; **rag·ing** **1.** to be very angry **2.** to continue in a fury (the winds *raged*)

raid (rād) *n.* **1.** a sudden and hostile attack (an air *raid*) **2.** a forced entrance by the police (a drug *raid*) —*vb.* **1.** to attack **2.** to make a forceful entry

rail (rāl) *n.* **1.** a bar parallel with the ground or floor, serving as a support or barrier **2.** one side of a railroad track **3.** a wading bird related to the crane —*vb.* **1.** to put up a railing **2.** to complain

rail·road (rāl′ rōd′) *n.* **1.** two parallel rails on which trains are run for moving passengers and freight **2.** the tracks along with all the engines, cars, and property **3.** the organization owning and running the railroad

rail·way (rāl′ wā′) *n.* railroad

rain (rān) *n.* **1.** drops of water falling from the clouds **2.** anything falling (a *rain* of beetles) —*vb.* **1.** to fall as water from a cloud **2.** to give freely (to *rain* favors)

rain·bow (rān′ bō′) *n.* an arc of colors appearing in the sky opposite the sun caused by the sun's rays reflecting in the drops of rain

rain·coat (rān′ kōt′) *n.* a waterproof or water-resistant coat made as a protection against rain

rain·drop (rān′ dräp′) *n.* a drop of rain

rain·fall (rān′ fȯl′) *n.* the rain or the amount of rain

raise (rāz) *vb.* **raised**; **rais·ing** **1.** to lift **2.** to build (*raise* the walls) **3.** to breed, care for (*raise* cattle) **4.** to collect (*raise* funds) **5.** to promote (*raise* to grade ten) —*n.* **1.** the act of raising (the *raise* in salary) **2.** an increase in amount

rai·sin (rāz′ n) *n.* a special kind of grape that is dried for use as a food

rake (rāk) *n.* a long-handled garden tool with teeth or prongs for gathering leaves and brush or breaking up garden soil —*vb.* **raked**; **rak·ing** to gather, loosen, or smooth using a rake

Rake

ral · ly (ral′ ē) *vb.* **ral · lied**; **ral · ly · ing** to bring together to restore order, spirit, hope, enthusiasm (to *rally* the spirit of the campaign) —*n., pl.* **ral · lies** **1.** the act of rallying **2.** a mass meeting to build spirit for a team or group effort (pep *rally*)

ram (ram) *n.* a male sheep —*vb.* **rammed**; **ram · ming** **1.** to strike or butt against in an effort to crush (*rammed* his socks into the already full drawer) **2.** to use excessive pressure (*ram* a bill through Congress)

ram · ble (ram′ bəl) *vb.* **ram · bled**; **ram · bling** **1.** to wander around without purpose (*rambled* all over the countryside) **2.** to talk or write aimlessly, going from one topic to another (His letter *rambled* on for pages without really saying anything important.)

ranch (ranch) *n.* in the western United States, a farm for raising large numbers of cattle on the open range —*vb.* to manage or work on a ranch

ran · dom (ran′ dəm) *n.* **1.** something that occurs without a definite aim **2.** in statistics, a process of selection in which each item in a set has an equal chance of being selected (This student was chosen at *random*.) —*adj.* lacking a definite pattern (the use of *random* numbers)

range (rānj) *n.* **1.** things arranged in a line or chain (mountain *range*) **2.** a stove for cooking (electric *range*) **3.** open grasslands (out on the *range*) **4.** the distance a thing will go or operate (the *range* of an airplane on a tank of fuel) —*vb.* **ranged**; **rang · ing** **1.** to roam on a grassland (Buffalo *ranged* there.) **2.** to vary within limits (The price of meat has *ranged* widely.)

rank (rangk) *adj.* **1.** tall, coarse, and plentiful in growth (tall, *rank* weeds) **2.** having a strong, offensive smell (a *rank* cigar) **3.** coarse or vulgar (*rank* language) —*n.* **1.** in lines or rows (the *rank*s of marchers) **2.** the place a person or thing holds in a line (Her *rank* is second in her class.) **3.** military grade (*rank* of captain) **4.** social position (of high *rank*) **5.** the masses (rose from the *rank*s) —*vb.* to put into lines, classes, order of importance, or achievement

rap·id (rap′ əd) *adj.* very fast

rare (raər) *adj.* **rar·er**; **rar·est** **1.** partially cooked (*rare* steak) **2.** thin (The air is *rare* at high altitudes.) **3.** unusual, not common (a *rare* bird)

rare·ly (raər′ lē) *adv.* seldom, not common

rasp·ber·ry (raz′ ber′ ē) *n., pl.* **rasp·ber·ries** a sweet, cup-shaped berry, usually black or red

rat (rat) *n.* **1.** a gnawing rodent shaped like but much larger than a mouse **2.** a person who betrays others —*vb.* **rat·ted**; **rat·ting** **1.** to hunt rats **2.** to betray or desert others for one's own benefit

rate (rāt) *n.* an amount of one thing in relation to units of another thing, as dollars per hour, miles per gallon, or words per page (a *rate* of forty miles an hour) —*vb.* **rat·ed**; **rat·ing** to decide the rank, class, or value of

rath·er (rath′ ər) *adv.* **1.** sooner (*rather* not go) **2.** somewhat (*rather* nice) **3.** instead (walk barefoot *rather* than put on shoes)

rat·ing (rāt′ ing) *n.* **1.** placement in a class (a *rating* of ninth grade) **2.** placement in a rank order (His *rating* placed him third in the class.)

ra·tio (rā′ shō) *n., pl.* **ra·tios** a proportional relation between two measures (selling two-pound cans in a *ratio* of 5:4 over one-pound cans)

ra·tio·nal (rash′ ən l) *adj.* **1.** having the power to reason **2.** sensible

rat·tle (rat′ l) *vb.* **rat·tled**; **rat·tling** **1.** to make a number of clicking sounds, one after the other **2.** to talk in a rapid manner (*rattle* off the list of numbers) **3.** confuse (The noise *rattled* him.) —*n.* a baby's toy for making a rattling sound

rat·tle·snake (rat′ l snāk′) *n.* a poisonous American snake with hard rings on the tail which rattle

ra·vine (rə vēn′) *n.* a narrow, steep-sided gorge, usually worn out by a stream of water

raw (rȯ) *adj.* **1.** not cooked **2.** not having the usual finish (*raw* edge) **3.** not processed (*raw* materials) **4.** cold and damp (*raw* weather)

ray (rā) *n.* **1.** a single beam of light or energy **2.** a broad, flat fish such as the skate

ray·on (rā′ än′) *n.* a fabric made from cellulose which has a luster similar to silk

ra·zor (rā′ zər) *n.* an instrument with a sharp edge used for shaving hair off the skin

reach (rēch) *vb.* **1.** to extend a hand or foot as though to touch something **2.** to extend as far as (This runway *reach*es the river's edge.) **3.** to get to (*reach* Omaha by noon) **4.** to talk to (*reach* them by phone) —*n.* the act of reaching to touch or grasp

re·act (rē akt′) *vb.* to respond in some way to what has just happened (He *react*ed calmly to the change in plan.)

re·ac·tion (rē ak′ shən) *n.* **1.** a response to an action (His difficulty in breathing was a *reaction* to the medicine.) **2.** the result of combining certain chemicals (The chemical *reaction* changed the color of the liquid.)

read (rēd) *vb.* **read** (red); **read·ing** (rēd′ ing) **1.** to look at attentively and understand the meaning of something such as a text (*read* a book) **2.** to utter aloud with appropriate inflections and pauses (*read* to someone) **3.** to study (*read* textbooks)

read·er (rēd′ ər) *n.* **1.** one who reads **2.** a book from a series used to teach reading (a basal *reader*)

read·ing (rēd′ ing) *n.* **1.** making an attempt to understand the meaning of printed matter or other written material **2.** the way a person orally interprets printed matter (Ted's *reading* of that line is different from Ann's interpretation.) **3.** the act of reading before an audience (give *reading*s from Dickens)

read·y (red′ ē) *adj.* **read·i·er**; **read·i·est** **1.** prepared to be used (The hot chocolate is *ready.*) **2.** mentally willing (*ready* to discuss the problem) **3.** in a state to be likely (The bridge is *ready* to collapse.) —*vb.* **read·ied**; **read·y·ing** to prepare

re·al (rē′ əl) *adj.* actually existing (*real* property; *real* estate)

re·al·ism (rē′ ə liz′ əm) *n.* the tendency to deal with facts and experiences in a practical way

re·al·is·tic (rē′ ə lis′ tik) *adj.* seeing things as they really are, true to life

re·al·i·ty (rē al′ ət ē) *n., pl.* **re·al·i·ties** the state of being real or actual

re·al·ize (rē′ ə līz′) *vb.* **re·al·iz·ing** **1.** to make something real or actual (to *realize* the dream of owning a home) **2.** to be aware of (to *realize* how much influence he had)

re·al·ly (rē′ ə lē) *adv.* **1.** actually **2.** in reality

realm (relm) *n.* region, domain, sphere, kingdom (in the *realm* of music)

reap (rēp) *vb.* to cut down in order to harvest (to *reap* the grain)

rear (riər) *vb.* **1.** to bring up (*rear* children) **2.** to lift upright **3.** to build up or erect **4.** to rise up on the hind legs (The horse *rear*ed in fright.) —*n.* **1.** the area at the back (coming up from the *rear*) **2.** a military unit farthest from the enemy (took a message to the *rear*)

rea·son (rēz′ n) *n.* **1.** the mental ability to understand (Use sanity and *reason* in handling this problem.) **2.** the cause for a decision or action (For what *reason* did you do it?) —*vb.* **1.** to argue or discuss (He *reasoned* that there was too little time for any other action.) **2.** to think

reb·el (reb′ əl) *adj.* **1.** defiant **2.** disobedient —*n.* a person who refuses to obey —*vb.* (rib el′) **re·belled**; **re·bel·ling** **1.** to resist authority (*rebelled* against the leader) **2.** to take up arms against (*rebelled* against the government)

re·bel·lion (ri bel′ yən) *n.* the state of revolting against one's government

re·build (rē′ bild′) *vb.* **re·built** (rē bilt′); **re·build·ing** **1.** to build again (The church that burned down was *rebuilt.*) **2.** to take apart and put together again using some new parts and possibly making changes in structure (They *rebuilt* the kitchen using oak cabinets.)

re·call (ri kȯl′) *vb.* **1.** the act of calling back (The cars with poor brakes were *recall*ed.) **2.** to remember (can't *recall* the new girl's name) **3.** to take back or cancel (to *recall* the attack) —*n.* **1.** a call to return **2.** an act of remembering **3.** the act of canceling

re·cede (ri sēd′) *vb.* **re·ced·ed**; **re·ced·ing** **1.** to move back (The tide *receded.*) **2.** to slope backward (a forehead that *recede*s from his thick eyebrows)

re·ceipt (ri sēt′) *n.* **1.** the act of receiving **2.** that which is taken in (cash *receipt*s for the day) **3.** a written statement that goods or money have been received (rent *receipt*s) —*vb.* to stamp or mark as paid

re·ceive (ri sēv′) *vb.* **re·ceived**; **re·ceiv·ing** **1.** to get something that is given (*receive* a report card) **2.** to welcome to one's home (*receive* friends) **3.** to change radio waves into sounds or pictures (to *receive* a good picture on a television)

re·cent (rēs′ nt) *adj.* **1.** relating to a short time ago (a *recent* letter) **2.** new (a *recent* discovery)

re·cep·tion (ri sep′ shən) *n.* **1.** a way of receiving (a tearful *reception* of the news) **2.** a large formal gathering (the *reception* after the wedding) **3.** the act of receiving radio or television broadcasts

re·cess (rē′ ses′) *n.* **1.** a break between classes **2.** a place where a surface is indented or grooved —*vb.* to put into a depression or recess (to *recess* the lighting)

rec·i·pe (res′ ə pē′) *n.* the directions for making something (*recipe* for fish soup)

re·cite (ri sīt′) *vb.* **re·cit·ed; re·cit·ing** **1.** to say aloud from memory (*recite* the Gettysburg Address) **2.** to give many details (*recite* the facts about robins) **3.** to answer when called upon in class

reck·on (rek′ ən) *vb.* **1.** to calculate or compute (*reckon* the cost of the jacket and boots) **2.** to consider (I *reckon* him as one to watch.)

rec·og·ni·tion (rek′ əg nish′ ən) *n.* **1.** the act of recognizing something previously known (word *recognition*) **2.** special attention or commendation (He was given *recognition* for his bravery.)

rec·og·nize (rek′ əg nīz′) *vb.* **rec·og·nized; rec·og·niz·ing** **1.** to see and remember (to *recognize* his former teacher) **2.** to see and admit (*recognize* he was wrong) **3.** to give special notice to (*recognize* with an award those who did well)

rec·om·mend (rek′ ə mend′) *vb.* **1.** to speak in favor of (*recommend* her for a job) **2.** to advise (*recommend* that they do more studying) **3.** to earn attention (Her ability to lead people *recommends* her for promotion.)

re·cord (ri kȯrd′) *vb.* **1.** to put in writing (*record* in a notebook) **2.** to make a permanent notation (*record* at the City Hall) **3.** to make a tape or disk —*n.* **rec·ord** (rek′ ərd) **1.** the written account of facts and events for future reference (historical *record*) **2.** a public document —*adj.* remarkable, outstanding, something to be remembered (a *record* year for school athletics)

re·cord·er (ri kȯrd′ ər) *n.* **1.** a person or device that records **2.** a flute with a whistle-type mouthpiece, eight finger holes, and a soft, mellow tone

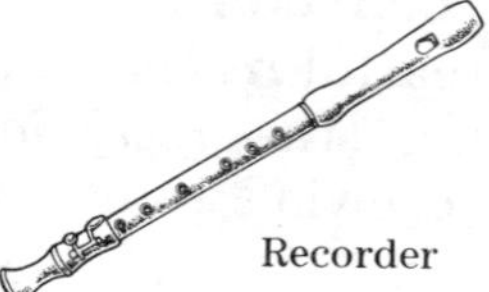
Recorder

re·cov·er (ri kəv′ ər) *vb.* to get back something one once had (*recover* one's pen, one's health, or one's home)

re·cov·er·y (ri kəv′ ə rē) *n., pl.* **re·cov·er·ies** the act of recovering or getting something back

rec·re·a·tion (rek′ rē ā′ shən) *n.* a pastime, game, or other activity that gives relaxation and enjoyment

rec·tan·gle (rek′ tang′ gəl) *n.* a flat, four-sided figure having right angles and opposite sides parallel

Rectangle

rect·an·gu·lar (rek tang′ gyə lər) *adj.* shaped like a rectangle

red (red) *adj.* **red·der**; **red·dest** **1.** of the color red, one of the primary colors **2.** relating to communism or a revolutionary —*n.* **1.** the color of blood or a ruby **2.** *(capital)* a person who is a Communist

red·coat (red′ kōt′) *n.* a British soldier, especially during the American Revolution

red·dish (red′ ish) *adj.* somewhat like the color red

re·duce (ri düs′) *vb.* **re·duced**; **re·duc·ing** to make smaller in size, quantity, value, or importance (*reduce* hostility)

re·duc·tion (ri dək′ shən) *n.* **1.** the act or state of being reduced **2.** the amount by which something is made smaller (a fifty percent *reduction* in the price of tools) **3.** a smaller copy (a *reduction* of the map)

red·wood (red′ wu̇d′) *n.* a cone-bearing California evergreen tree, the sequoia, which grows to the immense height of 200 to 300 feet or higher

reed (rēd) *n.* **1.** certain tall coarse grasses with jointed hollow stems that grow in wet places **2.** a thin strip of reed, wood, or metal placed at the opening of a pipe, as in an organ, or fastened to a mouthpiece, as in an oboe or clarinet, which vibrates as air passes over it causing the air in the hollow tube of the instrument to vibrate

reef (rēf) *n.* **1.** a ridge of rock, sand, or coral on the ocean floor that extends upward to the surface or nearly to the surface of the water **2.** in mining, a layer or vein of ore

re·fer (ri fər′) *vb.* **re·ferred; re·fer·ring** **1.** to go to another source for help or information (*refer* to the encyclopedia for facts about transportation) **2.** to send someone somewhere else for help (*Refer* the patient to a specialist in allergies.)

ref·er·ence (ref′ ə rəns) *n.* **1.** the act of referring **2.** anything that directs the attention to another source for information (This article makes *reference* to a booklet on fructose, a type of sugar.) **3.** a statement about a person's training, ability, and character (The teacher gave him a good *reference* for the job.)

re·fine (ri fīn′) *vb.* **re·fined; re·fin·ing** **1.** to make pure (to *refine* sugar) **2.** to educate or improve (to *refine* her writing)

re·flect (ri flekt′) *vb.* **1.** to bounce back waves of light, sound, or heat (The mirror *reflect*s sunlight onto the opposite wall.) **2.** to come back as a result (Her success in college *reflect*s credit on her high school.) **3.** to ponder deeply (He *reflect*ed long on the problem.)

re·flec·tion (ri flek′ shən) *n.* **1.** the return of light and sound from a surface **2.** that which is returned or thrown back (your *reflection*) **3.** casting one's thoughts back to past experiences or ideas (in a state of *reflection*) **4.** an indicator (His offenses are a *reflection* of his character.)

re·flex (rē′ fleks′) *n.* an automatic action of certain muscles when a related sensory nerve is activated (When something comes close to your eye, your *reflex* is to blink. When someone taps the base of your kneecap, your *reflex* is to kick.)

re·form (ri fȯrm′) *vb.* to improve by getting rid of faults —*n.* a removal or correction of what is bad, wrong, corrupt, or abusive

re·frain (ri frān′) *vb.* to keep oneself from doing something —*n.* the part of a poem or song that is repeated frequently

re·fresh·ment (ri fresh′ mənt) *n.* **1.** the act of reviving or making fresher **2.** a light meal

re·frig·er·a·tor (ri frij′ ə rāt′ ər) *n.* a chest or room where perishable foods, and other things that spoil when warm, are kept cold

ref·uge (ref′ yüj) *n.* a place of safety and protection against danger (a wetlands animal *refuge*)

re·fuse (ri fyüz′) *vb.* **re·fused**; **re·fus·ing** **1.** to decline to take (*refuse* the cigarette) **2.** to decline to do or grant (*refuse* to work) —*n.* **ref·use** (ref′ yüs′) worthless trash

re·gain (ri gān′) *vb.* **1.** to get back, get again (*regain* control of the Senate) **2.** to get back to (*regain* the northern region)

re·gard (ri gärd′) *n.* **1.** relation (to hurry with *regard* to chores) **2.** concern or consideration (high *regard* for the young people in the unit) **3.** friendly feelings (my *regards* to your family) —*vb.* **1.** to pay attention to (to *regard* him fondly) **2.** to show respect or esteem (We *regard* him highly.) **3.** to consider (*regard* him as an excellent worker)

re·gard·less (ri gärd′ ləs) *adj.* careless, showing no regard (*regardless* of warnings)

reg·i·ment (rej′ ə mənt) *n.* a military unit composed of a headquarters, two or more battalions, and supporting units

re·gion (rē′ jən) *n.* **1.** a large area with indefinite boundaries (the temperate *region*) **2.** an area of the body (the pelvic *region*) **3.** an area in space (the *region* of the Milky Way galaxy)

reg·is·ter (rej′ əs tər) *n.* **1.** an official written record (a *register* of births) **2.** a school record of enrollment and attendance (mark the *register*) **3.** a device for regulating the heat coming into a room (adjust the hot air *register*) **4.** a mechanical device for recording items (cash *register*) **5.** the range of a voice or instrument (singing in the alto *register*) —*vb.* **1.** to enroll in a register **2.** to show (*register* surprise) **3.** to secure (*register* a letter)

reg·u·lar (reg′ yə lər) *adj.* **1.** according to rule or custom **2.** balanced, even, orderly (a *regular* pattern) **3.** relating to a permanent army —*n.* a player on a team who usually starts every game

reg·u·late (reg′ yə lāt′) *vb.* **reg·u·lat·ed**; **reg·u·lat·ing** **1.** to conduct according to rule **2.** to control **3.** to fix or adjust

reg·u·la·tion (reg′ yə lā′ shən) *n.* the act or state of being regulated

reign (rān) *n.* **1.** the period of time a sovereign rules **2.** the controlling influence (the *reign* of terror) —*vb.* **1.** to rule as a sovereign **2.** to have control (Silence *reign*ed in the library.)

rein (rān) *n.* **1.** a leather strap attached to the bit of the bridle to control a horse **2.** a controlling influence —*vb.* to control by or as if by reins

rein·deer (rān′ diər′) *n., pl.* **rein·deer** a large deer with antlers found in northern parts of North America, Europe, and Asia, raised for its milk, meat, and hide

re·ject (ri jekt′) *vb.* **1.** to refuse to take (to *reject* the offer of money) **2.** to refuse to give (to *reject* the request to borrow the typewriter) **3.** to throw away (to *reject* all bruised fruit) —*n.* (rē′ jekt′) *n.* a person or thing that has been rejected

re·joice (ri jȯis′) *vb.* **re·joiced**; **re·joic·ing** **1.** to feel or express joy **2.** to give joy to another

re·late (ri lāt′) *vb.* **re·lat·ed**; **re·lat·ing** **1.** to tell or recite (*relate* the events of the day) **2.** to connect (*related* his experience to a story he had read)

re·la·tion (ri lā′ shən) *n.* **1.** the act of telling or reciting **2.** the connection or relationship **3.** a person who is related by blood or marriage **4.** affairs or associations (foreign *relations*)

re·la·tion·ship (ri lā′ shən ship′) *n.* a connection by blood, marriage, business association, or thinking process (the *relationship* of ideas)

rel·a·tive (rel′ ət iv) *n.* a person connected with another by blood or marriage —*adj.* considered in relation to something else as in comparing (considering work to be done *relative* to a planned vacation)

re·lax (ri laks′) *vb.* **1.** to loosen one's muscles **2.** to make less strict (to *relax* the rules) **3.** to lessen the tension (*relax* for a few minutes)

re·lay (rē′ lā′) *n.* **1.** a race between teams where each team member runs a part of the race in turn **2.** a fresh supply of persons or animals to relieve those who have been active —*vb.* **re·layed**; **re·lay·ing** to pass along from one to another (*relay* a message)

re·lease (ri lēs′) *vb.* **re·leased**; **re·leas·ing** **1.** to set free (*release* the hostage) **2.** to free from pain or obligation **3.** to make free to circulate (*release* the story about the movie star)

re·lent (ri lent′) *vb.* to become less strict

re·lent·less (ri lent′ ləs) *adj.* harsh, pitiless, indifferent to the pain of others

re·lief (ri lēf′) *n.* **1.** the act of releasing from pain and discomfort **2.** assistance, as money, for people in need or trouble **3.** provision of time off from a difficult job for rest or refreshment **4.** the showing of mountains and valleys (a map showing *relief*) **5.** artwork with figures that stand out from the background

re·lieve (ri lēv′) *vb.* **re·lieved**; **re·liev·ing** **1.** to remove or lessen a burden of pain, trouble, or obligation **2.** to provide a substitute for a time to give a regular worker a break or time off

re·li·gion (ri lij′ ən) *n.* belief in God shown through a system of faith and worship

re·luc·tant (ri lək′ tənt) *adj.* unwilling, opposed (*reluctant* to work with a bad-mannered person)

re·ly (ri lī′) *vb.* **re·lied**; **re·ly·ing** to trust, have confidence (*rely* on her family)

re·main (ri mān′) *vb.* **1.** to stay when others go **2.** to stay or last (The image of her beautiful face *remains* with me.) **3.** to stay in the same condition (He *remains* a fisherman.)

re·main·der (ri mān′ dər) *n.* **1.** the number left after a subtraction **2.** the final part, less than the divisor, left after a division **3.** what is left after anything is taken away

re·mark (ri märk′) *vb.* to notice or make a comment about something —*n.* an observation or a passing comment

re·mark·a·ble (ri mär′ kə bəl) *adj.* unusual or extraordinary enough to make a comment about

rem·e·dy (rem′ ə dē) *n., pl.* **rem·e·dies** **1.** any medicine or treatment given to relieve sickness or pain **2.** anything that is given or done to cure, repair, or correct a sickness or evil —*vb.* **rem·e·died**; **rem·e·dy·ing** to cure

re·mem·ber (ri mem′ bər) *vb.* **1.** to bring to mind (tried to *remember* the name of the ship) **2.** to keep in mind (*Remember* to stop at the store for milk.) **3.** to bring greetings (*Remember* us to Dick.)

re·mind (ri mīnd′) *vb.* to bring to mind (*Remind* me to stop at the card shop. This *reminds* me of a place I visited in Michigan.)

rem·nant (rem′ nənt) *n.* something that is left over (a *remnant* of drapery material)

re·mote (ri mōt′) *adj.* **1.** far off in time or place (a *remote* hunting lodge in Wisconsin, the cliff-dwelling Pueblos who lived in a *remote* period of our history) **2.** distant or alien (The artist's portrait was only a *remote* likeness of my sister.)

re·move (ri müv′) *vb.* **re·moved**; **re·mov·ing** **1.** to move something off or away (*remove* clothing from the chair) **2.** to dismiss (*remove* the secretary) **3.** to get rid of (*remove* poverty from this nation)

re·nais·sance (ren′ ə säns′) *n.* a coming to life again, rebirth (a *renaissance* of learning)

ren·der (ren′ dər) *vb.* **1.** to give (*render* loyalty to your country) **2.** to state as final (*render* a decision) **3.** to separate out (*render* the fat) **4.** to become (*rendered* helpless by the accident)

rent (rent) *n.* money paid for the use of property —*vb.* **1.** to use property with an agreement to pay **2.** to allow others to use property in return for rent (to *rent* an apartment)

re·pair (ri paər′) *vb.* to fix or restore to a former condition —*n.* **1.** the process of fixing **2.** general condition (a building in poor *repair*)

re·pay (rē pā′) *vb.* **re·paid** (rē pād′); **re·pay·ing** to pay back (to *repay* money borrowed, to *repay* a friend for his kindness)

re·peat (ri pēt′) *vb.* **1.** to say or do again (*repeat* the exercises twenty times) **2.** to say from memory (to *repeat* the poem, "Old Ironsides")

rep·e·ti·tion (rep′ ə tish′ ən) *n.* **1.** the act of repeating **2.** the thing that is said or done more than once

re·place (ri plās′) *vb.* **re·placed**; **re·plac·ing** **1.** to put something back in the right place (*replace* the record in the cabinet) **2.** to take the place of (new cards to *replace* the old ones)

re·ply (ri plī′) *vb.* **re·plied; re·ply·ing** to give an answer, respond —*n., pl.* **re·plies** answer, response

re·port (ri pōrt′) *n.* **1.** an oral or written account of facts or details (weather *report*) **2.** an explosive noise (the *report* of the cannon) —*vb.* **1.** to tell or give an account **2.** to go back to work (*report* for duty)

rep·re·sent (rep′ ri zent′) *vb.* **1.** to show a likeness or image (to *represent* a hunting scene) **2.** to serve as a symbol or sign (Letters *represent* sounds in our language.) **3.** to act in place of (*represent* the member who is ill) **4.** to take the part of (*represents* the witch in the play) **5.** to serve as an example of

rep·re·sen·ta·tion (rep′ ri zen′ tā′ shən) *n.* **1.** the act of representing **2.** the use of words, pictures, symbols, or signs, to present an idea or opinion **3.** actions or speech on the part of another person or group **4.** the state of being represented by another

re·pro·duce (rē′ prə düs′) *vb.* **re·pro·duced; re·pro·duc·ing** **1.** to produce again **2.** to bear offspring

rep·tile (rep′ təl, -tīl′) *n.* an air-breathing, cold-blooded vertebrate that usually has scales or bony plates on the skin (Snakes, lizards, and alligators are *reptiles*.)

re·pub·lic (ri pəb′ lik) *n.* a representative democracy in which the chief of state is usually called the president and supreme power is held by the people who are entitled to vote

rep·u·ta·tion (rep′ yə tā′ shən) *n.* the opinion people have of a person, whether good or bad

re·quest (ri kwest′) *n.* **1.** the act of asking for something **2.** the thing asked for **3.** the condition of being asked for (He will come to speak on *request*.) —*vb.* to ask for something

re·quire (ri kwīr′) *vb.* **re·quired; re·quir·ing** **1.** to demand (Drivers are *required* to know and observe traffic signals.) **2.** to need (Playing an instrument *requires* talent as well as skill.)

re·quire·ment (ri kwīr′ mənt) *n.* **1.** something that an authority demands (Attendance at school is a *requirement* for a child of school age.) **2.** something that is needed (Many nutrients are *requirements* for good health.)

res·cue (res′ kyü) *vb.* **res·cued**; **res·cu·ing** to save (He *rescue*d the skater who fell through the ice.) —*n.* the act of rescuing by saving from danger, violence, or imprisonment

re·search (ri sərch′, rē′ sərch) *n.* inquiry aimed at discovering new information in any of the fields of knowledge

re·sem·ble (ri zem′ bəl) *vb.* **re·sem·bled**; **re·sem·bling** to look like or similar to someone or something else (He *resemble*s his father.)

re·sent·ment (ri zent′ mənt) *n.* strong feelings of displeasure because of what someone has done, or appears to have done, that is looked upon as an insult or injury

res·er·va·tion (rez′ ər vā′ shən) *n.* **1.** the act of reserving (a *reservation* for a private bedroom in the sleeping car) **2.** land kept for a special use (Indian *reservation*) **3.** a keeping of rights for one's own use (the *reservation* that no part of this book may be copied) **4.** a limiting condition (accept without *reservation*)

re·serve (ri zərv′) *vb.* **re·served**; **re·serv·ing** **1.** to set aside for special use **2.** to keep for one's own use —*n.* **1.** something, such as supplies, kept on hand **2.** land set apart, as a reservation **3.** an act of reserving, as a hotel room or table for dinner at a restaurant **4.** *pl.* military forces available for use (Call up the *reserve*s.)

res·er·voir (rez′ ərv wär′) *n.* a place where something, especially water, is stored in large quantities for use by people in that region or area

re·side (ri zīd′) *vb.* **re·sid·ed**; **re·sid·ing** **1.** to live in a place for a long time (He has *reside*d in California since 1970.) **2.** to be present in (Trust *reside*s in their agreement to work together.)

res·i·dence (rez′ ə dəns) *n.* **1.** the home in which one lives on a permanent basis **2.** the period in which one lives in one's home

res·i·dent (rez′ ə dənt) *adj.* **1.** living permanently in a place (the *resident* population) **2.** working on a permanent basis in a place (*resident* nurse)

re·sist (ri zist′) *vb.* to exert some effort to oppose or stay away from (*resist* sweets)

re·sist·ance (ri zis′ təns) *n.* **1.** an act of resisting **2.** the ability to resist **3.** a force that opposes (the *resistance* of the water to the boat) **4.** the opposition of a conductor to an electric current

re·solve (ri zälv′) *vb.* **re·solved**; **re·solv·ing** **1.** to promise oneself or others that something will be done (*resolve* to quit smoking) **2.** to break up into component parts (*resolved* the mystery by studying each clue) —*n.* **1.** something resolved **2.** steadfast purpose

re·sort (ri zȯrt′) *n.* **1.** a person or thing to whom one goes for help (a friend who was his last *resort*) **2.** a place for people on vacation (a mountain *resort*) —*vb.* **1.** to go to often or as a habit (*resort*ed to coffee to keep him awake) **2.** to have recourse (*resort*ed to the court to solve his problem)

re·source (rē′ sōrs′) *n.* **1.** supplies held in reserve for later use **2.** money or possessions that can be exchanged for money (financial *resource*s) **3.** forests, minerals, petroleum, and other valuable stores supplied naturally (natural *resource*s) **4.** a person's natural talents and disposition (depended upon his personal *resource*s to get him through hard times)

re·spect (ri spekt′) *n.* **1.** relation to something else (with *respect* to your question) **2.** honor and esteem (*respect* for this famous statesman) **3.** greetings (Give my *respects* to your dear aunt.) **4.** detail (wonderful in all *respects*) —*vb.* **1.** to esteem **2.** to pay attention to (*respect* their concerns)

res·pi·ra·tion (res′ pə rā′ shən) *n.* **1.** the act of breathing **2.** the process of breathing to take in the oxygen needed to live

re·spond (ri spänd′) *vb.* **1.** to reply (*respond* to the question) **2.** to react (*respond* to the physical therapy treatments)

re·sponse (ri späns′) *n.* **1.** the act of answering **2.** the reaction of the human body to a medical treatment (a *response* to the shot)

re·spon·si·bil·i·ty (ri spän′ sə bil′ ət ē) *n., pl.* **re·spon·si·bil·i·ties** **1.** the state of being responsible or accountable, as for something promised **2.** the thing for which one is accountable (nervous about his *responsibility*) **3.** a duty or obligation (the *responsibility* of caring for the children after school)

re·spon·si·ble (ri spän′ sə bəl) *adj.* **1.** involving duty and obligation (*responsible* position) **2.** morally or legally liable to carry out a duty or trust (*responsible* to the owner for the damage)

rest (rest) *n.* **1.** sleep **2.** a state of repose **3.** a quiet place for resting **4.** in music, a silence **5.** something that is left over —*vb.* **1.** to relax or take a nap **2.** to depend (pay *rests* on amount of work done) **3.** to place (*rest*ed her elbow on the desk)

res·tau·rant (res′ tə rənt) *n.* a place where food is served

rest·ing (res′ ting) *adj.* not active

rest·less (rest′ ləs) *adj.* active, never resting (the *restless* winds)

re·store (ri stōr′) *vb.* **re·stored**; **re·stor·ing** **1.** to give back to the owner **2.** to put back into a former position **3.** to put back into good condition

re·strict (ri strikt′) *vb.* **1.** to confine or hold within certain boundaries (*Restrict* all visitors to the display rooms.) **2.** to limit (*restrict* his use of the family car)

re·sult (ri zəlt′) *vb.* to happen as an effect (Pride will *result* from this community effort.) —*n.* an effect or consequence (I've had good *results* from this product.)

re·tain (ri tān′) *vb.* to hold or keep (*Retain* this stub to show you paid for your ticket.)

re·tire (ri tīr′) *vb.* **re·tired**; **re·tir·ing** **1.** to go to bed (He *retired* early.) **2.** to withdraw to a quiet place **3.** to go away from what one was doing

re·treat (ri trēt′) *n.* **1.** an act of withdrawing or going back, often from something dangerous **2.** in the military, bringing troops further back from the enemy **3.** a place of shelter, refuge, or privacy

re·turn (ri tərn′) *vb.* **1.** to come or go back to a place (*return* to school) **2.** to come or go back to an idea (*return* to the subject) **3.** to give or send back something received (*return* an object, a comment, a courtesy, or a benefit) —*n.* **1.** coming or going back to a place, a situation, or a condition (a *return* to business as usual) **2.** the act of returning something **3.** the profit one receives from business or financial activity

re·veal (ri vēl′) *vb.* to make known something that was secret or hidden (*reveal* their hiding place)

re·venge (ri venj′) *vb.* **re·venged**; **re·veng·ing** to hurt someone in return for the harm that person caused —*n.* the act of returning injury for injury in a spirit of vengeance or anger

re·verse (ri vərs′) *adj.* opposite (in *reverse* gear) —*n.* **1.** the opposite of the previous action or idea (No, the answer is the *reverse* of what you are saying.) **2.** the back or underside of an object **3.** a decline in health or fortune (His financial condition is in *reverse.*) —*vb.* **re·versed**; **re·vers·ing** **1.** to go in an opposite direction or condition **2.** to change places with something else (*reverse* the order) **3.** to take back, revoke (*reverse* the decision)

re·view (ri vyü′) *n.* **1.** a second look at something, such as a lesson (a *review* of the chapter) **2.** a summary and opinion of a book, play, or work of art (a book *review*) **3.** a formal inspection of troops (military *review*) —*vb.* **1.** to look at again **2.** to give a summary and an opinion of a literary or artistic work **3.** to make a formal inspection of troops

re·vise (ri vīz′) *vb.* **re·vised**; **re·vis·ing** **1.** to go over for the purpose of making corrections in organization and wording (*revise* a report) **2.** to make a new edition

re·volt (ri vōlt′) *vb.* **1.** to rise up against authority **2.** to turn away in disgust (*revolt*ed at their coarse language) —*n.* **1.** rebellion **2.** disgust

rev·o·lu·tion (rev′ ə lü′ shən) *n.* **1.** a complete cycle of a heavenly body as it travels around another heavenly body (The earth makes one *revolution* around the sun every 365.25 days.) **2.** a complete change in actions or conditions **3.** a forceful overthrow of a government by some of the people within the country

rev·o·lu·tion·ar·y (rev′ ə lü′ shə ner′ ē) *adj.* relating to revolution or complete change (*revolutionary* uprisings)

re·volve (ri välv′) *vb.* **re·volved**; **re·volv·ing** **1.** to move in a circle around an object (The moon *revolve*s around the earth.) **2.** to turn over in the mind

re·ward (ri wȯrd′) *vb.* to give something in appreciation —*n.* something given in return for a service, a lost article, or other merit

re·write (rē rīt′) *vb.* **re·wrote** (rē rōt′); **re·writ·ten** (rē rit′ n); **re·writ·ing** (rē rīt′ ing) to write in a different way, reorganizing to make the point more clear and well-stated

rhi·noc·er·os (rī näs′ ə rəs) *n. pl.* **rhi·noc·er·os·es** or **rhi·noc·er·os** a huge, thick-skinned, three-toed, plant-eating mammal having one or two horns curving upward from the snout, that live in the tropical regions of Asia and Africa

rhyme (rīm) *n.* in poetry, two or more lines that end with the same sound —*vb.* **rhymed**; **rhym·ing** to write poetry or verse in which some lines end with the same sound according to a pattern

rhythm (ri<u>th</u>′ əm) *n.* **1.** in music, a regular flow of accented beats **2.** in poetry, a regular flow of stressed and unstressed syllables **3.** any regular recurrence (the *rhythm* of the tides, rising and ebbing)

rib (rib) *n.* **1.** one of the twelve pairs of curved bones attached to the spine, some of which are also attached to the breastbone, that form the chest wall of the human body **2.** a piece of meat containing a rib (barbecued *rib*s) **3.** any stiff material that is used to support a structure (the *rib* of an umbrella) **4.** a ridge in woven or knitted fabric —*vb.* **ribbed**; **rib·bing** **1.** to form ribs as in knitting **2.** to use ribs in shaping a structure

rib·bon (rib′ ən) *n.* **1.** a long, narrow strip of fabric with finished edges used for tying presents, decorating clothing, or making badges **2.** any long narrow strip similar to ribbon (typewriter *ribbon*)

rice (rīs) *n.* a cereal grass grown in warm, wet regions, mainly in the Eastern Hemisphere, that provides a valuable grain used as the principal food in that part of the world

rich (rich) *adj.* **1.** having a lot of money and costly possessions (*rich* people) **2.** having many desirable qualities **3.** fertile (*rich* soil) **4.** abundant (*rich* crops) **5.** expensive (*rich* clothing)

rick·et·y (rik′ ət ē) *adj.* shaky, ready to fall apart (a *rickety* table)

rid (rid) *vb.* **rid** also **rid·ded**; **rid·ding** **1.** to remove (Get *rid* of this trash.) **2.** to be or become free (*rid* this house of ants)

rid·dle (rid′ l) *n.* **1.** a question with clues that are puzzling **2.** anything difficult to understand —*vb.* **rid·dled**; **rid·dling** to fill with holes as in a coarse sieve (The moths *riddled* this sweater with holes.)

ride (rīd) *n.* **1.** a trip on a vehicle or a horse (a *ride* on the monorail at Disneyland) **2.** a mechanical device for riding at an amusement park (a *ride* on the roller-coaster) —*vb.* **rode** (rōd); **rid·den** (rid′ n); **rid·ing** (rīd′ ing) **1.** to go in a vehicle (*ride* the bus) **2.** to go by sitting on and controlling (to *ride* a horse, bicycle, or sled)

ridge (rij) *n.* a raised line or strip in a structure (a *ridge* of hills, the *ridge* of the roof)

rid·i·cule (rid′ ə kyül) *n.* the act of making fun of —*vb.* **rid·i·culed**; **rid·i·cul·ing** to laugh at scornfully, to make fun of (*ridiculed* her very short haircut)

ri·dic·u·lous (rə dik′ yə ləs) *adj.* absurd, laughable, worthy of ridicule (a *ridiculous* idea)

ri·fle (rī′ fəl) *vb.* **ri·fled**; **ri·fling** to search through someone's belongings looking for something to steal and leaving everything in a mess —*n.* a gun with a long barrel (a National Guard *rifle*)

right (rīt) *adj.* **1.** not wrong (*right* answer) **2.** not left (*right* hand) **3.** suitable (*right* person; *right* clothing) **4.** having more color or a better finish (*right* side of the material) —*n.* **1.** that which is correct, suitable, true, or just (fight for his *rights*) —*adv.* **1.** directly (Go *right* to class.) **2.** justly (to conduct his business *right*) **3.** correctly —*vb.* to bring back to a proper state or condition (to *right* what is wrong)

rig·id (rij′ əd) *adj.* **1.** stiff (a *rigid* pole) **2.** strict (a *rigid* manner or attitude)

rim (rim) *n.* the border or outer edge of something curved (the *rim* of the cup) —*vb.* **rimmed**; **rim·ming** **1.** to add a border **2.** to serve as a border (A fine edging of gold *rims* the plate.)

ring (ring) *n.* **1.** a circular band worn on the finger **2.** a circular band for holding things together, such as notebook paper or keys **3.** anything round in shape **4.** a place for an athletic contest (boxing *ring*) or entertainment (circus *ring*) —*vb.* **ringed**; **ring·ing** **1.** to put a ring around something (to *ring* the stake with the horseshoe) **2.** to make the sound of a bell **3.** to have a clear sound (cheers *ring* out) **4.** to have an honest sound (That story *ring*s true.)

rink (ringk) *n.* a clear expanse of ice for skating, often inside an arena

rinse (rins) *vb.* **rinsed**; **rins·ing** **1.** to wash lightly with water, especially to remove the soap used in a previous wash **2.** to treat the hair with color —*n.* **1.** the act of rinsing **2.** the water or other liquid used for rinsing **3.** a preparation for adding color to the hair

rip (rip) *vb.* **ripped**; **rip·ping** to tear —*n.* a tear, as in fabric

ripe (rīp) *adj.* **rip·er**; **rip·est** **1.** fully grown (*ripe* vegetables or fruits) **2.** mature, having the knowledge and judgment of a fully grown person (*ripe* for a promotion)

rip·en (rī′ pən) *vb.* to become ripe

rise (rīz) *vb.* **rose** (rōz); **ris·en** (riz′ n); **ris·ing** (rī zing) **1.** to go from a lower to a higher position (*rise* in fame) **2.** to get up from a lying, sitting, or crouching position **3.** to go up (Warm air *rise*s.) **4.** to increase (Prices are *rising.*) —*n.* **1.** an act of rising **2.** an upward slope (the *rise* in the land) **3.** an emotional reaction

risk (risk) *n.* the chance of danger or injury —*vb.* to expose to the chance of injury or danger

rit·u·al (rich′ ə wəl) *n.* a special set of things to say or do in a ceremony, especially a religious one

ri·val (rī′ vəl) *n.* a person who is competing for the same goal, prize, or claim to fame as another —*adj.* competing (a *rival* player) —*vb.* **ri·valed**; **ri·val·ing** to compete, to try to surpass another's score or record

riv·er (riv′ ər) *n.* a large stream of water flowing from high land down to a lake, an ocean, or to another river

road (rōd) *n.* **1.** a usually paved way on which vehicles may travel **2.** a safe place away from the shore where ships may ride at anchor (Hampton *Roads*, Virginia) **3.** route (*road* to success)

road·way (rōd′ wā′) *n.* a road, including the land beneath it, the traveled surface, and the breakdown lane, or the shoulder

roam (rōm) *vb.* to wander from place to place without any set purpose

roar (rōr) *vb.* to make a deep loud rumble in the throat like the sound of a lion —*n.* a loud, rumbling sound

roast (rōst) *vb.* to cook a large piece of meat or a whole peeled potato in a hot oven until it is brown and cooked through —*n.* a piece of meat that is or is about to be roasted —*adj.* roasted (*roast* turkey)

rob (räb) *vb.* **robbed**; **rob·bing** **1.** to take something from another person unjustly by stealing or by force **2.** to deny a person his or her rights as through fraud or other illegal action

rob·ber·y (räb′ ə rē) *n., pl.* **rob·ber·ies** taking another person's property by stealing, violence, or causing fear

robe (rōb) *n.* **1.** a long, loose garment worn by men or women for some official act (a judge's *robe*, a professor's *robe*) **2.** any long, loose garment (bath*robe*) **3.** a small blanket used to keep one's legs warm (lap *robe*)

rob·in (räb′ ən) *n.* a large, North American thrush with a grayish back and reddish breast

ro·bot (rō′ bät′) *n.* a machine that sometimes looks like a person and does simple things on command

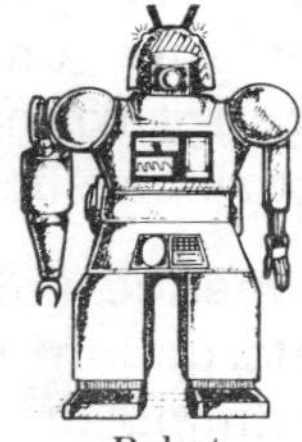

Robot

rock (räk) *vb.* to move back and forth —*n.* **1.** a forward and backward movement (The *rock* of the ship made it hard to walk.) **2.** a large chunk of stone

rock·er (räk′ ər) *n.* **1.** a curved piece on which something rocks, as a rocking chair **2.** a rocking chair

Rocker

rock·et (räk′ ət) *n.* **1.** a firework that shoots up into the air and bursts into a shower of sparks **2.** a device that when set afire is shot forward by gases that escape in the rear (A *rocket* works like a jet engine.) **3.** a bomb, missile, or space vehicle propelled by a rocket

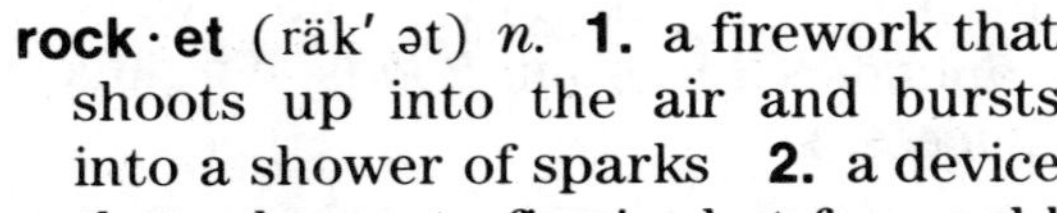

rod (räd) *n.* **1.** a straight, thin stick of wood or metal (a fishing *rod*) **2.** a measure of length equal to 16 1/2 feet

ro·de·o (rōd′ ē ō′) *n., pl.* **ro·de·os** **1.** a show of bronco riding, calf roping, and other cowboy skills **2.** a cattle roundup

role (rōl) *n.* **1.** a part or character in a show played by an actor or actress **2.** the work of a person in a particular job (the *role* of the school principal)

roll (rōl) *n.* **1.** the names of all those who belong to a group (The teacher called the *roll* to take attendance.) **2.** a small piece of bread dough baked into a round bun (hamburger *roll*) **3.** the sound of many quick beats on a drum (the *roll* of the drum) —*vb.* **1.** to turn over and over along a surface (to *roll* across the grass) **2.** to wind a flat piece of something such as paper into a tube shape **3.** to move along on rollers or wheels

Roll

roll·er (rō′ lər) *n.* **1.** a turning cylinder or tube on which something is moved **2.** a turning cylinder used to flatten a surface such as a lawn or a road

A Lawn Roller

ro·mance (rō mans′) *n.* **1.** a love story **2.** a special attraction between one person and another person, animal, or thing (He felt the *romance* of the tropical island.) **3.** a story of brave and noble characters who do heroic things —*vb.* to think about love or noble deeds

roof (rüf, rủf) *n., pl.* **roofs** the part of a building that covers the top —*vb.* to cover with a roof

room (rüm) *n.* a space in a building having four walls

roost·er (rüs′ tər) *n.* a full-grown, male, barnyard fowl (The *rooster* crowed at sunrise.)

root (rüt, rủt) *n.* **1.** the part of a plant that grows underground **2.** source (the *root* of the problem) **3.** a word from which other words can be made by adding a prefix, suffix, or ending (Pure is the *root* of purely, purity, and impure.) —*vb.* **1.** to enable the formation of roots (She *root*ed the plant cutting.) **2.** to dig up with the snout (The pig *root*ed in the mud.) **3.** to cheer (They *root*ed for their team.)

rope (rōp) *n.* **1.** a thick cord made of twisted or braided strands of fiber **2.** a string of beads (a *rope* of pearls) —*vb.* to tie with a rope

rose (rōz) *n.* a thorny plant with showy flowers, voted by Congress in 1986 to be our national flower

ros·y (rō′ zē) *adj.* **ros·i·er; ros·i·est** **1.** having a purplish-red color **2.** bright, hopeful (a *rosy* outlook)

ro·tate (rō′ tāt′) *vb.* **ro·tat·ed; ro·tat·ing** **1.** to turn around a center axis (The earth *rotate*s once every twenty-four hours.) **2.** to take turns doing something (They *rotated* the ball so that everyone could pitch.)

ro·ta·tion (rō tā′ shən) *n.* **1.** the act of turning as on an axis **2.** the act of moving one at a time through a series (the *rotation* of the seasons)

ro·tor (rōt′ ər) *n.* **1.** a part of a machine that turns around and around **2.** the overhead rotating blades on a helicopter

rough (rəf) *adj.* **1.** uneven (*rough* road) **2.** harsh (*rough* voice) **3.** violent (*rough* seas) **4.** coarse and crude (*rough* character) **5.** shaggy (*rough* texture) —*n.* **1.** uneven ground with tall grass (The ball fell in the *rough*.) **2.** an unfinished state (This term paper is still in the *rough* stage.) —*vb.* to handle roughly

round (raůnd) *adj.* **1.** having the shape of a circle or globe **2.** nearly exact, except for fractional parts (in *round* or whole numbers) —*adv.* around —*prep.* around —*n.* **1.** a definite route (The paperboy made his *rounds*.) **2.** one shot from a firearm, or the ammunition for one shot (fired one *round*) —*vb.* **1.** to make round **2.** to finish (*round* out his program with an art course)

rouse (raůz) *vb.* **roused**; **rous·ing** **1.** to awaken (*rouse* from sleep) **2.** to stir up excitement (to *rouse* their spirits)

route (rüt, raůt) *n.* a chosen way or road to travel (She went on the interstate *route.*) —*vb.* **rout·ed**; **rout·ing** to send by a chosen route (She *routed* the package by freight train through Detroit.)

rou·tine (rü tēn′) *n.* a usual procedure or course of action (Her normal *routine* was to answer her mail before beginning work.) —*adj.* ordinary or common

row (rō) *vb.* to push a boat onward through the water by using oars —*n.* **1.** an act of rowing (The *row* was tiring but fun.) **2.** several things lined up (six seats in a *row*)

row (raů) *n.* a noisy fight

row·boat (rō′ bōt′) *n.* a small boat made for rowing

roy·al (ròi′ əl) *adj.* **1.** relating to a king **2.** suitable for a king or a member of the king's or queen's family

rub (rəb) *vb.* **rubbed**; **rub·bing** to move one thing over another with pressure and friction —*n.* something that causes difficulty or friction (Our problem is boredom; that's the *rub.*)

rub·ber (rəb′ ər) *n.* **1.** a flexible material made from the milky juice of rubber plants **2.** a waterproof covering for a shoe, usually made of rubber (Wear your *rubbers* when it rains.)

rub·bish (rəb′ ish) *n.* trash

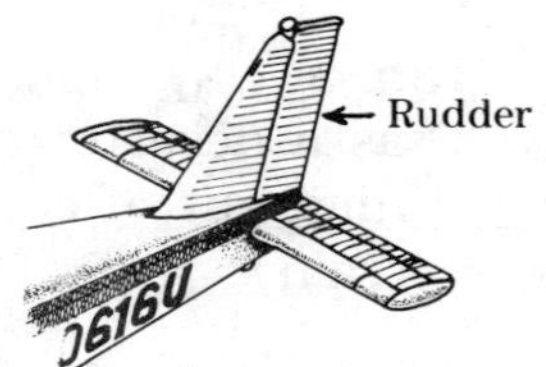

rud·der (rəd′ ər) *n.* a movable blade at the back of a ship or aircraft used for steering the craft to the left or right

rude (rüd) *adj.* **rud·er**; **rud·est** **1.** not polite (a *rude* answer) **2.** roughly made (a *rude* piece of furniture)

rug (rəg) *n.* a floorcovering made of thick fabric, usually having a pile

ru·in (rü′ ən) *n.* the remains of something that has been destroyed —*vb.* to destroy or severely damage

rule (rül) *n.* **1.** a guide for action (follow the *rule*) **2.** the time of the reign of a king or queen (under Queen Elizabeth's *rule*) —*vb.* **ruled**; **rul·ing** **1.** to govern (He *ruled* with a firm hand.) **2.** to make a formal decision (The judge *ruled* for the defendant.) **3.** to draw a straight line using a ruler

rul·er (rü′ lər) *n.* **1.** a king or queen **2.** a straight edge for drawing lines

rum·ble (rəm′ bəl) *vb.* **rum·bled**; **rum·bling** to make a deep rolling sound like thunder —*n.* a continuous, deep muffled sound

ru·mor (rü′ mər) *n.* gossip, as a story that is going around without any certainty about the facts —*vb.* to spread a rumor

run (rən) *vb.* **ran** (ran); **run**; **run·ning** **1.** to go at a fast pace **2.** to escape **3.** to take part in a race **4.** to campaign for election (*run* for the state senate) **5.** to go under power (The car *ran* smoothly.) **6.** to flow (The water *ran* all over the floor.) **7.** to mix (The colors *ran* in the wash.) **8.** to pass (*run* into difficulty) —*n.* **1.** an act of running **2.** a period of time (a *run* of bad weather) **3.** a usual trip (finished his *run*) **4.** an enclosure for animals (the dogs in the *run*) **5.** a dropped stitch or snag (a *run* in the stocking)

run·a·way (rən′ ə wā′) *n.* **1.** one who runs away, such as a deserter or a fugitive **2.** one or more horses running out of control —*adj.* having run away (*runaway* train)

rung (rəng) *n.* **1.** a crossbar between two legs of a chair **2.** a crossbar between the uprights of a ladder, used as a step for climbing (Step on each *rung* of the ladder.)

run·ner (rən′ ər) *n.* **1.** one who runs **2.** a messenger **3.** a thin bar on which something slides as on a sled **4.** a plant that makes new plants by sending out runners (the strawberry plant *runners*)

run·way (rən′ wā′) *n.* **1.** a paved strip on which airplanes land and take off **2.** a path made by animals leading to their feeding grounds

ru·ral (rür′ əl) *adj.* having to do with country life and country people (*rural* farmstead)

rush (rəsh) *n.* **1.** a hollow-stemmed grasslike marsh plant used in chair seats and baskets **2.** a fast forward movement (in a *rush*) **3.** the fast movement of people to a place of opportunity (the gold *rush,* the *rush* for jobs at the new factory) —*vb.* to hurry —*adj.* needing fast action (a *rush* order)

rust (rəst) *n.* **1.** a brownish-orange coating that forms on iron in the presence of air and water **2.** a plant disease that causes spots on leaves

rus·tle (rəs′ əl) *vb.* **rus·tled**; **rus·tling** **1.** to make a soft sound as of crisp material rubbing together (The taffeta skirt *rustled.*) **2.** to steal cattle from the range —*n.* a soft, squeaky sound

rust·y (rəs′ tē) *adj.* **rust·i·er**; **rust·i·est** **1.** covered with rust **2.** out of practice (*rusty* at tennis)

rye (rī) *n.* a cereal grass, the seeds of which are used in making flour, animal feed, and whiskey

S

sac (sak) *n.* a baglike part of an animal or plant often containing a fluid

sack (sak) *n.* **1.** a flexible container made of paper, cloth, or plastic for carrying goods **2.** the amount held by a sack (a *sack* of potatoes) **3.** the act of stealing from the people in a captured land —*vb.* **1.** to put into a sack **2.** to steal from the captured people (The conquerors *sack*ed the city.)

sa·cred (sā′ krəd) *adj.* **1.** holy **2.** religious **3.** worthy of reverence (*sacred* book)

sac·ri·fice (sak′ rə fīs′) *n.* **1.** an offering to God **2.** something offered unselfishly (a *sacrifice* of one's time as a volunteer) —*vb.* **sac·ri·ficed**; **sac·ri·fic·ing** to give up something for the sake of something else (He *sacrificed* his weekends to work in a drug rehabilitation center.)

sad (sad) *adj.* **sad·der**; **sad·dest** unhappy, sorrowful, or depressed

sad·dle (sad′ l) *n.* **1.** a padded leather seat for a horseback rider **2.** a cut of meat including the back and both loins (a *saddle* of lamb) —*vb.* **1.** to put a saddle on **2.** to place a burden on (*saddle* him with making all the arrangements)

safe (sāf) *adj.* **1.** free from harm **2.** free from risk **3.** in baseball, reaching base without being put out —*n.* a heavy metal chest for keeping valuable things

safe·ty (sāf′ tē) *n.* freedom from harm or risk

sail (sāl) *n.* a piece of canvas attached to the mast of a sailboat and used to catch the wind to move the boat —*vb.* to travel in a boat, especially one propelled by the wind pushing against a sail

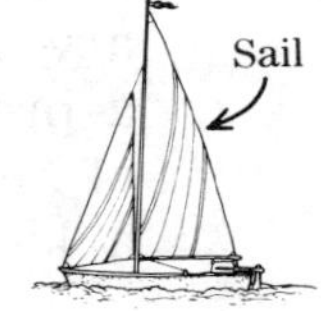

sail·boat (sāl′ bōt′) *n.* a boat that is propelled by the wind pushing against one or more sails

sail·or (sā′ lər) *n.* one who sails

sake (sāk) *n.* **1.** benefit **2.** aim or purpose (for the *sake* of good will)

sal·ad (sal′ əd) *n.* a dish of usually cold cut-up food that is served with dressing (garden *salad*; tuna *salad*)

sal·a·ry (sal′ ə rē) *n., pl.* **sal·a·ries** a fixed amount of money paid to a worker on a regular basis, such as weekly or monthly, for work done

sale (sāl) *n.* **1.** the selling of property or goods (The ranch house is for *sale.*) **2.** selling goods at a lower than usual price (Plant pots are on *sale* today at the garden shop.)

sales·man (sālz′ mən) *n.,pl.* **sales·men** (-mən) **sales·wo·man** (-wu̇m′ ən) one who sells in a store or in a territory (The book *salesman* is here.)

salm·on (sam′ ən) *n.* a large food fish with pinkish-orange flesh found near the mouths of large rivers where it returns to deposit its eggs

Salmon

salt (sȯlt) *n.* a white crystalline substance, *sodium chloride*, used in seasoning and in preserving foods, especially meat and fish —*vb.* to season or preserve with salt —*adj.* salty or salted

salt·y (sȯl′ tē) *adj.* **salt·i·er**; **salt·i·est** tasting of salt or containing salt (This soup is too *salty.*)

sa·lute (sə lüt′) *vb.* **sa·lut·ed**; **sa·lut·ing** **1.** the raising of a hand to one's cap as a gesture of respect as customary among military personnel **2.** a discharge of cannon, a presentation of arms, or dipping of flags as a gesture of respect to dignitaries **3.** a greeting with kind wishes, a kiss, or a bow

sal·vage (sal′ vij) *n.* **1.** the act of saving a ship that is in danger, or its cargo **2.** the saving of possessions that are in danger of being lost or wrecked —*vb.* **sal·vaged**; **sal·vag·ing** to save from wreckage, fire, or other danger

same (sām) *adj.* **1.** identical (the *same* apartment I rented last year) **2.** equal (the *same* flavoring he used in the cookies) **3.** unchanged in many ways (The *same* theme comes through in all her stories.)

sam·ple (sam′ pəl) *n.* a piece given to show the quality of the whole —*vb.* **sam·pled**; **sam·pling** to take a small part to check on the quality of the whole

sand (sand) *n.* loose, grainy material formed when larger rocks break up —*vb.* **1.** to sprinkle with sand **2.** to scrub with sand or sandpaper

san·dal (san′ dəl) *n.* a foot covering made up of a sole with straps to hold it on

sand·pa·per (sand′ pā′ pər) *n.* paper with sand glued to one side that is used in rubbing surfaces to smooth them or to remove a finish such as paint —*vb.* to rub with sandpaper

sand·stone (sand′ stōn′) *n.* a rock made up chiefly of quartz sand hardened into a solid mass with silica, calcium carbonate, iron oxide, and clay

sand·wich (sand′ wich′) *n.* two slices of bread with meat, cheese, or other filling between them

sap (sap) *n.* the juice circulating through a plant carrying nutrients —*vb.* **sapped**; **sap·ping** to undermine or weaken (Working ten hours a day *sapped* her strength.)

sat·el·lite (sat′ l īt′) *n.* **1.** a moon revolving around a planet **2.** a vehicle revolving around the earth or other heavenly body **3.** a country under the influence of a more powerful country

sat·in (sat′ n) *n.* cloth, as of silk or rayon, with a glossy surface, often used for wedding gowns or special occasion dresses

sat·is·fac·tion (sat′ əs fac′ shən) *n.* **1.** the act of giving what is wanted, expected, or owed **2.** the condition of being fulfilled or appeased

sat·is·fy (sat′ əs fī′) *vb.* **sat·is·fied**; **sat·is·fy·ing** **1.** to make content **2.** to fulfill one's needs and expectations

sauce (sȯs) *n.* a thickened liquid mixture to pour over foods to add more flavor (vanilla *sauce* for the pudding; spaghetti with tomato *sauce*)

sau·cer (sȯ′ sər) *n.* a shallow dish on which to rest a cup of tea, coffee, or hot chocolate

sau·sage (sȯ′ sij) *n.* ground meat such as pork mixed with seasonings and usually stuffed into a casing

sav·age (sav′ ij) *adj.* **1.** wild, untamed (*savage* animals) **2.** cruel, brutal (*savage* person) **3.** rugged and without roads (*savage* wilderness) —*n.* **1.** a primitive, uncivilized person **2.** a cruel, brutal person (a *savage* criminal)

save (sāv) *vb.* **saved**; **sav·ing** **1.** to rescue from danger or violence (to *save* them from drowning) **2.** to keep from being lost (*saved* pictures of their childhood) **3.** to avoid waste (to *save* by shopping wisely) —*prep.* except (all the boys *save* Donald)

saw (sȯ) *n.* a tool with a sharp edge or a series of sharp teeth —*vb.* **sawed**; **sawed** or **sawn** (sȯn); **saw·ing** to cut with a saw

saw·dust (sȯ′ dəst′) *n.* fine particles of wood produced when sawing wood

say (sā) *vb.* **said** (sed); **say·ing** to express in words —*n.* an expression of opinion (He had his *say* before he left.)

scale (skāl) *n.* **1.** a device for weighing **2.** one of the small, stiff plates on the bodies of some animals such as fish and snakes **3.** in music, a series of eight tones within an octave **4.** the size of a picture or plan in relation to the real thing (*scale*: 1 in. = 10 ft.) **5.** a standard for judging (mark on a *scale* from 1 to 10) —*vb.* **scaled**; **scal·ing** **1.** to weigh on a scale **2.** to scrape off the scales (*scale* the fish) **3.** to climb up or over (*scale* the wall) **4.** to raise or lower by a certain percentage or amount (to raise wages according to *scale*)

scalp (skalp) *n.* the skin, flesh, and hair on the top of the head —*vb.* to remove the scalp

scam·per (skam′ pər) *vb.* to run quickly or playfully

scar (skär) *n.* **1.** a mark left on the skin after a wound has healed **2.** a scratch or dent on furniture

scarce (skeərs) *adj.* **scarc·er**; **scarc·est** in short supply, not enough to meet the need (Fresh fruits are *scarce* in northern villages.)

scare (skeər) *vb.* **scared**; **scar·ing** to frighten —*n.* a state of alarm

scare·crow (skeər′ krō′) *n.* usually a figure dressed in old pants, shirt, and hat, set up in a garden to scare the crows and other birds away

Scarecrow

scarf (skärf) *n., pl.* **scarves** (skärvz) or **scarfs** **1.** a long or square piece of cloth worn about the neck or head as an ornament or protection against wind or cold **2.** a fancy rectangle of material or handwork used on a flat surface of furniture, such as a bureau or chest of drawers

scar·let (skär′ lət) *n.* bright red —*adj.* having a bright red color (a *scarlet* dress)

scar·y (skeər′ ē) *adj.* **scar·i·er**; **scar·i·est** causing fright or alarm (a *scary* book)

scat·ter (skat′ ər) *vb.* **1.** to throw here and there (*scatter* seeds) **2.** to go in different directions (the crowd soon *scatter*ed)

scene (sēn) *n.* **1.** a part of a play happening at one time and in one place (The *scene* took place at noontime, in the garden.) **2.** an emotional outbreak (She caused a *scene* in the office.) **3.** scenery (From the balcony, the *scene* was breathtaking.)

scen·er·y (sē′ nə rē) *n.* **1.** the painted background and furniture on a stage **2.** outdoor views

sce·nic (sē′ nik) *adj.* relating to scenery (a *scenic* tour up the river)

scent (sent) *vb.* **1.** to fill with an odor (The bayberry candle will *scent* the room.) **2.** to detect an odor (to *scent* an animal nearby) —*n.* a lingering odor (The dogs picked up the *scent.*)

sched·ule (skej′ ül) *n.* **1.** a list of times when classes or other events will take place **2.** a program —*vb.* **sched·uled**; **sched·ul·ing** to make up a timetable of events

scheme (skēm) *n.* **1.** a plan (a *scheme* for a cultural fair) **2.** a secret plot (an evil *scheme*) —*vb.* **schemed**; **schem·ing** to form a scheme

schol·ar (skäl′ ər) *n.* **1.** a student in school **2.** a well-educated person who has broad knowledge of one or more subjects

school (skül) *n.* **1.** a place for teaching and learning **2.** the teachers and students in the school (The whole *school* supported the principal.) **3.** a large number of fish feeding and swimming together —*vb.* to teach (They were *school*ed to think and question.)

school·house (skül′ haùs′) *n.* a building used as a school

school·ing (skü′ ling) *n.* education

school·room (skül′ rüm, -rùm) *n.* a room where classes are held

schoo·ner (skü′ nər) *n.* a sailing vessel with two or more masts with fore-and-aft sails on each

sci·ence (sī′ əns) *n.* an area of study dealing with the facts and laws governing the physical or material world set forth in an orderly arrangement

sci·en·tif·ic (sī′ ən tif′ ik) *adj.* relating to science or scientists (a *scientific* study of ear mites in animals)

sci·en·tist (sī′ ən təst) *n.* an expert in science

scis·sors (siz′ ərz) *n., sing.* or *pl.* a cutting instrument for thin pieces of paper or cloth, made so that its two sharp blades cut one against the other

scold (skōld) *vb.* to find fault with or criticize —*n.* a person who often finds fault and gives unfriendly criticism

scoop (sküp) *n.* a utensil for lifting a portion of a soft substance such as sugar or flour (a sugar *scoop*) —*vb.* to lift out with a scoop (*scoop* up some flour)

Scoop

scope (skōp) *n.* the extent or range of the topic or activity (The *scope* of this course will be from the early explorers through the Revolutionary War.)

scorch (skȯrch) *vb.* to burn slightly so as to turn brown on the surface of cloth, or to cause a bitter taste in food

score (skōr) *n.* **1.** twenty (four *score* and seven years ago) **2.** a line made with a sharp instrument **3.** the points made by each team in a game (a *score* of 4 to 2) —*vb.* **scored**; **scor·ing** **1.** to mark with a line or a scratch **2.** to keep the score in a game **3.** to earn one or more points in a game (She *scored* in the first period.)

scorn (skȯrn) *n.* disdain or contempt —*vb.* to reject or hold in disdain

scout (skaůt) *vb.* to look for, search —*n.* **1.** the act of searching **2.** a person who searches **3.** a girl scout or boy scout

scout·ing (skaůt′ ing) *n.* **1.** the general activities of girl scouts and boy scouts **2.** exploring activities for the military

scowl (skaůl) *vb.* frown —*n.* a gloomy or angry look

scram·ble (skram′ bəl) *vb.* **scram·bled**; **scram·bling** **1.** to climb quickly using both hands and feet (He scram*bled* over the boxes.) **2.** to cook beaten eggs, stirring often (to *scramble* eggs) —*n.* the end result of mixing things up (The wind blew the neat pile of papers into a *scramble.*)

scrap (skrap) *n.* **1.** a small piece **2.** *pl.* leftover pieces of food or material —*vb.* **scrapped**; **scrap·ping** to throw away as useless

scrap·book (skrap′ bůk′) *n.* an album of blank pages in which pictures or clippings may be pasted

scrape (skrāp) *vb.* **scraped**; **scrap·ing** **1.** to rub clean or smooth with a sharp tool **2.** to damage by rubbing against something rough **3.** to get by with difficulty (By cutting back their expenses, they managed to *scrape* by.) —*n.* **1.** a scratch **2.** a sound made by scraping **3.** a difficult situation (got into a *scrape*)

scratch (skrach) *vb.* **1.** to rub with one's fingernails (*scratch* a mosquito bite) **2.** to erase or draw a line through (*Scratch* the rest of the things on the list.)

scream (skrēm) *vb.* to let out a loud shrill cry —*n.* a long, loud cry

screech (skrēch) *vb.* to make a harsh, shrill sound (The brakes *screech.*) —*n.* **1.** a shrill sound **2.** a shriek as in fright or pain (to hear a *screech*)

screen (skrēn) *n.* **1.** a fine mesh material set in a window frame to keep out insects **2.** a movable partition for decoration or to block one's view **3.** a surface on which to show a motion picture **4.** the front part of a television set —*vb.* **1.** to partition with a screen **2.** to sort out by passing through a screen

screw (skrü) *n.* a metal rod threaded with a winding coil —*vb.* to fasten with a screw

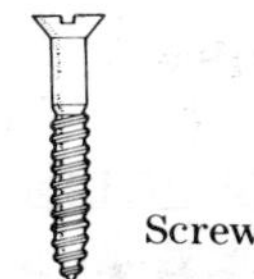
Screw

script (skript) *n.* **1.** handwriting **2.** a style of print that looks like handwriting **3.** the lines to be said by actors in a play or motion picture (Study the *script.*)

scrub (skrəb) *n.* a thick growth of stunted trees and bushes; a thicket —*vb.* **scrubbed**; **scrub·bing** to rub hard or brush while washing

sculp·tor (skəlp′ tər) *n.* one who makes a statue by carving, chiseling, or forming in clay, wood, or marble

sculp·ture (skəlp′ chər) *n.* **1.** the process of making a statue **2.** the work produced by this process (Her *sculpture* won a prize.)

sea (sē) *n.* **1.** ocean **2.** sometimes, a body of salt water not as large as an ocean and nearly surrounded by land (Caribbean *Sea*)

sea·coast (sē′ kōst′) *n.* the shore of the sea

seal (sēl) *n.* **1.** a fish-eating, salt-water mammal found in polar regions, including the true seal and the sea lion, hunted for their hides and oil **2.** a small stamp for making an impression on paper or wax

seam (sēm) *n.* **1.** the line made by stitching the edges of two pieces of material together **2.** a layer of ore in the surrounding rock (a *seam* of iron ore) —*vb.* **1.** to join with a seam **2.** to mark with a crease (his face, *seam*ed by the sun and the wind)

sea·man (sē′ mən) *n., pl.* **sea·men** (sē′ mən) a person who works on a ship at sea, a sailor

sea·port (sē′ pōrt′) *n.* **1.** a harbor open to ships at sea **2.** a town or city having such a harbor

search (sərch) *vb.* to spend time looking carefully for something —*n.* an effort to find something

sea·shore (sē′ shōr) *n.* the land at the edge of the sea

sea·son (sēz′ n) *n.* one of the four periods into which a year is divided depending upon the position of the sun overhead at noon; spring in the northern hemisphere being from the time the sun crosses the equator coming north until it reaches the Tropic of Cancer and starts back

sea·son·al (sēz′ n əl) *adj.* relating to a certain season

seat (sēt) *n.* **1.** a chair, bench, or other place to sit **2.** the place where a person sits (This is your *seat.*) **3.** a capital (the *seat* of government) **4.** a center (a *seat* of learning) —*vb.* to provide seats

sea·weed (sē′ wēd′) *n.* an alga such as kelp or any sea plant

sec·ond (sek′ ənd) *adj.* coming next after first —*adv.* in second place (He came in *second.*) —*n.* **1.** one who is second **2.** a sixtieth part of a minute or a degree —*vb.* to give support to a motion so that it can be discussed at a meeting (I *second* the motion.)

sec·ond·ar·y (sek′ ən der′ ē) *adj.* **1.** second in rank or value **2.** lesser in value **3.** following primary **4.** higher than elementary; the secondary grades, usually seven through twelve

se·cret (sē′ krət) *adj.* hidden from public view or knowledge (a *secret* meeting) —*n.* **1.** information intended for a small number of people (a military *secret*) **2.** something difficult to explain (the *secret* of long life)

sec·re·tar·y (sek′ rə ter′ ē) n., pl. **sec·re·tar·ies** **1.** a person who takes care of the letters, orders, and records of a business **2.** a government official in charge of a department (*Secretary* of State) **3.** a writing desk with a book cabinet, pigeon holes for supplies, and drawers below

Secretary

sec·tion (sek′ shən) *n.* **1.** a natural or logical division of something (an orange *section*, in the *section* of the report about accidents) **2.** a drawing showing the inner part (a cross-*section*) **3.** an area with special characteristics (rural *section* of the state) —*vb.* to divide into sections

se·cure (si kyůr′) *adj.* causing no worry (a *secure* relationship) —*vb.* **se·cured**; **se·cur·ing** **1.** to make safe (to *secure* a place for her jewelry) **2.** to lock carefully (*secure* the doors and windows)

se·cu·ri·ty (si kyůr′ ət ē) *n., pl.* **se·cu·ri·ties** **1.** safety **2.** a person or possession used as a guarantee that a debt will be paid (*security* for a loan) **3.** *pl.* stocks and bonds

sed·i·ment (sed′ ə mənt) *n.* **1.** matter that settles to the bottom of a liquid, dregs **2.** matter such as stones and sand deposited by water or a glacier

sed·i·men·ta·ry (sed′ ə ment′ ə rē) *adj.* relating to or formed from sediment (sandstone, a *sedimentary* rock)

see (sē) *vb.* **saw** (sȯ); **seen** (sēn); **see·ing** **1.** to have the power of sight **2.** to understand the meaning of **3.** to meet with or attend —*n.* the city in which a bishop's church is located, diocese

seg·ment (seg′ mənt) *n.* **1.** any of the parts into which a thing naturally separates or is logically divided **2.** a part cut off from a circle by a straight line called a chord **3.** a part of a straight line between two points

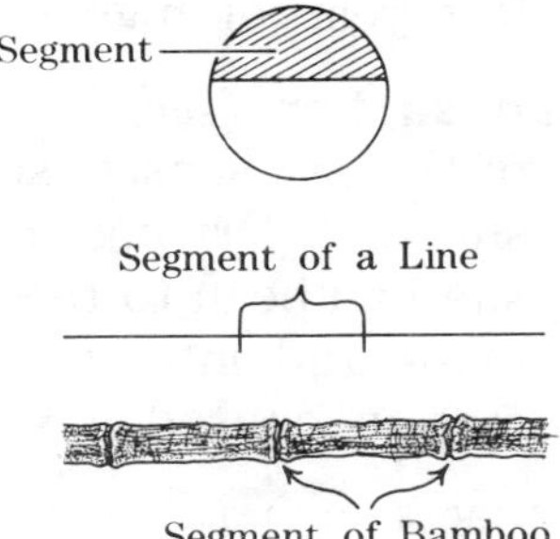

seize (sēz) *vb.* **seized**; **seiz·ing** **1.** to take by force or legal authority (The police *seized* their weapons.) **2.** to grasp suddenly (The boy *seized* the opportunity to work for the scientist.)

sel·dom (sel′ dəm) *adv.* not often

se·lect (sə lekt′) *adj.* **1.** chosen (This store carries a *select* quality of goods.) **2.** choice (a *select* group of people) —*vb.* to choose from among a number (*Select* those you like.)

se·lec·tion (sə lek′ shən) *n.* **1.** the act of selecting (The *selection* was difficult.) **2.** the thing selected (Bill liked my *selection.*)

self (self) *n., pl.* **selves** (selvz) a person's individuality, character, nature, identity (one's own *self*)

self·ish (sel′ fish) *adj.* putting one's own interests and advantages first before those of others in a self-centered way

sell (sel) *vb.* **sold** (sōld); **sell·ing** to give in return for money (*sell* health foods)

send (send) *vb.* **sent** (sent); **send·ing** **1.** to cause to leave (*Send* them away.) **2.** to cause to go from one place to another (*sent* his brother to help them) **3.** to throw, cast, or drive (*sent* the ball over the fence)

se·nior (sē′ nyər) *n.* **1.** someone older or higher in rank (She was his *senior* by five years.) **2.** a student in the last year of high school or college

sen·sa·tion (sen sā′ shən) *n.* **1.** the stimulation of one of the five senses: seeing, hearing, touching, tasting, and smelling (Driving into town, she had the *sensation* that she had been to this place before.) **2.** a state of excitement and interest (The movie cameras in the railroad station caused a *sensation.*)

sense (sens) *n.* **1.** the ability to take in information through the senses **2.** a recognition of what is right (*sense* of justice or duty)

sen·si·ble (sen′ sə bəl) *adj.* **1.** capable of being perceived correctly (The message is not *sensible.*) **2.** showing good reasoning (a *sensible* plan)

sen·si·tive (sen′ sət iv) *adj.* **1.** affecting the senses (My arm is *sensitive.*) **2.** easily affected (a *sensitive* nature)

sen·tence (sent′ ns) *n.* **1.** a judgment or punishment (His *sentence* was set at three years in prison.) **2.** a group of words that expresses a complete thought —*vb.* **sen·tenced**; **sen·tenc·ing** to tell what the punishment will be (The judge will *sentence* her today.)

sen·ti·ment (sent′ ə mənt) *n.* **1.** a state of mind or judgment based on feeling rather than reason (What is their *sentiment* about this?) **2.** opinion

sep·a·rate (sep′ ə rāt′) *vb.* **sep·a·rat·ed**; **sep·a·rat·ing** to set apart (*Separate* the fresh and packaged foods.) **sep·a·rate** (sep′ ə rət) *adj.* **1.** not connected or shared (Study at *separate* tables.) **2.** individual (the *separate* pieces)

sep·a·ra·tion (sep ə rā′ shən) *n.* **1.** the act of separating **2.** a line, point, or barrier that divides

se·quence (sē′ kwəns) *n.* **1.** a series **2.** the order of arrangement based on time, space, or logic

ser·geant (sär′ jənt) *n.* **1.** a non-commissioned officer in the army **2.** an officer in the police force

se·ries (siər′ ēz) *n., pl.* **se·ries** a number of things related in some way and arranged in order according to time, space, or logic (Joe's team will play in the World *Series.*)

se·ri·ous (sir′ ē əs) *adj.* **1.** showing deep thought (a *serious* attitude) **2.** important and earnest (*serious* business) **3.** dangerous, causing sadness or anxiety (a *serious* accident)

ser·mon (sər′ mən) *n.* **1.** a religious talk, often based on the Bible, given publicly by a clergyperson **2.** a serious talk to someone about his or her behavior

ser·pent (sər′ pənt) *n.* a large snake

ser·vant (sər′ vənt) *n.* a person hired to perform personal and household tasks such as cleaning, cooking, and laundry

serve (sərv) *vb.* **served; serv·ing** **1.** to work for or wait on (*serve* meals) **2.** to work for one's country (*serve* in the army) **3.** to perform one's duties (*serve* as a librarian; *serve* on the jury) **4.** to hit the ball, putting it in play, as in tennis —*n.* the act of putting a ball in play, as in tennis

ser·vice (sər′ vəs) *n.* **1.** the act of serving **2.** a religious ceremony (a prayer *service*) **3.** a set of dishes (a china tea *service*) **4.** the armed forces (the *service*) **5.** a business that provides a convenience to the public (bus *service*; repair *service*)

ses·sion (sesh′ ən) *n.* **1.** a meeting (Congress was in *session* today.) **2.** a whole series of meetings (School is in *session* for 180 days.)

set (set) *vb.* **set; set·ting** **1.** to put something in a particular place (*Set* it there.) **2.** to cover and warm eggs (Hens *set* on the eggs to hatch them.) **3.** to get something into a position of readiness (*set* a fire) **4.** to get something ready for use (to *set* the table) **5.** to go down below the horizon (The sun is *setting.*) —*adj.* **1.** fixed or established **2.** ready —*n.* **1.** the act of setting **2.** a group of tennis games **3.** the scene for a play made up usually of a painted background and furnishings (Arrange the *set.*)

set·ting (set′ ing) *n.* **1.** the act of one who sets (the *setting* of stones in jewelry) **2.** the time and place of the events in a story or play **3.** the disappearance of the sun below the horizon (the *setting* of the sun)

set·tle (set′ l) *n.* a long, high-backed bench with arms and sometimes a storage place under the seat —*vb.* **set·tled; set·tling** **1.** to agree upon (*settled* on the work the carpenter would do) **2.** to pay up what is owed (*settle* the bill) **3.** to find a permanent home, job, and way of life (*settled* in Iowa) **4.** to calm something down (*settled* the argument; medicine *settled* his stomach) **5.** to sink down or come to rest (The particles in the liquid *settled.* The dust *settled* as it rained.)

set·tle·ment (set′ l mənt) *n.* **1.** the act of settling **2.** final payment **3.** establishing a home **4.** an institution that helps people in a crowded area

set·tler (set′ lər) *n.* a person who settles in a new area, a colonist

sev·er·al (sev′ ə rəl) *adj.* **1.** single, individual (a union of the *several* subject areas) **2.** more than two but not many (*several* teachers) —*pron.* more than two but not many (*Several* of them are here.)

se·vere (sə viər′) *adj.* **se·ver·er**; **se·ver·est** **1.** serious, strict (*severe* penalty) **2.** plain (*severe* style) **3.** sharp, distressing (*severe* headache) **4.** violent (*severe* storm)

sew (sō) *vb.* **sewed**; **sewed** or **sewn** (sōn); **sew·ing** to stitch with needle and thread

sew·age (sü′ ij) *n.* waste matter carried away by sewers

sex (seks) *n.* **1.** the characteristics that make a person, animal, or plant either male or female **2.** sexual activity —*adj.* relating to sex

shab·by (shab′ ē) *adj.* **shab·bi·er**; **shab·bi·est** **1.** faded and worn out (*shabby* clothes) **2.** run-down and neglected (a *shabby* building) **3.** mean and unfair

shack (shak) *n.* a shabby house or hut

shade (shād) *n.* **1.** a place sheltered from the sun (in the *shade* of the tree) **2.** a color slightly different than the one it relates to (two *shade*s of navy blue) **3.** a small degree of difference (Their interpretations have different *shade*s of meaning.) **4.** a curtain on a roller used to shut out the light or provide privacy (window *shade*) —*vb.* **shad·ed**; **shad·ing** **1.** to shelter from the sun's light and heat **2.** to change by slight degrees in color, quality, or meaning

shad·ow (shad′ ō) *n.* **1.** shade in the shape of whatever blocks the sun, lengthened or shortened by the position of the sun (The late afternoon sun cast long *shadows*.) **2.** trace (not a *shadow* of truth to it) —*vb.* **1.** to cast a shadow upon **2.** to follow and keep under close watch

shad·y (shād′ ē) *adj.* **shad·i·er**; **shad·i·est** **1.** sheltered from the sun **2.** dishonorable, not open to public knowledge (a *shady* deal)

shaft (shaft) *n.* **1.** a long, slender rod, as the thin part of an arrow **2.** a narrow beam of light **3.** a tall, narrow, vertical opening in a building (elevator *shaft*) **4.** the vertical entrance to a mine (mine *shaft*)

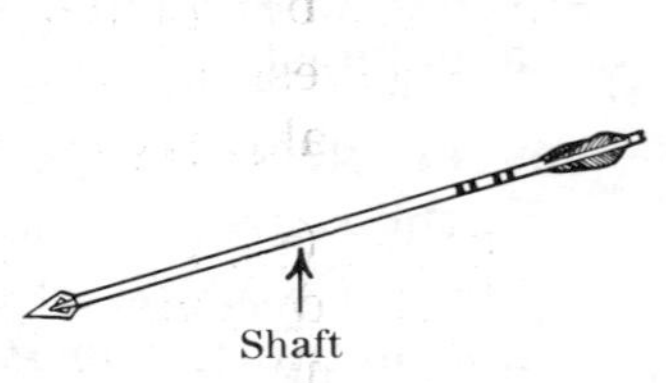

shag·gy (shag′ ē) *adj.* **shag·gi·er**; **shag·gi·est** having long and tangled fur or hair (an animal with *shaggy* fur)

shake (shāk) *vb.* **shook** (shu̇k); **shak·en** (shā′ kən); **shak·ing** **1.** to tremble or shiver (to *shake* with cold) **2.** to move up and down or back and forth (*Shake* your head "yes" or "no." *Shake* some apples from the tree.)

shak·y (shā′ kē) *adj.* **shak·i·er**; **shak·i·est** **1.** unsteady or unsound (a *shaky* stepladder) **2.** weak, feeble (The elderly person took a few *shaky* steps.)

shall (shəl, shal) *helping vb.* **should** (shəd, shu̇d); **shall** **1.** am to, are to (I *shall* be home next week. We *shall* be here until June.) **2.** must (You *shall* not leave. They *shall* turn in their papers by 10 P.M.)

shal·low (shal′ ō) *adj.* not deep (*shallow* water) —*n.* a shallow place, usually used in the plural (Stay in the *shallows*.)

shame (shām) *n.* a feeling of guilt (She felt *shame* after her sarcastic remark.) —*vb.* **shamed**; **sham·ing** **1.** to make ashamed **2.** to disgrace (His fear *shamed* him.)

shape (shāp) *vb.* **shaped**; **shap·ing** **1.** to make into a particular form (to *shape* the clay into a turtle) **2.** to organize (to *shape* up these office procedures) —*n.* **1.** form (the *shape* of a bird) **2.** condition (In what kind of *shape* is your old piano?)

share (sheər) *n.* **1.** one of the equal parts into which something is divided (his *share* of the family business) **2.** an interest in a corporation (One hundred *shares* of stock) —*vb.* **shared**; **shar·ing** **1.** to divide into a number of parts and distribute (*shared* her candy) **2.** possess in common (*share* a room with her sister) **3.** to take part (*share* in planning)

shark (shärk) *n.* a long fish, some of which are large, greedy eaters of smaller fish and sometimes dangerous to man

sharp (shärp) *adj.* **1.** having a thin edge, as a knife, or a fine point, as a needle **2.** angular (*sharp* features) **3.** biting or piercing (a *sharp* wind) **4.** keen (a *sharp* intellect) **5.** attentive (a *sharp* watch) —*vb.* to raise a note by a half step —*adv.* **1.** in a sharp way **2.** exactly —*n.* a tone that is one-half step higher than the note named (Play the song in F *sharp*.)

shat·ter (shat′ ər) *vb.* **1.** to break into little pieces **2.** to wreck (*shatter* her plans)

shawl (shȯl) *n.* a square or rectangle of cloth used by some women to cover the head or shoulders

she (shē) *pron.* that woman

shears (shiərz) *n., pl.* a cutting tool that works like scissors but is larger and more powerful

shed (shed) *vb.* **shed**; **shed·ding** **1.** to pour out (*shed* tears) **2.** to run off without sinking in (Plastic *shed*s water.) **3.** to get rid of (The lobster *shed*s its shell.) —*n.* a small storage building (a tool*shed*)

sheep (shēp) *n., pl.* **sheep** a domesticated animal related to the goat and raised for its meat, wool, and skin

sheet (shēt) *n.* **1.** an article of bedding used next to the body **2.** a broad, thin piece of any material (*sheet* of paper) **3.** an expanse (*sheet*s of water)

shelf (shelf) *n., pl.* **shelves** (shelvz) a long, narrow piece of board or metal attached to a wall or to the inside of a cabinet or closet for storing articles such as books

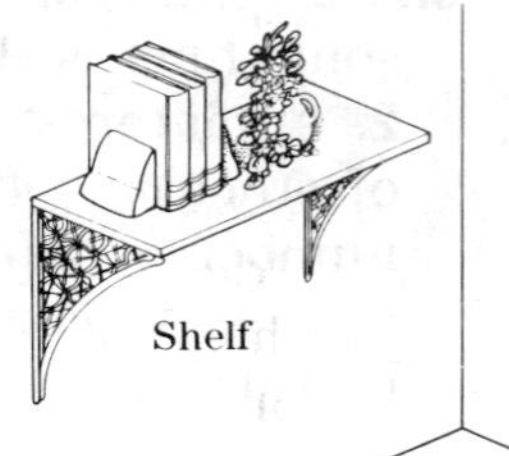
Shelf

shell (shel) *n.* **1.** the hard outer covering of certain sea animals, including mollusks such as clams and crustaceans such as lobsters **2.** the hard outer covering of an egg or a nut **3.** the case of certain ammunition (shotgun *shell*) —*vb.* **1.** to remove the shell **2.** to shoot shells at (to *shell* the fort)

shel·ter (shel′ tər) *n.* something that protects one from weather or danger —*vb.* to provide with a shelter

shep·herd (shep′ ərd) *n.* **1.** a man who tends sheep **2.** one who watches over one or more people —*vb.* **1.** to take care of sheep **2.** to take care of as a shepherd does

sher·iff (sher′ əf) *n.* a county law-enforcement officer whose duty it is to keep the peace

shield (shēld) *n.* **1.** a piece of armor, a metal plate, worn on the left arm as a protection in battle **2.** something that serves as a protection —*vb.* to protect from danger or discomfort (*shield*ed them from the wind)

shift (shift) *vb.* **1.** to change or transfer from one person or place to another **2.** to manage alone (*shift* for himself)

shil·ling (shil′ ing) *n.* a British coin equal to 1/20 pound sterling (a measure of money)

shine (shīn) *vb.* **shone** (shōn) or **shined**; **shin·ing** **1.** to be bright with light (The sun *shone.*) **2.** to make glossy (*Shine* your shoes.) —*n.* **1.** brightness **2.** polish

shin·gle (shing′ gəl) *n.* a piece of building material —*vb.* **shin·gled**; **shin·gling** to cover with shingles in overlapping rows

shin·y (shī′ nē) *adj.* **shin·i·er**; **shin·i·est** bright, glossy (She polished her shoes until they were *shiny.*)

ship (ship) *n.* **1.** a sea-going vessel large enough to navigate in deep water **2.** an airship or airplane **3.** a space vehicle (a rocket *ship*) —*vb.* **shipped**; **ship·ping** to put on a ship to be transported

shirt (shərt) *n.* a garment for the upper part of the body usually having a collar, tails for tucking in, and a buttoned front

shiv·er (shiv′ ər) *vb.* to tremble with cold —*n.* an instance of shivering

shock (shäk) *n.* **1.** sheaves of grain or corn stalks set up straight in the field **2.** an earthquake **3.** the effect of an electric current passing through the body **4.** severe mental strain **5.** the collapse of certain bodily functions caused by serious injury **6.** a stroke of paralysis

shoe (shü) *n.* **1.** an outer covering for the human foot **2.** a U-shaped metal bar applied to a horse's hoof (horse*shoe*) **3.** the part of a brake that presses against a wheel —*vb.* **shod** (shäd); **shoe·ing** to put a shoe on (*shoe* a horse)

shoot (shüt) *vb.* **shot** (shät); **shoot·ing** **1.** to fire a weapon **2.** to hit with a missile **3.** to let fly quickly (*shoot* questions at the speaker) **4.** to pass rapidly (*shoot* the rapids) **5.** to throw or propel (*shoot* the ball) **6.** to take photographs (*shoot* some pictures) —*n.* a new sprout on a plant

shop (shäp) *n.* **1.** a store **2.** a place where a particular kind of work is done (a repair *shop*) —*vb.* **shopped**; **shop·ping** to look at goods offered for sale in stores

shore (shōr) *n.* the land around the edge of a large body of water —*vb.* **shored**; **shor·ing** to support with props (*Shore* up that far wall.)

short (shȯrt) *adj.* **1.** not long **2.** brief in time (a *short* wait) **3.** not measuring up to average standards (a *short* measure) **4.** less than needed or expected (a *short* supply) **5.** flaky (*short* biscuits)

short·age (shȯrt′ ij) *n.* a lack of something needed (a *shortage* of money)

shot (shät) *n.* **1.** the act of shooting **2.** a bullet **3.** something thrown (That was a good *shot.*) **4.** attempt (Take a *shot* at the answer.) **5.** an injection (a flu *shot*)

shoul·der (shōl′ dər) *n.* **1.** the part of a person or animal where the arm or foreleg is joined to the body **2.** a part that slopes like a shoulder (the *shoulder* of a road) —*vb.* **1.** to push with one's shoulder (*shoulder* his way through a crowd) **2.** to put on one's shoulders (*shoulder* a load)

shout (shau̇t) *vb.* to call loudly —*n.* a loud cry

shove (shəv) *vb.* **shoved**; **shov·ing** **1.** to push from behind **2.** to move a boat offshore by pushing with a pole or oar (*shove* off) —*n.* an act of shoving

shov·el (shəv′ əl) *n.* a long-handled scoop used to dig and remove loose material such as dirt, sand, or snow —*vb.* **shov·eled**; **shov·el·ing** to lift or toss with a shovel (He *shoveled* snow all morning.)

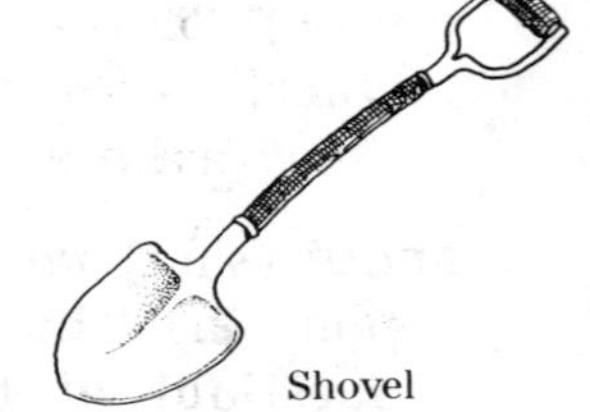
Shovel

show (shō) *vb.* **showed**; **shown** (shōn) or **showed**; **show·ing** **1.** to put on display (*show* his coin collection) **2.** to teach (*Show* them how to knead the dough.) **3.** give (*Show* them a good time.) **4.** lead (*Show* her to a seat.) **5.** to be noticeable (Her happiness *shows.*) —*n.* **1.** an entertainment (a Broadway *show*) **2.** a demonstration (a *show* of physical fitness) **3.** pretense (put on a *show*)

show·er (shau̇′ ər) *n.* **1.** a short, light rainfall **2.** a party for a woman about to be married or to have a baby **3.** a bath in which water is sprayed from above —*vb.* **1.** to wet with a fine spray **2.** to give freely (*shower*ed her with gifts)

shrill (shril) *vb.* to scream —*adj.* having a high, piercing sound (a *shrill* whistle)

shrimp (shrimp) *n.* a small crustacean related to the lobster

Shrimp

shrine (shrīn) *n.* **1.** an altar, chapel, church, or temple dedicated to God or a holy person, where people go to pray **2.** a place considered sacred because of its connection with a nation's history and beliefs, such as the Lincoln Memorial in Washington, D.C. and the Tomb of the Unknown Soldier in the Arlington National Cemetery

shrub (shrəb) *n.* a woody plant with many stems that is shorter than a tree; a bush

shrug (shrəg) *vb.* **shrugged**; **shrug·ging** to raise the shoulders meaning a lack of knowing or caring

shut (shət) *vb.* **shut**; **shut·ting** **1.** to close or become closed (The wind *shut* the door.) **2.** to confine (*Shut* him in his room.)

shut·ter (shət′ ər) *n.* **1.** a movable cover for a window **2.** a device in a camera that regulates the length of the exposure

Shutters

shy (shī) *adj.* **shi·er** or **shy·er**; **shi·est** or **shy·est** **1.** bashful, timid, or retiring (too *shy* to speak to strangers) **2.** cautious or suspicious (*shy* of money deals that offer big profits) **3.** lacking (*shy* of money today) —*vb.* **shied**; **shy·ing** to turn away in fear or distrust (The horses *shied* at the noise.)

sick (sik) *adj.* **1.** having a disease or poor health **2.** relating to illness (*sick*room supplies) **3.** disgusted (*sick* of waiting in line)

sick·ness (sik′ nəs) *n.* a disease or poor health

side (sīd) *n.* **1.** the right part or the left part of the body or any object **2.** one surface of an object (top *side* or bottom *side*) **3.** a position in favor or against a proposal (the affirmative *side*) **4.** each team in a sports contest (the winning *side*) **5.** a quiet comment (a *side* remark) —*vb.* **sid·ed**; **sid·ing** to take or support a side (*side*d with the home team)

side·walk (sīd′ wȯk) *n.* a usually paved walk along the side of a street

sigh (sī) *vb.* to take a deep breath and let it out with a soft, weary sound —*n.* the act or sound of sighing

sight (sīt) *n.* **1.** the sensation of seeing **2.** something worth seeing (A *sight* to behold!) **3.** that which is seen (the *sight* of land) **4.** visual attention (fix one's *sight* upon the horizon) **5.** a device on a gun for aiming (Take *sight* of the target before firing.) —*vb.* to see (to *sight* the Canada geese with his binoculars)

sign (sīn) *n.* **1.** a symbol that stands for something else (A flag is a *sign* of a nation.) **2.** a motion or gesture used to express meaning (An up-and-down nod is a *sign* of approval.) **3.** a large printed notice (a *sign* giving the sale price) **4.** trace (no *sign* of trouble)

sig·nal (sig′ nəl) *n.* **1.** something that starts or stops an action (A whistle is the *signal* to begin the game.) **2.** a warning or command (The traffic officer held up his hand as a *signal* to stop.) **3.** a traffic light (A green light is a *signal* to go.) —*vb.* **sig·naled**; **sig·nal·ing** to use a signal to give information (He *signaled* the start of the race.)

sig·na·ture (sig′ nə chu̇r′) *n.* **1.** a person's name written by himself; an autograph **2.** in music, the signs at the beginning of the staff to show the key and the time in which the music is written

sig·nif·i·cance (sig nif′ i kəns) *n.* **1.** importance **2.** meaning

sig·nif·i·cant (sig nif′ i kənt) *adj.* **1.** important (*significant* amounts of money) **2.** having meaning, sometimes hidden (a *significant* smile)

si·lence (sī′ ləns) *n.* **1.** a quiet state **2.** stillness (the *silence* of the north woods) **3.** secrecy or absence of mention (sworn to *silence*) —*vb.* **si·lenced**; **si·lenc·ing** **1.** to stop the noise or talking (*Silence* the crowd.) **2.** to put to rest or suppress (*Silence* their fears.)

si·lent (sī′ lənt) *adj.* **1.** not talking or making noise **2.** unspoken (*silent* grief) **3.** inactive (*silent* partner)

sil·i·con (sil′ i kən) *n.* a non-metallic element making up more than one-fourth of the earth's crust, found abundantly in quartz, sand, and sandstone, and used in making glass, steel, pottery, and other things

silk (silk) *n.* **1.** fiber spun by the silkworm to form its cocoon **2.** thread, yarn, or cloth made from this fiber

silk·en (sil′ kən) *adj.* **1.** made of silk **2.** having the luster and smoothness of silk

sill (sil) *n.* **1.** the wooden piece that forms the bottom of a window frame (Put this small plant on the window *sill.*) **2.** the wooden piece at the bottom of a doorway (Don't trip on the door*sill.*)

sil·ly (sil′ ē) *adj.* **sil·li·er**; **sil·li·est** **1.** lacking enough thought (I was *silly* to come without a coat.) **2.** lacking common sense (too *silly* to benefit from the advice)

sil·ver (sil′ vər) *n.* a whitish metal that takes a high polish and is used in coins, tableware, jewelry, and fancy objects —*vb.* to coat with a layer of silver

sim·i·lar (sim′ ə lər) *adj.* almost alike

sim·i·lar·i·ty (sim′ ə lar′ ət ē) *n., pl.* **sim·i·lar·i·ties** likeness

sim·ple (sim′ pəl) *adj.* **sim·pler**; **sim·plest** **1.** plain (a *simple* design) **2.** having few parts (a *simple* machine) **3.** not well educated (*simple* folks) **4.** clear and uninvolved (a *simple* explanation)

sim·plic·i·ty (sim plis′ ət ē) *n., pl.* **sim·plic·i·ties** **1.** the quality of being simple and easy **2.** clearness and plainness

sim·ply (sim′ plē) *adv.* clearly, plainly, and sincerely

si·mul·ta·ne·ous (sī′ məl tā′ nē əs) *adj.* existing or happening at the same time

since (sins) *adv.* **1.** from a time in the past until now (*since* World War II) **2.** after a time in the past (has *since* moved away) **3.** before the present (long *since* finished the book) —*prep.* from the time of (*since* last Monday) —*conj.* **1.** because (*since* he was late) **2.** from the time when (*since* I was sixteen)

sing (sing) *vb.* **sang** (sang); **sung** (səng); **sing·ing** **1.** to make musical sounds with the voice **2.** to talk with enthusiasm (*sing* out about)

sing·er (sing′ ər) *n.* one who sings

sin·gle (sing′ gəl) *adj.* **1.** unmarried **2.** being the only one (had a *single* piece) **3.** involving only one person (reserved a *single* seat) —*n.* **1.** a separate person or thing (items wrapped in *singles* or in pairs) **2.** a one-base hit in baseball —*vb.* **sin·gled**; **sin·gling** to select one from many (*singled* out the one he wanted)

sin·gu·lar (sing′ gyə lər) *adj.* **1.** being the only one of its kind **2.** exceptional (of *singular* beauty) **3.** relating to one (a *singular* noun) —*n.* the form meaning one (Use the *singular*.)

sink (singk) *vb.* **sank** (sangk); **sunk** (səngk); **sink·ing** **1.** to go underwater (The canoe *sank*.) **2.** to descend (The sun *sank*.) **3.** to become weaker (His spirits *sank*.) **4.** to go into (The water *sank* into the sand.) —*n.* a basin with faucets and a drain

Sink

sip (sip) *vb.* **sipped**; **sip·ping** to drink a small amount at a time —*n.* the act of sipping (Take a *sip*.)

sir (sər) *n.* **1.** a title of respect used in talking to a man (Yes, *sir*.) **2.** a British title given to a knight or baronet (*Sir* John Jones)

sis·ter (sis′ tər) *n.* **1.** a female related to another person by having the same parents **2.** a member of a religious order of women; a nun

sit (sit) *vb.* **sat** (sat); **sit·ting** **1.** to occupy a seat **2.** to hold a session (The court *sat.*) **3.** to be a member of an official body (He *sat* on the council.) **4.** to rest (The letter *sits* on the bar.)

site (sīt) *n.* the location of something (the *site* of the famous treaty)

sit·u·a·tion (sich′ ə wā′ shən) *n.* **1.** place of employment and position there (one's job *situation*) **2.** one's status in relation to what is happening (a rewarding *situation*) **3.** location

size (sīz) *n.* **1.** mass or bulk (of great *size*) **2.** the measurements of something (3′ × 4′ × 8′ is the *size.*) **3.** a standard measure (a *size* twelve)

skate (skāt) *n.* **1.** a flat fish with long fins **2.** a shoe with metal runner used for gliding on ice **3.** a shoe with rollers for gliding on a hard, smooth surface such as wood or concrete (roller *skate*)

skel·e·ton (skel′ ət n) *n.* a structure or framework that gives firm support, as the bones in man or the steel frame in a large building

sketch (skech) *n.* a rough, quickly-made outline giving the main features of something to be drawn, built, or written —*vb.* to make a sketch or outline

ski (skē) *n., pl.* **skis** one of a pair of long, narrow strips of wood, metal, or plastic attached to the foot and used for gliding over snow or water —*vb.* **skied**; **ski·ing** to slide or travel on skis

skill (skil) *n.* mastery of an ability or procedure acquired through practice (woodworking *skills*)

skil·let (skil′ ət) *n.* a frying pan

skill·ful (skil′ fəl) *adj.* **1.** having or requiring skill (a *skillful* dancer) **2.** showing skill (a *skillful* demonstration)

skim (skim) *vb.* **skimmed**; **skim·ming** **1.** to remove floating matter such as fat from a liquid **2.** to read rapidly to find the main idea and the way information is organized **3.** to throw so as to make a series of leaps on the surface of the water (The flat stone *skimmed* the water.)

skin (skin) *n.* **1.** the pelt of an animal **2.** the outer covering of a vertebrate (such as man) made up of two layers, the *dermis,* or inner layer and the *epidermis,* or outer layer **3.** the rind or peel of a fruit or vegetable —*vb.* **skinned**; **skin·ning** to remove the skin

skin·ny (skin′ ē) *adj.* **skin·ni·er**; **skin·ni·est** very thin, like skin and bone

skip (skip) *vb.* **skipped**; **skip·ping** **1.** to step and hop lightly on one foot and then the other (*skip* down the path) **2.** to pass over or omit (*skip* a page, *skip* a grade in school) —*n.* **1.** a light bounding step **2.** an omission

skip·per (skip′ ər) *n.* the master of a ship

skirt (skərt) *n.* a woman's garment that covers the body from the waist down —*vb.* to go around the outer edge of (the road that *skirts* the town)

skull (skəl) *n.* the bony skeleton of the head and face, protecting the brain and supporting the jaws

skunk (skəngk) *n.* a small black and white animal that squirts a very offensive odor

sky (skī) *n., pl.* **skies** the heavens or upper atmosphere, the region of clouds and winds

sky·scrap·er (skī′ skrā′ pər) *n.* a very tall building

slab (slab) *n.* a thick slice of something (a *slab* of stone)

slam (slam) *vb.* **slammed**; **slam·ming** **1.** to bang something shut (*slam* the door) **2.** to put something in place with force (*slam* the cards down) —*n.* **1.** a noisy bang **2.** in bridge, the taking of more than eleven tricks

slang (slang) *n.* popular but non-standard language filled with coined words and humorous or grotesque figures of speech

slant (slant) *vb.* to place something in a tilted position —*n.* **1.** an inclined or sloping position **2.** something that slants

slap (slap) *n.* a blow with the open hand —*vb.* **slapped**; **slap·ping** **1.** to strike with the open hand **2.** to place something with force (*slap* it together)

slash (slash) *vb.* **1.** to cut a gash **2.** to reduce greatly (*slash* prices)

slate (slāt) *n.* a fine-grained rock, usually bluish gray but sometimes having shades of brown, green, rusty-red, or black

slave (slāv) *n.* **1.** a person who is owned by another person and can be bought and sold **2.** anyone who is not his own master (*slave* to alcohol) —*vb.* **slaved**; **slav·ing** to work like a slave

slav·er·y (slā′ və rē) *n.* long, tiring labor or drudgery as directed by the will of another

sled (sled) *n.* a vehicle on runners for carrying people or goods over the snow —*vb.* **sled·ded**; **sled·ding** to travel by sled

sleek (slēk) *vb.* to make smooth and glossy —*adj.* having a smooth and well-groomed look (*sleek* hair)

sleep (slēp) *n.* a natural loss of consciousness, occurring at regular times, during which the body rests —*vb.* **slept** (slept); **sleep·ing** to rest through a normal loss of consciousness

sleep·y (slē′ pē) *adj.* **sleep·i·er**; **sleep·i·est** drowsy, slow in movement and in need of sleep

sleet (slēt) *n.* partly frozen rain or a mixture of rain and snow —*vb.* to shower with partly frozen rain

sleeve (slēv) *n.* **1.** the part of a garment that covers the arm **2.** a tubelike shape resembling a sleeve

sleigh (slā) *n.* a vehicle with runners used for traveling over snow and ice —*vb.* to travel in a sleigh

slen·der (slen′ dər) *adj.* **1.** long and thin, slim (a style for *slender* figures) **2.** swaying and unsteady (*slender* hope) **3.** not enough (*slender* support)

slice (slīs) *n.* a thin, broad piece of something (a *slice* of meat) —*vb.* **sliced**; **slic·ing** to cut into slices

slick (slik) *vb.* to make something smooth and shiny (*slick*ed his hair down) —*adj.* **1.** smooth and slippery (a *slick* spot on the floor) **2.** sly and tricky (a *slick* character) —*n.* a smooth surface (an oil *slick*)

slide (slīd) *vb.* **slid** (slid); **slid·ing** (slīd′ ing) **1.** to move smoothly over a surface with little effort (*slide* across the ice) **2.** to move smoothly into position (*slid* into line) —*n.* **1.** the act of sliding (a long *slide*) **2.** a sliding mass of material (a snow *slide* or avalanche) **3.** a slanted surface for sliding (played on the *slide*) **4.** a framed piece of film (showed *slide*s of the America's Cup Races) **5.** a small piece of matter on a glass plate for study under a microscope (a *slide* of skin tissue)

slight (slīt) *adj.* **1.** slim and frail (a *slight* frame) **2.** small in amount or importance (a *slight* problem) —*vb.* to treat as unimportant (*slight*ed their efforts) —*n.* an act of slighting (The *slight* angered them.)

slim (slim) *adj.* **slim·mer**; **slim·mest** thin or scanty —*vb.* **slimmed**; **slim·ming** **1.** to make thin **2.** to become slender

slip (slip) *vb.* **slipped**; **slip·ping** **1.** to move easily (*Slip* the coin into her pocket.) **2.** to pass without notice (The days *slipped* by.) **3.** to slide out of place (*slipped* to the floor) **4.** to take cuttings from a plant —*n.* **1.** a dock (Put the boat in the *slip.*) **2.** a mistake (a *slip* of the tongue) **3.** a fall (a *slip* in prices) **4.** a case for a pillow (pillow*slip*) **5.** a piece of a plant for rooting **6.** a small piece of paper (a *slip* of paper, a sales *slip*)

slip·per (slip′ ər) *n.* **1.** a low, comfortable shoe for indoor wear that slips on and off easily **2.** a fancy dress shoe for special occasions such as dancing

slip·per·y (slip′ ə rē) *adj.* **slip·per·i·er**; **slip·per·i·est** **1.** having a surface that can cause slipping **2.** having a wet, oily, or slimy surface

slit (slit) *vb.* **slit**; **slit·ting** **1.** to cut a long opening **2.** to cut into long strips

slope (slōp) *vb.* **sloped**; **slop·ing** to slant or tilt —*n.* an upward or downward slant

slot (slät) *n.* a long, narrow opening (a mail *slot*) —*vb.* **slot·ted**; **slot·ting** to cut a slot in

sloth (slȯth, slōth) *n.* **1.** laziness **2.** a slow-moving mammal of Central and South America

slow (slō) *adj.* **1.** dull (a *slow* learner) **2.** going below the usual speed (*slow* traffic) **3.** behind time (Your watch is *slow.*) **4.** taking a long time (*slow* in getting here) —*adv.* slowly —*vb.* to make slow or slower

slum (sləm) *n.* a poor, thickly populated, dirty, and run-down section of a city

sly (slī) *adj.* **sli·er** or **sly·er**; **sli·est** or **sly·est** slick, tricky, or crafty (a *sly* fox)

small (smȯl) *adj.* **1.** little in size or amount **2.** few in number (a *small* group) **3.** limited (*small* shipment) **4.** gentle (*small* voice) **5.** modest (a *small* investment) —*n.* a part that is smaller than the rest

small·pox (smȯl′ päks′) *n.* a contagious virus disease marked by vomiting, fever, and skin eruptions over the entire body

smart (smärt) *vb.* **1.** to cause or feel a stinging pain **2.** to suffer from hurt feelings —*adj.* **1.** bright and able (a *smart* lawyer) **2.** stylish in appearance (*smart*-looking outfit) **3.** having a stinging sensation (a *smart* slap) —*n.* a stinging pain

smash (smash) *vb.* **1.** to crush to pieces **2.** to shatter violently (*smash*ed the vase) **3.** to hit hard (*Smash* the ball over the net.) —*n.* **1.** a violent blow (One *smash* and it was over.) **2.** the ruin or collapse

smell (smel) *vb.* **smelled** (smeld) or **smelt** (smelt); **smell·ing** **1.** to get the scent or odor of something **2.** to give forth an odor —*n.* the sense of smell

smile (smīl) *vb.* **smiled**; **smil·ing** **1.** to have a pleasant facial expression with upturned lips **2.** to look with favor (Her parents *smiled* upon her success.) **3.** to look with disdain or contempt (to *smile* in contempt) —*n.* a bright, pleasant expression of pleasure or amusement (A *smile* lit her face.)

smog (smäg) *n.* a mixture of smoke and fog in the air causing a haze

smoke (smōk) *n.* gases rising from burning materials containing particles of carbon and ash —*vb.* **smoked**; **smok·ing** **1.** to give off smoke **2.** to inhale and exhale the smoke of burning tobacco **3.** to cure by smoking, as meat and fish **4.** to drive out by smoke (to *smoke* the woodchuck out of its hole)

smooth (smüth) *adj.* **1.** not rough or hairy (*smooth* skin) **2.** free and clear (*smooth* path) **3.** mild and pleasant (*smooth* taste) **4.** flattering (*smooth* words) —*vb.* **1.** to make smooth **2.** to remove difficulties **3.** to soothe

snack (snak) *n.* a light lunch

snail (snāl) *n.* a slow-moving mollusk with a spiral shell from which the head and a foot protrude when in motion

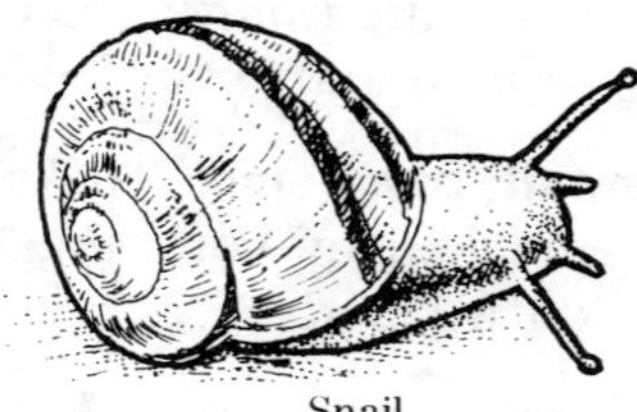
Snail

snake (snāk) *n.* a long, slim reptile without limbs that generally eats insects or small animals and birds —*vb.* **snaked**; **snak·ing** to crawl or zigzag along as a snake

snap (snap) *vb.* **snapped**; **snap·ping** **1.** to grab suddenly with the teeth or lips (frog *snapping* at a fly) **2.** to grasp at something eagerly (*snapped* at the chance to see his brother) **3.** to make a clicking noise (*snapped* her finger) **4.** to break something brittle (*snapped* the branch) **5.** to become alert (*snapped* to attention) —*n.* **1.** the sound or act of snapping **2.** a fastener that closes with a click **3.** a period of the same weather (a cold *snap*) **4.** something easy (Homework was a *snap.*) —*adj.* **1.** made without much thought (*snap* decision) **2.** closing with a click (a *snap* latch) **3.** very easy

snare (snaər) *n.* **1.** a noose for catching small animals **2.** anything that traps or deceives **3.** a gut or spiraled metal string on a snare drum —*vb.* **snared**; **snar·ing** to capture or deceive

snarl (snärl) *n.* **1.** a tangle of hair or thread **2.** a growling noise **3.** any tangled situation (a traffic *snarl*) —*vb.* **1.** to growl **2.** to speak in surly tones **3.** to get into a tangle

sneak (snēk) *vb.* to act in a sly or fearful way —*n.* a person who acts sly or fearful

sneeze (snēz) *vb.* **sneezed**; **sneez·ing** to let out the breath in a violent spasm with the sound *ah-choo* —*n.* an act of sneezing

sniff (snif) *vb.* **1.** to catch the scent of something by taking short, quick breaths **2.** the act or sound of sniffing

snort (snȯrt) *vb.* to blow out through the nose with a harsh sound —*n.* the act or sound of snorting

snout (snaủt) *n.* the long nose or muzzle of certain animals such as the pig

snow (snō) *n.* small white crystals frozen directly from water vapor in the air —*vb.* to fall as snow

snow·flake (snō′ flāk′) *n.* a feathery mass of snow containing one or more snow crystals

snow·storm (snō' stȯrm') *n.* a heavy fall of snow, often accompanied by high winds

snug (snəg) *adj.* **snug·ger**; **snug·gest** **1.** fitting exactly with no extra roominess (a *snug* vest) **2.** sheltered and comfortable (a *snug* little home)

so (sō) *adv.* **1.** as stated (said she would get it and did *so*) **2.** very much (tries *so* to do well) **3.** thus (is honest and *so* told the truth)

soak (sōk) *vb.* **1.** to wet thoroughly in a liquid (*soak*ed the dirty clothes) **2.** to get through to the inside or the depths of something (Rainwater *soak*ed through the basement walls. The meaning of what she said finally *soak*ed in.) —*n.* the act or process of soaking (A seven-minute *soak* loosens the dirt.)

soap (sōp) *n.* a product made from fat and alkali and used in washing —*vb.* to put soap on something or in the wash water

soar (sōr) *vb.* **1.** to move through the air as a bird **2.** to rise above what is normal or average (Interest rates *soar*ed.)

sob (säb) *vb.* **sobbed**; **sob·bing** to let the air out of the lungs while crying, then catch the breath with a heave of the chest —*n.* an act or sound of sobbing

so·ber (sō' bər) *adj.* **1.** calm, steady, serious (a *sober* person) **2.** moderate or restrained in the use of alcohol (always *sober* at parties) —*vb.* to make or become sober

soc·cer (säk' ər) *n.* a kind of football game in which a round ball is propelled by any part of the body except the hands and arms

so·cial (sō' shəl) *adj.* **1.** friendly and inclined to enjoy talking and being with other people (a *social* attitude) **2.** suited to live cooperatively with others (Ants are *social* insects.) **3.** relating to the welfare of people (a *social* service) **4.** events where people may meet and talk (a tea and *social*) **5.** relating to a particular rank in society based on material wealth (a *social* circle)

so·ci·e·ty (sə sī′ ət ē) *n., pl.* **so·ci·e·ties** **1.** people in general (in today's *society*) **2.** a group of persons joined for some purpose (Leukemia *Society* of America) **3.** a group of people with the same living standards or interests (middle-class *society*)

sock (säk) *n., pl.* **socks** (säks) a knitted foot-covering put on before the shoe

sock·et (säk′ ət) *n.* a hollow place into which something fits (The hip *socket* holds the thigh bone.)

sod (säd) *n.* a piece of turf, or soil held together with grass roots —*vb.* **sod·ded**; **sod·ding** to cover with pieces of turf

so·da (sōd′ ə) *n.* **1.** sodium carbonate, or washing soda, used commonly as a mild bleach as well as in the manufacture of glass, soap, paper, and other products **2.** sodium bicarbonate, or baking soda, used in or instead of baking powder, in the refrigerator to prevent odors and in industry **3.** a carbonated drink, usually with added flavoring, often called soda pop

so·di·um (sōd′ ē əm) *n.* a silver-white element always found in nature combined with one or more other elements such as in sodium chloride, common table salt

so·fa (sō′ fə) *n.* a long, upholstered seat with back and arms, often long enough to seat three people

Sofa

soft (sȯft) *adj.* **1.** not hard (*soft* pillow) **2.** not harsh (*soft* voice) **3.** not glaring (*soft* colors) **4.** not firm or crisp (*soft* fabric) **5.** containing no alcohol (*soft* drink) —*adv.* softly

soft·ball (sȯft′ bȯl′) *n.* **1.** a game similar to baseball but played on a smaller diamond with a larger and softer ball **2.** the ball used in softball

soft·en (sȯf′ ən) *vb.* to make soft or softer

soft·ly (sȯft′ lē) *adv.* quietly and gently

soil (sȯil) *vb.* to stain or make dirty —*n.* **1.** stain **2.** the finely broken rock and humus on the earth's surface that supports plant life

so·lar (sō′ lər) *adj.* **1.** relating to the sun (*solar* system) **2.** coming from the sun (*solar* rays) **3.** using the light or heat of the sun (*solar* power)

sol·dier (sōl′ jər) *n.* **1.** an enlisted person in the army **2.** someone who works for a specific cause (a *soldier* of fortune)

sole (sōl) *n.* **1.** an edible flatfish (fillet of *sole*) **2.** the bottom of a foot, also of a shoe, boot, or slipper —*vb.* **soled**; **sol·ing** to put on a sole (*sole* the shoes) —*adj.* **1.** acting alone (*sole* responsibility) **2.** only (*sole* survivor)

sol·emn (säl′ əm) *adj.* **1.** sacred (*solemn* religious rites) **2.** formal and impressive (a *solemn* occasion) **3.** serious and earnest (my *solemn* word)

sol·id (säl′ əd) *adj.* **1.** dense, not hollow (*solid* rock) **2.** without a break (a *solid* hour) **3.** firm and compact (*solid* earth) **4.** heavy and well-built (*solid* furniture) **5.** united (a *solid* front)

sol·i·tar·y (säl′ ə ter′ ē) *adj.* **1.** single or lone (a *solitary* student) **2.** lonely, seldom traveled (*solitary* place)

so·lu·tion (sə lü′ shən) *n.* **1.** the act or result of solving, consisting of looking at the parts and determining how a problem can be fixed or a question answered **2.** a preparation made by dissolving a solid, liquid, or gas in a liquid

solve (sälv) *vb.* **solved**; **solv·ing** to find a solution to a problem or an answer to a question

some (səm) *adj.* **1.** a person or thing not named (*Some* toys are safe.) **2.** an unnamed amount or number (*some* coins) —*pron.* a portion or part of the whole (*some* of our citizens) —*adv.* approximately (*some* five years ago)

some·bod·y (səm′ bäd′ ē) *pron.* some person

some·how (səm′ hau̇′) *adv.* in one way or another

some·one (səm′ wən′) *pron.* some person

some·thing (səm′ thing) *pron.* a thing not definitely known or not named

some·time (səm′ tīm′) *adv.* **1.** at a time in the future (will visit *sometime*) **2.** at a time not known or not named

some·times (səm′ tīmz) *adv.* now and then

some·what (səm′ hwät′) *pron.* a little bit (She is *somewhat* of a comedian.) —*adv.* in some degree (*somewhat* tired of it)

some·where (səm′ hweər) *adv.* **1.** in, at, or to a place not named (going *somewhere*) **2.** at a time not named (*somewhere* around four o'clock)

son (sən) *n.* **1.** a male offspring (her *son*) **2.** a man or boy closely allied with a group or a belief (*sons* of freedom)

so·nar (sō′ när) *n.* an acronym, or word formed from initial letters, for "*so*und *na*vigation *r*anging," a method for finding underwater objects, such as submarines or sunken vessels, by bouncing sound waves off them

song (so̊ng) *n.* **1.** music intended to be played and sung, or vocal music **2.** a small amount (You can have it for a *song*.)

soon (sün) *adv.* **1.** quickly (will need it *soon*) **2.** willingly (They would as *soon* work as waste time.)

sore (sōr) *adj.* **1.** causing pain (*sore* arm) **2.** angered (*sore* about it) —*n.* a part of the body having a spot that hurts because of a bruise or infection

sor·row (sär′ ō) *n.* **1.** sadness or grief **2.** a feeling of sadness or regret because of what one has done

sor·ry (sär′ ē) *adj.* **sor·ri·er**; **sor·ri·est** feeling or causing sorrow or regret

sort (sȯrt) *n.* a group of persons or things alike in some way (this *sort* of wood) —*vb.* to put into groups or piles based on the ways things are alike (*sort* the mail by zip code) **—out of sorts** not the same as usual

soul (sōl) *n.* **1.** the spiritual part of a person as distinguished from the body; the center of feelings, ideals, and morals **2.** the essential part of anything (the *soul* of the project)

sound (saůnd) *adj.* **1.** free from flaw, in good condition (a *sound* house frame) **2.** healthy (*sound* of mind and body) **3.** basically good, true, honorable, and legal (a *sound* contract) —*n.* a noise —*vb.* **1.** to make a noise (*sound* the fire alarm) **2.** utter or say (*sound* your words) **3.** seem (That doesn't *sound* right.) **4.** to measure the depth of water **5.** to try to figure out a person's thinking (*sound* him out)

soup (süp) *n.* a liquid food made by simmering meat, fish, or vegetables, and serving either the broth from this or the broth with cut-up food in it

sour (saůr) *adj.* having an acid or tart taste caused by fermentation (*sour* milk) or decay —*vb.* to make or become sour

source (sōrs) *n.* the beginning or origin of something (the river *source*, the *source* of the information)

south (saůth) *adv.* to or toward the south —*adj.* lying toward or coming from the south (*south* of the city) —*n.* the compass point opposite north

south·east (saůth ēst′) *adv.* to or toward the southeast (going *southeast*) —*n.* the direction or compass point between south and east —*adj.* lying in, going to, or coming from the southeast (a *southeast* wind)

south·east·ern (saůth ēs′ tərn) *adj.* lying toward or coming from the southeast

south·ern (sə<u>th</u>′ ərn) *adj.* lying toward or coming from the south

south·ward (saůth′ wərd) *adv.* or *adj.* toward the south —*n.* a southward direction, part or point

south·west (saůth west′) *adv.* to or toward the southwest (traveling *southwest*) —*n.* the direction or compass point between south and west —*adj.* lying in, going to, or coming from the southwest (a *southwest* wind)

south·west·ern (saůth wes′ tərn) *adj.* lying toward or coming from the southwest

sow (saů) *n.* an adult female swine

sow (sō) *vb.* **sowed**; **sown** or **sowed**; **sow·ing** to scatter or spread widely (*sow* seeds)

soy·bean (sȯi′ bēn′) *n.* a plant related to clover having edible seeds widely used for soybean oil and soybean meal which is left after the seeds are pressed

space (spās) *n.* **1.** something that has length, width, and height (a parking *space*, *space* for a building) **2.** the region beyond the earth's atmosphere (outer *space*) **3.** a definite place (I need my own *space*.) **4.** a period of time (*space* to think) —*vb.* **spaced**; **spac·ing** to place at a certain distance apart

space·craft (spās′ kraft′) *n.* a vehicle for carrying people beyond the earth's atmosphere

space·ship (spās′ ship′) *n.* spacecraft

spa·ghet·ti (spə get′ ē) *n.* a food made chiefly of flour and water paste and dried in long strings

span (span) *n.* **1.** the distance between the end of the thumb and the end of the little finger when the hand is stretched out **2.** the time or distance between two points (long *span* of time) —*vb.* **spanned**; **span·ning** to reach or extend across (to *span* the river with a bridge)

spar (spär) *n.* a stout pole on a sailboat used for a mast, yard, or boom, to which a sail is fastened —*vb.* **sparred**; **spar·ring** **1.** to fit with spars **2.** to box with the fists without hitting any hard blows **3.** to get into a contest of words

spare (spaər) *vb.* **spared**; **spar·ing** **1.** to keep free from punishment or harm (*Spare* him!) **2.** to save (*Spare* them from worry.) **3.** to use rarely (*spare* the rod) **4.** to avoid (to *spare* no effort) **5.** to live cheaply (to be *sparing* with your money) **6.** to give or lend (I can *spare* a few slices of bread.) —*adj.* **1.** scanty or frugal (*spare* meal) **2.** extra (*spare* parts) —*n.* **1.** an extra thing or part of a thing (four tires and a *spare*) **2.** in bowling, knocking down ten pins on the first two balls

spark (spärk) *n.* **1.** a small burning particle thrown off from a fire **2.** a sudden flash **3.** a short flash of electricity between two conductors **4.** a small sign of something (a *spark* of interest) —*vb.* **1.** to produce sparks **2.** to stir up (to *spark* a revolt)

spar·kle (spär′ kəl) *vb.* **spar·kled**; **spar·kling** **1.** to give off flashes of light (The diamond *sparkled* in the sunlight.) **2.** to bubble up (to *sparkle* like champagne) **3.** to glisten from within (eyes that *sparkle* with friendliness) —*n.* **1.** a spark **2.** a sparkling appearance

spar·row (spar′ ō) *n.* a small bird in the finch family, usually a brown color with gray or black markings

speak (spēk) *vb.* **spoke** (spōk); **spo·ken** (spō′ kən); **speak·ing** **1.** to talk **2.** to convey in speech or writing **3.** to convey other than through speech (Her dry, wrinkled skin *spoke* of an outdoor life.)

speak·er (spē′ kər) *n.* **1.** one who speaks **2.** an electronic device to make the sounds of speech or music loud enough to be heard by an audience

spear (spiər) *n.* **1.** a weapon with a sharp pointed shaft for thrusting or throwing **2.** a device with barbs like a fishhook for spearing fish

spe·cial (spesh′ əl) *adj.* **1.** unusual (a *special* gift) **2.** different from others (a *special* friend) **3.** extra (a *special* treat)

spe·cial·ist (spesh′ ə ləst) *n.* a person who confines his work and study to a limited subject, occupation, or profession (an allergy *specialist*)

spe·cial·ize (spesh′ ə līz′) *vb.* **spe·cial·ized**; **spe·cial·iz·ing** to limit one's attention or study to a narrow field (*specialize* in repairing jet engines)

spe·cial·ty (spesh′ əl tē) *n., pl.* **spe·cial·ties** **1.** a branch of work or study to which one is devoted **2.** something one does particularly well (Baked chicken is her *specialty*.)

spe·cies (spē′ shēz) *n., pl.* **spe·cies** a class of things with common characteristics (The human race forms a *species*.)

spe·cif·ic (spi sif′ ik) *adj.* **1.** relating to or constituting a species **2.** definite (*specific* time)

spec·i·fy (spes′ ə fī′) *vb.* **spec·i·fied**; **spec·i·fy·ing** **1.** to give exact details (*specify* the size and color) **2.** to name or state (*specify* 100 percent cotton)

spec·i·men (spes′ ə mən) *n.* a small sample that shows what the whole thing is like (a termite *specimen*)

speck (spek) *n.* **1.** a tiny bit or piece (a *speck* of dust) **2.** a small spot (a *speck* of decay on the tomato)

spec·ta·cle (spek′ tə kəl) *n.* anything presented for public viewing such as a show or parade

spec·tac·u·lar (spek tak′ yə lər) *adj.* pertaining to a display with scenic, dramatic, or showy qualities (a *spectacular* view of the erupting volcano)

spec·ta·tor (spek′ tāt′ ər) *n.* one who watches (a *spectator* at the football game)

spec·trum (spek′ trəm) *n., pl.* **spec·tra** (-trə) or **spec·trums** the colors of the rainbow including red, orange, yellow, green, blue, indigo, and violet which are also seen when light passes through a prism

speech (spēch) *n.* **1.** the ability to say understandable words **2.** a formal talk **3.** a manner of speaking (Her *speech* is low and musical.)

speed (spēd) *n.* **1.** rate of moving **2.** quickness —*vb.* **sped** (sped) or **speed·ed**; **speed·ing** **1.** to hurry **2.** to drive above the speed limit

spell (spel) *n.* an influence or charm (His dramatic entrance cast a *spell* upon the audience.) —*vb.* **1.** to say or write the letters of a word **2.** to indicate (Skipping school *spells* trouble.) **3.** to take the place of (I'll *spell* you while you have lunch.)

spell·ing (spel′ ing) *n.* **1.** the way a word is spelled **2.** the act of saying or writing the letters in a word

spend (spend) *vb.* **spent** (spent); **spend·ing** **1.** to pay out, usually for purchases or bills (*spent* on groceries) **2.** to make use of (*spend* time reading a novel) **3.** to exhaust (*spent* themselves trying to finish before nightfall) **4.** to waste (*spent* his salary on the lottery)

sperm (spərm) *n.* a male reproductive cell

sphere (sfiər) *n.* **1.** a ball-shaped object such as the earth or moon **2.** a field of interest, knowledge, or activity (The stock market is beyond my *sphere* of understanding.)

spice (spīs) *n.* **1.** a sharp-tasting or fragrant plant product such as mustard or clove used to give foods an interesting flavor **2.** anything that adds flavor or excitement (a hobby that adds *spice* to your life) —*vb.* **spiced**; **spic·ing** to add seasoning or excitement

spi·der (spīd′ ər) *n.* an insect-like animal having two body parts instead of three and eight legs instead of six that spins silken webs for catching prey

Spider

spike (spīk) *n.* **1.** a large nail **2.** a firm, pointed object such as put on the bottom of certain sports shoes to prevent slipping **3.** an ear of grain (a *spike* of wheat) —*vb.* **spiked**; **spik·ing** **1.** to put on spikes **2.** to cut with a spike

spill (spil) *vb.* **spilled** (spild) or **spilt** (spilt); **spill·ing** **1.** to allow to run over the edge or fall from a container (to *spill* milk) **2.** to be wasted by dripping or pouring out (The flour *spilled* on the floor.) **3.** to reveal, as a secret

spin (spin) *vb.* **spun** (spən); **spin·ning** **1.** to twist or twirl **2.** to draw out and twist into yarn or thread (*spin* wool) **3.** to have a whirling sensation —n. **1.** the act of whirling or twirling **2.** a short drive in a vehicle

spin·ach (spin′ ich) *n.* a green leafy plant eaten raw in salad or cooked as a hot vegetable

spi·nal (spīn′ l) *adj.* relating to the backbone or spine

spin·dle (spin′ dəl) *n.* **1.** a tapered rod used for twisting fibers into thread and for holding the spun thread **2.** a rod on which something turns

spine (spīn) *n.* **1.** the backbone or spinal column **2.** a pointed growth on a plant as on a rose or a cactus

spi·ral (spī′ rəl) *n.* **1.** a curve that circles around a point or line like a spring or the thread of a screw **2.** a single turn of a spiral object —*adj.* circling around a center —*vb.* **spi·raled**; **spi·ral·ing** to shape or be shaped in a spiral

Spiral

spir·it (spir′ ət) *n.* **1.** one's soul **2.** a supernatural being **3.** a mood, humor, or disposition (played with a lively *spirit*) **4.** underlying meaning or intent (Judge not the words, but the *spirit.*) **5.** an alcoholic solution —*vb.* to carry off secretly (to *spirit* away)

spir·i·tu·al (spir′ i chə wəl) *adj.* **1.** relating to the soul, not the body **2.** religious —*n.* an emotional religious song native to the black people in southern states

spit (spit) *n.* **1.** a rod to hold meat for roasting over an open fire **2.** a small point of land or a long, narrow sand bar that juts out into a body of water **3.** saliva, a secretion in the mouth —*vb.* **spit** or **spat** (spat); **spit·ting** to expel from the mouth (*Spit* out the prune stone.)

spite (spīt) *n.* a feeling of dislike or ill will toward another

splash (splash) *vb.* **1.** to hit a liquid with the hand or an object, causing some of the liquid to fly around (The car went through the puddle and *splash*ed us.) **2.** to scatter with marks as if splashed (The sunlight *splash*ed through the trees.) **3.** to make noticeable —*n.* **1.** a splatter of liquid **2.** a spot made by a splatter

splen·did (splen′ dəd) *adj.* **1.** very bright, inspiring (a *splendid* wedding) **2.** excellent (a *splendid* piece of artwork)

splen·dor (splen′ dər) *n.* **1.** brilliance (the *splendor* of the marble palace) **2.** glorious achievement (the *splendor*s of that ancient civilization)

split (split) *vb.* **split**; **split·ting** **1.** to divide lengthwise (*split* wood with the grain) **2.** to burst (The sack *split.*) **3.** to separate into parts —*n.* **1.** a crack or tear (The *split* in the fabric was hard to mend.) **2.** separation (the *split* in the union over health benefits) —*adj.* cracked, torn, or divided (*split* fingernail)

spoil (spȯil) *n.* a thing taken by force, especially during war (destroyed the town and took the *spoil*s) —*vb.* **spoiled** (spȯild); **spoil·ing** **1.** to rob **2.** to damage, or harm (*spoiled* their children) **3.** to become rotten, sour, or unfit to eat (The food left on the table *spoiled.*)

spoke (spōk) *n.* **1.** one of the bars connecting the center of a wheel with the rim **2.** a rung of a ladder

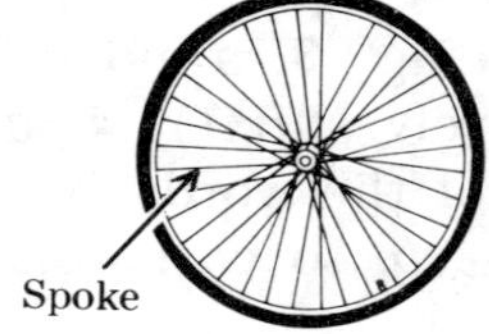

sponge (spənj) *n.* **1.** a springy, hole-filled mass of hard fibers, forming the skeleton of a group of sea animals, which is able to hold water, making it useful in cleaning **2.** a product with the useful qualities of natural sponge —*vb.* **sponged**; **spong·ing** **1.** to wash or bathe with or as if with a sponge **2.** to get something from another by imposing on hospitality or good nature

spool (spül) *n.* a small cylinder with a raised rim on which thread or wire is wound —*vb.* to wind on a spool

Spool

spoon (spün) *n.* a utensil with a long handle and shallow bowl used in eating liquid, juicy, or soft foods and also for stirring and mixing (a soup *spoon*) —*vb.* to take up or out in a spoon (*Spoon* some berries over the ice cream.)

spore (spōr) *n.* a reproductive cell of a lower organism such as a fungus, capable of developing into a new organism under the proper conditions

sport (spōrt) *vb.* **1.** to wear or display in a showy way (*sport* a new suit) **2.** to play or amuse oneself —*n.* **1.** physical activity, as athletic games **2.** fun or jest (said in *sport*) **3.** a person who enjoys flashy clothes and an easy life (quite the *sport*) **4.** one who loses a game or contest gracefully (a good *sport*) **5.** an animal or plant that shows a sudden change from the usual or normal type, as the absence of spines on a spine-type cactus **6.** ridicule (made *sport* of him)

spot (spät) *n.* **1.** a stained area (ink *spot*) **2.** a fault **3.** a place (a good *spot* for a candy store) —*vb.* **spot·ted; spot·ting** **1.** to be marked or stained **2.** to recognize (*spot* his uncle at the mall)

spout (spaůt) *vb.* **1.** to eject a stream of liquid **2.** to say in a self-important way (always *spout*ing off about something) —*n.* **1.** a pipe to carry off rainwater (a water*spout*) **2.** a spurt of liquid

spray (sprā) *n.* **1.** one or more flowering branches in a flat arrangement (a *spray* of pink flowers) **2.** a fine mist of liquid or vapor as from an atomizer **3.** a device, as an atomizer, for ejecting a mist or vapor (a *spray* of perfume) —*vb.* to squirt out (*spray* the peach tree)

spread (spred) *vb.* **spread**; **spread·ing** **1.** to open, extend, or stretch out (to *spread* the tablecloth) **2.** to divide among people or over time (to *spread* the prizes among different age groups) **3.** to apply a thin layer (*spread* jelly) **4.** to scatter (*spread* lime on the grass) **5.** to pass from one to another (*spread* the flu) —*n.* **1.** the act of spreading **2.** the extent of the spread (wing*spread*) **3.** a feast (a delicious *spread*) **4.** a bed cover

spring (spring) *vb.* **sprang** (sprang) or **sprung** (sprəng); **sprung**; **spring · ing** **1.** to leap or bound **2.** to shoot upward or appear **3.** to warp or bend (The car hood was *sprung* due to the crash.) **4.** to split (The pipe *sprang* a leak.) **5.** to release (*spring* a trap) —*n.* **1.** a natural issue of water (A *spring* fed the brook.) **2.** the season between winter and summer (a wet *spring*) **3.** an elastic device that gives under stress and rebounds when stress is released (a coil *spring*)

sprin · kle (spring′ kəl) *vb.* **sprin · kled**; **sprin · kling** **1.** to scatter in small drops or bits **2.** to rain lightly —*n.* a light shower

spruce (sprüs) *n.* a cone-shaped evergreen tree with short needles for leaves and drooping cones —*adj.* **spruc · er**; **spruc · est** neat and trim (a *spruce* outfit) —*vb.* **spruced**; **spruc · ing** to make oneself, a place, or an object, spruce (to *spruce* up before dinner, *spruce* up the living room)

Spruce

spur (spər) *n.* **1.** a pointed object worn on the heel of a rider to urge on a horse **2.** anything that urges action **3.** a ridge extending sideways from a mountain range **4.** a short branch of railroad track attached at only one end to the main line —*vb.* **spurred**; **spur · ring** **1.** to spur a horse **2.** to urge to action

spy (spī) *vb.* **spied**; **spy · ing** to watch closely and secretly to uncover information for the enemy —*n., pl.* **spies** one who watches the conduct of others in secret; a secret agent

squad (skwäd) *n.* any small group of persons taking part in a common effort

squad·ron (skwäd′ rən) *n.* **1.** a group of navy vessels smaller than a fleet, working together on a particular duty **2.** a unit of an airplane fleet **3.** any group of persons working in regular formation

square (skwaər) *n.* **1.** an instrument for drawing or testing a square **2.** a figure with four equal sides and four right angles **3.** the product or answer when a number is multipled by itself (The *square* of five is twenty-five.) —*adj.* **1.** having four equal sides and four right angles **2.** square in shape **3.** honest **4.** satisfying (a *square* meal) —*vb.* **squared**; **squar·ing** **1.** to make something square **2.** to form a right angle **3.** to multiply a number by itself

squash (skwäsh) *vb.* **1.** to mash or crush **2.** to put down or silence (to *squash* his opponent's argument) —*n.* the fruit of any of several vines of the gourd or cucumber family that is cooked and served as a vegetable

squeak (skwēk) *vb.* **1.** to make a high shrill sound (The mouse *squeak*ed.) **2.** to barely pass (*squeak*ed by) —*n.* **1.** a shrill sound **2.** escape

squeal (skwēl) *vb.* **1.** to make a long shrill sound (The tires *squeal*ed.) **2.** to give out information about another, especially for a reward **3.** to protest —*n.* a long, shrill cry

squeeze (skwēz) *vb.* **squeezed**; **squeez·ing** **1.** to press together (*squeezed* his hand) **2.** to press out the juice (*squeezed* a lemon) **3.** to force into a small space (*squeezed* one more into the box) —*n.* an act of squeezing, as in a handshake or embrace

squir·rel (skwər′ əl) *n.* a bushy-tailed rodent that lives in trees and is prized mainly for its fur

Squirrel

sta·ble (stā′ bəl) *n.* a building used mainly to house and feed horses —*vb.* **sta·bled**; **sta·bling** to keep in a stable —*adj.* **sta·bler**; **sta·blest** **1.** steady, firm (a *stable* organization) **2.** lasting (a *stable* relationship)

stack (stak) *n.* **1.** a heap (*stack* of hay) **2.** a neat pile (*stack* of papers) **3.** a tall chimney (smoke*stack*) **4.** a large number (a *stack* of things to do)

sta·di·um (stād′ ē əm) *n., pl.* **sta·di·ums** or **sta·di·a** (stād ē ə) a usually oval enclosed area with sloping rows of seats for spectators at sports events

staff (staf) *n., pl.* **staffs** or **staves** (stavz, stāvz) **1.** a pole on which a flag is displayed **2.** a sign of authority (a bishop's *staff*) **3.** something that supports **4.** a group of assistants (the office *staff*) **5.** the lines on which music is written

stage (stāj) *n.* **1.** a raised platform on which speakers or actors perform **2.** a single step in a process (an early *stage* of growth) —*vb.* **staged**; **stag·ing** to put in a show

stage·coach (stāj′ kōch′) *n.* a horse-drawn coach that ran on a regular schedule, as a bus, to carry people and mail

stain (stān) *vb.* **1.** to soil or discolor **2.** to spot with guilt (the *stain* of guilt) —*n.* **1.** a spot **2.** guilt **3.** a dye used to color wood (used an oak *stain*)

stair (staər) *n.* one step of a staircase

stair·case (staər′ kās) *n.* a flight of stairs including the framework and handrail

stake (stāk) *n.* **1.** a pointed stick driven into the ground to mark a boundary or serve as a support (a tent *stake*) **2.** a post (tied to the *stake*) **3.** an interest or share (a *stake* in the candy store) —*vb.* **staked**; **stak·ing** **1.** to mark with stakes (*staked* the corners of his lot) **2.** to support with stakes (*staked* the young trees) **3.** to invest money in (*staked* his son's business)

stalk (stȯk) *vb.* **1.** to follow so as not to be seen (He *stalk*ed the deer.) **2.** to walk off in a stiff manner (She *stalk*ed off in anger.) —*n.* **1.** the act of stalking **2.** a tender plant stem (a *stalk* of celery)

stall (stȯl) *n.* **1.** an enclosed space for one animal in a stable **2.** a booth where goods are sold **3.** a scheme to delay —*vb.* **1.** to stop by accident (*stall* the engine) **2.** to delay for a hidden reason

stal·lion (stal′ yən) *n.* a male horse

stamp (stamp) *vb.* **1.** to strike hard with the bottom of the foot **2.** to put on a postage stamp **3.** to press with a rubber stamp —*n.* **1.** a device for stamping **2.** a mark made by a stamp **3.** a small piece of paper showing a fee has been paid (a postage *stamp*)

stand (stand) *vb.* **stood** (stu̇d); **stand·ing** **1.** to take an erect position (to *stand* up) **2.** to hold a position or rank (to *stand* in line) **3.** to take a position (to *stand* for freedom of the press) **4.** to remain unchanged (The order *stands*.) **5.** to bear patiently (must *stand* the heat) —*n.* **1.** an act of standing **2.** a platform **3.** a stall (a fruit *stand*) **4.** a place for something to stand (a taxi *stand*)

stan·dard (stan′ dərd) *n.* **1.** a flag **2.** an accepted guide for weights and measures —*adj.* **1.** serving as a basis for judgment (a *standard* mile) **2.** commonly used (*standard* dress length) **3.** having an accepted value (*standard* classics)

stan·za (stan′ zə) *n.* a number of lines, often having a rhyming scheme, that form a division of a poem

sta·ple (stā′ pəl) *n.* **1.** a U-shaped piece of wire used to fasten things together **2.** something in common and constant use (Bread is a food *staple*.) —*adj.* **1.** used constantly **2.** produced regularly (The pineapple is a *staple* product in their economy.)

star (stär) *n.* **1.** a heavenly body such as our sun that shines by its own light **2.** a shape with five or more points **3.** an outstanding actor or actress —*vb.* **starred**; **star·ring** **1.** to sprinkle with stars **2.** to mark with a star **3.** to play a leading role (*star* in the play)

star·board (stär′ bərd) *n.* looking forward, the right side of a ship or airplane

starch (stärch) *vb.* to use starch to make fabric stiff (to *starch* the curtains) —*n.* a white carbohydrate that is an important substance in food and is also used to make cloth stiff

stare (staər) *vb.* **stared**; **star·ing** to look at one person or thing for some time —*n.* the act of staring

star·fish (stär′ fish′) *n.* a sea animal with five arms coming out from the center that eats mainly mollusks such as clams

start (stärt) *vb.* **1.** to begin (*start* a job) **2.** to move suddenly (At the noise, he *start*ed.) —*n.* **1.** a sudden, unplanned movement **2.** a beginning (got a late *start*)

star·tle (stärt′ l) *vb.* **star·tled**; **star·tling** to jump in surprise or fright

star·va·tion (stär vā′ shən) *n.* an act of starving

starve (stärv) *vb.* **starved**; **starv·ing** **1.** to become weak or die from lack of food **2.** to hunger for something (*starve*d for attention)

state (stāt) *n.* **1.** the condition of someone or something as to its health or wholeness, substance, rank, or value **2.** one of the territories united under a central government (United *States* of America) —*vb.* **stat·ed**; **stat·ing** **1.** to say (*stated* his opinion) **2.** to set forth formally (the rules *stated* here) —*adj.* relating to the state (*state* politics)

state·ment (stāt′ mənt) *n.* **1.** a single sentence **2.** an account or report (monthly *statement*) **3.** a communication in speech or writing

stat·ic (stat′ ik) *adj.* **1.** relating to something that is not moving (remained *static*) **2.** an electric charge caused by rubbing things together (*static* electricity) **3.** acting by weight without motion (a *static* pressure) —*n.* crackling sounds that interfere with a radio broadcast, caused by electrical discharges in the air

sta·tion (stā′ shən) *n.* **1.** the place where a train or bus stops **2.** the place assigned for a person to work (All workers, go to your *stations*!) **3.** a location of a public service (police, fire, or weather *station*) **4.** a broadcasting location (radio or television *station*) —*vb.* to assign or be assigned to a station (*station*ed in Rome)

sta·tion·ar·y (stā′ shə ner′ ē) *adj.* not moving or changing

sta·tio·ner·y (stā′ shə ner′ ē) *n.* writing materials such as paper and envelopes

stat·ue (stach′ ü) *n.* a sculptured or cast likeness of a person or animal

sta·tus (stāt′ əs, stat′ əs) *n.* **1.** a person's position or rank (had the *status* of a hospital volunteer) **2.** the state or condition (*status* of the flower fund)

stay (stā) *n.* a brace to hold something in position or keep it stiff (had *stay*s in the points of his shirt collar) —*vb.* **1.** to fasten or hold **2.** to hold back or remain (*stay* a moment) **3.** to stop something (*stay* an execution)

stead·y (sted′ ē) *adj.* **stead·i·er**; **stead·i·est** **1.** firm and well balanced (in a *steady* position) **2.** regular and even (the *steady* tick of the clock) **3.** dependable (a *steady* friend) —*vb.* **stead·ied**; **stead·y·ing** to make something steady

steak (stāk) *n.* a slice of meat or fish (sirloin *steak*; swordfish *steak*)

steal (stēl) *vb.* **stole** (stōl); **sto·len** (stō′ lən); **steal·ing** **1.** to rob (*stole* her necklace) **2.** to take more than one's share **3.** to come and go without being noticed (*stole* outside to see the dogs) —*n.* **1.** an act of stealing **2.** a bargain (a *steal* at $2.99)

steam (stēm) *n.* **1.** the vapor into which water is changed when boiled **2.** energy (cut wood using his own *steam*) —*vb.* **1.** to give off steam or vapor **2.** to move by or as if by the power of steam —*adj.* operated by steam (*steam* heat)

steam·boat (stēm′ bōt′) *n.* a boat operated by steam

steel (stēl) *n.* a hard alloy of iron that can be made tough and strong, used as a framework for high buildings, for vehicles, cutlery, and many other products —*adj.* made of steel —*vb.* **1.** to make with or to look like steel **2.** to make hard and tough

steep (stēp) *adj.* **1.** having a sharp rise (a *steep* hill) **2.** being very high (*steep* prices) —*vb.* **1.** to soak (*steep* tea) **2.** to saturate (*steep*ed in ancient history)

steer (stiər) *n.* a castrated domestic bull raised for beef —*vb.* **1.** to guide a vehicle using a wheel or rudder **2.** to follow a course of action (to *steer* toward a goal)

stem (stem) *n.* **1.** the main stalk of a plant that supports leaves and flowers **2.** anything that resembles a stem —*vb.* **stemmed**; **stem·ming** **1.** to stop or hold back (a dam to *stem* the river) **2.** to arise (a fever that *stem*s from a virus) **3.** to remove the stem from (*stem* the grapes) **4.** to make headway against (*stem* the tide)

step (step) *n.* **1.** a place for the foot in going up or down a ladder or stairs **2.** the sound or way of walking (heard her *step* on the walk) **3.** one part of a series (the first *step* of the plan) —*vb.* **stepped**; **step·ping** **1.** to lift the foot and move it forward (*step* ahead) **2.** to resign or give up leadership (*step* down) **3.** to dance or walk (*step* along)

ster·ile (ster′ əl) *adj.* **1.** free from germs (*sterile* bandages) **2.** not able to bear crops or offspring, not fertile **3.** not producing any results (a *sterile* meeting)

stern (stərn) *adj.* **1.** hard and strict (a *stern* parent) **2.** firm (a *stern* tone of voice) —*n.* the rear part of a boat

stew (stü) *vb.* **1.** to cook at a slow boil (*stew* the meat) **2.** to worry (always *stew*ing about something) —*n.* **1.** chunks of meat and vegetables cooked slowly **2.** worry or uneasiness (in a *stew* about the news)

stick (stik) *n.* **1.** a small branch of wood **2.** something shaped like a stick (a *stick* of peppermint candy) —*vb.* **stuck** (stək); **stick·ing** **1.** to pierce (*stuck* a pin in her thumb) **2.** to put out (*stuck* out his head) **3.** to cheat (gotten *stuck* by the prices) **4.** to burden (*stuck* with the worst job **5.** to become jammed in (*stuck* behind the car.) **6.** hang out **7.** to adhere (*stick* it on with glue)

stick·y (stik′ ē) *adj.* **stick·i·er**; **stick·i·est** **1.** tending to adhere like glue (*sticky* fingers) **2.** hot and humid (*sticky* weather) **3.** involving opposing views (*sticky* problem)

stiff (stif) *adj.* **1.** firm or rigid (*stiff* muscles) **2.** stubborn (a *stiff* argument) **3.** formal (*stiff* manners) **4.** severe (a *stiff* punishment) **5.** difficult (a *stiff* test)

still (stil) *adj.* being calm, peaceful, and motionless —*adv.* **1.** until then or now (*still* doing it) **2.** nevertheless (It was wrong; *still* they did it.) **3.** quiet, motionless (Keep *still.*) —*n.* quiet (the *still* of the night)

stim·u·late (stim′ yə lāt′) *vb.* **stim·u·lat·ed**; **stim·u·lat·ing** **1.** to arouse to more activity **2.** to produce more spirit and interest

sting (sting) *vb.* **stung** (stəng); **sting·ing** **1.** to bite or inject a poison (A hornet *stung* him.) **2.** to cause a sharp, burning feeling (A cold wind *stung* their faces.) **3.** to feel the pain of sorrow —*n.* an act of stinging

stir (stər) *vb.* **stirred**; **stir·ring** **1.** to move or put into motion (Wind *stirred* the leaves.) **2.** to mix (*stir* the batter) **3.** to arouse (*stir* up trouble) —*n.* activity or excitement (The news created a *stir.*)

stir·rup (stər′ əp) *n.* foot support for a horseback rider that hangs by straps from the saddle

Stirrup

stitch (stich) *n.* **1.** one in-and-out movement of the needle in sewing **2.** one complete movement of the needle in knitting, crocheting, or other handwork with thread or yarn **3.** a sharp pain in the side —*vb.* to put together or decorate with stitches

stock (stäk) *n.* **1.** the goods kept in a store for sale to customers (low on *stock*) **2.** the shares of a company or corporation (ten shares of *stock*) **3.** ancestors (from good *stock*) **4.** handle (whip*stock*; gun*stock*) —*vb.* **1.** to provide with supplies (*stock* the shelves) **2.** to put into the stock (*stock*s pocket radios) —*adj.* commonly used (a *stock* item)

stock·ade (stäk ād′) *n.* an enclosure made of strong posts set into the ground as a barrier for defense

stock·ing (stäk′ ing) *n.* a knit covering for the foot and leg

stom·ach (stəm′ ək) *n.* a pouch in the abdomen where food goes when swallowed and is digested —*vb.* to put up with or endure (cannot *stomach* his actions)

stone (stōn) *n.* **1.** a piece of rock (threw *stone*s at the can on the fence) **2.** a rock cut and shaped for a special purpose (a grave*stone*; a flag*stone*) **3.** a hard mass formed in a diseased organ (gall*stone*; kidney *stone*) **4.** the hard seed covering in some fruits (peach *stone*) —*vb.* **stoned**; **ston·ing** **1.** to throw stones **2.** to remove the stones (*stone* peaches) —*adj.* made of stone

stoop (stüp) *vb.* **1.** to bend forward, down, or over **2.** to act below one's level of dignity (*stoop*ed to stealing) —*n.* **1.** an act of bending **2.** a forward tilt of the head and shoulders (walks with a *stoop*) —*n.* a small porch or platform between a stairway and an outside door (the newspaper on the *stoop*)

stop (stäp) *vb.* **stopped**; **stop·ping** **1.** to halt progress or motion (*stop* the bus) **2.** to prevent (*stop* him from running) **3.** to interrupt (*stop* a minute) **4.** to plug up (*stop* the leak) **5.** to visit (*Stop* in when you are in town.) —*n.* **1.** a halt in a journey (a *stop* for refreshments) **2.** end (work came to a *stop*) **3.** a control for organ pipes (Pull out that *stop*.)

stop·per (stäp′ ər) *n.* a cork or plug to fill an opening

stor·age (stor′ ij) *n.* **1.** the state of being stored (*Storage* is costly.) **2.** space for storing (small room for *storage*)

store (stōr) *vb.* **stored**; **stor·ing** **1.** to supply (*store* food for the camping trip) **2.** to put away for the future (*store* blankets until winter) —*n.* **1.** a shop (buy milk at the *store*) **2.** a large supply (a *store* of ammunition)

store·house (stōr′ haůs) *n.* a building where goods are stored, as a warehouse

Stork

stork (stȯrk) *n.* a wading bird, related to the heron, with long legs and neck and a long, sharp bill, that often nests on roofs and chimneys

storm (stȯrm) *n.* **1.** a weather disturbance involving wind, rain, or snow, thunder and lightning, sand, or dust in any combination **2.** any strong outburst (a *storm* of praise) —*vb.* **1.** to blow hard and rain or snow **2.** to make a mass attack (*storm* the hill) **3.** to say angry words (*storm*ed at the crowd)

storm·y (stȯr′ mē) *adj.* **storm·i·er**; **storm·i·est** **1.** relating to a storm (a *stormy* night) **2.** having a high level of emotion (a *stormy* discussion)

sto·ry (stōr′ ē) *n., pl.* **sto·ries** **1.** an anecdote or a narrative with characters and a plot (a folk *story*) **2.** a rumor —*n.* a set of rooms between two floors making one floor level of a building (a three-*story* house)

stout (staůt) *adj.* **1.** large, bulky, or fat (a *stout* person) **2.** brave and fearless (*stout*-hearted)

stove (stōv) *n.* an iron or steel structure that uses fuel to provide heat for cooking or to warm one or more rooms

straight (strāt) *adj.* **1.** direct, not curved or bent (a *straight* line) **2.** staying on the topic (*straight* thinking) **3.** open and honest (*straight* talk) **4.** organized and in good order (keep the house *straight*) **5.** in a straight line or manner (Tell it to us *straight.*)

strain (strān) *n.* **1.** a line of descent or bloodline (from a hardy *strain* of people) **2.** a race of people or a variety of plant **3.** strong physical effort (put a *strain* on his arm) **4.** an injury caused by a twisted or stretched muscle —*vb.* **1.** to pull, stretch, or twist beyond a proper limit **2.** to try as hard as possible (*strain* to move the load) **3.** to injure or become injured by too much effort **4.** to press through a strainer (*strain* the gravy)

strange (strānj) *adj.* **strang·er**; **strang·est** **1.** not familiar (a *strange* place) **2.** odd or unusual (a *strange* color) **3.** shy or ill at ease (felt *strange* in that group)

strap (strap) *n.* **1.** a narrow strip of material such as leather used to attach, bind, or fasten something **2.** a narrow strip of material used for whipping —*vb.* **strapped**; **strap·ping** to attach, bind, or fasten with a strap (*Strap* the stirrups to the saddle.)

stra·te·gic (strə tē′ jik) *adj.* **1.** pertaining to strategy **2.** planned so as to achieve a goal (a *strategic* move)

strat·e·gy (strat′ ə jē) *n., pl.* **strat·e·gies** **1.** the art and science of directing large military operations to win a war **2.** skill in planning and managing any affair

straw (stró) *n.* **1.** a slender tube for sipping a drink **2.** a dry stalk of a plant, especially of wheat, rye, oats, or barley **3.** a thing of little worth —*adj.* made of or stuffed with straw

straw·ber·ry (stró′ bėr′ ē) *n., pl.* **straw·ber·ries** a low-growing plant with runners, white flowers, and red, juicy berries used fresh or in jams and preserves

Strawberry

stray (strā) *vb.* **1.** to go beyond the limits **2.** to wander off course (*stray* from the topic) —*adj.* **1.** wandering (a *stray* dog) **2.** casual or random (a few *stray* comments) —*n.* a person or animal that strays

streak (strēk) *n.* **1.** a line or stroke of color or grime **2.** one trait in a person's character (a *streak* of selfishness) **3.** a flash of light **4.** a series of happenings (a *streak* of luck) **5.** a layer (a *streak* of ore in the rock) —*vb.* **1.** to rush **2.** to make streaks on

stream (strēm) *n.* **1.** a brook or river **2.** a flow (a *stream* of baseball fans) —*vb.* **1.** to flow (water *streaming* from the faucet) **2.** to stretch or float out (banners *stream*ing overhead)

street (strēt) *n.* a public road in a town or city

strength (strength) *n.* **1.** physical, mental, moral, or political power **2.** power as measured in numbers (the *strength* of one hundred horses) **3.** the intensity of color, sound, light, flavor, odor, or heat **4.** the power to resist wear and strain (material having *strength*)

stress (stres) *n.* **1.** pressure **2.** something that makes a person tense (Her work causes *stress.*) —*vb.* **1.** to put under pressure **2.** to accent (*stress* the second syllable)

stretch (strech) *vb.* **1.** to draw out or pull out (to *stretch* out the net) **2.** to reach (*stretch*ed out her hand) **3.** to exaggerate (tends to *stretch* the story a little) —*n.* **1.** the act of pushing or pulling out **2.** an extent (a *stretch* of rough road)

strict (strikt) *adj.* **1.** rigid (*strict* rules) **2.** absolute (a *strict* blackout of news) **3.** exact and accurate

stride (strīd) *vb.* **strode** (strōd); **strid·den** (strid′ n); **strid·ing** (strīd′ ing) to take long steps —*n.* **1.** a long step **2.** a step forward (made *stride*s in learning to sing)

strike (strīk) *vb.* **struck** (strək); **struck** or **strick·en** (strik′ ən); **strik·ing** (strī′ king) **1.** to hit or crash into **2.** to cause a sound (The clock *struck* two.) **3.** to agree upon (*struck* a deal) **4.** to stop work to bring about a change in working conditions (to go on *strike*) **5.** to reach (*strike* oil) —*n.* **1.** a work stoppage **2.** a blow **3.** in baseball, failure to hit a fair ball **4.** in bowling, knocking down all the pins with one ball

string (string) *n.* **1.** a thin cord **2.** the gut or cord on a musical instrument **3.** a series or line of things (*string* of bicycles on the highway) —*vb.* **strung** (strəng); **string·ing** **1.** to put strings on **2.** to put on a cord (*string* pearls) **3.** to remove strings, as on beans

strip (strip) *vb.* **stripped**; **strip·ping** **1.** to undress **2.** to peel (*strip* bark) **3.** to rob (*stripped* them of their treasures) **4.** to clear of trees (*stripped* the land) —*n.* a long narrow piece (a *strip* of land)

stripe (strīp) *n.* **1.** a narrow strip of color **2.** strips of braid worn on the sleeves or shoulders of uniforms to show rank —*vb.* **striped**; **strip·ing** to make stripes on

stroke (strōk) *vb.* **stroked**; **strok·ing** to rub gently (*stroke* her puppy) —*n.* **1.** the act of striking (got the bee in a single *stroke*) **2.** a quick action (a *stroke* of lightning) **3.** a light rub in one direction (a *stroke* of the hand) **4.** a clot or break in a blood vessel in the brain (paralyzed from the *stroke*) **5.** a movement of a tool (a *stroke* of the pen)

stroll (strōl) *vb.* to walk slowly (*stroll* through the park) —*n.* a leisurely walk

strong (strȯng) *adj.* **strong·er** (strȯng′ gər); **strong·est** (strȯng′ gəst) **1.** physically, mentally, morally, or politically powerful **2.** having the power of a specified number (Volunteers were sixty *strong.*) **3.** convincing (*strong* reasons)

struc·ture (strək′ chər) *n.* **1.** something built in an organized way **2.** the arrangement and position of parts (*structure* of an atom)

strug·gle (strəg′ əl) *vb.* **strug·gled**; **strug·gling** **1.** to put forth great effort (*struggle* to get away) **2.** to strive or work hard (*struggle* to pay his bills) —*n.* a great effort

strut (strət) *vb.* **strut·ted**; **strut·ting** to walk proudly as with a feeling of self-importance —*n.* **1.** a proud way of walking **2.** a lengthwise brace (the *struts* on the airplane)

stub·born (stəb′ ərn) *adj.* **1.** determined, not flexible (a *stubborn* attitude) **2.** difficult to manage or treat (a *stubborn* cold)

stu·dent (stüd′ nt) *n.* **1.** one who goes to school **2.** one who studies and observes in a particular field (a *student* of sea life)

stu·di·o (stüd′ ē ō′) *n., pl.* **stu·di·os** **1.** the place where an artist works **2.** rooms equipped for radio or television broadcasts **3.** the land and buildings where motion pictures are made

stud·y (stəd′ ē) *n., pl.* **stud·ies** **1.** the mental effort to gain knowledge **2.** careful examination of a topic (the *study* of ants) **3.** a room set apart as a place to study —*vb.* **1.** to think deeply, to ponder **2.** to apply the mind to learn something

stuff (stəf) *n.* **1.** goods or baggage **2.** the material of which something is made, such as the fabric, the ideas, the substance (Is the *stuff* useful or worthless?)

stum·ble (stəm′ bəl) *vb.* **stum·bled**; **stum·bling** **1.** to trip or walk unsteadily (*stumble* along) **2.** to speak in a faltering manner **3.** to come upon by chance (*stumbled* upon a deep cavern in the forest) —*n.* **1.** the act of tripping **2.** a blunder or mistake

stump (stəmp) *n.* **1.** the root and bottom of a tree that remains when the tree is cut down **2.** the base or stub of anything —*vb.* **1.** to confuse (*stump* the experts) **2.** to support a cause with political speeches (*stump* his district)

stunt (stənt) *vb.* to slow the normal growth (an illness *stunt*ed his growth in childhood.) —*n.* a skillful performance (a high-wire *stunt*)

stu·pid (stü′ pəd) *adj.* **1.** senseless (a *stupid* answer) **2.** boring (a *stupid* book) **3.** slow-learning

stur·dy (stərd′ ē) *adj.* **stur·di·er**; **stur·di·est** strongly built

style (stīl) *n.* **1.** a pointed instrument used for engraving **2.** a manner of speaking or writing (clear *style*) **3.** a way of living (fashionable *style*) —*vb.* **styled; styl·ing** **1.** to make something in a new design (She *styles* dresses.) **2.** to give someone a title or rank (He *styles* himself an artist.)

sub·ject (səb′ jikt) *n.* **1.** a person under the control of another (a British *subject*) **2.** the person or thing treated or discussed (the *subject* of the demonstration) **3.** the part of a sentence that tells who or what the sentence is about —*adj.* dependent upon (*subject* to change, without notice)

sub·ject (səb jekt′) *vb.* **1.** to bring under control **2.** to expose (*subjected* the film to light) **3.** to lay open (*subject* himself to their anger)

sub·ma·rine (səb′ mə rēn′) *adj.* underwater (*submarine* photography) —*n.* **1.** a naval ship that operates underwater (nuclear *submarine*) **2.** a research submarine such as the *Alvin* that explored the Titanic

sub·merge (səb mərj′) *vb.* **sub·merged; sub·merg·ing** to put under or cover with water

sub·se·quent (səb′ si kwənt) *adj.* following (the *subsequent* meetings)

sub·stance (səb′ stəns) *n.* **1.** the material of which something is made **2.** the main points of an article or speech (the *substance* of her message) **3.** character or importance (an argument that lacks *substance*)

sub·stan·tial (səb stan′ chəl) *adj.* **1.** well built **2.** important **3.** of real worth **4.** responsible

sub·sti·tute (səb′ stə tüt′) *n.* a person or thing that takes the place of another —*vb.* **1.** to put in the place of another **2.** to act as a substitute

sub·tle (sət′ l) *adj.* **sub·tler** (sət′ lər); **sub·tlest** (sət′ ləst) **1.** delicate (a *subtle* fragrance) **2.** tactful (a *subtle* reminder) **3.** sly (a *subtle* thief)

sub·tract (səb trakt′) *vb.* to take away (*subtract* ten from thirty-two)

sub·urb (səb′ ərb′) *n.* an outlying part of a city or town, especially a residential area

sub·way (səb′ wā′) *n.* **1.** an underground passage **2.** an underground electric railway (ride the *subway* to one's job in the city)

suc·ceed (sək sēd′) *vb.* **1.** to follow (President Reagan *succeed*ed President Carter.) **2.** to be successful (finally *succeed*ed in winning a game)

suc·cess (sək ses′) *n.* **1.** the act of reaching a goal or a favorable outcome **2.** a person or thing that does well

suc·ces·sion (sək sesh′ ən) *n.* a series of persons or things following in order

such (səch) *adj.* **1.** similar to the one just mentioned (bought two *such* billfolds) **2.** so much (*such* joy) **3.** of that kind (a book *such* as Jim is reading) —*pron.* that (finished ten of them, but *such* was not my goal)

suck (sək) *vb.* to draw in liquid or air with the mouth using the action of the tongue and lips (*suck* through a straw; *suck* an orange or a Popsicle)

sud·den (səd′ n) *adj.* coming quickly without notice (a *sudden* storm)

suf·fer (səf′ ər) *vb.* **1.** to feel pain **2.** to endure or experience (to *suffer* a loss of money)

suf·fi·cient (sə fish′ ənt) *adj.* equal to the need or purpose

suf·fix (səf′ iks′) *n.* one or more letters added to the end of a word to alter its meaning

sug·ar (shu̇g′ ər) *n.* **1.** a sweet carbohydrate found in sugarcane, sugarbeet, or maple syrup **2.** one of the sweet substances found in fruits, corn, and milk —*vb.* **1.** to add sugar **2.** to use sweet-sounding words or flattery **3.** to form granules of sugar

sug·gest (səg jest′) *vb.* **1.** to hint at something **2.** to propose an idea

sug·ges·tion (səg jes′ chən) *n.* **1.** the act of suggesting **2.** the hint or idea that is proposed

suit (süt) *n.* **1.** a court action that seeks justice **2.** certain clothing used together (a business *suit*) **3.** playing cards of one type such as spades, hearts, diamonds, or clubs —*vb.* **1.** adapt (*suit* the hours to your available time) **2.** to please (*suit* yourself) **3.** to be satisfactory (*suit*ed our purpose)

suit·a·ble (süt′ ə bəl) *adj.* appropriate or proper

suit·case (süt′ kās′) *n.* a rectangular bag for carrying clothing and personal items when traveling

Suitcase

sul·fur or **sul·phur** (səl′ fər) *n.* a yellow, non-metallic element found widely in nature that produces a suffocating odor when burned and that is used in making many products such as matches, rubber, and paper

sul·len (səl′ ən) *adj.* **1.** ill-humored (a *sullen* disposition) **2.** gloomy (a *sullen* day)

sul·tan (səlt′ n) *n.* a Mohammedan ruler

sum (səm) *n.* **1.** the total when everything is added together (the *sum* of an addition problem, the *sum* of one's expenses) **2.** an indefinite amount (a large *sum*) —*vb.* **summed**; **sum·ming** **1.** to get a total by adding **2.** to review and give the main points (to *sum* up)

sum·ma·ry (səm′ ə rē) *adj.* **1.** briefly stating the main points (a *summary* statement) **2.** immediate, without delay (*Summary* action was taken.) —*n., pl.* **sum·ma·ries** a brief statement of the main points or the facts that were covered

sum·mer (səm′ ər) *n.* a season between spring and fall beginning at the June solstice when the sun is over the Tropic of Cancer and extending to the September equinox when the sun crosses the equator going south

sum·mit (səm′ ət) *n.* **1.** the highest point, as of a mountain **2.** a meeting at the highest level (The leaders of the countries planned a *summit* to discuss arms control.) **3.** the highest degree of achievement (Winning the Tchaikovsky Competititon in Moscow was the *summit* of his musical career.)

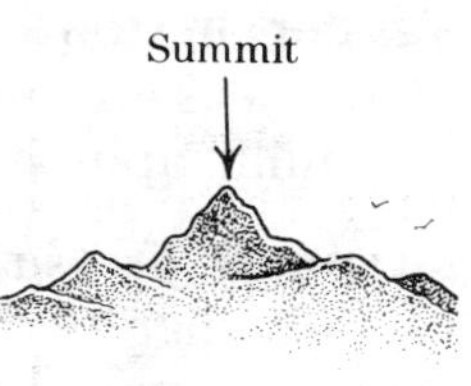

sum·mon (səm′ ən) *vb.* **1.** to order someone to appear at a specified time and place (*summon* the defendant to court) **2.** to call an official body for deliberation or action (*summon* the legislature) **3.** to arouse or excite (*summon* one's energies)

sun (sən) *n.* **1.** a star, the center of our solar system, whose light makes our day **2.** sunshine —*vb.* **sunned**; **sun·ning** to expose to the rays of the sun

sun·down (sən′ daůn′) *n.* sunset

sun·flow·er (sən′ flaů′ ər) *n.* a tall, straight-stemmed garden flower with showy yellow ray flowers, the centers of which are packed with oily seeds used for edible oil, stock feed, bird feed, and snacks

Sunflower

sun·light (sən′ līt′) *n.* sunshine

sun·ny (sən′ ē) *adj.* **sun·ni·er**; **sun·ni·est** bright and warm from or like the sun (a *sunny* day; a *sunny* greeting)

sun·rise (sən′ rīz′) *n.* **1.** the appearance of the morning sun along with the light and color in the sky **2.** the time of sunrise

sun·set (sən′ set′) *n.* **1.** the disappearance of the sun below the horizon in the evening, along with the light and color in the sky **2.** the time of sunset

sun·shine (sən′ shīn′) *n.* **1.** the light and warmth of the sun **2.** something that gives off warmth (the *sunshine* of her presence)

su·per·in·tend·ent (sü′ pər in ten′ dənt) *n.* one who oversees or directs an organization or district such as a mill, apartment building, or school system

su·pe·ri·or (sů pir′ ē ər) *adj.* **1.** higher in position, rank, dignity, or office **2.** above average in intelligence or achievement —*n.* **1.** one that is higher than another in any quality **2.** the head of a religious house

su·per·mar·ket (sü′ pər mär kət) *n.* a large and well-stocked food store that is operated on a self-serve, cash-and-carry basis

su·per·sti·tion (sü′ pər stish′ ən) *n.* **1.** a belief, act, or practice, often of a religious nature, based on fear and not on reason or knowledge **2.** belief in charms and magic

sup·per (səp′ ər) *n.* **1.** a light evening meal, when dinner is eaten earlier **2.** the regular evening meal

sup·ple·ment (səp′ lə mənt) *n.* something added to fill a need, complete a supply, or add to the whole

sup·ply (sə plī′) *vb.* **sup·plied**; **sup·ply·ing** **1.** to provide what is needed (*supply* the food) **2.** to add to the stores of provisions (*supplied* an extra basket of apples) —*n., pl.* **sup·plies** the goods on hand for use or for sale at any given time

sup·port (sə pōrt′) *vb.* **1.** to bear the weight (the walls that *support* the roof) **2.** to strengthen or give reasons (*support* an argument) **3.** to bear the expense (*support* her mother) **4.** to work for (*support* a candidate for public office) —*n.* **1.** the act of supporting **2.** the one who supports

sup·pose (sə pōz′) *vb.* **sup·posed**; **sup·pos·ing** **1.** to assume something is true for the sake of argument (*suppose* someone gives me a thousand dollars) **2.** to think or believe (I *suppose* we'll go on a picnic if it is a nice day.)

su·preme (sü prēm′) *adj.* **1.** highest in power, rank, or authority **2.** utmost (of *supreme* value to me) **3.** final (the *supreme* sacrifice)

sure (shür) *adj.* **sur·er**; **sur·est** **1.** firm and steady (*sure*-footed) **2.** certain (a *sure* way to recognize him) **3.** dependable (a *sure* cure) —*adv.* surely

sure·ly (shür′ lē) *adv.* without doubt (I will *surely* be there.)

surf (sərf) *n.* ocean waves breaking on the shore (riding the *surf* on a surfboard)

sur·face (sər′ fəs) *n.* the outside part of anything —*adj.* relating to or acting on a surface (*surface* mail)

surge (sərj) *vb.* **surged**; **surg·ing** to swell (The group *surged* into the office.) —*n.* an onward rush, roll, or swell (*surge* of interest in the computer program)

sur·geon (sər′ jən) *n.* **1.** a doctor who specializes in surgery **2.** one who operates on patients

sur·ger·y (sər′ jə rē) *n., pl.* **sur·ger·ies** the branch of medical science that treats injuries, deformities, and diseased organs through operative procedures

sur·plus (sər′ pləs) *n.* something left over, not used —*adj.* extra (*surplus* grain)

sur·prise (sər prīz′) *n.* **1.** a sudden or unexpected happening such as a gift or the visit of a friend or relative **2.** the feeling of excitement when pleasantly surprised —*vb.* **sur·prised**; **sur·pris·ing** **1.** to fill with amazement **2.** to capture by an unexpected attack

sur·ren·der (sə ren′ dər) *vb.* to give oneself into the control of another under force (*surrender* the ship) —*n.* the act of giving up oneself or a possession to another under force

sur·round (sə raünd′) *vb.* to enclose on all sides (*surround* the swimming pool with a fence)

sur·vey (sər vā′) *vb.* **sur·veyed**; **sur·vey·ing** **1.** to view broadly (*survey* the countryside) **2.** to view closely to determine condition, value **3.** to determine exact boundaries (*survey* the property) —*n., pl.* **sur·veys** **1.** the act of surveying **2.** a careful examination to determine condition **3.** the process of determining a position on the earth's surface **4.** a brief summary of the history or structure of a topic

sur·viv·al (sər vī′ vəl) *n.* **1.** a staying alive, especially under difficult conditions **2.** the continuing presence of a person or thing from an earlier period (*survival* of the fittest)

sur·vive (sər vīv′) *vb.* **sur·vived**; **sur·viv·ing** to outlive an event or another person (*survived* his wife)

sus·pect (səs′ pekt′) *adj.* under suspicion (His excuse is *suspect.*) —*n.* a person who is suspected —*vb.* **sus·pect** (sə spekt′) **1.** to doubt or distrust **2.** to believe someone is guilty with little or no proof **3.** to guess or suppose

sus·pend (sə spend′) *vb.* **1.** to stop a physical or mental action for a time (*suspend* judgment) **2.** to hang (*suspend* the plant from the ceiling hook)

sus·pense (sə spens′) *n.* **1.** the state of waiting for an event or a response with some anxiety **2.** an interruption (the *suspense* of activity)

sus·pi·cion (sə spish′ ən) *n.* **1.** the feeling, on little evidence, that something is wrong **2.** the act of suspecting or being suspected

sus·tain (sə stān′) *vb.* **1.** to keep someone or something alive (*sustain* life, *sustain* the campaign) **2.** to keep up courage, spirit, faith (*sustain* hope)

swal·low (swäl′ ō) *vb.* any one of a family of small birds with long, pointed wings and a forked tail, noted for their swift, graceful flight and useful for the eating of large numbers of insects

swal·low (swäl′ ō) *vb.* **1.** to move food, drink, or saliva from the mouth to the stomach by using throat muscles **2.** to absorb or overwhelm (*swallow*ed by the raging river) **3.** to bear or hold back (*swallow*ed his sorrow) —*n.* **1.** an act of swallowing **2.** the amount of one swallow (I'll take just a *swallow* of it.)

swamp (swämp) *n.* wet, spongy land —*vb.* **1.** to fill with water and sink **2.** to overwhelm with things to do (*swamp*ed with holiday mail)

swan (swän) *n.* a large, heavy, white, long-necked bird similar to but heavier than a goose

Swan

swarm (swȯrm) *n.* a large crowd, usually moving in a body (A *swarm* of honeybees left the hive.) —*vb.* to go in a swarm (The sidewalk was *swarm*ing with ants.)

sway (swā) *vb.* **1.** to swing slowly from side to side **2.** to be influenced (Her opinion can *sway* from one side to the other.) —*n.* **1.** the act of swaying **2.** control or influence (under the *sway* of their leader)

swear (swaər) *vb.* **swore** (swōr); **sworn** (swōrn); **swear·ing** **1.** to promise to tell the truth with an appeal to God or some religious object as confirmation of the truth of what is stated **2.** to administer an oath **3.** to use language that is not decent

sweat (swet) *vb.* **sweat** or **sweat·ed**; **sweat·ing** **1.** to give off moisture through the pores of the skin **2.** to collect moisture from the air, as on a pitcher of ice water **3.** to work very hard (*sweat* over a problem) —*n.* **1.** perspiration **2.** moisture gathering on a cold surface

sweat·er (swet′ ər) *n.* a jacket or pullover, knit or crocheted of yarn, worn as casual dress

sweep (swēp) *vb.* **swept** (swept); **sweep·ing** **1.** to clean by brushing or as if by brushing (to *sweep* a floor, *swept* clean by the wind) —*n.* **1.** an act or instance of sweeping **2.** a curving movement (a *sweep* of his hand)

sweep·ing (swē′ ping) *n.* a collection of things that were swept —*adj.* **1.** having wide effect (*sweeping* changes) **2.** moving over a wide area (a *sweeping* tour of the park)

sweet (swēt) *adj.* **1.** containing sugar **2.** pleasing to the taste **3.** agreeable, mild, or dear —*n.* a candy, or dessert, made with sugar (*sweets* for dessert)

swell (swel) *vb.* **swelled**; **swelled** or **swol·len** (swō lən); **swell·ing** **1.** to get bigger **2.** to bulge (The ball will *swell* as it fills with air.) **3.** to fill with emotion (*swelled* with pride) —*n.* an increase in size, value, importance, or emotion —*adj.* excellent or fashionable

swift (swift) *adj.* moving or happening with great speed —*adv.* swiftly —*n.* one of a family of birds that are extremely speedy in flight, related to the hummingbird but similar to the swallow in appearance

swim (swim) *vb.* **swam** (swam); **swum** (swəm); **swim·ming** **1.** to propel oneself through the water by moving the limbs **2.** to glide smoothly or be in liquid as if swimming (the clams *swimming* in butter) —*n.* **1.** the act of swimming (went for a *swim*) **2.** current affairs (in the *swim* of things)

swim·mer (swim′ ər) *n.* one who swims

swing (swing) *vb.* **swung** (swəng); **swing·ing** **1.** to move quickly in a sweeping motion (to *swing* the bat) **2.** to move to and fro in a hanging seat **3.** to move on hinges (The gate *swung* shut.) —*n.* **1.** the act of swinging **2.** a swaying movement **3.** a swinging seat **4.** a style of jazz

swirl (swərl) *n.* a circular motion or design —*vb.* to move in a circular or twisting path

swish (swish) *vb.* to move with a rustling or a *shhhh* sound —*n.* a swishing or sweeping movement that makes a *shhhh* sound (The whip cut the air with a *swish.*)

switch (swich) *n.* **1.** a thin, flexible whip or shoot used for whipping **2.** in railroading, a movable section of track that can be used to send cars to another track **3.** a device for making or breaking an electrical circuit

sword (sōrd) *n.* a weapon with a long, sharp blade extending from a handle

Swords

syl·la·ble (sil′ ə bəl) *n.* a word or part of a word having one vowel sound

sym·bol (sim′ bəl) *n.* a sign or emblem that stands for something else (The sign ÷ is the *symbol* for division.)

sym·pa·thy (sim′ pə thē) *n., pl.* **sym·pa·thies** the act or capacity for entering into or sharing the feelings and emotions of another (I feel *sympathy* with your sorrow; *sympathy* for your misfortune)

sym·pho·ny (sim′ fə nē) *n., pl.* **sym·pho·nies** **1.** a musical composition for full orchestra, usually having three or more parts, similar to a sonata in form but on a much grander scale **2.** a large orchestra of wind, string, and percussion instruments that gives public performances

syn·o·nym (sin′ ə nim′) *n.* one of two or more words having about the same meaning

syn·thet·ic (sin thet′ ik) *adj.* relating to something that is produced chemically as opposed to something that is found in nature (*Synthetic* gems can look like rubies and diamonds.)

syr·up (sər′ əp) *n.* the juice of a fruit or plant that has been concentrated by boiling it down (corn or maple *syrup*)

sys·tem (sis′ təm) *n.* a group of organs or units that work together to perform an important function (a lighting *system*; a digestive *system*)

T

ta·ble (tā′ bəl) *n.* **1.** a flat piece of furniture set on legs **2.** the food on a table (set a plentiful *table*) **3.** an arrangement of information in rows and columns **4.** a summary of topics (*table* of contents)

tack (tak) *n.* **1.** a small, sharp nail with a large head **2.** the direction a ship is sailing **3.** a policy or course of action (Take a new *tack.*) —*vb.* **1.** to fasten with tacks **2.** to change from one direction to another in sailing

tack·le (tak′ əl) *n.* **1.** the ropes and pulleys used for raising and lowering heavy objects **2.** equipment and gear, especially for fishing **3.** the act of tackling **4.** a football player in the line next to either end —*vb.* **1.** to deal with **2.** to knock down

tac·tic (tak′ tik) *n.* a plan or procedure for achieving an end

tad·pole (tad′ pōl′) *n.* the larva of frogs and toads that lives in the water and breathes with gills

Tadpoles

tag (tag) *n.* a small ticket or tab hanging on something (price *tag*) —*vb.* **tagged**; **tag·ging** **1.** to put a tag on **2.** to follow closely (to *tag* along) **3.** to touch in a game of tag —*n.* children's game in which the one who is tagged is "it" and must do the chasing

tail (tāl) *n.* **1.** the extension of the backbone that hangs from the back of most animals **2.** the end of a line **3.** a tail-like part on an object such as an airplane or a kite

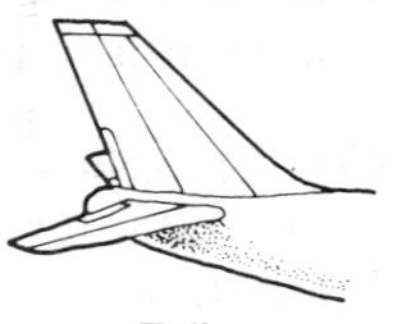

Tail

tai·lor (tā′ lər) *n.* a person whose occupation is to make or alter men's and women's outer garments such as suits and coats —*vb.* to make outer garments

take (tāk) *vb.* **took** (tu̇k); **tak·en** (tā′ kən); **tak·ing** **1.** to accept **2.** to win (*Take* a prize.) **3.** to get possession (*Take* a stateroom on the boat.) **4.** to grasp **5.** to subtract (*Take* two from five.) **6.** to get a reading (*Take* her temperature.) **7.** to choose (*Take* the red one.) **8.** to occupy (*Take* a seat.) **9.** to submit to (*Take* the treatment.) —*n.* the act of taking

tale (tāl) *n.* **1.** a story or an account of what happened **2.** an account that is gossip or an untruth

tal·ent (tal′ ənt) *n.* a natural ability or gift for achieving something especially of an artistic nature

talk (tȯk) *vb.* **1.** to speak or discuss **2.** to gossip —*n.* **1.** the act of speaking **2.** a formal discussion **3.** an informal lecture (a *talk* about job opportunities)

tall (tȯl) *adj.* **1.** high (a *tall* person) **2.** large in amount or degree (a *tall* order) **3.** unbelievable (a *tall* tale)

tame (tām) *adj.* **tam·er**; **tam·est** **1.** changed from a wild to a gentle state (a *tame* elephant) **2.** dull and quiet (a *tame* afternoon) —*vb.* **tamed**; **tam·ing** to make gentle and subdued

tan (tan) *vb.* **tanned**; **tan·ning** **1.** to change hide into leather by a process such as soaking it in a tannic acid solution **2.** to become tan from exposure to the sun —*n.* **1.** the color of skin browned by the sun **2.** a yellowish-brown color

tan·gle (tang′ gəl) *vb.* **tan·gled**; **tan·gling** **1.** to twist and snarl (Wind *ιangled* her hair.) **2.** to involve in a difficult situation (to *tangle* with the tax law) —*n.* **1.** a snarl **2.** a confused situation

tank (tangk) *n.* **1.** a large container for a liquid (full oil *tank*) **2.** an armored war vehicle armed with cannon and guns and running on caterpillar tread —*vb.* to put in a tank

Tank

tap (tap) *n.* a faucet or spigot —*vb.* **tapped**; **tap·ping** **1.** to allow or cause a liquid to flow out of a container (to *tap* the keg for a drink) **2.** to take from (*tap* the money they had saved)

tap (tap) *n.* a light rap or the sound it makes —*vb.* **tapped**; **tap·ping** **1.** to knock or rap lightly **2.** to repair a shoe by adding a thickness of leather to the sole

tape (tāp) *n.* **1.** a narrow strip of woven fabric **2.** a band of clear plastic with a sticky side for mending or sealing **3.** a plastic band used for recording sound —*vb.* **taped**; **tap·ing** **1.** to bind, fasten, or furnish with tape **2.** to record sound on a tape

tar (tär) *n.* **1.** a sailor **2.** a dark, thick, oily substance obtained from wood, coal, or peat —*vb.* **tarred**; **tar·ring** to cover with tar

tar·get (tär′ gət) *n.* **1.** a goal to be achieved **2.** a bull's eye surrounded by circles used for shooting practice **3.** a person who is the object of criticism

Target

task (task) *n.* work that is given to a person to do

taste (tāst) *vb.* **tast·ed**; **tast·ing** **1.** to take a small amount into the mouth to test the flavor **2.** to perceive a flavor (to *taste* basil in the sauce) —*n.* **1.** a small amount tested or experienced **2.** a flavor **3.** the ability to judge what is attractive or good (has good *taste*)

tax (taks) *vb.* **1.** to require a payment to support the government **2.** to cause a strain (to *tax* one's energy) —*n.* **1.** money required to support the government **2.** a difficult duty causing a strain

tax·i (tak′ sē) *n., pl.* **tax·is** taxicab —*vb.* **tax·ied**; **tax·i·ing** or **tax·y·ing** **1.** to ride in a taxicab **2.** to run an airplane slowly along the ground to get into position for take-off or, after landing, to proceed to the gate

tea (tē) *n.* **1.** the dried leaves of an Asian shrub **2.** a drink made by steeping the leaves in boiling water **3.** afternoon refreshments at which tea is served

teach (tēch) *vb.* **taught** (tȯt); **teach·ing** **1.** to give lessons in a subject of study **2.** to instruct by showing or explaining

teach·er (tē′ chər) *n.* **1.** a person who teaches **2.** a professional educator

tea·ket·tle (tē′ ket′ l) *n.* a covered kettle with a spout, for heating and pouring water

team (tēm) *n.* a group of persons who work, play, or act together (a softball *team*) —*vb.* to form a team

tea·pot (tē′ pät′) *n.* a covered container with a handle and a spout for brewing and serving tea

tear (tiər) *n.* a drop of the liquid that moistens the eye which overflows under the stress of emotion or irritation

tear (taər) *vb.* **tore** (tōr); **torn** (tōrn); **tear·ing** to rip or separate by force —*n.* **1.** the act of tearing **2.** a rip

tease (tēz) *vb.* **teased**; **teas·ing** to annoy, distract, or engage in good-natured ridicule, usually in sport —*n.* the one who teases

tea·spoon (tē′ spün) *n.* a small spoon used for stirring beverages and for eating from a small cup-shaped dish

tech·ni·cal (tek′ ni kəl) *adj.* **1.** belonging to a particular art, science, profession, or trade (*technical* skill) **2.** according to a strict interpretation of the rules (a *technical* decision)

tech·nique (tek nēk′) *n.* the manner in which a writer, artist, athlete, dancer, or mechanic uses technical skill in practicing his or her area of performance

tech·nol·o·gy (tek näl′ ə jē) *n., pl.* **tech·nol·o·gies** **1.** a branch of knowledge dealing with an applied science **2.** the ways in which society provides itself with the material objects of its civilization (a high level of *technology*)

te·di·ous (tēd′ ē əs, tē′ jəs) *adj.* long and tiresome

teen·ag·er (tēn′ ā′ jər) *n.* a person between the ages of thirteen and nineteen

teens (tēnz) *n., pl.* the years thirteen through nineteen of a person's life

tel·e·gram (tel′ ə gram′) *n.* a message sent by telegraph

tel·e·graph (tel′ ə graf′) *n.* a system for sending messages over long distances between two electrically operated stations connected by a communications channel

tel·e·phone (tel′ ə fōn′) *n.* an instrument or system for sending the sounds of a human voice over long distances to an electric device, often including transmission by radio beams bounced off a satellite

tel·e·scope (tel′ ə skōp) *n.* a long, tube-shaped instrument with lenses for viewing distant objects, but especially heavenly bodies

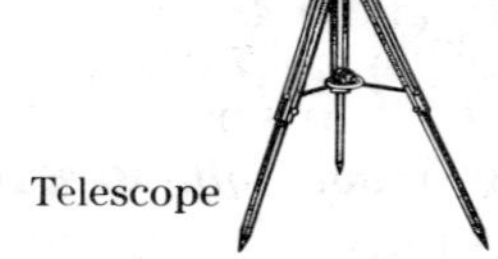
Telescope

tel·e·vi·sion (tel′ ə vizh′ ən) *n.* **1.** the broadcasting of images by radio waves to receivers which change them back to images or pictures on a screen **2.** a set for receiving such a broadcast

tell (tel) *vb.* **told** (tōld); **tell·ing** **1.** to say, relate, or report (*tell* what happened) **2.** to order, command, or direct (*told* him to do it) **3.** to be an informer (*told* on the guilty one)

tem·per (tem′ pər) *vb.* **1.** to regulate, soften, or tone down (to *temper* her outburst of anger) **2.** to bring to a degree of hardness or stiffness (*temper* steel) —*n.* a state of mind (a raging *temper*)

tem·per·ate (tem′ pə rət) *adj.* moderate, calm, or self-controlled (a *temperate* person or a *temperate* climate)

tem·per·a·ture (tem′ pə rə chůr′) *n.* **1.** the degree of heat or cold as measured by a thermometer **2.** a fever (a body *temperature* above 98.6 degrees)

tem·ple (tem′ pəl) *n.* **1.** a building dedicated to the worship of a deity (the *temple* in Jerusalem) **2.** the flat part of the face on either side between the eye and the top of the ear

tem·po (tem′ pō) *n., pl.* **tem·pi** (tem′ pē) or **tem·pos** **1.** the rate of speed at which music is performed **2.** a normal rate, rhythm, or pattern of activity (the *tempo* of college life)

tem·po·rar·y (tem′ pə rer′ ē) *adj.* continuing for a limited time only (a *temporary* permit)

tempt (tempt) *vb.* to persuade someone to do wrong by offering the possiblity of gain

tend (tend) *vb.* **1.** to manage or take care of (*tend* the campfire) **2.** to move or lean toward (He *tends* to support the independent candidate.)

tend·en·cy (ten′ dən sē) *n., pl.* **tend·en·cies** a trend or leaning toward a particular kind of thought or action (a *tendency* toward classical music)

ten·der (ten′ dər) *adj.* **1.** easily cut or chewed (*tender* meat) **2.** delicate (a *tender* bud) **3.** emotional; easily touched (a *tender* nature)

ten·der (ten′ dər) *n.* **1.** a person who tends to some activity (the fire *tender*) **2.** something that takes care of things, such as supplies or repairs (the ship's *tender*)

ten·der (ten′ dər) *n.* something that is offered or proposed (legal *tender*) —*vb.* **1.** to offer in payment **2.** to present for consideration (to *tender* an offer)

ten·nis (ten′ əs) *n.* a game played on a court divided by a net in which two or four players hit a ball with a racket back and forth across the net

Tennis Player

ten·or (ten′ ər) *n.* **1.** the general idea (the *tenor* of her speech) **2.** the highest adult male voice (sang *tenor* in the chorus)

tense (tens) *n.* a form of the verb used to show the time of the action (present *tense*; past *tense*)

tense (tens) *adj.* **1.** feeling or showing nervous strain (having a *tense* day) **2.** pulled tight (stretched the cord until it was *tense*) —*vb.* **tensed**; **tens·ing** to pull something tight (*tensed* it until it was rigid)

ten·sion (ten′ chən) *n.* **1.** a state of mental strain or emotional anxiety (filled with *tension*) **2.** a state of strained relations (*tension* between countries) **3.** the act of stretching or straining

tent (tent) *n.* a canvas shelter supported on poles and anchored by ropes —*vb.* to live or camp in a tent

term (tərm) *n.* **1.** a fixed period of time (*term* of office) **2.** a word or phrase that has a special meaning in a field (The *term* "mouth" has different meanings in anatomy and geography.) **3.** *pl.* conditions (*terms* of the lease)

ter·mi·nal (tər′ mən l) *adj.* forming an end or limit (*terminal* illness) —*n.* **1.** a part that forms the end (bus *terminal*) **2.** one end of an electrical circuit where a connection to equipment is made (battery *terminal*) **3.** railroad facilities where trains start or end (railroad *terminal*)

ter·mite (tər′ mīt′) *n.* a pale-colored, chewing insect similar to the ant that lives in large colonies and feeds on wood, often being very destructive to buildings or furniture

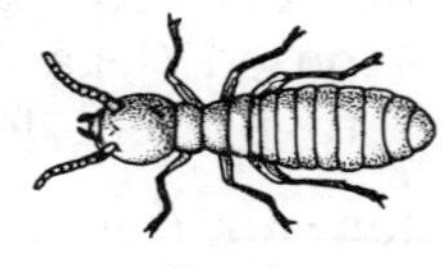
Termite

ter·rain (tə rān′) *n.* the natural features or advantages of a piece of land (good *terrain* for an airfield)

ter·ri·ble (ter′ ə bəl) *adj.* **1.** causing fear or terror (a *terrible* storm) **2.** extremely bad or horrible (a *terrible* cut of meat)

ter·rif·ic (tə rif′ ik) *adj.* **1.** great, wonderful, exciting (a *terrific* party) **2.** terrible, alarming (a *terrific* earthquake)

ter·ri·fy (ter′ ə fī′) *vb.* **ter·ri·fied; ter·ri·fy·ing** to frighten (*terrified* by the dog)

ter·ri·to·ry (ter′ ə tōr′ ē) *n., pl.* **ter·ri·to·ries** **1.** the land and water under the control of one government (Alaskan *territory*) **2.** a large region (woodland *territory*)

ter·ror (ter′ ər) *n.* **1.** extreme fear (filled with *terror*) **2.** a mischief maker (a little *terror*)

test (test) *n.* **1.** an examination (taking the achievement *test*) **2.** a trial (gave the process a fair *test*) —*vb.* to take a test

tes·ti·mo·ny (tes′ tə mō′ nē) *n., pl.* **tes·ti·mo·nies** **1.** a statement of a witness in court under oath **2.** a statement made to establish a fact

text (tekst) *n.* **1.** a textbook **2.** the printed words in a book (Read the headings in the *text.*)

text·book (tekst′ bu̇k′) *n.* a book used by students as a basis of study

tex·tile (tek′ stīl′) *n.* fabric that is woven (*textile* fabric)

tex·ture (teks′ chər) *n.* the roughness or silkiness or the smoothness or coarseness of any material (the fine *texture* of sandstone)

than (t͟hən, t͟han) *conj.* when compared to (colder *than* yesterday)

thank (thangk) *vb.* to express appreciation or gratitude

thank·ful (thangk′ fəl) *adj.* grateful (*thankful* for all your help)

that (t͟hat) *pron., pl.* **those** (t͟hōz) **1.** the one indicated or understood (*That*'s the last piece.) **2.** the one farther away (This is mine; *that* is yours.) **3.** something already mentioned (so *that* was the last trip) **4.** the one —*adj., pl.* **those** **1.** being the one mentioned or understood (*that* girl) **2.** being the one farther away (*that* pen) —*conj.* **1.** for this reason, namely (sorry *that* you lost) **2.** so as (called *that* all might hear) —*adv.* so (about *that* long)

the (t͟hə before consonant, t͟hē before vowel sounds) *definite article* used before a noun to point out a particular one —*adv.* **1.** before comparatives (*the* more, *the* merrier) **2.** than before (none *the* richer)

the·a·ter (thē′ ət ər) *n.* a building with many seats and a stage or screen where plays or motion pictures are presented

their (t͟hər, t͟heər) *adj.* relating to them (*their* skates)

theirs (t͟heərz) *pron.* one or ones belonging to them (The car is *theirs*.)

them (t͟həm, t͟hem) *pron.* objective case of THEY (for *them*)

theme (thēm) *n.* **1.** the subject of a presentation in writing or art form **2.** a short essay or composition (a *theme* about the last motion picture you saw)

them·selves (t͟həm selvz′) *pron.* their own selves

then (t͟hen) *adv.* **1.** at that time (I was younger *then*.) **2.** next in time or place (first Meg and *then* Ann) **3.** in that case (Since you have a car, *then* we can go.) **4.** besides (It's useful; and *then*, it's also on sale.) —*n.* that time (I won't go before *then*.) —*adj.* prevailing at that time (the *then* president)

the·o·ry (thē′ ə rē) *n., pl.* **the·o·ries** **1.** a statement that is an attempt to explain how, when, where, or why certain observable things happen (Newton's *Theory* of Gravity) **2.** the general principles and knowledge gained from experience in any established art or science (*theory* of government) **3.** an explanation developed by thinking and speculation as opposed to trying it out (That's your *theory*, but will it work?)

there (thaər) *adv.* **1.** in or at that place (He is *there.*) **2.** to or into that place (Go *there.*) **3.** in that matter (He's wrong *there.*) —*pron.* used to introduce a sentence (*There*'s a salad in the refrigerator.) —*n.* that place (Don't hide in *there.*) —*interj.* expressing feeling or emotion (*There*! I did it! *There, there,* don't take it so hard.)

there·af·ter (thaər af′ tər) *adv.* after that (*Thereafter*, I did better.)

there·by (thaər′ bī′) *adv.* by that means (*thereby* having a good meal)

there·fore (thaər′ fōr′) *adv.* for that reason (I felt sick; *therefore* I went home.)

ther·mom·e·ter (thər mäm′ ət ər) *n.* an instrument for measuring temperature

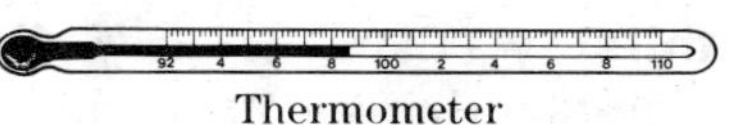

Thermometer

these (thēz) *adj., pl.* of THIS

they (thā) *pron.* people (*They* say the house is nice inside.)

thick (thik) *adj.* **1.** being of a greater than average depth (a *thick* board) **2.** closely packed (a *thick* crowd) **3.** dense (a *thick* fog) **4.** not clear in thinking (He's *thick* today.) —*n.* the most crowded or densest part (in the *thick* of it)

thick·et (thik′ ət) *n.* a small area thick with bushes and small trees (the rabbits living in the *thicket*)

thief (thēf) *n., pl.* **thieves** (thēvz) one who steals

thigh (thī) *n.* the part of the leg between the knee and the hip (bruised his *thigh*)

thim·ble (thim′ bəl) *n.* a metal cover for the finger that pushes the needle when sewing

Thimble

thin (thin) *adj.* **thin·ner; thin·nest** **1.** having a less than average depth **2.** scattered, not packed closely (a *thin* growth of grass) **3.** slim and lean (a *thin* body) —*vb.* **thinned; thin·ning** to make or become thin or thinner (She *thinned* the sauce.)

thing (thing) *n.* **1.** an object (found a strange *thing*) **2.** event (The accident was a sad *thing.*) **3.** state of affairs (*Things* are better now.) **4.** activity (one *thing* to finish) **5.** *pl.* belongings (took his *things*) **6.** a piece of clothing (not one *thing* to wear)

think (thingk) *vb.* **thought** (thȯt); **think·ing** to recall, analyze, form a judgment, ponder, or invent in the mind (*think* of an answer)

thirst (thərst) *n.* **1.** a feeling of dryness in the mouth and throat **2.** a longing (a *thirst* for a good book) —*vb.* **1.** to feel thirsty **2.** to long for

thirst·y (thərs′ tē) *adj.* **thirst·i·er; thirst·i·est** **1.** needing a drink **2.** having a longing

this (t̲his) *pron., pl.* **these** (t̲hēz) **1.** the one nearest in time or space (*This* is my pen.) **2.** present events (*This* is hard on her.) —*adj., pl.* **these** being the one present or just mentioned (*this* time) —*adv.* to the degree or extent stated (*this* far; *this* often)

thorn (thȯrn) *n.* the briers or spines on a plant (a *thorn* on the rose)

thor·ough (thər′ ō) *adj.* careful and complete (*thorough* job)

those (t̲hōz) *pron., pl.* of THAT

though (t̲hō) *adv.* however —*conj.* **1.** in spite of the fact that (I went, *though* I was tired.) **2.** even if (She smiles *though* it hurts.)

thought (thȯt) *vb. past* of THINK —*n.* the act or process of thinking, such as recalling, analyzing, deciding, imagining, or planning

thought·ful (thȯt′ fəl) *adj.* given to attention to others and concern for their welfare

thou·sand (thau̇z′ nd) *n.* ten times one hundred, a very large number —*adj.* being one thousand

thread (thred) *n.* **1.** a fine cord used for sewing **2.** the ridge that winds around a screw —*vb.* **1.** to put a thread through the eye of a needle or through its path in a machine **2.** to make one's way through a crowd (*thread* their way to a door)

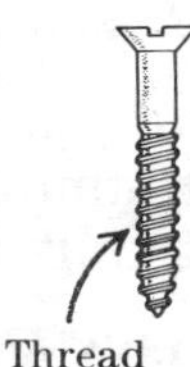

threat (thret) *n.* **1.** a statement that someone will be harmed or injured **2.** something that presents an indication of causing harm (Lightning is a *threat* to swimmers.)

threat·en (thret′ n) *vb.* **1.** to say an intent to hurt someone **2.** to warn of danger

thrill (thril) *vb.* to fill with excitement —*n.* a shiver of excitement

thrive (thrīv) *vb.* **thrived**; **thriv·ing** **1.** to grow well **2.** to make progress in one's work

throat (thrōt) *n.* **1.** the passageway from the mouth to the upper part of the windpipe **2.** in anatomy, the pharynx into which the nostrils, gullet, and windpipe open

throne (thrōn) *n.* the chair of a king, queen, or bishop

through (thrü) *prep.* **1.** in one side and out the other (*through* the door) **2.** by means of (*through* hours of study) **3.** from one end to the other (*through* town) **4.** during the whole of —*adv.* **1.** from side to side or from end to end (Read the chapter *through.*) **2.** to the finish (worked the problem *through*) **3.** to the middle (cold *through* and *through*) **4.** to the outside (broke *through*) —*adj.* going from one place to another (a *through* train to Washington, D.C.)

throw (thrō) *vb.* **threw** (thrü); **thrown** (thrōn); **throw·ing** **1.** to propel through the air by pitching or hurling (to *throw* the ball) **2.** to push over **3.** to put clothing on quickly (*threw* on a jacket) **4.** to cast (*throw* dice)

thrust (thrəst) *vb.* **thrust**; **thrust·ing** **1.** to push or shove (*thrust* the car into gear) **2.** to press someone (*thrust* an invitation upon him) —*n.* **1.** a lunge with a weapon **2.** a strong forward or upward push

thud (thəd) *vb.* **thud·ded**; **thud·ding** to make a low thumping sound (He *thudded* along with his cane.) —*n.* a dull, thumping sound (The box dropped with a *thud.*)

thumb (thəm) *n.* the short, thick finger next to the forefinger —*vb.* **1.** to turn pages with the thumb (*thumb* through the book) **2.** to hold out one's thumb to request a ride (To *thumb* a ride is very dangerous.)

thump (thəmp) *vb.* to pound or knock (*Thump* on the heavy door.) —*n.* a blow with something heavy (gave it a *thump*)

thun·der (thən′ dər) *n.* the rumbling sound that follows lightning —*vb.* to roar like thunder

thus (t͟həs) *adv.* **1.** in this way **2.** to this degree **3.** so or therefore

tick (tik) *n.* a blood-sucking insect related to the spider

tick (tik) *n.* **1.** a soft, rhythmic beat (the *tick* of the clock) **2.** a small check mark to mark an item on a list —*vb.* **1.** to make a tick **2.** to mark with ticks **3.** to operate (What makes it *tick*?)

tick·et (tik′ ət) *n.* **1.** a card showing a fee has been paid for such activities as entrance to entertainment, transportation on an airplane, train, or bus, or a chance on a lottery or drawing **2.** a notice of warning or fine for a traffic violation **3.** a list of candidates endorsed for election by one party **4.** a sales slip —*vb.* **1.** to attach a ticket to **2.** to give a ticket to

tick·le (tik′ əl) *vb.* **tick·led**; **tick·ling** **1.** to have or cause a tingling feeling **2.** to amuse (The story *tickled* her.) —*n.* a tickling feeling

tid·al (tīd′ l) *adj.* relating to or having the action of tides (A huge *tidal* wave flooded the shore.)

tide (tīd) *n.* **1.** the regular rise and fall of the ocean due to the pull of the moon and sun **2.** a time, usually surrounding a special day or a critical event (Christmas*tide*; even*tide*; the *tide* of her illness) —*vb.* to help someone through a difficulty (to *tide* him through his difficulty)

tid·y (tīd′ ē) *adj.* **ti·di·er; ti·di·est** **1.** trim and neat (a *tidy* house) **2.** large (a *tidy* amount of money) —*vb.* **ti·died; ti·dy·ing** to make neat or put things in order (*tidied* up the kitchen)

tie (tī) *n.* **1.** a ribbon or cord used for binding **2.** a beam holding two pieces of a structure together **3.** one of the cross pieces on a railroad to which the rails are attached **4.** a bond (family *ties*) **5.** equality in votes or scores **6.** a necktie —*vb.* **tied; ty·ing** (tī ing) **1.** to fasten with a cord or ribbon **2.** to unite (*tie* together) **3.** to have an equal score

ti·ger (tī′ gər) *n.* a large tan and black-striped flesh-eating animal of the cat family

tight (tīt) *adj.* **1.** permitting no passing of liquid (a *tight* seal) **2.** firm (a *tight* weave) **3.** close-fitting (a *tight* sweater) **4.** stretched to the limit (a *tight* rope) **5.** hard to get (*tight* money)

tile (tīl) *n.* **1.** a thin square of clay, baked either flat or bent, used for roofing, floor covering, or other purposes **2.** squares made of other material for similar purposes **3.** clay pipe used for draining land —*vb.* **tiled; til·ing** to cover with tiles

till (til) *prep.* or *conj.* until (wait *till* Monday)

till (til) *vb.* to plow land, sow seeds, and raise crops (*till* the land)

till (til) *n.* a drawer for money such as in a cash register or counter (take money from the *till*)

tilt (tilt) *vb.* **1.** to put at an angle (Don't *tilt* your chair.) **2.** to strike or charge at someone

tim·ber (tim′ bər) *n.* **1.** wood prepared as building material **2.** growing trees from which wood may be cut

time (tīm) *n.* **1.** a definite period during the past, present, or future **2.** spare time (*time* to exercise) **3.** a set hour (came on *time*) **4.** an age or era (the *time* of Columbus) **5.** the reading on a clock (What is the *time*?) **6.** multiplied by (five *times* five) —*vb.* **timed**; **tim·ing** to be aware of how long something takes (*Time* the cake as it is baking.)

tim·id (tim′ əd) *adj.* shy or fearful

tin (tin) *n.* **1.** a rust-free metal used as a protective covering for other metals **2.** a can or box made from tin plate (*tin* cans)

ti·ny (tī′ nē) *adj.* **ti·ni·er**; **ti·ni·est** very small

tip (tip) *n.* **1.** a narrow or pointed end (*tips* of her toes) **2.** an act of tipping **3.** a light tap or blow (foul *tip*) —*vb.* **tipped**; **tip·ping** **1.** to cover or decorate the tip (*Tip* it with gold paint.) **2.** to cause to fall over (*tipped* the paint can over) **3.** to tilt (*tip* to one side)

tip (tip) *vb.* **tipped**; **tip·ping** **1.** to give a small sum of money, a gratuity, for a service (*Tip* the waiter.) **2.** to give a piece of good advice —*n.* **1.** a small sum given as a gratuity **2.** a piece of good advice (a *tip* on how to invest money)

tire (tīr) *vb.* **tired**; **tir·ing** **1.** to make weary or sleepy (Cutting wood *tired* him.) **2.** to make bored (Driving on the turnpike *tired* her.) —*n.* an air-filled rubber ring that surrounds a wheel (new *tires* for her car)

tis·sue (tish′ ü) *n.* **1.** a piece of soft, thin paper (wiped off the cream with a *tissue*) **2.** a mass or layer of similar cells in a plant or animal (bone *tissue*)

ti·tle (tīt′ l) *n.* **1.** a name of rank or office (now has the *title* of governor) **2.** the name of something such as a composition or work of art (The *title* of the composition is “The Spirit to Win.”) **3.** a legal right to property (holds *title* to a ranch house)

to (tə, tü) *prep.* **1.** in the direction of (going *to* Kansas City) **2.** on (put her hand *to* the wheel) **3.** as far as (up *to* the corner) **4.** until (nine *to* four-thirty) **5.** along with (dance *to* the music) **6.** compared with (two games *to* one) **7.** within (*to* their liking) **8.** connecting an action with its recipient (Give it *to* me.) —*adv.* **1.** in a certain direction (landed backside *to*) **2.** into a usual position (blew the gate *to*) **3.** to a state of awareness (came *to*)

toad (tōd) *n.* a tailless, hopping, insect-eating amphibian that is able to live on land or in water, as the frog, but unlike the frog, usually stays on land and has rough skin

toast (tōst) *vb.* to heat until brown and crisp —*n.* sliced bread that is toasted

toast (tōst) *n.* **1.** an act of drinking in a person's honor (I propose a *toast* to) **2.** the person named in a toast —*vb.* to drink a toast to

to·bac·co (tə bak′ ō) *n.* a plant of the nightshade family having leaves that are dried for use in smoking

to·day (tə dā′) *adv.* on or for this day (I need it *today.*) —*n.* the present day (*Today* is warmer than yesterday.)

toe (tō) *n.* one of the digits at the end of a person's foot —*vb.* **toed**; **toe·ing** to touch or move with the toes

to·geth·er (tə ge<u>th</u>′ ər) *adv.* **1.** in a group (came *together*) **2.** in or into contact (bumped *together*) **3.** in or into agreement

toil (tȯil) *n.* very hard work —*vb.* to work very hard

to·ken (tō′ kən) *n.* **1.** a sign (a flower as a *token* of my affection) **2.** a sample (a *token* of what I can get) **3.** a metal disk used as money for paying a toll or fare (My bridge *token*s and subway *token*s are in this box.)

toll (tōl) *n.* **1.** a tax paid for using a highway or bridge **2.** a heavy payment in wealth or welfare (paid a *toll* for his poor eating habits) **3.** the sound of a bell ringing slowly —*vb.* to sound slowly and evenly (The bell *toll*s.)

to·ma·to (tə māt′ ō, tə mät′ ō) *n., pl.* **to·ma·toes** a red or yellow pulpy fruit used as a vegetable or in salads

tomb (tüm) *n.* a grave or vault for the dead

to·mor·row (tə mär′ ō) *adv.* on or for the day after today —*n.* the day after today

ton (tən) *n.* a measure of weight equal to two thousand pounds (a short *ton*) or two thousand, two hundred forty pounds (a long *ton*)

tone (tōn) *n.* **1.** a sound or the quality of a sound **2.** a way of speaking (a stern *tone*) **3.** a color or the quality of a color **4.** the health and firmness of the body (good muscle *tone*) —*vb.* **toned**; **ton·ing** **1.** to give firmness or strength to (*tone* up the body) **2.** to blend or bring into harmony (*tone* the colors down)

tongue (təng) *n.* **1.** the organ in the mouth used in tasting, swallowing, and speaking **2.** a language (a foreign *tongue*) **3.** something that looks like an animal tongue (*tongue* of his shoe)

to·night (tə nīt′) *adv.* at the end of this day, this night —*n.* the present or coming night

too (tü) *adv.* **1.** in addition or also **2.** very **3.** more than usually (*too* noisy today)

took (tu̇k) *vb. past tense* of TAKE

tool (tül) *n.* an implement such as a hammer, saw, screwdriver, needle, scissors, or knife used to make work possible or easier to do (Find a *tool* to remove the screw from the latch.)

tooth (tüth) *n., pl.* **teeth** (tēth) **1.** a hard bony formation, many of which grow in a row from each jaw, made up of three layers: a soft pulp in the center surrounded by dentin and covered with a layer of enamel and used for biting and chewing **2.** a toothlike part such as a cog on a wheel

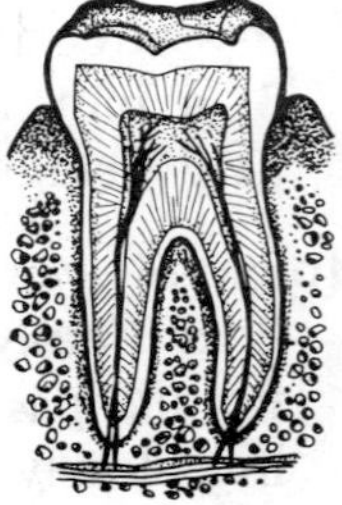

Tooth

top (täp) *n.* **1.** the highest part of something **2.** a lid

top · ic (täp′ ik) *n.* **1.** the title or subject of a composition or talk **2.** a heading in a textbook or other written material

torch (tȯrch) *n.* **1.** a flaming light fastened to a pole to carry in the hand, made of heavy plant fibers soaked in grease or oil and set afire **2.** anything that gives out a flame or flare, such as a plumber's torch (carrying the Olympic *torch*)

tore (tōr) *vb.* past tense of TEAR

Tornado

tor · na · do (tȯr nād′ ō) *n., pl.* **tor · na · does** a funnel-shaped cloud and whirlwind that drops down out of the sky and moves along a narrow path causing destruction

tor · rent (tȯr′ ənt) *n.* **1.** a deep rushing stream caused by heavy rainfall or snow melting in the higher elevattions **2.** a heavy rain (raining in *torrents*) **3.** a steady downhill flow of lava

toss (tȯs) *vb.* **1.** to throw out lightly (to *toss* the beanbag) **2.** to glide up and down (*toss* on the rough sea) **3.** to mix lightly (to *toss* the pasta and sauce)

to · tal (tōt′ l) *adj.* **1.** relating to the whole of something (the *total* bill) **2.** complete (a *total* blackout) —*n.* **1.** the sum (The *total* of 3+4+5 is 12.) **2.** the entire mass (The *total* of it stretched three miles.) —*vb.* **to · taled; to · tal · ing** to add up (to *total* the bill)

touch (təch) *vb.* **1.** to feel by contacting with the hand (to *touch* the kitten's fur) **2.** to be next to (a chair *touch*ing the wall) **3.** to handle or abuse (don't dare *touch* you) **4.** to mention (*touch*ed upon the subject) **5.** to improve (*touch*ed up the old table) **6.** moved emotionally (*touch*ed by your kind deeds) —*n.* **1.** the act of touching or being touched **2.** a state of contact (in *touch* with her family) **3.** information perceived through contact (rough to the *touch*) **4.** a small amount (a *touch* of nutmeg)

tough (təf) *adj.* **1.** strong and hardy (*tough* material) **2.** hard to chew (*tough* meat) **3.** hard to endure (*tough* schedule) —*n.* a rough person

tour (tu̇r) *n.* **1.** a trip covering some chief points of interest **2.** a period of duty following a set pattern —*vb.* to make a trip as a tourist

tour·ist (tu̇r′ əst) *n.* a person who travels to see the points of interest and enjoy the change of scenery

tour·na·ment (tu̇r′ nə mənt) *n.* **1.** in the Middle Ages, a contest of skill between armed knights on horseback **2.** a series of athletic events or games for a championship (tennis *tournament*)

tow (tō) *vb.* to drag along behind on a rope or line —*n.* **1.** an act of towing **2.** a line or rope for towing something

tow (tō) *n.* the coarse fibers of flax, hemp, or jute

to·ward (tō′ ərd) or **to·wards** (tō′ ərdz) *prep.* **1.** in the direction of (*toward* Omaha) **2.** leading to (*toward* an agreement) **3.** near (*toward* dawn) **4.** with respect to (feelings *toward* his studies)

tow·el (tau̇′ əl) *n.* a piece of soft cloth or paper for wiping or drying

tow·er (tau̇′ ər) *n.* a tall structure that is neither very wide nor very deep

Tower

town (tau̇n) *n.* a settled area, larger than a village but smaller than a city, with a local government

toy (tȯi) *n.* a plaything for a child —*vb.* to amuse oneself as if playing with a toy (*toy*ed with the lace on her scarf)

trace (trās) *n.* **1.** a mark left by something that went by **2.** a tiny amount (a *trace* of salt) —*vb.* **traced; trac·ing** **1.** to copy on thin paper placed over the original **2.** to study the history or progress (*traced* the settlement of the town back to 1640)

track (trak) *n.* **1.** a mark left by something that went by (deer *tracks*, tire *tracks*) **2.** rails with crossties (railroad *track*) **3.** a course of action (got off on the wrong *track*) **4.** awareness (keep *track* of time) **5.** in athletics, running events (*track* and field sports) —*vb.* to follow the tracks of

tract (trakt) *n.* **1.** a leaflet on a political or religious subject **2.** a stretch of land **3.** a body system (respiratory *tract*)

trac·tor (trak′ tər) *n.* **1.** a short truck used for hauling a trailer **2.** a vehicle with large rear wheels for hauling farm equipment

trade (trād) *n.* **1.** a business or line of work **2.** the people working in one line of work (the hardware *trade*) **3.** the business of buying and selling

tra·di·tion (trə dish′ ən) *n.* beliefs and customs handed down from generation to generation

tra·di·tion·al (trə dish′ ən l) *adj.* handed down from one's ancestors (*traditional* egg hunt at Easter)

traf·fic (traf′ ik) *n.* **1.** the movement of vehicles on the highway **2.** the business of moving people or goods —*vb.* **traf·ficked**; **traf·fick·ing** to trade

trag·e·dy (traj′ ə dē) *n., pl.* **trag·e·dies** **1.** a crime or disaster (*tragedy* of the earthquake) **2.** a serious play with a sad ending

trag·ic (traj′ ik) *adj.* **1.** pertaining to tragedy (a *tragic* accident) **2.** sad

trail (trāl) *vb.* **1.** to hang or let hang down to the ground in the rear **2.** lag behind —*n.* **1.** the thing that trails or is trailed **2.** a trace or marker left behind (a *trail* of peanut shells)

trail·er (trā′ lər) *n.* **1.** a vehicle for hauling goods pulled by a tractor **2.** a vehicle equipped for light housekeeping that can be pulled by another vehicle

train (trān) *n.* **1.** a part of a gown that trails on the floor (wedding gown with a *train*) **2.** the people and vehicles that come with an important person (the queen and her *train*) **3.** a line of thinking or acting (*train* of events) —*vb.* **1.** to teach procedures and skills (*train* assembly workers) **2.** to direct growth (*train* the plant to grow on the wall)

train·ing (trā′ ning) *n.* **1.** the course of study followed by one in training **2.** the level of skill of a trained person

trait (trāt) *n.* a quality or characteristic

tramp (tramp) *vb.* to walk with heavy footsteps —*n.* **1.** a homeless person who lives on what he can beg or find **2.** a hike (a *tramp* through the woods) **3.** the sound of marching feet (Hear the *tramp* of the soldiers.) **4.** a cargo ship that is not on a regular schedule

trans·fer (trans fər′) *vb.* **trans·ferred**; **trans·fer·ring** **1.** to pass from one person or place to another **2.** to pass ownership of property to another **3.** to pass a design from one surface to another (*transferred* the design to the T-shirt with heat) **4.** to move from one vehicle to another (*transferred* from the train to a bus in Boston) —*n.* **trans·fer** (trans′ fər′) **1.** the change of title to property from one person to another **2.** a ticket for continuing a trip on another public conveyance (a bus *transfer*) **3.** the act of transferring

trans·form (trans fȯrm′) *vb.* to change completely (*transform* wind power to electricity)

tran·sis·tor (tran zis′ tər) *n.* a device using a semi-conductor for controlling the flow of current between two terminals

trans·late (trans lāt′) *vb.* **trans·lat·ed**; **trans·lat·ing** to change from one language into another (to *translate* his speech into English)

trans·la·tion (trans lā′ shən) *n.* **1.** the act of changing a communication from one language to another **2.** the text of the communication in the new language

trans·mit (trans mit′) *vb.* **trans·mit·ted**; **trans·mit·ting** **1.** to pass on from one person to another **2.** to send by radio waves

trans·par·ent (trans par′ ənt) *adj.* **1.** clear enough to see through **2.** apparent or obvious (His evil scheme is *transparent* to everyone.)

trans·port (trans pōrt′) *vb.* to carry from one place to another —*n.* **1.** the act of carrying **2.** a vehicle for carrying

trans·por·ta·tion (trans′ pər tā′ shən) **1.** an act of carrying **2.** a means of travel **3.** a public moving of people or goods (the city with good *transportation*)

trap (trap) *n.* **1.** a snare for catching animals **2.** a device that catches some things and allows others to pass (a *sink* trap) —*vb.* **trapped**; **trap·ping** **1.** to catch or snare in a trap (to *trap* the groundhog) **2.** to set traps for animals (no hunting or *trapping* allowed)

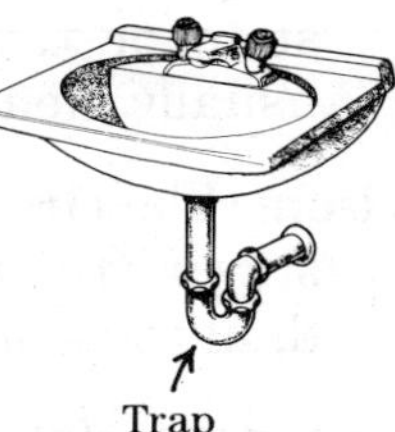

trash (trash) *n.* something of little or no worth (Get rid of the *trash.*)

trav·el (trav′ əl) *vb.* **trav·eled**; **trav·el·ing** to go from place to place for enjoyment or business —*n.* **1.** the act of traveling **2.** a trip, tour, or journey

tray (trā) *n.* a flat object with low sides for carrying objects, especially dishes of food or drink

treach·er·ous (trech′ ə rəs) *adj.* **1.** not loyal, not to be trusted (a *treacherous* person) **2.** looking safe but really unstable (a *treacherous* boat)

treas·ure (trezh′ ər) *n.* **1.** a hoard of valuable things such as money, jewels, and art works **2.** a thing of great value (a ring that is my *treasure*) —*vb.* **trea·sured**; **trea·sur·ing** **1.** to put aside for future use **2.** to look upon as precious

treat (trēt) *vb.* **1.** to handle, deal with, develop or manage (to *treat* the workers well) **2.** to provide food or entertainment (*treat*ed them to sandwiches and tea) **3.** to provide medical care (*treat* her patients) **4.** to provide a chemical solution (*Treat* the water with chlorine.)

treat·ment (trēt′ mənt) *n.* **1.** the act of treating **2.** the substance or method prescribed (the *treatment* of the sprain)

trea·ty (trēt′ ē) *n., pl.* **trea·ties** a formal agreement between two or more nations on matters of international relations such as peace or trade

tree (trē) *n.* a woody plant with one main stem or trunk and most of the branches usually near the top

Tree

trem·ble (trem′ bəl) *vb.* **trem·bled**; **trem·bling** **1.** to shiver (to *tremble* with cold) **2.** to shake with fear or doubt —*n.* a spell of shaking

tre·men·dous (tri men′ dəs) *adj.* **1.** fearful or terrible (a *tremendous* flash of lightning) **2.** wonderful, astounding, or awesome (a *tremendous* Broadway hit)

trend (trend) *vb.* to move in a general direction —*n.* a tendency or drift (The *trend* is toward loose, comfortable clothing.)

tri·al (trī′ əl) *n.* **1.** the process of trying or testing (three elimination *trials* before the race) **2.** a court case (on *trial* for stealing) **3.** events that test one's faith or patience (The family illnesses were a terrible *trial.*)

tri·an·gle (trī′ ang′ gəl) *n.* **1.** a figure with three sides and three angles **2.** a musical instrument made of a triangle-shaped steel rod with one open angle

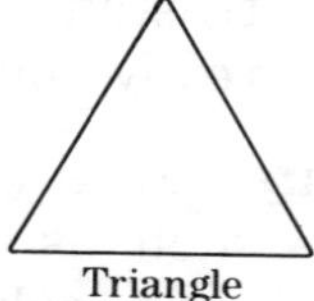

Triangle

trib·al (trī′ bəl) *adj.* relating to a tribe

tribe (trīb) *n.* a group of many families under one chief (a nomad *tribe*)

trick (trik) *n.* **1.** a sly act intended to deceive **2.** an act performed to puzzle or amuse (a magic *trick*) **3.** a particular skill (knowing the *tricks* of the trade) **4.** the cards played in one round of a card game (won five *tricks*) —*vb.* to cheat

trick·y (trik′ ē) *adj.* **trick·i·er; trick·i·est** **1.** tending to use tricks to cheat people **2.** requiring skill or careful procedures (Taming horses is a *tricky* business.)

tri·fle (trī′ fəl) *n.* something small in amount or importance (took only a *trifle*) —*vb.* **tri·fled; tri·fling** **1.** to waste time **2.** to talk jokingly

trig·ger (trig′ ər) *n.* a lever or catch that, when moved, releases the hammer of a gun

trim (trim) *vb.* **trimmed; trim·ming** **1.** to make fancy with ornaments (to *trim* a Christmas tree) **2.** to make trim by clipping (to *trim* the shrubs) **3.** to make lean and barebone (*trim* expenses) **4.** to level off a plane or ship —*adj.* **trim·mer; trim·mest** neat and clean in line and structure —*n.* **1.** good condition (in *trim*) **2.** ornaments for decorating (a box of *trim*) **3.** the inside woodwork in a building (putting *trim* around the doorway)

trip (trip) *vb.* **tripped; trip·ping** **1.** to step lightly as in dancing **2.** to catch the foot and stumble **3.** to make a mistake **4.** to set free a spring or catch in order to operate (*trip* the control lever) —*n.* **1.** a voyage or tour (a *trip* to Alaska) **2.** an errand (a *trip* to the grocery store) **3.** a lever or catch for tripping a machine or mechanism

tri·ple (trip′ əl) *vb.* **tri·pled; tri·pling** to make three times as great —*n.* **1.** a triple quantity **2.** in baseball, a hit that enables a batter to reach third base —*adj.* **1.** having three parts (a *triple* cone of ice cream) **2.** being three times as great (a *triple* share)

Triple Cone

tri·umph (trī′ əmf) *n.* a victory or achievement —*vb.* **1.** to win a victory **2.** to celebrate a success

troop (trüp) *n.* **1.** a unit of boy scouts or girl scouts **2.** *pl.* soldiers (moving the *troops*) **3.** a group of people (ballet *troop*) —*vb.* to collect, move, or march in a body (*troop* along)

trop·ic (träp′ ik) *n.* **1.** either of two lines parallel to the equator, one at 23°27′ north called the Tropic of Cancer and the other at 23°27′ south called the Tropic of Capricorn, being the boundaries of the Torrid Zone, and the boundaries within which the sun travels between the summer and winter solstices **2.** *pl.* the hot region of the earth lying between the two tropics

trop·i·cal (träp′ i kəl) *adj.* relating to the tropics (*tropical* fish)

trot (trät) *n.* **1.** a human jogging pace between a run and a walk **2.** the gait of a four-footed animal such as the horse, which is faster than a walk, and in which a front foot and the opposite hind foot move together —*vb.* **trot·ted**; **trot·ting** **1.** to go at a trot **2.** to go at a pace between a walk and a run

trou·ble (trəb′ əl) *vb.* **trou·bled**; **trou·bling** **1.** to worry or annoy **2.** to cause physical or mental distress —*n.* **1.** misfortune (money *trouble*) **2.** effort (Don't go to any *trouble.*)

trough (tròf) *n.* **1.** a shallow feed container for livestock **2.** a gutter or runway for water **3.** a long depression between ridges

trou·sers (traủ′ zərz) *n.,pl.* pants or slacks

trout (traủt) *n.* a dark speckled fish related to the salmon

truck (trək) *vb.* to transport on a truck —*n.* a vehicle for carrying heavy articles

trudge (trəj) *vb.* **trudged**; **trudg·ing** to travel on foot wearily, with much effort (to *trudge* up the hill)

true (trü) *adj.* **tru·er**; **tru·est** **1.** faithful, loyal, and reliable (a *true* friend) **2.** accurate (*true* measurement) **3.** rightful (a *true* heir) **4.** conforming to a type (A spider is not a *true* insect.)

tru·ly (trü′ lē) *adv.* **1.** sincerely (yours *truly*) **2.** truthfully (*truly* an accurate measure) **3.** indeed (*Truly,* the hours are going faster than usual.)

trum·pet (trəm′ pət) *n.* **1.** a metal wind instrument made of a single looped tube with a flare at the end **2.** something similar to the sound of a trumpet such as the cry of an elephant —*vb.* to blow a trumpet

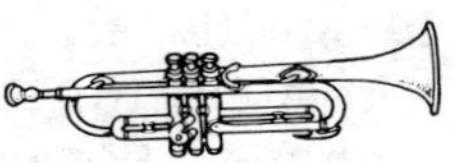
Trumpet

trunk (trəngk) *n.* **1.** the main stem of a tree **2.** the body of a person or animal except for the head, arms, and legs **3.** a chest for storing or carrying clothes **4.** a storage area in the rear of an automobile **5.** the long nose of an elephant

trust (trəst) *n.* **1.** confidence (a position of *trust*) **2.** a financial arrangement in which property is held by one person for the benefit of another **3.** something cared for in the interest of another (left her home in their *trust* while traveling)

truth (trüth) *n., pl.* **truths** (trüt͟hz) **1.** a fact or principle accepted as true **2.** honesty or correctness

try (trī) *vb.* **tried** (trīd); **try·ing** **1.** to make an effort (*try* to swim well) **2.** to test or experiment (*Try* honey in the tea.) **3.** to examine before a court (*try* the prisoner)

tub (təb) *n.* **1.** bathtub (got into the *tub*) **2.** a deep sink or washtub **3.** a slow boat (an old *tub*) —*vb.* **tubbed**; **tub·bing** to wash or bathe in a tub

tube (tüb) *n.* **1.** a long, hollow cylinder (bronchial *tubes*, test *tube*) **2.** a flexible container with a narrow opening from which a paste may be squeezed (toothpaste *tube*)

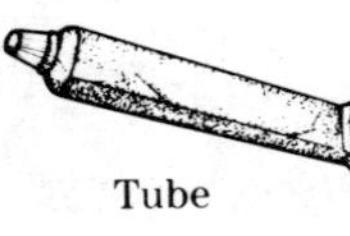
Tube

tuck (tək) *vb.* **1.** to lap or sew into a fold **2.** to push in the loose ends snugly (*tuck* in the sheets) —*n.* a fold sewed into a garment

tug (təg) *vb.* **tugged**; **tug·ging** **1.** to use effort to pull or drag **2.** to tow by means of a tugboat —*n.* **1.** an act of tugging or pulling **2.** a struggle between two teams to pull a rope (*tug*-of-war) **3.** a tugboat

tu·lip (tü′ ləp) *n.* a spring-flowering bulb related to the lily that produces cup-shaped flowers of many colors

Tulip

tum·ble (təm′ bəl) *vb.* **tum·bled**; **tum·bling** **1.** to fall headlong (*tumble* down the stairs) **2.** to perform acrobatic feats of rolling feet over head —*n.* an act of tumbling

tu·na (tü′ nə) *n.* a large ocean fish related to the mackerel valued for food, especially the canned product, and for sport

tun·dra (tən′ drə) *n.* a plain of the far north including northern Siberia where only moss and lichens grow

tune (tün) *n.* **1.** a melody (a pretty *tune*) **2.** the state of having good pitch (being in *tune*) **3.** harmony (in *tune* with his friends) —*vb.* **tuned**; **tun·ing** **1.** to adjust the pitch **2.** to bring into harmony **3.** to adjust so as to improve performance

tun·nel (tən′ l) *n.* a passage under the earth such as through a hill or under a river —*vb.* **tun·neled**; **tun·nel·ing** to form a tunnel

tur·bine (tər′ bən) *n.* a machine with a central shaft turned by the pressure of a liquid on the blades of the drive wheel

turf (tərf) *n.* the top few inches of soil bound together by plant roots into a thick mat

tur·key (tər′ kē) *n., pl.* **tur·keys** a large, domesticated American game bird raised for food

Turkey

turn (tərn) *vb.* **1.** to go around, or rotate, as a wheel **2.** to seem to be turning as in dizziness **3.** to flip over (*turn* the potato cakes) **4.** to upset (The sweetness of the pie *turn*ed my stomach.) **5.** to change to an opposite direction (*turn* around) —*n.* **1.** one complete trip around a center point **2.** a change in direction, conditions, or trend (a *turn* for the better) **3.** a place for turning around or changing direction (Take the next *turn*.)

tur·nip (tər′ nəp) *n.* the rounded yellow or white root of a plant related to the cabbage and used as a vegetable

tur·tle (tərt′ l) *n.* a reptile with bony toothless jaws and a soft body encased in a horny shell, having two parts, the upper being the *carapace* and the lower, the *plastron*

Turtle

tusk (təsk) *n.* a long, pointed tooth extending below the mouth from either side of the jaw, such as on the elephant or walrus, used in digging and fighting

twice (twīs) *adv.* two times (I read the book *twice*.)

twig (twig) *n.* a small branch

twi·light (twī′ līt′) *n.* the light in the sky just before sunrise and just after sunset that varies between full light and full darkness

twin (twin) *adj.* **1.** consisting of a pair (*twin* engine airplane) **2.** being a double birth (*twin* girls) —*n.* **1.** either of two offspring at a birth **2.** one of two related or similar things (*twin* lamps)

twin·kle (twing′ kəl) *vb.* **twin·kled**; **twin·kling** to gleam with a flickering light (Stars seem to *twinkle*.)

twirl (twərl) *vb.* **1.** to revolve rapidly **2.** to twist —*n.* a quick circular motion

twist (twist) *vb.* **1.** to turn two or more strands one around the other **2.** to turn too far so as to sprain (to *twist* an ankle) **3.** to turn away from the intended meaning (*twist*ing one's words) —*n.* **1.** a thread made by twisting fibers **2.** an act of twisting **3.** an unexpected turn

type (tīp) *n.* **1.** a description of a person or thing that represents a group (a religious *type* of person) **2.** a raised metal figure that produces a letter or symbol when inked and pressed against paper (the *type* on a typewriter) —*vb.* **typed**; **typ·ing** **1.** to typify or represent (He is *typed* as aggressive and domineering.) **2.** to typewrite (*type* a letter)

type·writ·er (tīp′ rīt′ ər) *n.* a machine for writing letters or characters like those in print

typ·i·cal (tip′ i kəl) *adj.* **1.** like others of its type or kind (a *typical* "A" student) **2.** having the one or more characteristics that describes a group (*typical* of the plastic film on the market today)

U

ug·ly (əg′ lē) *adj.* **ug·li·er; ug·li·est** **1.** unpleasant to the senses (an *ugly* sight; an *ugly* smell) **2.** suggesting trouble (an *ugly* mood)

ul·ti·mate (əl′ tə mət) *adj.* **1.** the last in a progression through time or space (touring Southeast Asia, with our *ultimate* stop in Peking, China) **2.** fundamental (our *ultimate* purpose in life)

ul·tra·vi·o·let (əl′ trə vī′ ə lət) *adj.* relating to ultraviolet light which is composed of waves beyond the violet end of the spectrum, found in sunlight and filtered by the ozone layer in the upper air

um·brel·la (əm′ brel′ ə) *n.* a device for protection against rain or sun, composed of material stretched over a metal frame which can be folded to a closed position when not in use

Umbrella

um·pire (əm′ pīr′) *n.* a sports official who rules on plays and decides disputes

un·a·ble (ən′ ā′ bəl) *adj.* not able

un·a·ware (ən′ ə waər′) *adv.* unawares —*adj.* not aware, not conscious (*unaware* of the accident)

un·a·wares (ən′ ə waərz′) *adv.* without warning or by surprise (caught *unawares* by the storm)

un·be·liev·a·ble (ən′ bə lē′ və bəl) *adj.* too unlikely to believe

un·bro·ken (ən′ brō′ kən) *adj.* **1.** whole (The vase fell, but remained *unbroken.*) **2.** not tamed (wild, *unbroken* horse) **3.** continuous (silence, *unbroken* even by the sound of a falling leaf)

un·cer·tain (ən′ sərt′ n) *adj.* **1.** not fixed (with an *uncertain* number of them in each sack) **2.** not dependable (*uncertain* reaction to foreign foods)

un·cle (əng′ kəl) *n.* the brother of one's mother or father, or the husband of one's aunt

un·com·mon (ən′ käm′ ən) *adj.* **1.** rare (rock that is *uncommon* in this region) **2.** outstanding (a musician with *uncommon* talent on the piano)

un·cov·er (ən′ kəv′ ər) *vb.* **1.** to find or make known (*uncover* the truth) **2.** to remove a cover (*uncover* the piece of equipment)

un·der (ən′ dər) *adv.* **1.** below or beneath something (then the frog went *under*) **2.** below a fixed level or quantity (Get one if they are five dollars or *under.*) —*prep.* **1.** in a position below or beneath something that is higher (*under* the sea, *under* his coat) **2.** subject to (worked *under* the director) **3.** conforming with (*under* military regulations) **4.** subject to the effect of (*under* investigation) —*adj.* placed below or beneath (the *under* portion of the box of fruit)

un·der·brush (ən′ dər brəsh′) *n.* small shrubs and plants growing among trees

un·der·go (ən′ dər gō′) *vb.* **un·der·went** (-went′); **un·der·gone** (-gȯn′); **un·der·go·ing** (-gō′ ing) to submit to (*undergo* questioning)

un·der·ground (ən′ dər graủnd′) *adv.* **1.** below the surface of the earth **2.** secretly (published the newsletter *underground*) —*adj.* **1.** below the surface of the earth (*underground* river) **2.** acting in secret (*underground* movement of supplies) —*n.* **1.** a space under the surface **2.** a secret political movement

un·der·line (ən′ dər līn′) *vb.* **un·der·lined**; **un·der·lin·ing** **1.** to draw a line beneath **2.** to emphasize (*underline* the importance of being here on time)

un·der·neath (ən′ dər nēth′) *prep.* directly under (Look *underneath* the newspaper.) —*adv.* beneath (Look *underneath.*)

un·der·side (ən′ dər sīd′) *n.* the side lying underneath

un·der·stand (ən′ dər stand′) *vb.* **un·der·stood** (-stu̇d′); **un·der·stand·ing** **1.** to get the meaning or significance of (*understand* the directions) **2.** to feel sympathy (*understand* his grief)

un·eas·y (ən′ ē′ zē) *adj.* **un·eas·i·er**; **un·eas·i·est** **1.** awkward (*uneasy* on the telephone) **2.** restless (spent an *uneasy* night in the hospital)

un·e·qual (ən′ ē′ kwəl) *adj.* not the same in size, strength, or other characteristic (an *unequal* match)

un·e·ven (ən′ ē′ vən) *adj.* **1.** odd, or not divisible by 2 (*uneven* number) **2.** not smooth or uniform (on an *uneven* surface)

un·fair (ən′ faər′) *adj.* dishonest, tricky, or unjust (an *unfair* decision)

u·ni·form (yü′ nə fȯrm′) *adj.* not changing, always the same (*uniform* heat and pressure) —*vb.* to provide with a uniform —*n.* a special type of clothing worn by a particular group (a band *uniform*; a soldier's *uniform*)

u·ni·fy (yü′ nə fī′) *vb.* **u·ni·fied**; **u·ni·fy·ing** to make into a single group or unit (The celebration *unified* the town.)

u·nion (yü′ nyən) *n.* **1.** an act of combining parts or individuals into one unit **2.** a group of workers organized to improve their working conditions (a labor *union*)

u·nique (yu̇ nēk′) *adj.* **1.** existing as the only one of its kind (The kayak is *unique* among canoes.) **2.** limited to a region or situation (The camel is *unique* to the desert.)

u·nit (yü′ nət) *n.* **1.** a single person or thing forming part of the group or whole (The "yard" is the basic *unit* of measurement for fabric.) **2.** a part of a school course (The three *units* are: Background, Workers and Their Work, and Arts and Culture.)

u·nite (yu̇ nīt′) *vb.* **u·nit·ed**; **u·nit·ing** **1.** to link together into a single group or whole **2.** to bring together by treaty or legal agreement (to *unite* as allies)

u·ni·ty (yü′ nət ē) *n., pl.* **u·ni·ties** **1.** the state of being together as one (sharing a *unity* of purpose) **2.** peace and harmony

u·ni·ver·sal (yü′ nə vər′ səl) *adj.* **1.** pertaining to all without exception (*universal* truth) **2.** happening everywhere (food and shelter being *universal* needs)

u·ni·verse (yü′ nə vərs′) *n.* the earth, all the heavenly bodies, and all creatures

u·ni·ver·si·ty (yü′ nə vər′ sət ē) *n., pl.* **u·ni·ver·si·ties** an institution of higher learning that grants masters and doctoral degrees in special fields, as well as the usual undergraduate degrees, including the arts and sciences

un·less (ən les′) *conj.* **1.** except when **2.** except under the condition that (Nothing will help *unless* she tries.)

un·like (ən′ līk′) *prep.* **1.** different from (a dog *unlike* my dog) **2.** unusual for (It is *unlike* a good student to drop out of school.) —*adj.* different or unequal (*unlike* examples)

un·load (ən′ lōd′) *vb.* to remove or get rid of (*unload*ed boxes from the truck)

un·lock (ən′ läk′) *vb.* to open by releasing a lock (*unlock* the old chest)

un·nec·es·sar·y (ən′ nes′ ə ser′ ē) *adj.* not needed

un·seen (ən′ sēn′) *adj.* **1.** not seen **2.** invisible

un·tie (ən′ tī′) *vb.* **un·tied**; **un·ty·ing** **1.** to remove the tie **2.** to set free from something that fastens

un·til (ən til′) *prep.* **1.** up to (*until* nine o'clock) —*conj.* **1.** to the time when (*until* I get home) **2.** to the point that (*until* he fell)

un·to (ən′ tə, -tü) *prep.* to (I give it *unto* you.)

un·u·su·al (ən′ yü′ zhə wəl) *adj.* not usual; odd (An *unusual* light flashed across the sky.)

up (əp) *adv.* **1.** to a higher position (went *up*) **2.** to or with greater force (start *up*) **3.** so as to arrive (walked *up* the path) —*adj.* **1.** being higher than before (they are *up* now) **2.** equal (felt *up* to the job) **3.** happening (What's *up*?) —*prep.* **1.** to or toward a higher place (*up* the hill) **2.** to or toward a farther place (*up* the tracks) —*n.* a good period (had his *ups* and downs)

up·hill (əp hil′) *adv.* **1.** upward on an incline (traveled *uphill*) **2.** against difficulties (worked *uphill* all the way) —*adj.* **1.** going up (an *uphill* route) **2.** difficult (an *uphill* fight)

up·on (ə pȯn′ , -pän) *prep.* on

up·per (əp′ ər) *adj.* **1.** higher in place (*upper* floor of the house) **2.** superior in rank (the *upper* classes in the school)

up·right (əp′ rīt′) *adj.* **1.** straight up (an *upright* posture) **2.** honest, honorable (an *upright* woman)

up·roar (əp′ rōr′) *n.* a loud disturbance

up·set (əp′ set′, əp′ set′) *adj.* disturbed, not settled (an *upset* stomach from eating too much) —*vb.* **up·set**; **up·set·ting** **1.** to tip over **2.** to disturb —*n.* a state of being upset

up·side (əp′ sīd′) *n.* the upper or top side (tipped *upside* down)

up·stairs (əp′ staərz′) *adv.* on or to a higher floor (went *upstairs*) —*adj.* relating to an upper floor (the *upstairs* apartment) —*n.* the floors in a building above the ground floor (painted the *upstairs*)

up·ward (əp′ wərd) or **up·wards** (-wərdz) *adv.* toward a higher place or better condition (moved *upward* in his profession)

u·ra·ni·um (yu̇ rā′ nē əm) *n.* a radioactive element, some forms of which are used in atomic bombs and nuclear reactors

ur·ban (ər′ bən) *adj.* relating to a city (*urban* problems)

urge (ərj) *vb.* **urged**; **urg·ing** **1.** to encourage an action (*urge* him to run faster) **2.** to persuade (*urge* them to vote on the bond issue)

ur·gent (ər′ jənt) *adj.* pressing, needing attention right away (an *urgent* need)

us (əs) *pron.* objective case of WE

us·age (yü′ sij) *n.* **1.** the common way of using or treating something **2.** the way something is actually used (common *usage*)

use (yüs) *n.* **1.** the act or way of using (the *use* of a hammer) **2.** need or necessity (no *use* for that)

use (yüz) *vb.* **used**; **us·ing** **1.** to put into service or employ (to *use* Brand X) **2.** to practice (*use* a gentle approach) **3.** to treat (*Use* the china dishes carefully.)

used (yüzd) *adj.* second hand (*used* furniture)

use·ful (yüs fəl) *adj.* having some use (*useful* lumber)

use·less (yüs′ ləs) *adj.* having no use (Junk is *useless.*)

u·su·al (yü′ zhə wəl) *adj.* **1.** ordinary **2.** as in common use (at the *usual* time and place)

u·ten·sil (yü ten′ səl) *n.* **1.** useful articles such as kitchen tools and baking pans (kitchen *utensil*) **2.** any useful tools or vessels

ut·most (ət′ mōst′) *adj.* of the greatest, highest, farthest, or most extreme point, degree, or amount (handled the problem with *utmost* care) —*n.* the greatest degree or extent (I have given my *utmost* to the project.)

ut·ter (ət′ ər) *adj.* absolute and entire (*utter* enemies) —*vb.* **1.** to express in speech (to *utter* a calm explanation) **2.** to send forth a sound (*utter*ed a terrified cry)

V

va·cant (vā′ kənt) *adj.* **1.** empty (a *vacant* house) **2.** lacking thought (a *vacant* look in his eyes)

va·ca·tion (vā kā′ shən) *n.* **1.** a period for rest and/or recreation **2.** a time away from usual duties

vac·cine (vak sēn′) *n.* killed or weakened virus or bacteria used to prevent disease (a shot of flu *vaccine*)

vac·u·um (vak′ yə wəm) *n., pl.* **vac·u·ums** or **vac·u·a** (-yə wə) a completely empty space; a void —*adj.* containing or using a vacuum or partial vacuum (a *vacuum* bottle of hot soup) —*vb.* to use a vacuum cleaner (I'll *vacuum* the rug.)

vague (vāg) *adj.* **1.** not clear (a *vague* outline in the fog) **2.** not easily understood (a *vague* idea)

vain (vān) *adj.* **1.** without worth or value (a *vain* effort to hold back the flood) **2.** proud of one's abilities or looks (a *vain* person)

val·ley (val′ ē) *n., pl.* **val·leys** lowland between hills or mountains (a river that ran through the *valley*)

val·u·a·ble (val′ yə wə bəl) *adj.* **1.** costly in time or money (a *valuable* work of art) **2.** useful (not expensive, but *valuable* to me) —*n.* something that cost a lot of money, such as a diamond (my *valuables* were stolen)

val·ue (val′ yü) *n.* the worth or merit of an article or an idea (an idea of little *value*) —*vb.* **val·ued**; **val·u·ing** **1.** to hold dear (*valued* our friendship) **2.** to put a price on (*valued* the property at $100,000)

valve (valv) *n.* **1.** a device in a pipe or other structure to control the flow of liquid (a problem in a *valve* in her heart) **2.** one of the hinged shells of a bivalve, such as a clam

van (van) *n.* a usually closed wagon or truck for moving people, animals, or goods (a moving *van*)

vane (vān) *n.* a rotating device moved by the wind to show which way the wind is blowing (a weather *vane*)

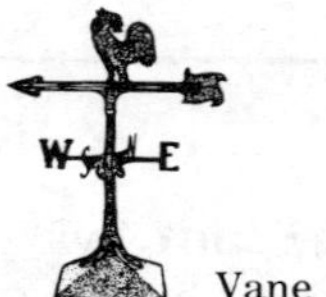

Vane

van·ish (van′ ish) *vb.* to disappear

va·por (vā′ pər) *n.* **1.** fine particles of moisture or smoke such as fog or smog clouding the air **2.** a substance in the form of a gas mixed into the air

var·i·a·ble (ver′ ē ə bəl) *adj.* changeable (The weather is *variable.*) —*n.* something that is changeable (The time students give to their work and the grades they get are both *variables.*)

var·i·a·tion (ver′ ē ā′ shən) *n.* **1.** a change (a *variation* in the schedule) **2.** something that is different from what is typical (a strange *variation* in color)

va·ri·e·ty (və rī′ ət ē) *n., pl.* **va·ri·e·ties** **1.** the state of being different **2.** a collection of unlike things (a large *variety* of gloves)

var·i·ous (ver′ ē əs) *adj.* **1.** being different from one another (*various* kinds of entertainers) **2.** uncertain or indefinite (*various* numbers of these postcards in the collection)

var·y (veər′ ē) *vb.* **var·ied**; **var·y·ing** **1.** to change from the typical or usual **2.** to make different from one another

Vase

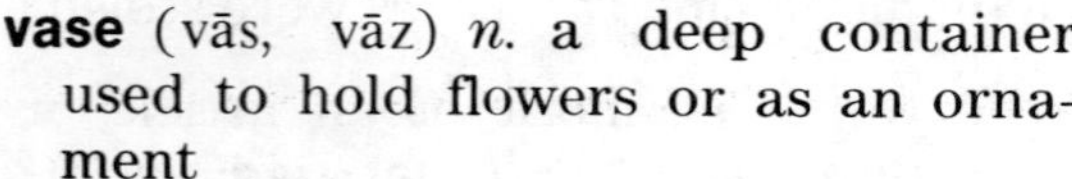

vase (vās, vāz) *n.* a deep container used to hold flowers or as an ornament

vast (vast) *adj.* very large in amount or degree (Alaska is a *vast* state.)

vault (vȯlt) *n.* **1.** an area with an arched roof **2.** a thick-walled room with a heavy door for safekeeping (bank *vault*) **3.** a leap —*vb.* **1.** to cover with a vault **2.** to leap high using the hands or a pole (pole *vault*)

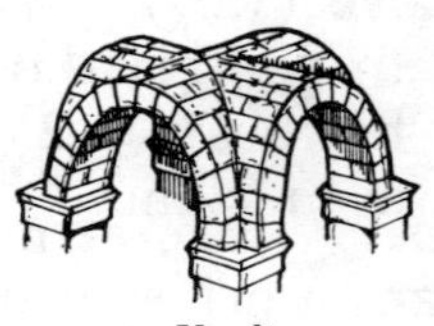
Vault

veg·e·ta·ble (vej′ ət ə bəl) *adj.* relating to plants raised for food (*vegetable* garden) —*n.* a plant raised to be eaten as part of meal

veg·e·ta·tion (vej′ ə tā′ shən) *n.* plant life in general (the *vegetation* on the hillside)

ve·hi·cle (vē′ ik′ əl) *n.* **1.** something that carries people or goods from one place to another (a gasoline-powered *vehicle*) **2.** a means of sending a message (the telephone as a *vehicle* for personal contact)

vein (vān) *n.* **1.** a layer of mineral matter in rock **2.** a blood vessel that carries blood back to the heart **3.** a streak of something different, such as a color or a mood

ve·loc·i·ty (və läs′ ət ē) *n.*, *pl.* **ve·loc·i·ties** speed (the *velocity* of a spaceship)

vel·vet (vel′ vət) *n.* a fabric with a short, thick, upright pile made from fibers such as cotton, rayon, or nylon, and used for decorative clothing or objects such as pillow covers

ven·geance (ven′ jəns) *n.* **1.** a forceful or violent act against a person in return for trouble, injury, or annoyance **2.** force or violence (with a *vengeance*)

ven·i·son (ven′ ə sən, -zən) *n.* the meat of a deer used as food

ven·ture (ven′ chər) *vb.* **ven·tured**; **ven·tur·ing** **1.** to face a risk or danger (*ventured* to save the men trapped in the mine) **2.** to dare to say at the risk of opposition or criticism (*ventured* a remark that was critical of some of the members)

verb (vərb) *n.* a word that expresses an action, such as *ran* (Tom *ran* home.) or state of being such as *are* (Bob and Ann *are* my friends.)

ver·bal (vər′ bəl) *adj.* **1.** oral rather than written (a *verbal* agreement) **2.** relating to a verb (a *verbal* noun)

verse (vərs) *n.* **1.** one metrical line of poetry **2.** one short division of a chapter in the Bible **3.** one part of a song, written usually as a solo, to be followed by a chorus that is repeated after each verse

ver·sion (vər′ zhən) *n.* a form or variation of an original as a translation (a *version* of the Bible), a shortened form (condensed *version*), or an individual point of view (his *version* of the robbery)

ver·ti·cal (vərt′ i kəl) *adj.* straight up (the *vertical* side of the triangle) —*n.* something that is vertical

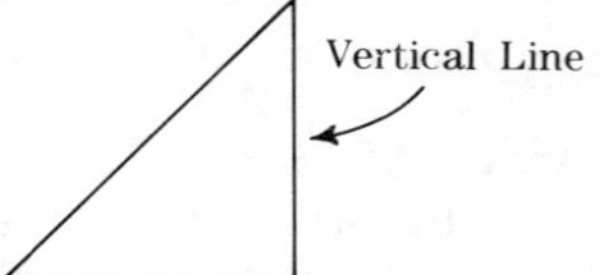

ver·y (ver′ ē) *adj.* **1.** exact, complete, or utter (the *very* bottom of the well) **2.** same (this *very* dog that was so good yesterday) —*adv.* extremely (a *very* fine job)

ves·sel (ves′ əl) *n.* **1.** a hollow container such as a cup or a saucepan **2.** a vehicle for traveling on water that is larger than a rowboat, such as a motorboat or ship **3.** a tube containing fluid (a blood *vessel*)

vest (vest) *n.* a sleeveless garment usually worn beneath a coat —*vb.* **1.** to put under the control of (That town is *vest*ed in its town meeting.) **2.** to be fixed or established by law (*vest*ed in the company's retirement plan)

vi·brate (vī′ brāt′) *vb.* **vi·brat·ed**; **vi·brat·ing** **1.** to move back and forth in a steady rhythm **2.** to quiver

vice (vīs) *n.* **1.** a fault or bad habit (the *vice* of gambling) **2.** a device with jaws for holding objects firmly

vi·cin·i·ty (və sin′ ət ē) *n.*, *pl.* **vi·cin·i·ties** the surrounding area or neighborhood

vi·cious (vish′ əs) *adj.* wicked or savage (a *vicious* temper; a *vicious* dog)

vic·tim (vik′ təm) *n.* **1.** a person who is killed or injured (*victim* of the crime) **2.** a person who is cheated or fooled (a *victim* of fraud)

vic·to·ry (vik′ tə rē) *n., pl.* **vic·to·ries** **1.** a triumph or conquest (to achieve a *victory* in the contest) **2.** the defeat of an opponent

view (vyü) *n.* **1.** the act of seeing, or that which is seen (a *view* of the countryside) **2.** an opinion or perception (his *view* of the situation) —*vb.* **1.** to look at (time to *view* the evidence) **2.** to form an opinion

vig·or (vig′ ər) *n.* physical or mental strength or energy (lacking in *vigor* since his illness)

vil·lage (vil′ ij) *n.* a settlement smaller than a town

vil·lain (vil′ ən) *n.* **1.** a wicked person **2.** the character in a play or story who opposes the hero **3.** often used humorously to mean a playful pest (That child is a *villain*!)

vine (vīn) *n.* a plant with a long stalk requiring support, often sending out tendrils to attach itself to a nearby object

vin·e·gar (vin′ i gər) *n.* a sour liquid used to flavor or preserve foods and made from fermenting cider or wine

vine·yard (vin′ yərd) *n.* a space used for growing grapevines

vi·o·lence (vī′ ə ləns) *n.* the use of great force to do harm to a person or thing (the *violence* of the attack)

vi·o·lent (vī′ ə lənt) *adj.* furious or intense (*violent* acts, *violent* hatred)

vi·o·let (vī′ ə lət) *n.* **1.** a wild, low-growing, flowering plant with white, blue, or purple flowers, also found cultivated in gardens **2.** the color at the end of the spectrum opposite red

Violet

vi·o·lin (vī′ ə lin′) *n.* a musical instrument with four strings played with a bow

Violin

vir·tue (vər′ chü) *n.* **1.** moral strength **2.** an excellent quality (the *virtue* of being honest)

vi·rus (vī′ rəs) *n.* **1.** something that infects people, animals, or plants that is too small to be seen by an ordinary microscope **2.** a disease caused by a virus

vis·i·ble (viz′ ə bəl) *adj.* **1.** open to view (no *visible* means of escape) **2.** being apparent

vi·sion (vizh′ ən) *n.* **1.** the sense of sight (good *vision*) **2.** a mental picture of how a plan will work out **3.** something seen in a dream or in a state of rapture

vis·it (viz′ ət) *vb.* the act of going to see someone for a short time, such as an hour or a few days —*n.* a brief stay, as a guest or as a professional (a doctor's *visit*)

vis·i·tor (viz′ ət ər) *n.* one who visits

vi·su·al (vizh′ ə wəl) *adj.* relating to vision (a *visual* signal)

vi·tal (vī′ tl) *adj.* **1.** relating to life (*vital* signs; *vital* organs) **2.** very important (*vital* necessity) **3.** full of life (a *vital* personality)

vi·tal·i·ty (vī tal′ ət ē) *n.*, *pl.* **vi·tal·i·ties** physical or mental strength or energy (the *vitality* of our delegates)

vi·ta·min (vīt′ ə mən) *n.* one of the organic substances found in natural foods, small quantities of which are essential to growth and body function

viv·id (viv′ əd) *adj.* **1.** strong, intense (a *vivid* color) **2.** producing clear images in the mind (a *vivid* imagination)

vo·cab·u·lar·y (vō kab′ yə ler′ ē) *n.*, *pl.* **vo·cab·u·lar·ies** a list of words, usually in alphabetical order with definitions, related to a topic, subject, or written selection (a science *vocabulary*)

vo·cal (vō′ kəl) *adj.* **1.** relating to the voice (*vocal* cords) **2.** composed to be sung (a *vocal* selection) **3.** using speech in great amounts to express a point of view (a *vocal* supporter of the bill in the legislature)

voice (vòis) *n.* **1.** sounds produced by the vocal cords (to hear his *voice*) **2.** the right to express an opinion (to have a *voice* in the decision) —*vb.* **voiced**; **voic·ing** to utter

void (vòid) *adj.* **1.** empty or vacant (a *void* space) **2.** useless (a *void* document) —*n.* **1.** an empty space **2.** an empty feeling (a death that left a *void* in her life) **3.** a lack of something (Her bridge hand was *void* of clubs.) —*vb.* **1.** to make empty (*void*ed the tank of liquid) **2.** to make useless (*void*ed the check)

vol·ca·no (väl kā′ nō) *n., pl.* **vol·ca·noes** or **vol·ca·nos** **1.** an opening in the earth's crust through which hot lava, steam, and ashes are pushed up from beneath forming a mountain of this material around the opening **2.** a mountain with a cup-shaped crater at the top that erupts occasionally while it is active

vol·ume (väl′ yəm) *n.* **1.** a book **2.** the space inside a three-dimensional figure measured in cubic units

vol·un·teer (väl′ ən tiər′) *n.* **1.** a person who enters into a military or naval service by choice **2.** a person who provides a free service (a literacy *volunteer*) —*adj.* relating to volunteers (a *volunteer* tutor) —*vb.* to choose to offer (*volunteer*ed as a campaign worker)

vote (vōt) *n.* **1.** the act or process of voting **2.** the right to vote **3.** the outcome of the balloting —*vb.* **vot·ed**; **vot·ing** **1.** to decide by voting **2.** to elect (*voted* her into office)

vow·el (vaù′ əl) *n.* an open speech sound made by the sounds of *a*, *e*, *i*, *o*, and *u*

voy·age (vòi′ ij) *n.* a journey by water, especially a long one —*vb.* to take a long trip

vul·ture (vəl′ chər) *n.* a large bird that eats animals found dead

W

wade (wād) *vb.* **wad·ed**; **wad·ing** **1.** to walk through water (*wade* in shallow water) **2.** to go through something with difficulty or boredom (*wade* through the dull parts of the book)

wag (wag) *vb.* **wagged**; **wag·ging** to move from side to side (Rover, *wagging* his tail) —*n.* **1.** a wagging motion **2.** a person who is full of jokes or tricks

wage (wāj) *vb.* **waged**; **wag·ing** to carry on or engage in (*wage* war) —*n.* the money paid to a worker for the work done (to earn a good *wage*)

wag·on (wag′ ən) *n.* a four-wheeled vehicle used for carrying goods

wail (wāl) *vb.* **1.** to make a sad cry (The child *wail*ed.) **2.** to make a moaning sound (Through the night the wind *wail*ed around the house.) —*n.* a sorrowful cry

waist (wāst) *n.* the narrow part of a body between the chest and the hips (wearing a belt at the *waist*)

wait (wāt) *vb.* **1.** to stay in a place expecting something to happen (*Wait* for the show to start.) **2.** to serve food at a meal (*wait*ed on table at the coffee shop) —*n.* an act of waiting (The *wait* was long and tiring.)

wait·er (wāt′ ər) *n.* a man who waits on tables at an eating place

wait·ress (wā′ trəs) *n.* a girl or woman who waits on tables

wake (wāk) *vb.* **waked** or **woke** (wōk); **waked** or **wo·ken** (wō′ kən); **wak·ing** to be or become awake (*Wake* me at seven o'clock.) —*n.* **1.** a watch or visiting period held over a dead body before a burial **2.** a trail left by a boat moving through the water

walk (wȯk) *vb.* **1.** to move along on foot at a natural gait **2.** in baseball, to move to first base on balls —*n.* **1.** a short trip on foot **2.** a path set aside for walking **3.** a base on balls

wall (wȯl) *n.* **1.** a vertical barrier intended to enclose a space (a stone *wall*) **2.** one of the four vertical sides of a room or building (the north *wall* of the room) —*vb.* to build a wall around

wal·nut (wȯl′ nət) *n.* a tree valued for its edible nuts and its wood which is used mainly for furniture

wal·rus (wȯl′ rəs) *n.* a large sea mammal related to the seal and valued for its hide, the ivory tusks of the males, and for its oil

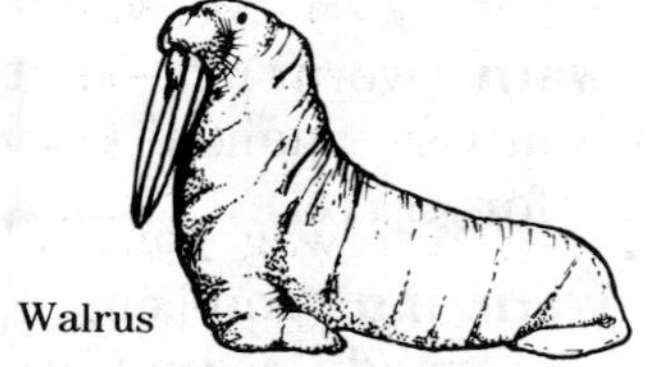
Walrus

waltz (wȯlts) *n.* **1.** music having three beats to a measure **2.** a dance done in waltz time —*vb.* to dance a waltz

wan·der (wän′ dər) *vb.* **1.** to move about without aim or purpose **2.** to move off a subject and talk or write about other things (*wander* from the subject)

want (wȯnt) *vb.* to desire or feel a need for (*want* a warm jacket for winter) —*n.* **1.** a shortage (to have many *wants*) **2.** great poverty (people in *want*) **3.** a wish (my one *want* is)

war (wȯr) *n.* **1.** a hostile contest (a *war* of words) **2.** armed conflict between opposing sides —*vb.* **warred**; **war·ring** to fight a war

ward (wȯrd) *n.* **1.** a person who is protected (a *ward* of the state) **2.** a voting district **3.** a section of a hospital —*vb.* **1.** to protect or keep watch over **2.** to turn away or prevent from happening (to *ward* off danger)

ware (waər) *n.* manufactured articles such as hardware, software, or earthenware (Display the *wares* for sale.)

ware·house (waər′ haủs′) *n.* a building for storing wares (the goods in the *warehouse*)

war·fare (wȯr′ faər′) *n.* a state of armed conflict

warm (wȯrm) *adj.* **1.** having a moderate level of heat (*warm* soup) **2.** giving off heat (*warm* stove) **3.** having a feeling of warmth (a *warm* greeting) —*vb.* **1.** to make warm (*warm* the pasta sauce) **2.** to give a warm feeling (*warm*ed the audience with a good story)

warmth (wȯrmth) *n.* **1.** moderate heat **2.** a comfortable and cordial attitude or feeling

warn (wȯrn) *vb.* **1.** to notify of possible danger **2.** to advise against (*warn*ed that the snow was too deep for travel)

warn·ing (wȯr′ ning) *n.* something that warns in advance (tornado *warning*)

war·rior (wȯr′ yər, wȯr′ ē ər) *n.* soldier

war·y (waər′ ē) *adj.* **war·i·er; war·i·est** careful at a time of danger

wash (wȯsh, wäsh) *vb.* to clean with water, often with soap or detergent added —*n.* clothing and other things to be washed

wasp (wäsp) *n.* an insect with wings, related to the bees and ants, often having yellow and black markings, the females and workers of which can give a painful sting

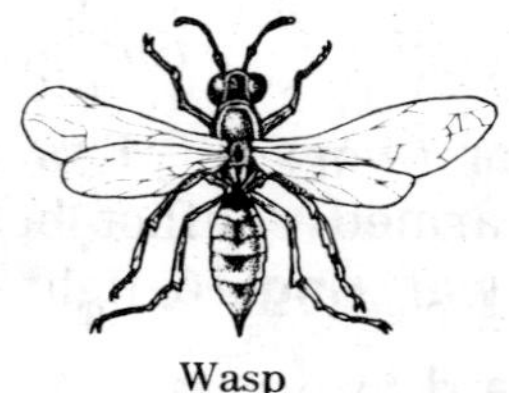
Wasp

waste (wāst) *n.* **1.** material or land that is not productive **2.** material that is useless or discarded —*vb.* **wast·ed; wast·ing** **1.** to ruin, destroy, or employ uselessly **2.** to fail to get full value from (to *waste* the apples by allowing them to rot) —*adj.* barren, useless (a *waste*land region, *waste* paper)

watch (wäch) *vb.* **1.** to stand guard **2.** to be on the lookout (*watch* for trouble) **3.** to tend (*watch* for the kettle to boil) —*n.* **1.** a small clock to be worn or carried **2.** a person on guard duty **3.** the time period a person must stand on guard (a four-hour *watch*)

wa·ter (wȯt′ ər, wät′-) *n.* the liquid that is evaporated to form clouds, then comes down as rain or snow to fill rivers, lakes, and seas —*vb.* to supply with water

wa·ter·fall (wȯt′ ər fȯl′, wät′-) *n.* a fall of water of a river or stream as from a cliff (Niagara Falls, a famous *waterfall*)

wa·ter·mel·on (wȯt′ ər mel′ ən, wät′-) *n.* a large edible fruit with a hard green rind and red juicy pulp with dark seeds

wave (wāv) *vb.* **waved**; **wav·ing** **1.** to float, as on a wave **2.** to move a hand back and forth as a greeting or signal (*wave* at them) —*n.* **1.** a swell of water moving toward the shore **2.** a signal **3.** a rise or surge (a *wave* of concern about our defenses)

wav·y (wā′ vē) *adj.* **wav·i·er**; **wav·i·est** having waves (*wavy* hair)

wax (waks) *n.* **1.** a substance made by bees to form a honeycomb; beeswax **2.** other waxy substances such as paraffin, made from crude petroleum and used as a waterproofing and preserving material; and carnauba, taken from the young leaves of the Brazilian wax palm and used as a polish for cars and furniture

way (wā) *n.* **1.** a path or road **2.** route or direction to follow (the *way* to the park) **3.** a method or means (an easy *way*) **4.** habit or attitude (your usual *way*) **5.** condition (in a better *way* today) —*adv.* to a great degree (*way* too large)

we (wē) *pron.* used by the person speaking to indicate himself and one or more other people (*We* came yesterday.)

weak (wēk) *adj.* **1.** lacking in strength (*weak* legs) **2.** lacking in force (a *weak* argument) **3.** lacking in some ingredients (*weak*, watery soup) **4.** lacking in mental or moral strength (*weak* character)

weak·ness (wēk′ nəs) *n.* **1.** defect (*weakness* in the material) **2.** a fault (*weakness* of character)

wealth (welth) *n.* **1.** property, money, and valuable possessions such as bonds or jewels (had great *wealth*) **2.** a large supply (a *wealth* of knowledge and ideas)

weap·on (wep′ ən) *n.* an instrument for hurting someone such as a gun or club (The police found a *weapon* on him.)

wear (waər) *vb.* **wore** (wōr); **worn** (wōrn); **wear·ing** **1.** to use as clothing (*wear* his new shirt) **2.** to put on an expression (*wear* a frown) **3.** to make thinner (*wear* away) **4.** to last (*wears* well) —*n.* the act of wearing (after all the *wear* and tear)

wea·ry (wiər′ ē) *adj.* **wea·ri·er**; **wea·ri·est** tired, worn out (*weary* after a long day of travel)

weath·er (weth′ ər) *n.* The state of the air: hot or cold, wet or dry, calm or stormy, clear or cloudy

weave (wēv) *vb.* **wove** (wōv); **wo·ven** (wō′ vən) to make fabric on a loom by threading the crosswise threads according to a pattern —*n.* a method or pattern of working the threads into cloth

web (web) *n.* **1.** a pattern of threads or fibers as in a cobweb **2.** an intricate pattern **3.** a membrane connecting the toes as in a duck —*vb.* **webbed**; **web·bing** to make or connect with a web

wed·ding (wed′ ing) *n.* a marriage ceremony

wedge (wej) *n.* **1.** a long, thin triangle of metal used to split logs **2.** something shaped like a wedge (a *wedge* of cake) —*vb.* **wedged**; **wedg·ing** **1.** to split with a wedge **2.** to tighten with a wedge

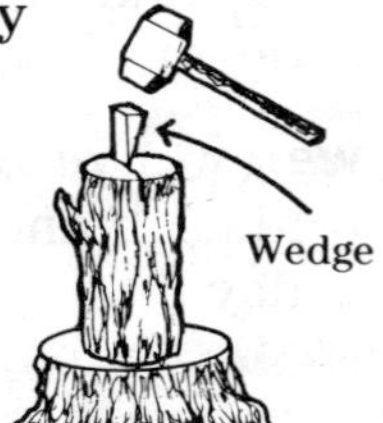

weed (wēd) *n.* a worthless plant that grows wild —*vb.* to remove weeds

week (wēk) *n.* the seven days from Sunday to Saturday, or the school and workdays of Monday to Friday with Saturday and Sunday being called the weekend

week·end (wēk′ end′) *n.* Saturday and Sunday

week·ly (wēk′ lē) *adj.* **1.** pertaining to a week (*weekly* pay) **2.** happening every week (our *weekly* trip to the supermarket) —*n.* a newspaper or magazine published once a week

weep (wēp) *vb.* **wept** (wept); **weep·ing** to cry in sorrow

weigh (wā) *vb.* **1.** to put on a scale to determine the weight **2.** to pull up (*weigh* anchor) **3.** to have weight (*weigh* ninety pounds)

weird (wiərd) *adj.* strange or mysterious (a *weird* costume for Halloween)

wel·come (wel′ kəm) *vb.* **wel·comed**; **wel·com·ing** to receive and greet as guests, with pleasure —*adj.* received gladly (a *welcome* break from routine) —*n.* a friendly greeting

wel·fare (wel′ faər′) *n.* **1.** a state of happiness, satisfaction, and well-being **2.** relief money or services to improve the life of the poor or disabled

well (wel) *n.* **1.** a hole dug in the earth to reach water, oil, or gas **2.** an open shaft in a building for an elevator or stairway —*vb.* to flow, as from a spring —*adj.* healthy —*adv.* **bet·ter** (bet′ ər); **best** (best) **1.** in a suitable or just manner **2.** easily, without difficulty (rode *well* on that horse) —*interj.* to express wonder, relief, or other feeling (*Well, well*!)

west (west) *adv.* to or toward the west —*adj.* placed near or coming from the west —*n.* the direction of the setting sun

west·ern (wes′ tərn) *adj.* lying toward or coming from the west (*western* jeans)

west·ward (west′ wərd) *adv.* or *adj.* toward the west —*n.* a westward direction or point

whale (hwāl) *n.* a large, warm-blooded, air-breathing sea mammal that suckles its young but looks like a fish —*vb.* **whaled**; **whal·ing** to catch whales and prepare the whalebone and oil for sale

wharf (hwȯrf) *n., pl.* **wharves** (hwȯrvz) or **wharfs** a landing place built on the shore near a channel for loading and unloading people and goods from ships

what (hwät) *pron.* **1.** which thing or things **2.** which sort of person or thing (*What* is this?) **3.** that which (say *what* you think) —*adv.* **1.** how, how much, in what way **2.** partly (*What* with the accident and the darkness, we decided to stay in town.) —*adj.* **1.** which (*What* computer games do you have?) **2.** whatever

wheat (hwēt) *n.* a widely grown and used cereal grass in the temperate zones, used in making flour and animal feed

wheel (hwēl) *n.* a circular frame revolving on an axis used as a means of moving vehicles or transmitting power —*vb.* **1.** to move on wheels **2.** to rotate (*wheel* around)

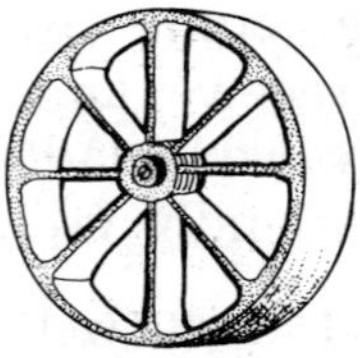

Wheel

when (hwen) *adv.* **1.** at what time **2.** at or during which (a time *when* we were busy) **3.** as soon as (*when* our work is done) —*conj.* **1.** whereas **2.** if **3.** at or during the time that —*pron.* what time

when·ev·er (hwen ev′ ər) *conj.* or *adv.* at whatever time

where (hweər) *adv.* **1.** at, in, or to what place (*Where* is the book?) **2.** at or in which (*where* supplies are stored) —*conj.* in or to the place —*pron.* what place (*Where* are you going?)

where·as (hwer az′) *conj.* **1.** since it is true that **2.** while on the contrary (*whereas* she goes home weekends)

wheth·er (hwe<u>th</u>ʹ ər) *conj.* if (*whether* or not it is raining)

which (hwich) *adj.* what specific one or ones —*pron.* which one or ones

while (hwīl) *n.* a period of time (a *while*) —*conj.* **1.** during the time that (*while* you were at school) **2.** although —*vb.* **whiled**; **whil·ing** to spend or pass

whip (hwip) *vb.* **whipped**; **whip·ping** **1.** to snatch quickly (*Whip* it away.) **2.** to hit with something thin such as a switch **3.** to beat hard (*whip* egg whites) —*n.* **1.** a device for whipping **2.** a fluffy dessert made with whipped cream or egg whites

whirl (hwərl) *vb.* to turn quickly in circles (*whirl* around) —*n.* the act of whirling

whis·per (hwisʹ pər) *vb.* **1.** to speak softly with the breath and without the vocal cords **2.** to make a soft sound like a whisper (the breeze *whisper*ing so softly through the trees) —*n.* the act of whispering

whis·tle (hwisʹ əl) *n.* **1.** a device for making a shrill sound **2.** a shrill sound made by forcing air through a small opening —*vb.* **whis·tled**; **whis·tling** **1.** to make a shrill sound by forcing air through a whistle or through the teeth or lips **2.** to produce by whistling (*whistle* a melody)

Whistle

white (hwīt) *adj.* **1.** having a white or near-white color **2.** being blank (*white* spaces on the page) —*n.* **1.** the color of clean fresh snow **2.** the white part of something (the *white* of your eye)

whiz (hwiz) *vb.* **whizzed**; **whiz·zing** to move very fast with a buzzing or hissing sound (A car *whizzed* by.) —*n.* a whizzing sound

who (hü) *pron.* **1.** what person **2.** the relative pronoun referring to persons (the girl *who* comes)

who·ev·er (hü ev′ ər) *pron.* **1.** whatever person **2.** anyone who (giving it to *whoever* comes)

whole (hōl) *adj.* **1.** sound and intact (box of *whole* cloves) **2.** having all its members or parts (the *whole* collection)

whom (hüm) *pron.* objective case of WHO

whose (hüz) *adj.* to whom or of whom (the girl *whose* book I borrowed) —*pron.* that which belongs to whom (Tell me *whose* it is.)

why (hwī) *adv.* for what reason or purpose (*Why* did he go?)

wick·ed (wik′ əd) *adj.* evil, vicious, or morally wrong (a *wicked* crime)

wide (wīd) *adj.* **wid·er; wid·est** **1.** broad **2.** extensive on a dimension at right angles to length **3.** far from a given point (*wide* of the target) **4.** including a large number of people or things (*wide* knowledge)

wid·ow (wid′ ō) *n.* a woman whose husband has died —*vb.* to make a widow of

wid·ow·er (wid′ ə wər) *n.* a man whose wife has died

width (width) *n.* the dimension at right angles to the length

Width

Length

wife (wīf) *n., pl.* **wives** (wīvz) a woman joined in marriage to a man

wig·gle (wig′ əl) *vb.* **wig·gled; wig·gling** to move parts of the body back and forth without necessarily moving the feet (The dog wagged its tail and *wiggled* with delight.)

wild (wīld) *adj.* living in a natural untamed or uncultivated state as the animals and plants in the forest —*n.* wilderness

wil·der·ness (wil′ dər nəs) *n.* an uncultivated and uninhabited region

wild·life (wīld′ līf′) *n.* living things that are neither human nor domesticated (the *wildlife* in the field and forest)

will (wəl, wil) *helping verb, past* **would** (wəd, wu̇d) *pres. sing.* and *pl.* **will** **1.** am, is, or are about to or going to **2.** am, is, or are determined to (You *will* do it.)

will (wil) *n.* **1.** the power to decide and direct one's energies (Everyone has freedom of the *will.*) **2.** a legal document indicating how one's property should be disposed of at one's death (my *will*) —*vb.* **1.** to command or order (Her father *wills* that she go to school.) **2.** to give at death (*will*ed it to her children)

wil·low (wil′ ō) *n.* **1.** a tree, usually growing near water, with narrow leaves and tough, flexible shoots used in making baskets **2.** the wood of the willow tree used in making baseball bats

win (win) *vb.* **won** (wən); **win·ning** **1.** to achieve with effort or skill (to *win* approval) **2.** to gain the victory in a contest or battle (to *win* the game; to *win* the war)

wind (wind) *n.* **1.** any movement of an air mass, from a light breeze to a gale **2.** breath (knock the *wind* out of) **3.** a wind instrument (music for the *winds*)

wind (wīnd) *vb.* **wound** (wau̇nd); **wind·ing** **1.** to twist around something (*wind* yarn into a ball) **2.** to tighten a spring (*wind* the old clock) **3.** to curve (the river *winds* through the valley)
—*n.* one loop or coil

wind·mill (wind′ mil′) *n.* a mill for grinding grain or pumping water, driven by the wind which turns the vanes, thereby turning the mill wheel

Windmill

win·dow (win′ dō) *n.* **1.** an opening in the wall of a building to let in light and sometimes air **2.** the glass, frame, and casing that fills a window

wing (wing) *n.* **1.** a broad flat part or structure that supports flight **2.** the forelimb, as on a bird **3.** the fold of skin between the hind and fore limbs as on a bat **4.** the wide supporting surfaces of an airplane **5.** a thin appendage on the back of an insect **6.** a part of a building on the side of the main building **7.** a platform or room on either side of a stage —*vb.* to fly

wink (wingk) *vb.* **1.** to close and open an eyelid quickly as a signal **2.** to pretend not to notice (*wink* at his curious manners) —*n.* **1.** a short nap (catch forty *winks*) **2.** an act of winking, especially as a signal

win·ner (win′ ər) *n.* one that wins

win·ter (wint′ ər) *n.* the season between autumn and spring extending from the December solstice to the March equinox

wipe (wīp) *vb.* **wiped; wip·ing** **1.** to rub lightly to clean or dry **2.** to destroy (to *wipe* out crime) —*n.* an act of wiping

wire (wīr) *n.* **1.** a metal cord (an electric *wire*) **2.** a telegram or cablegram (just received a *wire*) —*vb.* **wired; wir·ing** **1.** to provide or equip with wire **2.** to telegraph (*wire* a message to our senator)

wise (wīz) *n.* way or manner (in no *wise* can it be done) —*adj.* **1.** being intelligent and informed **2.** having good sense

wish (wish) *vb.* **1.** to desire or long for (*wish* to go home for the holidays) **2.** to desire for another (*wish* her a happy holiday)

wit (wit) *n.* **1.** the ability to observe, reason, and decide **2.** good sense **3.** quick in connecting ideas and making amusing remarks (the *wit* of the party)

witch (wich) *n.* one, especially a woman, believed to be working with the devil or evil spirits in practicing black magic

with (wi<u>th</u>) *prep.* **1.** in association or connection (work *with* lawyers) **2.** in possession of (a girl *with* acting ability) **3.** by the use of (covered *with* bandages) **4.** because of (died *with* the cold) **5.** in spite of (*With* all his experience, he made a mistake.)

with·draw (wi<u>th</u> drȯ′) *vb.* **with·drew** (-drü); **with·drawn** (-drȯn); **with·draw·ing** **1.** to take back or remove (*withdraw* his offer) **2.** to retreat (The troops *with-drew.*)

with·in (wi<u>th</u> in′) *adv.* inside (apply *within*) —*prep.* inside of (Stay *within* hearing distance.)

with·out (wi<u>th</u> au̇t′) *prep.* **1.** beyond (*without* a doubt) **2.** lacking (*without* thought) —*adv.* outside (painted, within and *without*)

wit·ness (wit′ nəs) *n.* a person who gives evidence or testimony (a *witness* in court) —*vb.* **1.** to be a witness **2.** to give evidence

wolf (wu̇lf) *n., pl.* **wolves** (wu̇lvz) a flesh-eating wild animal that feeds on game and domestic animals when possible —*vb.* to eat quickly and greedily (Don't *wolf* down the food.)

wom·an (wu̇m′ ən) *n., pl.* **wom·en** (wim′ ən) an adult female person

won·der (wən′ dər) *n.* something that fills one with awe or surprise —*vb.* **1.** to feel awe or surprise **2.** to feel some doubt (to *wonder* what to do)

won·der·ful (wən′ dər fəl) *adj.* very exciting or remarkable (a *wonderful* event)

wood (wu̇d) *n.* **1.** a small forest **2.** the substance of the tree cut and ready for use —*adj.* being made of or used for wood (a *wood* stove)

wood·chuck (wu̇d′ chək′) *n.* a burrowing, hibernating rodent, also called a groundhog

wool (wu̇l) *n.* **1.** the soft, heavy hair, especially of sheep **2.** material made of or similar to wool

word (wərd) *n.* **1.** one or more meaningful sounds used in speech **2.** any series of letters that stands for a word **3.** information (received *word* of the accident) —*vb.* to put into words

work (wərk) *n.* **1.** labor, employment, or a job (on the way to *work*) **2.** the result of one's labor (his recent *work*) —*vb.* **worked** or **wrought** (rȯt); **work·ing** **1.** to labor for money rather than for pleasure **2.** to perform or operate (This tool *works* well.)

work·shop (wərk′ shäp′) *n.* **1.** a place where work, especially manual or mechanical work, is carried on **2.** a demonstration or discussion of new ideas and techniques

world (wərld) *n.* **1.** the earth **2.** the people on earth **3.** the universe **4.** a part of the earth (the third *world*)

worm (wərm) *n.* **1.** a soft, crawling animal **2.** *pl.* a parasitic disease (The dog has *worms*.) —*vb.* to move or work slowly like a worm (*worm* along)

wor·ry (wər′ ē) *vb.* **wor·ried**; **wor·ry·ing** **1.** to express or feel anxiety **2.** to shake with the teeth —*n., pl.* **wor·ries** anxiety

wor·ship (wər′ shəp) *n.* **1.** a feeling or show of adoration and respect to God or a sacred image **2.** a formal service giving worship (attended *worship*) **3.** extreme devotion to a public figure (hero *worship*) —*vb.* **wor·shipped**; **wor·ship·ping** **1.** to give adoring respect **2.** to attend a worship

worth (wərth) *n.* value or merit (the total *worth* of the property) —*prep.* **1.** deserving of (*worth* the effort) **2.** equal to (a gift *worth* a lot of money)

worth·less (wərth′ ləs) *adj.* useless

would (wəd, wu̇d) *past tense* of WILL wish, could, or should

wound (wünd) *n.* **1.** a break in one's bodily tissues as by accident or surgery (keeping the *wound* clean) **2.** an injury to one's feelings —*vb.* **1.** to hurt by making a cut or break in tissue **2.** to hurt one's feelings

wrap (rap) *vb.* **wrapped**; **wrap·ping** **1.** to wind around **2.** to hide by covering —*n.* a loose outer garment, such as a shawl or cape

wreck (rek) *n.* **1.** the broken remains of something **2.** a person in ill health —*vb.* to damage or ruin (You'll *wreck* the car.)

wrig·gle (rig′ əl) *vb.* **wrig·gled**; **wrig·gling** **1.** to twist, squirm, or wiggle **2.** to move along by squirming

wrin·kle (ring′ kəl) *n.* **1.** a ridge or fold on a surface due to creasing (iron out the *wrinkle*) **2.** a clever hint or innovation (Here's a new *wrinkle.*) —*vb.* **wrin·kled**; **wrin·kling** to crease

wrist (rist) *n.* the narrow joint between the hand and the arm

write (rīt) *vb.* **wrote** (rōt); **writ·ten** (rit′ n); **writ·ing** (rīt′ ing) **1.** to express ideas in the form of words on paper (to *write* a letter or *write* a grocery list) **2.** to produce a work such as a story or novel by putting it down on paper as an author (to *write* a book)

writ·er (rīt′ ər) *n.* a person who writes, especially to be published

wrong (ròng) *n.* harmful, evil, or unjust acts (caught him doing *wrong*) —*adj.* illegal, immoral, or false (the *wrong* way) —*adv.* in the wrong way or manner (He threw the ball *wrong.*)

wrought (ròt) *past tense* of WORK —*adj.* worked or shaped (*wrought* iron)

X

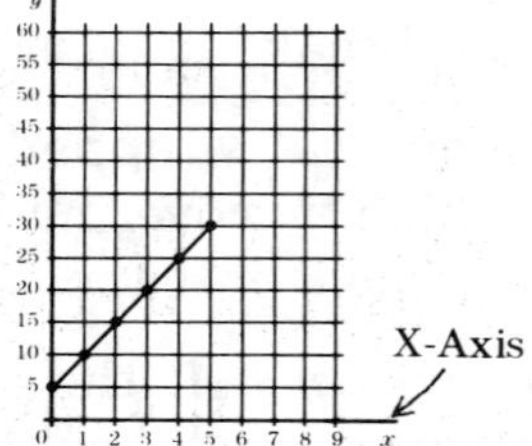

x-ax · is (eks′ ak′ sis) *n.*, *pl.* **x-ax · es** (-sēz) in a two-dimensional system, the horizontal axis along which the x value is measured and the y value is zero

x-ray (eks′ rā′) *n.* a form of electromagnetic radiation similar to light but of a shorter wave length, capable of penetrating solids, and useful in showing breaks in bones and growths in the body such as cancers

xy · lo · phone (zī′ lə fōn′) *n.* a musical instrument made of a series of parallel wooden bars from short to long and played with small flexible hammers

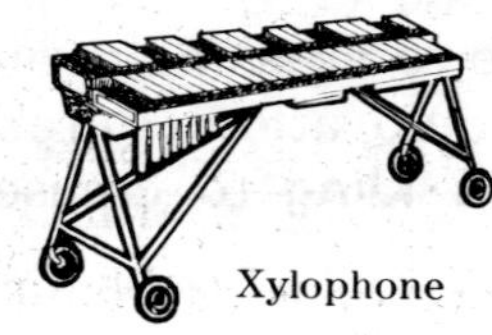
Xylophone

Y

yacht (yät) *n.* a sailing or motor vessel used for pleasure cruising

yam (yam) *n.* a starchy, moist, orange-fleshed sweet potato used as a staple food in many tropical areas

yard (yärd) *n.* **1.** a unit of linear measure equal to three feet or thirty-six inches **2.** a spar that spreads the top of a sail on a sailboat **3.** an area near a house used for family activities or a small garden **4.** an enclosure as for lumber or livestock

yard·age (yärd′ ij) *n.* the total measurement of something in yards

yard·stick (yärd′ stik′) *n.* **1.** a measuring stick, marked off into feet and inches usually **2.** a standard for measuring or judging (Wealth is not a good *yardstick* of happiness.)

yarn (yärn) *n.* **1.** a fiber spun into a continuous strand for weaving or knitting **2.** an incredible story of adventure

yawn (yȯn) *vb.* **1.** to exhale open-mouthed in sleepiness or boredom **2.** to be wide open (a large hole *yawn*ed before him)

y-ax·is (wī′ ak′ sis) *n., pl.* **y-ax·es** (wī′ ak′ sēs) in a two-dimensional system, the vertical axis along which the y value is measured and the x value is zero

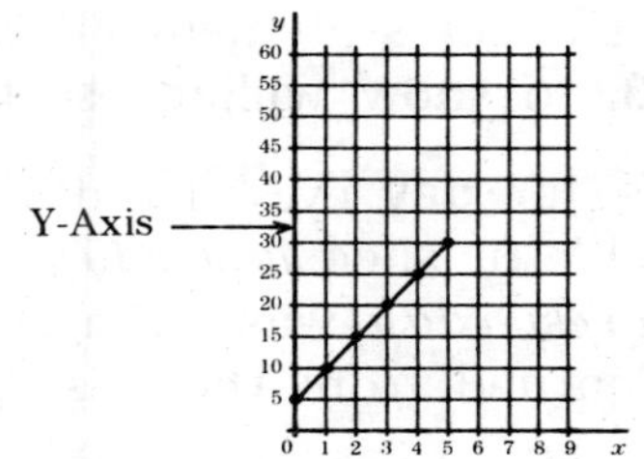

year (yiər) *n.* **1.** the number of days required for one revolution of the earth around the sun or 365.25 days, which for practical purposes is stated on calendars as 365 days with one day added every fourth year, or leap year, to make it 366 **2.** a calendar year from January 1 to December 31; a fiscal year, often July 1 to June 30; or a school year, usually September through June, or approximately 180 school days

year·ly (yiər′ lē) *adj.* annual or once a year (a *yearly* meeting) —*adv.* annually or once a year (had a physical examination *yearly*)

yearn (yərn) *vb.* to long for (to *yearn* for a close friendship)

yeast (yēst) *n.* a fungus causing sugary or starchy foods to ferment, used in making beer or in causing bread to rise

yell (yel) *vb.* to utter a shrill cry or scream —*n.* **1.** a loud scream as in fear or pain **2.** a shout or cheer for a team playing a sport

yel·low (yel′ ō) *adj.* **1.** having the color yellow **2.** having a yellow skin (bright *yellow* lemons) —*n.* the color in the spectrum between orange and green —*vb.* to make or to turn yellow (the pears *yellow*ed)

yes (yes) *adv.* **1.** used as a function word to express agreement (*Yes*, that is correct.) **2.** to introduce a stronger statement (Happy, *yes*, I'm very happy here.) **3.** to show willingness to help (*Yes*, may I help you?)

yes·ter·day (yes′ tər dā) *adv.* on the day before today (We finished *yesterday.*) —*n.* **1.** the day before today (*Yesterday* was sunny.) **2.** the recent past (We have learned from the mistakes of *yesterday.*)

yet (yet) *adv.* **1.** up until now (has not *yet* come) **2.** still (threw a *yet* faster ball) **3.** now (don't try *yet*) —*conj.* nevertheless (His work is good, *yet* it could be better.)

yield (yēld) *vb.* **1.** to produce or give a return (The land *yields* a good crop.) **2.** to give up or surrender (to *yield* to the enemy) **3.** to give in to (*yield*ed to his friend's wishes) **4.** to give way (The floor *yield*ed under the strain of the heavy furniture.) —*n.* the quantity returned or income produced (The *yield* of apples was higher than usual.)

yoke (yōk) *n.* **1.** a fitted piece at the shoulder or hip of a garment **2.** a frame for joining two farm animals for work such as drawing a load **3.** a frame that holds two parts together **4.** something that ties one down (a *yoke* of hardship) **5.** something that links two together (the *yoke* of marriage)

yolk (yōk) *n.* the yellow part of an egg

yon·der (yän′ dər) *adv.* there or in that place (I see him *yonder.*) —*adj.* within sight but at a distance (the *yonder* side of the field)

you (yü, yə) *pron.* **1.** the person or group spoken to (I hope *you* will enjoy this program.) **2.** one, or people in general (a tiny cell that *you* can't even see)

young (yəng) *adj.* **young·er** (yəng′ gər); **young·est** (yəng′ gəst) at an early stage of development (a *young* actress —*n., pl.* **young** **1.** *pl.* young persons (The future belongs to the *young.*) **2.** recently hatched or born (the mother and her *young*)

young·ster (yəng′ stər) *n.* a child or youth

your (yər, yůr) *adj.* **1.** belonging to you (*your* jacket) **2.** from you (*your* letter) **3.** relating to you or to one in general (facing forward, port is on *your* left, starboard on *your* right)

your·self (yər self′) *pron., pl.* **your·selves** (-selvz′) your own self

youth (yüth) *n., pl.* **youths** (yüt͟hz, yüths) the period between being a child and being an adult

Z

ze·bra (zē′ brə) *n.* a wild African animal related to the horse, with a black and white striped hide

ze·nith (zē′ nəth) *n.* **1.** the point in the sky that is directly overhead **2.** the highest point (reached the *zenith* of her career in her forties)

ze·ro (zē′ rō) *n., pl.* **ze·ros** nothing; a cipher, or the symbol 0

zig·zag (zig′ zag′) *n.* a line that changes direction at sharp angles

Zigzag

zinc (zingk) *n.* a bluish-white metal that tarnishes very little but is brittle, used in making brass and as a protective coating on iron

zip·per (zip′ ər) *n.* a fastener made of a sliding piece that is used to lock together the teeth on two pieces of tape

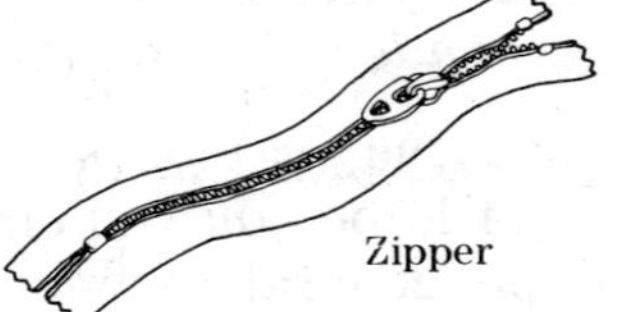

Zipper

zo·di·ac (zō′ dē ak) *n.* an imaginary belt in the heavens containing twelve constellations called the twelve signs of the zodiac: Aquarius, Pisces, Aries, Taurus, Gemini, Cancer, Leo, Virgo, Libra, Scorpio, Sagittarius, and Capricorn

zone (zōn) *n.* **1.** an area that is special because of its use (safety *zone*) **2.** a belt that circles around something (an evergreen *zone* around the mountain) **3.** any of the five temperature zones on the earth's surface: North Frigid Zone, North Temperate Zone, Torrid Zone, South Temperate Zone, and South Frigid Zone

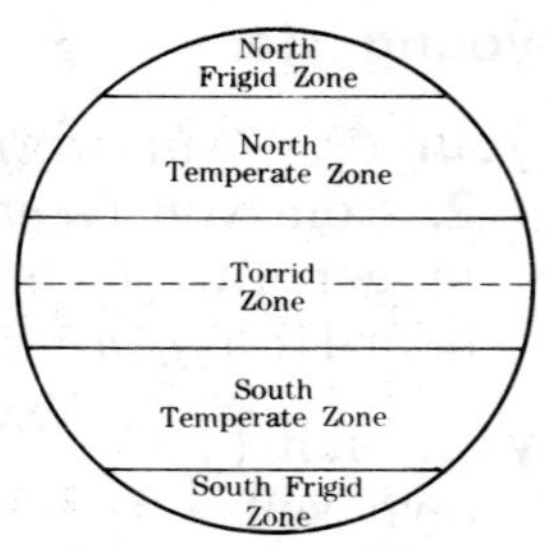

Temperature Zones

zoo (zü) *n., pl.* **zoos** a collection of living wild animals on display

Appendix A. Reading Numbers

CARDINAL NUMBERS

1 one (wən)

2 two (tü)

3 three (thrē)

4 four (fōr)

5 five (fīv)

6 six (siks)

7 seven (sev′ ən)

8 eight (āt)

9 nine (nīn)

10 ten (ten)

11 e·lev·en (i lev′ ən)

12 twelve (twelv)

13 thir·teen (thər′ tēn′)

14 four·teen (fōr′ tēn′)

15 fif·teen (fif′ tēn′)

16 six·teen (siks′ tēn′)

17 sev·en·teen (sev′ ən tēn′)

18 eight·teen (ā′ tēn′)

19 nine·teen (nīn′ tēn′)

20 twen·ty (twen′ tē)

- 21 twen·ty-one
- 22 twen·ty-two
- 23 twen·ty-three
- 24 twen·ty-four
- 25 twen·ty-five
- 26 twen·ty-six

27 twen·ty-seven

28 twen·ty-eight

29 twen·ty-nine

30 thir·ty (thirt′ ē)

40 for·ty (fōr′ tē)

50 fif·ty (fif′ tē)

60 six·ty (siks′ tē)

70 sev·en·ty (sev′ ən tē)

80 eight·ty (āt′ ē)

90 nine·ty (nīn′ tē)

100 one hun·dred (wən′ hən′ dred)

101 one hun·dred one (wən′ hən′ dred wən′)

102 one hun·dred two (wən′ hən′ dred tü′)

(and so on)

200 two hun·dred

300 three hun·dred

400 four hun·dred

500 five hun·dred

600 six hun·dred

700 seven hun·dred

800 eight hun·dred

900 nine hun·dred

1,000 one thou·sand (wən′ thaüz′ nd)

1,000,000 one mil·lion (wən′ mil′ yən)

1,000,000,000 one bil·lion (wən′ bil′ yən)

Reading Whole Numbers

The word *and* is never read into a whole number. See 101 and 102 above. This is true no matter how large the whole number.

Example: 1,692 is read "one thousand, six hundred ninety-two."

Reading Decimals and Fractions

The word *and* is read between a whole number and a decimal or fraction.

Example: $1\frac{3}{4}$ is read "one **and** three-fourths."

2.4 is read "two **and** four-tenths."

The rule is the same for reading dollars and cents.

Example: $2,305.89 is read "two thousand, three hundred five dollars **and** eighty-nine cents."

ORDINAL NUMBERS

1st first (fərst)

2nd sec·ond (sek′ ənd)

3rd third (thərd)

4th fourth (fōrth)

5th fifth (fifth)

6th sixth (siksth)

7th sev·enth (sev′ ənth)

8th eighth (āth)

9th ninth (nīnth)

10th tenth (tenth)

11th e·lev·enth (i lev′ ənth)

12th twelfth (twelfth)

13th thir·teenth (thər′ tēnth′)

14th four·teenth (fōr′ tēnth′)
15th fif·teenth (fif′ tēnth′)
16th six·teenth (siks′ tēnth′)
17th sev·en·teenth (sev′ ən tēnth′)
18th eigh·teenth (ā′ tēnth′)
19th nine·teenth (nīn′ tēnth′)
20th twen·ti·eth (twen′ tē əth)
21st twen·ty-first
22nd twen·ty-sec·ond
23rd twen·ty-third
24th twen·ty-fourth
25th twen·ty-fifth
26th twen·ty-sixth
27th twen·ty-sev·enth
28th twen·ty-eighth
29th twen·ty-ninth

30th thir·ti·eth (thər′ tē əth)
40th for·ti·eth (fōr′ tē əth)
50th fif·ti·eth (fif′ tē əth)
60th six·ti·eth (siks′ tē əth)
70th sev·en·ti·eth (sev′ ən tē əth)
80th eight·i·eth (āt′ ē əth)
90th nine·ti·eth (nīn′ tē əth)
100th one hun·dredth (wən hən′ dredth)
1,000th one thou·sandth (wən thaůz′ nth)
1,000,000th one mil·lionth (wən mil′ yənth)
1,000,000,000th one bil·lionth (wən bil′ yənth)

Appendix B. Pronouns

PERSONAL PRONOUNS

	Person	Nominative	Possessive	Objective	Compound
Singular	1. Speaker	I	my, mine	me	myself
	2. Spoken to	you	your, yours	you	yourself
	3. Spoken of	he	his	him	himself
		she	her, hers	her	herself
		it	its	it	itself
Plural	1. Speaker	we	our, ours	us	ourselves
	2. Spoken to	you	your, yours	you	yourselves
	3. Spoken of	they	their, theirs	them	themselves

Demonstrative Pronouns

this	that	these	those

Indefinite Pronouns

any	many	none	someone
one	neither	all	everyone
few	another	nobody	anyone
both	some	anybody	anything
each	several	somebody	something
other(s)	either	everybody	everything

Relative Pronouns

Nominative	*Possessive*	*Objective*
who	whose	whom
which		
what		
that		

Compound Relative Pronouns

whoever	whosever	whomever
whichever		
whatever		
whosoever	whosesoever	whomsoever
whatsoever		

Interrogative Pronouns

who	whose	whom
which		
what		

Appendix C. Verbs

Conjugation of the Verb "To Have"

Present	*Past*	*Future*	*Present Perfect*	*Past Perfect*	*Future Perfect*
I have	I had	I shall* have	I have had	I had had	I shall* have had
you have	you had	you will have	you have had	you had had	you will have had
he / she / it } has	he / she / it } had	he / she / it } will have	he / she / it } has had	he / she / it } had had	he / she / it } will have had
we have	we had	we shall* have	we have had	we had had	we shall* have had
you have	you had	you will have	you have had	you had had	you will have had
they have	they had	they will have	they have had	they had had	they will have had

*Traditionally, *shall* has been used as the auxiliary verb to form the first person singular and plural of the future and future perfect tenses. This practice still persists in formal usage and in many idiomatic expressions, such as *Shall we go now?* In informal usage, however, the distinction between *shall* and *will* is blurring, and *will* is more frequently chosen.

Conjugation of the Verb "To Be"

Present	*Past*	*Future*	*Present Perfect*	*Past Perfect*	*Future Perfect*
I am	I was	I shall* be	I have been	I had been	I shall* have been
you are	you were	you will be	you have been	you had been	you will have been
he / she / it } is	he / she / it } was	he / she / it } will be	he / she / it } has been	he / she / it } had been	he / she / it } will have been
we are	we were	we shall* be	we have been	we had been	we shall* have been
you are	you were	you will be	you have been	you had been	you will have been
they are	they were	they will be	they have been	they had been	they will have been

*See the note on page 449.

IRREGULAR VERBS

Verb	*Past Tense*	*Past Participle*
bear	bore	borne
beat	beat	beaten
begin	began	begun
blow	blew	blown
break	broke	broken
bring	brought	brought
build	built	built
burst	burst	burst
buy	bought	bought
cast	cast	cast
catch	caught	caught
choose	chose	chosen
come	came	come
cut	cut	cut
deal	dealt	dealt
do	did	done
draw	drew	drawn
drink	drank	drunk
drive	drove	driven
eat	ate	eaten
fall	fell	fallen
feed	fed	fed
feel	felt	felt
fight	fought	fought
find	found	found
fly	flew	flown
forget	forgot	forgotten
get	got	got or gotten
give	gave	given
go	went	gone
grow	grew	grown
hit	hit	hit
hold	held	held
know	knew	known
lay	laid	laid (to put)

Verb	*Past Tense*	*Past Participle*
lead	led	led
leave	left	left
let	let	let
lie	lay	lain (recline)
lie	lied	lied (tell an untruth)
lose	lost	lost
make	made	made
meet	met	met
put	put	put
read	read	read
ride	rode	ridden
ring	rang	rung
rise	rose	risen
run	ran	run
say	said	said
see	saw	seen
seek	sought	sought
sell	sold	sold
sent	sent	sent
set	set	set
show	showed	shown
sing	sang	sung
sit	sat	sat
sleep	slept	slept
speak	spoke	spoken
spring	sprang	sprung
stand	stood	stood
strike	struck	struck
take	took	taken
teach	taught	taught
tell	told	told
think	thought	thought
throw	threw	thrown
try	tried	tried
win	won	won
wind	wound	wound